THE STUDIA PHILONICA ANNUAL

THE STUDIA PHILONICA ANNUAL

STUDIES IN HELLENISTIC JUDAISM

EDITORIAL BOARD

EDITORS: David T. Runia, *Australian Catholic University and The University of Melbourne*
Gregory E. Sterling, *Yale University*

ASSOCIATE EDITOR: Sarah J. K. Pearce, *University of Southampton*

BOOK REVIEW EDITOR: Ronald Cox, *Pepperdine University*

ADVISORY BOARD

Thomas H. Tobin, S.J. (Loyola University Chicago) (chair)
Harold Attridge (Yale University)
Katell Berthelot (CNRS, Aix-en-Provence)
Ellen Birnbaum (Cambridge, MA)
Annewies van den Hoek (Harvard University)
Pieter van der Horst (Zeist, The Netherlands)
Adam Kamesar (Hebrew Union College)
Jutta Leonhardt-Balzer (University of Aberdeen)
Carlos Lévy (Paris)
Maren Niehoff (Hebrew University, Jerusalem)
Robert Radice (Sacred Heart University, Milan)
Jean Riaud (Angers, France)
James R. Royse (Claremont, CA)
Torrey Seland (Drammen, Norway)
Folker Siegert (Münster, Germany)
Abraham Terian (Fresno, CA)

Contributions should be sent to the Editor, Prof. G. E. Sterling, Yale Divinity School, 409 Prospect Street, New Haven, CT 06511, USA; email: gregory.sterling@yale.edu. Please send books for review to the Book Review Editor for 2018, Prof. Michael Cover, Department of Theology, Marquette University, P.O. Box 1881, Milwaukee, WI 53201-1881, U.S.A.; email michael.cover@marquette.edu.

Contributors are requested to observe the "Instructions to Contributors" located at the end of the volume. These can also be consulted on the Annual's website: http://divinity.yale.edu/philo-alexandria. Articles which do not conform to these instructions cannot be accepted for inclusion.

The Studia Philonica Monograph series accepts monographs in the area of Hellenistic Judaism, with special emphasis on Philo and his *Umwelt*. Proposals for books in this series should be sent to the Editor, Prof. Thomas H. Tobin, S.J., Theology Department, Loyola University Chicago, 1032 West Sheridan Road, Chicago, IL 60660-1537, U.S.A.; email: ttobin@luc.edu.

THE STUDIA PHILONICA ANNUAL
Studies in Hellenistic Judaism

Volume XXIX

2017

EDITORS
David T. Runia
Gregory E. Sterling

ASSOCIATE EDITOR
Sarah J. K. Pearce

BOOK REVIEW EDITOR
Ronald Cox

SBL Press
Atlanta

THE STUDIA PHILONICA ANNUAL
Studies in Hellenistic Judaism

The financial support of
C. J. de Vogel Foundation, Utrecht
Yale University
Pepperdine University
is gratefully acknowledged

Copyright © 2017 by the SBL Press

All rights reserved. No part of this work may be reproduced or transmitted in any form or by any means, electronic or mechanical, including photocopying and recording, or by means of any information storage or retrieval system, except as may be expressly permitted by the 1976 Copyright Act or in writing from the publisher. Requests for permission should be addressed in writing to the Rights and Permissions Office, SBL Press, 825 Houston Mill Road, Atlanta, GA 30329, USA
ISBN: 9781628371932 (hardcover: alk. paper)
ISBN: 9780884142553 (electronic book)
ISSN : 1052-4533

Printed on acid-free paper.

CONTENTS

BOOK REVIEW SECTION

NOTE. The editors wish to thank the typesetter Gonni Runia once again for her tireless work on this volume. They wish to express their thanks to Dr Lisa Marie Belz, OSU, Ph.D., and Zach Eberhart, for meticulously proof-reading the final manuscript. As in previous years we are deeply grateful to our publisher, SBL Press, and to its staff, with a special mention of Nicole Tilford.

ABBREVIATIONS

The abbreviations used for the citation of ancient texts and modern scholarly literature generally follow the guidelines of the Society of Biblical Literature as published in *The SBL Handbook of Style*, second edition (Atlanta: SBL Press, 2014) §8.4. For a list of abbreviations of particular relevance to this Annual, see the Instructions to Contributors at the back of the volume. In addition to that list, please note the following:

AGI	*Archivio Glottologico Italiano*
Ang	*Angelicum*
CHR	*Catholic Historical Review*
IJCT	*International Journal of the Classical Tradition*
PRSt	*Perspectives in Religious Studies*
RTP	*Revue de Théologie et de Philosophie*

The Studia Philonica Annual 29 (2017): 1–32

NUTRITIOUS MILK FROM HAGAR'S SCHOOL
Philo's Reception of Homer

GEERT ROSKAM

1. *By Way of Introduction: Philo and the Pagan Tradition*

Philo's familiarity with the age-old pagan tradition has been much examined in scholarly literature.[1] His indebtedness to Plato and the Platonic tradition is clear from nearly every page of his voluminous oeuvre,[2] but

[1] Seminal studies are Emile Bréhier, *Les idées philosophiques et religieuses de Philon d'Alexandrie* (Paris: Picard, 1907); Isaac Heinemann, *Philons griechische und jüdische Bildung: Kulturvergleichende Untersuchungen zu Philons Darstellung der jüdischen Gesetze* (Breslau: Marcus, 1932); and Harry A. Wolfson, *Philo: Foundations of Religious Philosophy in Judaism, Christianity, and Islam*, 2 vols. (Cambridge: Harvard University Press, 1948). Numerous later studies can be found in the rich bibliographies compiled by Roberto Radice and David T. Runia. *Philo of Alexandria: An Annotated Bibliography 1937–1986*, VCSup 8 (Leiden/New York/København/Köln: Brill, 1988); David T. Runia, ed. *Philo of Alexandria. An Annotated Bibliography 1987–1996, with Addenda for 1937–1986*, VCSup 57 (Leiden: Brill, 2000); Runia, ed., *Philo of Alexandria. An Annotated Bibliography 1997–2006, with Addenda for 1987–1996*, VCSup 109 (Leiden: Brill, 2012).

[2] See, e.g., the classic studies of John Dillon, *The Middle Platonists. A Study of Platonism 80 B.C. to A.D. 220* (London: Duckworth, 1977; rev. ed., Ithaca, NY: Cornell University Press, 1996), on Philo as a "Middle-Platonist" and David T. Runia, *Philo of Alexandria and the Timaeus of Plato*, PhA 44 (Leiden: Brill, 1986), on Philo's reception of the *Timaeus*; cf. the earlier study of Thomas H. Billings, *The Platonism of Philo Judaeus* (Chicago: University of Chicago Press, 1919). On the question of whether Philo can be regarded as a Middle Platonist, see David T. Runia, "Was Philo a Middle Platonist?" *SPhiloA* 5 (1993): 112–140; Gregory E. Sterling, "Platonizing Moses. Philo and Middle Platonism," *SPhiloA* 5 (1993): 96–111; Thomas H. Tobin, "Was Philo a Middle Platonist? Some Suggestions," *SPhiloA* 5 (1993): 147–50. The influence of Plato's imagery on Philo has been studied in detail by Anita Méasson, *Du char ailé de Zeus à l'Arche d'Alliance: Images et mythes platoniciens chez Philon d'Alexandrie* (Paris: Études augustiniennes, 1986). For the importance of later philosophical traditions, see esp. Francesca Alesse, ed., *Philo of Alexandria and Post-Aristotelian Philosophy*, SPhA 5 (Leiden: Brill, 2008); cf. also Carlos Lévy, ed., *Philon d'Alexandrie et le langage de la philosophie. Actes du colloque international organisé par le Centre d'études sur la philosophie hellénistique et romaine de l'Université de Paris XII-Val de Marne (Créteil, Fontenay, Paris, 26–28 octobre 1995)* (Turnhout: Brepols, 1998) and Francesca Calabi, *God's Acting, Man's Acting. Tradition and Philosophy in Philo of Alexandria*, SPhA 4 (Leiden/Boston: Brill, 2008).

other authors are important as well. Several poets, for instance, are often quoted in his treatises. In his youth, he was introduced to their works in the school of the grammarians (*Congr.* 74) and he never forgot their teaching. In his view, the whole field of pagan encyclical education is a preliminary stage that can contribute to the acquisition of wisdom: it is like milk for the children (*Agr.* 9; *Congr.* 19; *Prob.* 160). Philo was an enthusiastic milk drinker and remained so for his entire life. Throughout his oeuvre, numerous quotations from poets can be found:[3] Hesiod,[4] lyric and elegiac poetry,[5] tragedians,[6] and of course Homer.[7] The great number of Philo's references to both *Iliad* and *Odyssey* suggests that he considered Homer of special importance, yet the precise function and relevance of all these references is not completely clear. Several scholars are convinced that most of this Homeric material is little more than *ornatus*.[8] Others rather argue that in some passages, the quotations from Homer do add to Philo's argument. In this article, I'd like to develop the latter view, by examining

[3] See the list compiled by David Lincicum, "A Preliminary Index to Philo's Non-Biblical Citations and Allusions," *SPhiloA* 25 (2013): 139–67.

[4] Erkki Koskenniemi, "Philo and Greek Poets," *JSJ* 41 (2010): 301–22, esp. 312–15; Courtney J. P. Friesen, "Hannah's 'Hard Day' and Hesiod's 'Two Roads': Poetic Wisdom in Philo's *De ebrietate*," *JSJ* 46 (2015): 44–64.

[5] Koskenniemi "Philo and Greek Poets," 315–19; cf. also Stefan Radt, "Philon *de Plantatione* 127–29: ein übersehenes Testimonium zu Pindar fr. 31," *Mnemosyne* 67 (2014): 646–47.

[6] Erkki Koskenniemi, "Philo and Classical Drama," in *Ancient Israel, Judaism, and Christianity in Contemporary Perspective. Essays in Memory of K.-J. Illman*, ed. Jacob Neusner *et al.* (Lanham: University Press of America, 2006), 137; cf. David Lincicum, "Aeschylus in Philo, *Anim.* 47 and *QE* 2.6," *SPhiloA* 25 (2013): 65–68.

[7] See, e.g., Robert Lamberton, *Homer the Theologian: Neoplatonist Allegorical Reading and the Growth of the Epic Tradition*, The Transformation of the Classical Heritage 9 (Berkeley: University of California Press, 1986), 44–54; Koskenniemi, "Philo and Greek Poets," 305–11; Katell Berthelot, "Philon d'Alexandrie, lecteur d'Homère: quelques éléments de réflexion," in *Prolongements et renouvellements de la tradition classique*, ed. Anne Balansard, Giles Dorival and Mireille Loubet, Textes et documents de la Méditerranée antique et médiévale (Aix-en-Provence: Publications de l'Université de Provence, 2011); and Berthelot, "Philo and the Allegorical Interpretation of Homer in the Platonic Tradition (with an Emphasis on Porphyry's *De antro nympharum*," in *Homer and the Bible in the Eyes of Ancient Interpreters*, ed. Maren R. Niehoff (Leiden: Brill, 2012)), 155–74; Maren R. Niehoff, "Philo and Plutarch on Homer," in *Homer and the Bible*, 127–53; Pura Nieto Hernández, "Philo and Greek Poetry," *SPhiloA* 26 (2014): 135–49.

[8] See, e.g., Koskenniemi, "Philo and Greek Poets," 307–08 ("Here [*scil. Aet.* 37], as so often, the only reason for quoting seems to be that Philo liked to quote Homer. The reference does not add substance to his argumentation. Apparently, he happened to remember the verses, and willingly quoted them to decorate his own text. Philo here acts as any Greek writer writing a cultivated text.") and Lamberton, *Homer the Theologian*, 51 ("The vast majority of the Homeric words and phrases used by Philo are little more than poetic embellishments of the text.").

for what purposes Philo uses Homer (section 3) and which strategies he adopts in his Homer reception (section 4). These analyses will finally be placed in a broader perspective (section 5). I'd like to begin, though, with some "hard facts" (section 2).

2. *Quotations from and References to Homer in Philo*

Here is the list of passages where Philo quotes or refers to one or more verses from Homer's *Iliad* or *Odyssey*:

Philo	Homer	verbatim quotation?	explicit reference?
Sacr. 38	*Il.* 20.360–361	no	τὸ λεγόμενον δὴ τοῦτο
Det. 178	*Od.* 12.118	yes	-
Post. 151	*Il.* 20.360–361	no	τὸ λεγόμενον
Agr. 24	*Il.* 5.487	no	ὡς οἱ ποιηταί πού φασι
Agr. 41	several passages	no	τὸ ποιητικὸν γένος
Ebr. 103	*Il.* 2.489	no	κατὰ τοὺς ποιητὰς λεγομένῳ
Conf. 4	*Od.* 11.315–316	yes	ὁ μέγιστος καὶ δοκιμώτατος τῶν ποιητῶν Ὅμηρος
Conf. 170	*Il.* 2.204–205	yes	-
Migr. 156	*Il.* 6.484	yes	τὸ ποιητικόν
Migr. 195	*Od.* 4.392	yes	κατὰ τὸ ποιητικὸν γράμμα
Her. 189	*Il.* 9.97	yes	τὸ ποιητικὸν ἐκεῖνο
Congr. 171	*Il.* 18.104 and *Od.* 20.379	no	-
Fug. 31	*Od.* 21.294	no	ὡς οἱ ποιηταὶ λέγουσι
Fug. 61	*Od.* 12.118	yes	τὸ ποιητικόν
Mut. 179	*Od.* 7.36	yes	τῶν παρ' Ἕλλησι ποιητῶν ὁ δοκιμώτατος
Somn. 1.57	*Od.* 4.392	yes	κατὰ τὸ ποιητικὸν γράμμα
Somn. 1.150	*Od.* 11.303	no	ὡς ἔφη τις
Somn. 1.233	*Od.* 17.485–487	no	παλαιὸς μὲν οὖν ᾄδεται λόγος
Somn. 2.53	*Od.* 14.529	no	ὡς οἱ ποιηταί πού φασι
Somn. 2.70	*Od.* 12.219	yes	-
Somn. 2.144	*Od.* 4.535 and 11.411	no	τὸ λεγόμενον τοῦτο
Somn. 2.148	several passages	yes	-
Somn. 2.249	several passages	no	ποιητικοῖς ὀνόμασι
Somn. 2.260	*Il.* 2.212	no	ὡς εἶπέ τις
Somn. 2.275	*Il.* 2.246	no	ᾗ φασιν οἱ ποιηταί
Abr. 10	Homer himself	no	ποιητὴς Ὅμηρος, μυρίων ποιητῶν ὄντων, κατ' ἐξοχὴν λέγεται
Ios. 2	several passages	no	τὸ ποιητικὸν γένος
Ios. 265	*Il.* 3.277 = *Od.* 11.109 and 12.323	yes	-
Mos. 1.30	*Od.* 20.379	no	-

Mos. 1.61	several passages	no	-
Decal. 56	*Od.* 11.303	no	-
Decal. 69	*Il.* 17.32 and 20.198	yes	-
Spec. 1.74	*Il.* 18.104[9]	no	ὡς οἱ ποιηταί φασι
Spec. 2.6	*Il.* 6.266	yes	τὸ λεγόμενον δὴ τοῦτο
Spec. 3.50	*Il.* 18.104	no	ὡς εἶπέ τις
Prob. 31	several passages	no	Ὅμηρος
Prob. 112	*Il.* 6.407	yes	-
Prob. 122	*Il.* 24.602–604	yes	-
Prob. 125	*Il.* 1.180–181	yes	-
Contempl. 9	*Il.* 2.216–219	no	-
Contempl. 17	*Il.* 13.5–6	yes	Ὅμηρος ... ἐν Ἰλιάδι κατὰ τὴν ἀρχὴν τῆς τρισκαιδεκάτης
Contempl. 40	*Od.* 9.374	no	ᾗ φησιν ὁ ποιητής
Aet. 37	*Od.* 6.107–108	yes	-
Aet. 127	several passages	no	ᾗ φασιν οἱ ποιηταί
Aet. 132	*Il.* 6.147–148	yes	τὸ ποιητικὸν εὖ εἴρηται
Prov. 2.15	several passages	yes	apud probatissimum laudatissimumque poetarum Homerum
Prov. 2.16	*Il.* 20.234–235	yes	-
Prov. 2.19	several passages	no	ὡς οἱ ποιηταί που φασίν
Prov. 2.37	several passages	no	Homero
Prov. 2.37	*Il.* 5.336–540	no	Homero
Prov. 2.37	*Il.* 15.18–22	yes	Homero
Prov. 2.95	*Od.* 9.106–111	yes	poeta
Legat. 80	*Od.* 4.456–458	no	εἰσήγαγεν Ὅμηρος
Legat. 149	*Il.* 2.204	yes	λέλεκται δεόντως
QG 1.7	*Il.* 12.239–240	no	so the poet testifies
QG 1.76	*Od.* 12.118	yes	that which was said by the poet about Scylla
QG 2.27	*Il.* 4.299	yes	the poetic saying is not inaptly quoted
QG 3.3	*Od.* 12.39–46	no	as Homer says
QG 3.16	several passages	yes	a witness to this is the poet, who says
QG 4.2	*Od.* 17.485–487	yes	as the clever and considerably learned Homer with beauty of sound describes
QG 4.8	*Il.* 15.189	yes	Homer not ineptly says
QG 4.20	*Od.* 15.74	yes	what the poet fittingly says
QG 4.183	*Il.* 3.179	yes	according to the poet
QG 4.238	several passages	no	as the poet says
QE 2.102	several passages	no	Homer indeed shows this in (his poem about) the Trojan war
Anim. 54	*Il.* 20.170–171	yes	poeta certior factus dicit

9 Rather than *Od.* 20.379: see Nieto Hernández, "Philo and Greek Poetry," 146.

The above list indeed contains "hard facts," for the great majority of the cases leave little or no room for doubt. Yet there is a twilight zone, consisting of some passages where it is not clear whether they do or do not contain Homeric material. Since the list presented here differs in several respects from that compiled by Lincicum, it is appropriate to put my cards on the table and briefly discuss a few difficult cases.

• References to Homer that are neither accepted by Lincicum ("Preliminary Index") nor inserted in the above list

- *Leg.* 1.82, where Colson and Whitaker (PLCL 1:201, n. c) detect a Homeric use of the term φαίνειν (pointing to *Od.* 4.12 and 15.26). The parallel, however, is far from compelling, and Philo makes no suggestion at all that he is thinking of Homer here.
- *Gig.* 53, where Colson and Whitaker (PLCL 2:470–471, n. c) find an allusion to *Od.* 3.348. This, however, presupposes a change of the text (reading ἀνείμονι instead of ἀνειμένῃ). It is true that the word ἀνείμων ("without clothing") is also used in *Somn.* 1.99 and *Spec.* 1.83 (and in the Greek fragment from *Prov.* 2.26) and that it fairly seldom occurs in extant literature.[10] All of these passages, then, may contain a vague and learned echo of Homer's verse, although it remains odd that Philo in none of these passages signals the Homeric origin of the term (he could have done so easily by adding a phrase like τὸ ποιητικόν).
- *Ebr.* 201, which Colson and Whitaker (PLCL 3:422, n. 1) interpret as an allusion to the Homeric term εἶλαρ. This, however, requires a change of the text of the manuscripts (reading ὑπ' εἶλ<αρ> οὔσης instead of ὑπειλούσης).
- *Praem.* 146, where the term πανάπαλοι recalls *Od.* 13.223, as has been pointed out by Colson (PLCL 8:405, n. a). The term is a *hapax legomenon* in Homer and further occurs only here in Philo and in a few later texts (often discussing Homer's verse, or alluding to it). In that sense, this case is not so different from that of *Gig.* 53 discussed above. If this passage should be added to the list of references to Homer, it may be understood as an echo of the erudite tradition of Homeric exegesis with its particular interest in unusual words.

• References to Homer that are accepted by Lincicum ("Preliminary Index") but are not inserted in the above list

- *Leg.* 3.105: Philo deals with God's treasuries of good and evil things. Lincicum ("Preliminary Index," 154) refers to both Homer, *Il.* 24.527–528 (Achilles's famous words about the two urns of Zeus) and Plato, *Resp.* 379d, but Philo himself explicitly refers to Deut 28:12 and 32:34–35 as his reference texts.
- *Somn.* 2.50: here Philo recalls the behaviour of the heroes who roast their meat. This reference to ἡρωικῶν ὄντως ἀνδρῶν seems to point to Homer's poems indeed, even more so since there follows a clear reference to *Od.* 14.529 a few paragraphs later (2.53). Lincicum ("Preliminary Index," 147 and 155) thus refers to *Il.* 9.211–214, but this is hardly compelling. If we think about (Homeric) heroes roasting

10 A TLG search shows that many occurrences indeed concern Homeric exegesis. Callimachus, *Aet.* fr. 7.9 is no counter-example, as the *poeta doctus* of course very often alludes to Homer, esp. to rare words or *hapax legomena*.

sheep, we do not think of specific (Homeric) passages but rather call to mind a general image of the heroic world.

- *Aet.* 8: Lincicum ("Preliminary Index," 150 and 155) refers to *Il.* 5.4, but Philo's reference to the ἀκάματον πῦρ primarily concerns Stoic doctrine (it is inserted in von Arnim's *SVF* as 2:620) and may thus, at best, tell us more about the Stoic reception of Homer; there are, however, no further parallels in Stoic literature (the closest one is Cleanthes's ἀκάματον πρόνοιαν in *SVF* 1:549). And while ἀκάματον πῦρ is indeed a well-known Homeric phrase (it does not only occur at *Il.* 5.4 but also at *Il.* 15.597–598 and 731; 16.122; 18.225; 21.13 and 341; 23.52; *Od.* 20.123 and 21.181), it can also be found in many other authors (e.g., Hesiod, *Theog.* 563 and 566; Apollonius of Rhodes, *Argon.* 3.531; Theocritus, *Id.* 11.51; *Orphic Hymn* 66.1 and 12).
- *Aet.* 42: Philo evokes how children are playing on the beach. His description recalls *Il.* 15.362–364, but there is no explicit reference to Homer and the few verbal correspondences are not really compelling. Cf. Philostratus, *Vit. Apoll.* 2.22.2 and Gregory of Nyssa, *Against Eunomius* 2.469 (p. 363.14–16 J).
- *Anim.* 59: Philo alludes to the story of Ajax's anger concerning the arms of Achilles. This episode is briefly told in *Od.* 11.543–564, but it is a well-known story that was often discussed in ancient literature (e.g., in Sophocles's extant tragedy *Ajax*). Since Philo does not explicitly refer to Homer, there is no compelling reason to conclude that he has the particular passage from the *Odyssey* in mind.
- *Anim.* 69: Philo states that the hare is called timorous by the poets (*poetarum genus*). Terian (*Philonis Alexandrini De animalibus: The Armenian Text with an Introduction, Translation, and Commentary*, Studies in Hellenistic Judaism: Supplements to Studia Philonica 1 [Chico: Scholars Press, 1981], 181–82) argues that the Greek term was probably πτωκάς or πτώξ. If that is indeed true, this may be a reference to passages like *Il.* 17.676 and 22.310. But since the terms repeatedly occur in other poets as well (e.g., Aeschylus, *Ag.* 137 and *Eum.* 326; Theocritus, *Id.* 1.110; *Anth. Pal.* 9.14; Lycophron, *Alex.* 944; Nicander, *Ther.* 950; Babrius, 102.10; Oppian, *Cyn.* 1.165 and 3.504; cf. also Callimachus, *Hec.* fr. 266 Pf. = 84 H. and Horace, *Epod.* 2.35), Philo may well point to a poetic commonplace (cf. Aelian, *Nat. an.* 7.19: οἱ λαγῴ, οὓς δὴ καὶ πτῶκας οἱ ποιηταὶ καλοῦσιν; cf. 7.47).

- A final difference between the above list and that of Lincicum ("Preliminary Index") concerns Philo's references to repetitive verses. As it is impossible to decide which particular passage Philo has in mind (if any), I prefer to refer in such cases to "several passages." A few examples may suffice to illustrate the difference between my approach and that of Lincicum:

  - *Aet.* 127: Lincicum ("Preliminary Index," 150 and 155) refers to *Il.* 18.397, but omits *Il.* 18.411 and 417; 20.37; *Od.* 8.308 and 332, which are equally relevant.
  - *QG* 3.16: Lincicum ("Preliminary Index," 151 and 155) points to *Od.* 14.258 (= *Od.* 17.427), but equally relevant is *Od.* 4.477 and 4.581.
  - *Prov.* 2.15: Lincicum ("Preliminary Index," 150 and 155) only mentions *Il.* 1.544, but the famous phrase πατὴρ ἀνδρῶν τε θεῶν τε frequently occurs in both *Iliad* (apart from 1.544, see also 4.68; 5.426; 8.49, 132; 11.182; 15.12, 47; 16.458; 20.56; 22.167; and 24.103) and *Odyssey* (1.28; 12.445; and 18.137).

• References to Homer that are inserted in the above list but are absent from that of Lincicum ("Preliminary Index")

- *Sacr.* 38: the reference to *Il.* 20.360–361 in this passage is not mentioned in Lincicum ("Preliminary Index"), whereas the parallel use of the same Homeric verse in *Post.* 151 is included in his list.

- *Congr.* 171: Philo refers to Adam and Eve as τὰ γῆς ἄχθη. The same Homeric phrase occurs in *Spec.* 1.74 (with reference to "the poets") and 3.50 and in *Mos.* 1.30. The latter passages are inserted into Lincicum's list.
- *Somn.* 2.53: reference to *Od.* 14.529 (Lincicum, "Preliminary Index," 147 and 155 incorrectly has "*Somn.* 2.52: *Od.* 15.529").
- *Somn.* 2.249: a vague allusion to Homer's view of ambrosia (a term that frequently occurs in both *Iliad* and *Odyssey*). Philo's explicit reference to the ποιητικὰ ὀνόματα suggests that he is indeed thinking of Homer.
- *Mos.* 1.61: a clear reference to the Homeric phrase ποιμὴν λαῶν, which is also mentioned elsewhere (*Agr.* 41; *Ios.* 2; *Prob.* 31). In *Prob.* 31, Philo mentions Homer by name.

Several conclusions can already be drawn from this list. First, the great number of quotations and references suggests that Homer's epic poems were really important for Philo. That said, however, we should be cautious not to exaggerate. Scholars have compared Philo's knowledge and use of Homer with Plutarch's reception of Homer[11] and with the approach of the authors of the so-called "Second Sophistic."[12] There are undeniable similarities indeed, yet they should be placed in their correct perspective. The list of Plutarch's quotations from Homer compiled by Helmbold and O'Neil counts several hundreds of references to all the books of the *Iliad* and *Odyssey*.[13] This far outnumbers the sixty-six references in Philo's works. Homer was relevant to Philo, no doubt, but Philo was no Plutarch. Sixty-six quotations in a large oeuvre is significant, yet Homer was not omnipresent in Philo.

Second, the quotations from and references to Homer are scattered over the whole *Corpus Philonicum* and can be found at the outset, in the middle

[11] Maren R. Niehoff, 127–53.

[12] Koskenniemi, "Philo and Greek Poets," 311 and 322; Koskenniemi, "Philo and Classical Education," in *Reading Philo, A Handbook to Philo of Alexandria*, ed. Torrey Seland (Grand Rapids/Cambridge: Eerdmans, 2014), 102–28, esp. 126.

[13] See Wiliam C. Helmbold and Edward N. O'Neil, *Plutarch's Quotations*, Philological Monographs 19 (Baltimore: American Philological Association, 1959), 39–48. Plutarch's reception of Homer has been much discussed; see, e.g., Hans Schläpfer, *Plutarch und die klassischen Dichter: Ein Beitrag zum klassischen Bildungsgut Plutarchs* (Zürich: Junis-Verlag, 1950); Giacomo Bona, "Citazioni omeriche in Plutarco," in *Strutture formali dei "Moralia" di Plutarco: Atti del III Convegno plutarcheo. Palermo, 3–5 maggio 1989*, ed. Gennaro D'Ippolito and Italo Gallo (Naples: D'Auria, 1991), 151–62; E. Alexiou, "Die Funktion der Homerzitate in Plutarchs Biographien," in *Hortus litterarum antiquarum: Festschrift für Hans Armin Gärtner zum 70. Geburtstag*, ed. Andreas Haltenhoff and Fritz-Heiner Mutschler, Bibliothek der klassischen Altertumswissenschaften n. F. 2 Reihe 109 (Heidelberg: Winter, 2000), 51–65; Gennaro D'Ippolito, "L'Omero di Plutarco," in *La biblioteca di Plutarco: Atti del IX Convegno plutarcheo; Pavia, 13–15 giugno 2002*, ed. Italo Gallo (Naples: D'Auria, 2004), 11–35; J. M. Díaz Lavado, *Las citas de Homero en Plutarco* (Málaga: Libros Pórtico, 2010); and Niehoff, "Philo and Plutarch on Homer," 136–48.

and at the very end of separate works. A striking concentration of Homeric material is to be found in *On Dreams, On Providence,* and *Questions and Answers on Genesis,* for no obvious reason, as far as I can see.

Third, half of the passages contain verbatim quotations (33 out of 66, or exactly 50 percent). Even when the Homeric verses are not quoted, it is often very clear which specific passage Philo has in mind. Sometimes, he also refers to verses that recur several times in Homer's epics, or to the typically formulary terms or phrases. Since it makes little sense in my view to refer in such cases to one specific Homeric passage, I have preferred to use a more general reference like "several passages" in the above list.

Fourth, Homer is explicitly called by name no less than eleven times. Once we even find a precise reference to the beginning of book 13 of the *Iliad*. In most cases, however, Philo refers in a more general way to the poets (ποιηταί or τὸ ποιητικόν). This, presumably, is clear enough for his readers, even more so as Homer is the poet par excellence.[14] Occasionally, we have to do with a vague reference (such as τὸ λεγόμενον or ὡς εἶπέ τις) or even with none at all. In such instances, however, Philo nearly always provides a verbatim quotation, so that it is clear that he makes use of poetic material. In general, then, Philo is a secure guide in this respect: there are no cryptic or highly allusive references, and erudition never interferes with clearness (σαφήνεια).

The next list shows which specific Homeric passages are mentioned by Philo (leaving out the formulary verses; passages containing verbatim quotations are underlined):

Homer	Philo
Il.	
1.180–181	<u>*Prob.* 125</u>
2.204–205	<u>*Conf.* 170</u>
2.204	<u>*Legat.* 149</u>
2.212	*Somn.* 2.260
2.216–219	*Contempl.* 9
2.246	*Somn.* 2.275
2.489	*Ebr.* 103
3.179	<u>*QG* 4.183</u>
3.277	<u>*Ios.* 265</u>
4.299	<u>*QG* 2.27</u>
5.336–340	*Prov.* 2.37
5.487	*Agr.* 24
6.147–148	<u>*Aet.* 132</u>

[14] As Philo argues in *Abr.* 10, "we give the title of '*the* poet' to Homer in virtue of his pre-eminence, though there are multitudes of poets besides him." All translations, unless otherwise indicated, are borrowed from the Loeb Classical Library.

6.266	*Spec.* 2.6
6.407	*Prob.* 112
6.484	*Migr.* 156
9.97	*Her.* 189
12.239–240	*QG* 1.7
13.5–6	*Contempl.* 17
15.18–22	*Prov.* 2.37
15.189	*QG* 4.8
18.104	*Spec.* 1.74 and 3.50
20.170–171	*Anim.* 54
20.234–235	*Prov.* 2,16
20.360–361	*Sacr.* 38; *Post.* 151
24.602–604	*Prob.* 122
Od.	
4.392	*Migr.* 195; *Somn.* 1.57
4.456–458	*Legat.* 80
6.107–108	*Aet.* 37
7.36	*Mut.* 179
9.106–111	*Prov.* 2.95
9.374	*Contempl.* 40
11.109	*Ios.* 265
11.303	*Somn.* 1.150; *Decal.* 56
11.315–316	*Conf.* 4
12.39–46	*QG* 3.3
12.118	*Det.* 178; *Fug.* 61; *QG* 1.76
12.219	*Somn.* 2.70
12.323	*Ios.* 265
14.529	*Somn.* 2.53
15.74	*QG* 4.20
17.485–487	*Somn.* 1.233; *QG* 4.2
20.379	*Mos.* 1.30
21.294	*Fug.* 31

Whereas we often find the tendency in ancient authors to quote from the beginning of Homeric books, this is definitely not the case in Philo. As a matter of fact, quotations from the opening of books are quite rare. His use of Homer rather seems to encompass the whole spectre of both *Iliad* and *Odyssey*. It is true that he refers to well-known and popular books (such as book 1 and 24 of the *Iliad*, although both are mentioned only once) and to celebrated scenes (such as the farewell of Hector and Andromache or the encounter of Diomedes and Glaucon in the *Iliad*, and the episode of the Cyclops in the *Odyssey*), but we equally find references to inconspicuous verses that are at first sight of secondary importance but receive a new, rich meaning when read through the lens of Philo's philosophical or exegetical perspective. This whole picture already shows Philo's thorough familiarity with Homer. It has been supposed that Philo possessed a copy of the *Iliad* and the *Odyssey* in his personal library.[15] This cannot be proven of course, but it is surely plausible.

The last list shows how the quotations and references to Homer are distributed over Philo's different works:

Philo's works	*Iliad*		*Odyssey*		Homer alone	TOTAL
	quotations	references	quotations	references		
Allegorical Commentary	3	5	7	5	3	23
Exposition of the Law	2	0	0	1	4	7
Questions and Answers	3	1	4	1	2	11
Apologetic and historical writings	2	1	0	2	1	6
Philosophical works	7	3	2	0	3	15

This list leads to a surprising observation, that is, most Homeric material is to be found in the *Allegorical Commentary*. Although this is Philo's greatest work, the more frequent occurrence of Homer there is perhaps not what could be expected at first sight, in view of Philo's target reader. For the *Allegorical Commentary* was written for a specialised public of Jewish exegetes, and his approach there differs from what we find in the "Exposition of the Law," which was written for a broader reading public. We could a priori expect, then, that Homer would be more important in the Exposition, as an interesting *trait d'union* between pagan and Jewish readers and a welcome means to stimulate the dialogue between the exegesis of Jewish Scripture and the pagan Greek tradition. By reconciling Homer with Scripture, Philo could create the goodwill of pagans for the Jews. But precisely in the Exposition, references to Homer are relatively rare. This observation is important because it already undermines a possible hypothesis about Philo's agenda. Using Homer in order to make propaganda for Jewish faith, and negotiating between the Jewish and pagan intellectual traditions through a (re)interpretation of the *Iliad* and the *Odyssey* are apparently not Philo's prime concern. His interests lie elsewhere.

This raises the question of when and for what purpose Philo makes use of Homer. We are now ready to have a closer look at the relevant material.

[15] David Lincicum, "Philo's Library," *SPhiloA* 26 (2014): 99–114, esp. 114.

3. *Ad quid?*

3.1. Sometimes, Philo uses Homer's verses in order to illustrate a general philosophical insight, as appears from the following three examples.

In *Prov.* 2.95, Alexander points to Homer's description of the land of the Cyclopes (*Od.* 9.106–111) and uses this as an argument against providence. For whereas the barbarian Cyclopes are living in abundance thanks to the exceptional fertility of their land, the pious Greeks live on barren soil. Strikingly enough, Homer is taken very seriously in this passage, as he provides Alexander with a strong argument that is relevant within the context of a difficult philosophical discussion. Such an attitude towards Homer can be found in many pagan philosophers, yet in Philo it is to a certain extent an atypical passage. For the initiative to introduce Homer into the discussion comes from Alexander, who as a character in the dialogue adopts a critical stance towards providence.[16] In that respect, this use of Homer does not reflect Philo's own point of view, and Philo indeed replies to this argument further on in the dialogue (2.109). There, he significantly reduces its importance, emphasizing that the story about the Cyclopes is only a false fabrication of myth-makers, a πλάσμα μύθου,[17] and adding that the argument is anyhow less compelling than Alexander believes, since the Cyclopes also had to sow and cultivate their lands, given the fact that nothing is generated from nothing (*ex nihilo nihil*—a philosophical counterargument). This passage, then, should primarily be understood in light of a polemical discussion and as such illustrates the dynamics and subtleties of Philo's philosophical dialectics. It remains an isolated case though.

Our second example is to be found in *Contempl.* 17. Philo there argues that taking care of property is time-consuming and thus interferes with philosophical thinking. He finds the same idea in two Homeric verses about the Hippemolgi, who are characterized as milk drinkers (γλακτοφάγων), without means of life (ἀβίων), and as the most just of people (*Il.* 13.5–6). Unlike the previous passage, this one illustrates several typical features of Philo's approach towards Homer. First, it is a telling testimony to Philo's in-depth knowledge of Homer. That these verses should be selected is far

[16] Alexander's position may be influenced by pagan thinking. This is suggested by an interesting parallel in Plutarch, *Gryllus* 986F, where a similar opposition can be found, viz. between the fertile land of the Cyclopes and the infertile soil of Ithaca.

[17] The phrase πλάσμα μύθου very often occurs in Philo's works and reflects his generally critical view of Greek mythology. See esp. Anita Méasson, "Un aspect de la critique du polythéisme chez Philon d'Alexandrie: Les acceptions du mot μῦθος dans son œuvre," in *Centre Jean Palerne Mémoires II* (Saint-Étienne: Publications de l'Université de Saint-Étienne, 1980), 74–107.

from self-evident in a context such as this one. In all likelihood, the Alexandrian tradition of Homeric exegesis may have exerted some influence on Philo in this case. The scholia on the *Iliad* indeed mention several interpretations of these verses: some ancient scholars understood the term ἀβίων as a proper name, others proposed different interpretations.[18] Philo may well have been familiar with these philological discussions, and this may account for his use of these verses here. Yet no extant ancient explanation perfectly corresponds to Philo's interpretation. Philo, then, retains his independence and follows his own insights. Second, Philo's interpretation does not rest on an allegorical reading of Homer but on the connection between justice and being without means of life (ἄβιος). He does not develop a sophisticated explanation based on a deeper meaning but directly employs what Homer offers him. It is true that Philo uses the verb αἰνίξασθαι, a technical term that is often used for allegorical interpretations. Yet in this case, the word does not announce an allegorical understanding,[19] but simply indicates that the literal meaning of the passage is not immediately clear. After all, Homer himself does not explain the link between ἀβίων and δικαιοτάτων, but merely juxtaposes the two terms, and it is Philo's task to make Homer's idea explicit. Third, Philo's Homeric exegesis results in a win-win-situation. For, on the one hand, the verses from Homer perfectly illustrate and support Philo's own position; while, on the other hand, Philo's interpretation adds an interesting dimension to this Homeric passage. Without excessive sophistic ingenuity,[20] Philo indeed

[18] See on the ancient interpretations of these difficult Homeric verses, e.g., Félix Buffière, *Les mythes d'Homère et la pensée grecque,* Collection d'études anciennes (Paris: Belles Lettres, 1973), 362–64; A Ivančik, "Die hellenistischen Kommentare zu Homer Il. 13,3–6: Zur Idealisierung des Barbarenbildes. Ephorus und die Philologen der alexandrinischen Schule," in *Hellenismus. Beiträge zur Erforschung von Akkulturation und politischer Ordnung in den Staaten des hellenistischen Zeitalters. Akten des Internationalen Hellenismus-Kolloquiums, 9.–14. März 1994 in Berlin,* ed. Bernd Funck (Tübingen: Mohr Siebeck, 1996), 671–92; Steve Reece, "The Ἄβιοι and the Γάβιοι: An Aeschylean Solution to a Homeric Problem," *AJP* 122 (2001): 465–70; and Nieto Hernández, "Philo and Greek Poetry," 140–44.

[19] *Pace* Nieto Hernández, "Philo and Greek Poetry," 143: "The use of the verb αἰνίττομαι is a clear indication that Philo is launching one of his allegorical interpretations and here, as often, he uses an etymological analysis as his starting point."

[20] Exegetes were more than once blamed for over-sophisticated ingenuity (εὑρησιλογία) in interpreting the poets. See, e.g., Plutarch's attack on Chrysippus (*Adol. poet. aud.* 31E; cf. also Cornutus, 31, p. 64.15–17 Lang) and Porphyry's defence against a similar attack (*Antr. nymph.* 36; p. 81.1–2 Nauck). Philo likewise defends himself against εὑρεσιλογία in *Somn.* 2.301, and, quite remarkably, connects excessive ingenuity with literal interpretations rather than allegorical ones (*Agr.* 157).

succeeds in providing these rather inconspicuous and passing verses with a new and rich meaning.

The last passage to be discussed here is in several respects the counterpart of the previous one. In *Migr.* 156, Philo states that virtuous people often weep, either because they bewail the misfortunes of the unwise or because they are overjoyed by a pure delight that has unexpectedly fallen upon them. This reminds Philo of the Homeric phrase "laughing with tears" (δακρυόεν γελάσασα; *Il.* 6.484). This phrase, contrary to the verses quoted in the previous passage, stems from a famous scene, viz. the farewell of Hector and Andromache. Moreover, we here do not find clear influence of previous Homeric exegesis. The verse is discussed in the scholia on the *Iliad*, but the explanations that can be found there are much more closely related to the immediate context. Philo's general approach, however, is similar to that of *Contempl.* 17, in that he here as well selects one telling detail from Homer's work and creatively uses it to illustrate his own philosophical position. And here as well, he sticks to the literal meaning of the passage, avoiding to look for a deeper allegorical sense, and succeeds in adding a new dimension to the Homeric text. The same win-win-situation as in *Contempl.* 17 thus occurs in *Migr.* 156.

3.2. Often, Homer's verses also throw light on the meaning of Scripture. Philo's focus is then not so much on a general philosophical doctrine as on the exegesis of a particular passage from Scripture—although the difference between both is not always crystal clear. Sometimes, Homer can help in explaining a historical detail. Several passages from the *Odyssey* (4.477; 4.581; 14.258 = 17.427), for instance, can be used in order to demonstrate that the Nile was formerly also called Egypt (*QG* 3.16), and Homer's account of the Trojan War shows that the ancients used weapons of bronze (*QE* 2.102). Occasionally, then, Homer is employed for historical issues.[21]

Much more frequently, however, the Homeric verses are used to clarify the meaning of Scripture. In *QG* 4.20, for instance, Philo discusses how Abraham escorts his three visitors and suggests that he "took as his example what the poet fittingly said." The reference is to *Od.* 15.74, where Menelaus gives his opinion about the task of the good host. Philo's use of Homer in this context is not far-fetched, for every ancient *pepaideumenos* familiar with Homer would in all likelihood recall this passage, which thematises the Homeric ideal of hospitality. We may add in passing that here as well, Philo sticks to the literal interpretation of Homer.

[21] Cf. Nieto Hernández, "Philo and Greek Poetry," 137, n. 11 (*contra* Berthelot "Philon d'Alexandrie, lecteur d'Homère," 156).

A similar obvious connection between a particular passage from Scripture and another one from Homer occurs in *QG* 3.3, where Philo argues that heavenly music does not reach us because it would create madness in those who hear it. A comparison with the song of the Sirens is obvious, even more so since the episode from the *Odyssey* (12.39–46) was well-known and frequently discussed in ancient literature.[22]

Often, however, the link is far less obvious. A well-known example is Philo's exegesis of the Scriptural saying that Cain should not be killed (Gen 4:15). Philo repeatedly (*Det.* 178; *Fug.* 61; *QG* 1.76) connects this with Homer's characterization of Scylla, who is called an immortal evil (κακὸν ἀθάνατον) in the *Odyssey* (12.118).[23] Such a connection is far less evident and is in fact only established through Philo's allegorical understanding of the biblical figure of Cain. Moreover, it even interferes with Philo's exegesis and requires some further specification on his part: the whole idea only concerns this life on earth, for in immortal life, there is no place whatsoever for evil. To a certain extent, then, the reference to Homer muddles things up. But although the parallel is not really helpful, Philo uses it no less than three times, which suggests that he still deemed it an interesting hermeneutical tool for a correct understanding of the figure of Cain.[24] Finally, this passage is rather exceptional in that Philo here also develops an allegorical reading of Homer, since Scylla is, along with Cain, allegorically understood as evil.

Another example is to be found in *Mut.* 179, where Philo connects Abraham's instantaneous hesitation (Gen 17:17) with the Homeric comparison "like a bird's wing or a thought" (*Od.* 7.36). Again, the link between Homer and Scripture is not obvious as such, and the Homeric verses are not particularly famous either. The scholia on the *Iliad* regard

[22] See Buffière *Les mythes d'Homère et la pensée grecque*, 236–37, 380–86 and 474–79, for different interpretations. Esp. interesting are Plato, *Phaedr.* 259a6–c2 and Plutarch, *Quaest. conv.* 745C–746B; cf. Berthelot, "Philo and the Allegorical Interpretation of Homer in the Platonic Tradition, (with an Emphasis on Porphyry's *De antro nympharum*," 161–62.

[23] Philo's allegory has received a lot of attention in scholarly literature; see, e.g., Lamberton, *Homer the Theologian*, 51; Koskenniemi, "Philo and Greek Poets," 310; Berthelot, "Philon d'Alexandrie, lecteur d'Homère," 151–152 and Koskenniemi, "Philo and the Allegorical Interpretation of Homer in the Platonic Tradition (with an Emphasis on Porphyry's *De antro nympharum*," 158; and Niehoff, "Philo and Plutarch on Homer," 134–35).

[24] Cf. Berthelot, "Philo and the Allegorical Interpretation of Homer in the Platonic Tradition (with an Emphasis on Porphyry's *De antro nympharum*") 158: "This passage shows that Philo is so familiar with Homeric verses or expressions, which come so naturally to his mind, that he quotes them even when they tend to complicate his hermeneutical task."

Homer's phrase as proverbial (*ad loc.*), which suggests that the saying had become something of a commonplace, yet Philo is still familiar with its original source, as appears from his explicit reference to "the poet most highly esteemed among the Greeks." Moreover, he uses this quotation from Homer in a particularly appropriate way. For in Homer, the comparison with the bird's wing and with thought is used to underscore the fastness of the Phaeacians' ships. In other words, this is precisely what Philo needs in order to emphasise the swiftness and instantaneous character of Abraham's hesitation. In this case, there is no need of subtle allegorical interpretations, for the literal meaning of the phrase perfectly expresses the idea of speed which Philo needs. That Philo was able to catch this relevant phrase from a Homeric context that is entirely different from his own argument, again illustrates his in-depth knowledge of the Homeric epics.

In *QG* 2.27, Philo deals with the question of why Scripture talks about Noah, the beasts, and the cattle (Gen 8:1) in this strange order. The first explanation Philo borrows from Homer, notably from Nestor's strategy of placing the cowards in the middle (*Il.* 4.299). Just as these cowards would thus be forced to fight, even against their own will, so the wild beasts will benefit from both Noah and the cattle by being placed between them. Once again, a literal interpretation of the Homeric verses throws light on a specific passage from Scripture, and here too, there is no direct intrinsic connection between both passages. Moreover, Nestor's military strategy does not seem to have received special attention in ancient Homeric exegesis. It played an important role, however, in the rhetorical tradition, where the so-called *ordo Homericus* was recommended in the domain of *dispositio*. The orator had to place his weakest arguments somewhere in the middle, where he could quickly treat them, reserving his better points for the beginning and the end, imitating Demosthenes's approach in his famous *On the crown*.[25] Philo's familiarity with rhetoric[26] can have played

[25] Quintilian, 5,12,14 (with explicit reference to the Homeric passage); cf. also Cicero, *Orator* 50; Ps.-Cicero, *Rhet. Her.* 3.18; *Anon. Seguer.* 1:452.7–12 Sp.

[26] See, e.g., Alexandre, "La culture profane chez Philon," in *Philon d'Alexandrie: Colloques nationaux du Centre national de la Recherche Scientifique. Lyon, 11–15 Septembre 1966* (Paris: CNRS, 1967), 105–29, esp. 113–16; A. Michel, "Quelques aspects de la rhétorique chez Philon," in *Philon d'Alexandrie,* 81–103; Alan Mendelson, *Secular Education in Philo of Alexandria,* HUCM 7 (Cincinnati: Hebrew Union College Press, 1982), 7–10; J. Leopold, "Philo's Knowledge of Rhetorical Theory," in *Two Treatises of Philo of Alexandria: A Commentary on De Gigantibus and Quod Deus Sit Immutabilis,* ed. David Winston and John Dillon, BJS 25 (Chico: Scholars Press, 1983), 129–36; Thomas M. Conley, "Philo's Rhetoric: Argumentation and Style," *ANRW* 2.21.1:343–71 and Conley, "Philo of Alexandria," in *Handbook of Classical Rhetoric in the Hellenistic Period. 330 B.C.–A.D. 400,* ed. Stanley E. Porter (Leiden: Brill, 2001), 695–713; and Michael Martin, "Philo's Use of Syncrisis: An

its part, although he creatively uses the Homeric lines and introduces them into an entirely new context.

A last example is *QG* 1.7 concerning the question why Paradise is planted in Eden towards the East (Gen 2:8). As usual, Philo proposes different explanations. The second one is that the region of the East is the right side of the World, whereas the region of the West is the left. And this, so Philo argues, appears from Homer, who calls "the birds in the region of the East 'right,' and those which are in the region of the West 'on the left side.'" This is an allusion to the words of Hector in *Il.* 12.239–240. Hector's basic point there is that he disregards the omens of birds, whether they go to the right toward dawn and sun or to the left toward darkness, and only obeys Zeus. It is clear, then, that the distinction between left and right, West and East, is of secondary importance here: the full emphasis is on Zeus. Yet it is this distinction that Philo picks up and makes the core of his argument. Traditional Homeric exegesis may have exerted some influence, since the scholia *ad loc.* offer some close parallels, but even if that is true, the passage still testifies to Philo's eminent knowledge of Homer, much more indeed than a purely quantitative approach that is confined to a mere counting and listing of quotations.

3.3. But this is not all. Up to now, Philo's reception of Homer appeared to be a fairly theoretical, academic matter. Other passages from Philo's works, however, show that Homer could also be important for concrete life. Two charming anecdotes from *Every Good Person is Free* may serve as a point of departure. In *Prob.* 122, Philo tells how Diogenes was taking his dinner before he was sold as a slave and how he encouraged one of his companions with a well-chosen reference to Achilles's comforting words about Niobe, who also thought of food although she had lost twelve children (*Il.* 24.602–604). A few paragraphs further down (*Prob.* 125), he mentions Chaereas's frank reply to king Ptolemy: "Be king of the Egyptians —I care not for you, nor am I concerned about your anger," which is a clever adaptation of Agamemnon's reply to Achilles in *Il.* 1.180–181. Twice, we get an ingenious reception of Homeric verses that are directly applied to the present circumstances: Diogenes as it were becomes the new Achilles and Chaereas an Agamemnon *redivivus*. After all these centuries, Homer is still very much alive. Yet twice, this "update" of Homer comes from pagan intellectuals, who are the direct heirs of the great poet. Can we find instances of the same approach in Philo's own thinking as well?

Examination of Philonic Composition in the Light of the Progymnasmata," *PRSt* 30 (2003): 271–97.

Yes we can. Two examples can be found in *On the Embassy to Gaius*. In *Legat.* 80, Philo recalls how Gaius claimed honors of different gods, as a kind of Proteus who was able to transform into elements, animals, and plants—an explicit reference to *Od.* 4.456–458. In *Legat.* 149, he elaborates on a panegyric of Augustus, who demonstrated the truth of Homer's saying that "it is not well that many lords should rule" (*Il.* 2.204).[27] In both cases, Philo thus likewise applies Homeric verses to the contemporary situation. This application, however, is facilitated by the fact that he is twice dealing with pagans and thus talks about them in their own cultural idiom.

Yet a similar approach can also be found elsewhere. In *Prov.* 112, for instance, Philo tells the story of two athletes who were equally strong and were fighting until they both fell dead. This anecdote reminds Philo of Andromache's famous words to her husband: "thy own prowess will destroy thee" (*Il.* 6.407). Here too, we come across fundamentally the same dynamics: a particular scene from everyday life is directly connected with Homer. Thus, concrete reality is seen in a new light, whereas, vice versa, it also confirms the timelessness of Homer, who still proves relevant for real life. The same use of Homer also appears in *Anim.* 54, where Philo briefly points to the behaviour of animals during contests. These animals, so he says, lash themselves with their tails as if they urge themselves on to greater speed and thus show so many centuries later precisely the same conduct as the lion described by Homer in *Il.* 20.170–171.

Moreover, Homer can even be used as a source for concrete moral advice. The simple cloak of the swineherd Eumenes, for instance, contrasts with the purple clothing of the vainglorious rich (*Somn.* 2.53). For Homer presents the cloak as wind-proof (ἀλεξάνεμος [*Od.* 14.529]), that is, useful without being excessively luxurious, and in that sense provides his readers with useful moral advice. As usual, Philo takes over Homeric material without far-reaching allegorical interpretations, and again with the same win-win result, adding a new dimension to both his own argument and the Homeric text.

Bad behaviour at a symposium is another topic that can be illustrated through Homer's verses. The immoderate man "drinks with a yawning maw,"—a reference to Antinous's unjustified accusation of Odysseus (*Od.* 21.294). In this passage from *Fug.* (31), Homer's words, which are, as usual, understood in their literal sense, add a further twist to Philo's argument.

27 In the scholia *ad loc.*, the latter passage is also connected with historical figures. Cf. also Plutarch, *Ant.* 81.5, on Areius's use of the same verse in his political advice to Octavian.

The suggestion is that the virtuous man should not be afraid of participating in luxurious symposia, as he thus finds himself in the situation of righteous Odysseus. The point is not explicitly made by Philo—maybe because it would imply a straightforwardly positive picture of Odysseus as a model worthy of imitation—but the erudite reader, who is familiar with Homer's *Odyssey* and able to take into account the original context of the verse, can appreciate it as an additional argument. Furthermore, a similar use of Homer in order to illustrate blameworthy conduct during a symposium can be found in *Contempl.* 40. Here, Philo refers to the Cyclops eating "goblets of men" (cf. *Od.* 9.374). *Mutatis mutandis,* Philo adopts the same course as Diogenes and Chaereas: he detects an interesting parallel between a concrete situation of his own day (cf. *Plant.* 160) and what he can read in Homer. And this parallel results in a creative reception in which the reality of everyday life is seen in a new perspective. Passages such as this one interestingly show that Homer's epics were not merely relevant for a pagan's self-understanding and cultural identity, but to a certain extent even for that of cultivated Jews like Philo.

4. *Interpretative Strategies in Philo's Reading of Homer*

4.1. In the great majority of passages discussed so far, Philo preferred a literal interpretation of Homer's verses. At first sight, this observation is rather surprising in light of Philo's fondness for allegorical interpretations of Scripture. We might expect that he would apply the same allegorical approach towards Homer too. This, however, is not the case: as a matter of fact, we find very few examples of allegorical readings in which, for instance, the gods are conceived as physical powers or moral qualities. Philo is familiar with such interpretations and even defends them once in *On Providence* (2.40–41),[28] but his argument there is largely made *pour le besoin de la cause.* It is a traditional argument that in this particular context proves useful to undermine Alexander's foregoing criticism of Homer, but it should not be regarded as the theoretical foundation of Philo's own interpretative position. The principle of *testis unus testis nullus* is often problematic when dealing with ancient texts, but in this case it holds true. When Homer's verses are problematic for whatever reason, Philo does not explain them away by means of subtle allegories, but simply ignores them. Well-known allegorical interpretations of the gods are rejected in *Decal.* 54–

[28] Cf. also *Aet.* 127, which is inserted in our above list of references to Homer on the basis of this parallel with *Prov.* 2.40–41.

55 and *Contempl.* 3.[29] The astronomical allegory of the Dioscuri as the two hemispheres is likewise rejected (*Decal.* 56, referring to *Od.* 11.303). Even the famous allegory of the *Odyssey* as the story of the return of the soul to its celestial homeland has left (almost) no trace in Philo's works.[30] Such ideas could better be illustrated by Scripture.[31]

This does not imply, however, that allegorical interpretations of Homer nowhere occur in Philo's works. We have already discussed his allegorical understanding of Cain, which entailed a moral allegory of Scylla (cf. *supra* 3.2). A few passages also contain an interesting allegory of Ganymede as the logos outpouring from God.[32] But one of the clearest cases can be found in *Migr.* 195, where Philo deals with Abraham's gradual progress. When the latter has left behind the phase of astrology, he turns to self-examination, examining "what evil and what good has been done in his hall"—a verbatim quotation from Homer's *Odyssey* (4.392). The same quotation, similarly understood, also occurs in *Somn.* 1.57. In Homer, the words are said by Menelaus, who meets in Egypt Eidothea, Proteus' daughter. She tells him that her father can show him how he will return home and "what evil and what good had been done in his hall." The hall (μέγαρον), then, obviously refers to a real building. In Philo, however, it is understood as the house of man (τὸν ἴδιον οἶκον), that is, his body (σώματος), sense-perception and speech. For this allegorical interpretation, an interesting parallel can be found in Plutarch (who, by the way, was himself no enthusiast devotee of allegorical interpretation of poetry; cf. *Adol. poet. aud.* 19EF). In *Tu. san.* 122D, he explicitly connects the term μέγαρον in this Homeric quotation with σῶμα. This suggests that there may have existed a tradition in which this verse was allegorically understood,[33] especially in

[29] See on both passages J. Schwartz, "Philon et l'apologétique chrétienne du second siècle," in *Hommages à André Dupont-Sommer*, ed. André Caquot and Marc Philonenko (Paris: Adrien-Maisonneuve, 1971), 497–507.

[30] *Contra* Pierre Boyancé, "Écho des exégèses de la mythologie grecque chez Philon," in *Philon d'Alexandrie*, 169–88, esp. 169–73 and Méasson, *Du char ailé de Zeus à l'Arche d'Alliance*, 337–68, who both refer to *Agr.* 65 ("a wise man's soul ever finds heaven to be his fatherland and earth a foreign country") as the principal text; cf. also *Conf.* 77–78. Yet the idea of heaven as the homeland of the soul is nowhere directly connected with Homer's *Odyssey*.

[31] Thus Berthelot, "Philo and the Allegorical Interpretation of Homer in the Platonic Tradition (with an Emphasis on Porphyry's *De antro nympharum*," 172.

[32] *Deus* 155–158; *Somn.* 2.183 and 249; *Prov.* 2.7; see on this John Dillon, "Ganymede as the Logos: Traces of a Forgotten Allegorization in Philo?," *CQ* 31 (1981): 183–85. Another allegorical interpretation of Homer can be found in *QG* 4.183: see on this *infra*, 4.4b.

[33] Cf. also Plutarch, *Comm. not.* 1063D, where it is argued that a man who deliberates about life and death should not examine "what evil and what good had been done in his

philosophical circles (since it is not to be found in the scholia on Homer), and that this tradition may have exerted its influence on Philo here. However that may be, it is clear in any case that there is no *anathema* on allegorical interpretation of Homer in Philo's works. Such interpretations can occasionally be found, although they are few and far between.

4.2. More frequent are traces of previous Homeric scholarship in Alexandria. This is not surprising, for Niehoff has demonstrated that this scholarly tradition has influenced Philo's exegesis of Scripture.[34] Several traditional strategies of Homeric exegesis can indeed be found in Philo's works, especially in the *Allegorical Commentary*, where, as we have seen above (*supra* 2, *sub fin.*), references to Homer are more prominent than in Philo's other treatises. Moreover, traditional allegories of Homeric passages are more than once transformed and reoriented towards Philo's own Scriptural framework. The most obvious example is, of course, the Stoic allegory of Penelope and the suitors as the confrontation between virtue and encyclical education, which is applied by Philo to the relation between Sarah and Hagar.[35] An analogous example is that of the doctrine of the two λόγοι which is connected by Philo with Moses and Aaron. It has been argued on the basis of evidence from the scholia on Homer that this allegory should likewise be traced back to previous Homer interpretations, more precisely to Aristarchus's exegesis of the Homeric passage about the Aloadae (*Od.* 11.315–316).[36] This is possible, though not certain, for the doctrine of the two λόγοι was well-known[37] and played an important role in the inter-school polemics about the rationality of animals. That Philo was

---

hall." According to Diogenes Laertius 6.103, the verse was often quoted by Diogenes the Cynic.

34 See Maren R. Niehoff, "Homeric Scholarship and Bible Exegesis in Ancient Alexandria: Evidence from Philo's 'Quarrelsome' Colleagues," *CQ* 57 (2007): 166–82 and Niehoff, *Jewish Exegesis and Homeric Scholarship in Alexandria* (Cambridge: Cambridge University Press, 2011).

35 For the Stoic allegory, see, e.g., Ps.-Plutarch, *Lib. ed.* 7D; Diogenes Laertius 2.79; Stobaeus, 3.4.109; see further Wolfson, *Philo*, 1:145–46; Alexandre, "La culture profane chez Philon," 111–12; Albert Henrichs, "Philosophy, the Handmaiden of Theology," *GRBS* 9 (1968): 437–450, esp. 444–45; Samuel Sandmel, *Philo of Alexandria, An Introduction* (Oxford: Oxford University Press, 1979), 19–21; Mendelson, *Secular Education in Philo of Alexandria*, xxiii–xxiv and 81; and Annewies van den Hoek, "Mistress and Servant. An Allegorical Theme in Philo, Clement and Origin," in *Origeniana Quarta: Die Referate des 4. Internationalen Origineskongresses (Innsbruck, 2.–6. September 1985)*, ed. L. Lies (Innsbruck: Tyrolia, 1987), 344–48.

36 See Adam Kamesar, "The *Logos Endiathetos* and the *Logos Prophorikos* in Allegorical Interpretation: Philo and the D-Scholia to the *Iliad*," *GRBS* 44 (2004): 163–81.

37 Plutarch calls it a trivial commonplace in *Max. princ.* 777B.

familiar with this debate, appears from his dialogue *On the Animals*.[38] He thus did not need the specific exegetical tradition about Homer's Aloadae to apply the theory of the two λόγοι to the biblical figures of Moses and Aaron.

Nevertheless, we have already seen in our discussion of *Contempl.* 17 and *QG* 1.7 (cf. *supra*, 3.1 and 3.2 respectively) that Philo sometimes benefits from the previous Alexandrian exegesis of Homer. Moreover, Philo once explicitly refers to the exegetes (*Prov.* 2.40 on the *enarratores*). On several occasions, they are indeed present at the background, although they are never brought to the fore. Philo never explicitly takes issue with them and always follows his own insights. We may conclude, then, that there is a certain influence of the scholarly tradition of Homeric exegesis, but that it is less decisive than is sometimes suggested in scholarly literature.

4.3. We have seen that Philo relatively seldom proposes an allegorical interpretation of Homer. Yet this does not imply that he always takes Homer's words at face value. He rather makes use of several subtle strategies.

Firstly, he nearly always omits the original context of the verses which he quotes, so that the Homeric verse stands on itself. Sometimes, he inserts into his argument typically Homeric phrases such as "a witless infant knows" (*Decal.* 69; cf. Homer, *Il.* 17.32 and 20.198), "with hand and foot" (*Sacr.* 38 and *Post.* 151; cf. *Il.* 20.360–361), keeping away "from the smoke and wave" (*Somn.* 2.70; cf. *Od.* 12.219 on Charybdis), and "on the threshold of old age" (*Somn.* 2.148; the phrase repeatedly occurs in Homer). In all likelihood, such general phrases had taken on a proverbial character, and it may not be a coincidence that in none of the four cases, Philo explicitly refers to Homer or even to the poetic tradition.[39] In such cases—an absolute minority—the quotations hardly contribute to Philo's argument and their first function seems to concern *ornatus*.

[38] *Anim.* 13–15 deals with the λόγος προφορικός, 16–70 with the λόγος ἐνδιάθετος. Parallel discussions are to be found in Porphyry, *Abst.* 3.3.2–3.18.2 and Sextus Empiricus, *Pyr.* 1.65–75. See Georg Tappe, *De Philonis libro qui inscribitur Ἀλέξανδρος ἢ περὶ τοῦ λόγου ἔχειν τὰ ἄλογα ζῷα quaestiones selectae* (Diss. Göttingen, 1912), who suggests (along the lines of *Quellenforschung* that was very much *en vogue* at that moment) that the three authors made use of the same source (viz. an anti-Stoic work written by an Academic author, perhaps Carneades). Even though such *Quellenforschung* is nowadays strongly criticised, the parallels at least show that Philo's argument is rooted in a more general, traditional debate among different philosophical schools.

[39] In *Sacr.* 38 and *Post.* 151, he merely refers to τὸ λεγόμενον; in *Somn.* 2.70, the phrase is even connected with another such saying (τὸ τοῦ λόγου τοῦτο), viz. the "tip of the toe."

Yet even in such cases, the Homeric material is often not merely introduced for the sake of literary embellishment, as appears from the following series of examples. Four times in his oeuvre, Philo refers to the Homeric expression "shepherd of the people" (ποιμὴν λαῶν; *Agr.* 41; *Ios.* 2; *Mos.* 1.61; *Prob.* 31). This is a typically Homeric phrase, a kind of formulaic epithet of the king, yet it is taken very seriously by Philo and used to illustrate his own conception of good leadership. At the same time, his use of the phrase is one more example of his interpretive versatility, for whereas he usually approves of this characterisation of the king, he is more critical in *Every Good Man is Free*. There, he argues that the title applies to the good rather than to the king.

A somewhat similar case can be found in *Prov.* 2.19, where Philo recalls that clothes are called by Homer the "flower of the sheep." Again, a recurrent Homeric phrase is understood from a philosophical perspective. It entails a kind of "physical definition" which reduces objects to their very essence: costly clothes are nothing but wool of ordinary sheep. Close parallels can be found in Marcus Aurelius (6.13), where such physical definitions very often occur,[40] and in Lucian, *Demonax* 41. Philo adopts the same approach and cleverly takes advantage of a Homeric saying. Here as well, then, the Homeric material has a philosophical relevance that goes far beyond stylistic or literary concerns.

Other typical phrases are used to interpret passages from Scripture. In *QG* 4.238, for instance, Philo deals with the meaning of the words εἶπεν ἐν τῇ διανοίᾳ αὐτοῦ ("he said in his mind") in the Septuagint translation of Gen 27:41 and connects these words with Homeric idiom. This use of Homer can be compared with the cases discussed above in section 3, though here, Philo does not use one specific Homeric verse to explain Scripture but rather a well-known Homeric turn. A similar case can be found in *Spec.* 1.74, which concerns the reason why there is no grove within the walled area of the temple. Philo mentions several possible reasons; the third is that wild plants are useless and are only a "burden of the soil" (ἄχθος γῆς; referring to Homer, *Il.* 18.104: ἄχθος ἀρούρης). Philo's allusion to this famous[41] passage from Homer, where Achilles emphasises his own uselessness, has

[40] See, e.g., Pierre Hadot, "La physique comme exercice spirituel ou pessimisme et optimisme chez Marc Aurèle," *RTP* Ser. III, 22 (1972): 225–39, esp. 229–39; Aurèle, *La citadelle intérieure: Introduction aux Pensées de Marc Aurèle* (Paris: Fayard, 1992), 122–23; cf. also R. B. Rutherford, *The Meditations of Marcus Aurelius: A Study* (Oxford: Clarendon, 1989).

[41] It is often quoted or referred to in extant Greek literature; see, e.g., Plato, *Apol.* 28d4; Plutarch, *Tranq. an.* 465F; Lucian, *Icar.* 29 and *Apology* 14; Aelius Aristides, 28.25; Libanius, *Orat.* 1.101.

been understood as a kind of joke,[42] but this need not be the case. For the idea of uselessness that is expressed in the Homeric phrase is precisely what Philo needs for his own argument, and in a certain sense, the phrase is even more relevant for plants than for the hero, since plants directly get the nourishment from the soil and as such exhaust the soil more actively. In that sense, this is not a joke but a pertinent and adequate application of the Homeric verse to Philo's own argument.

In other instances, Philo's use of a Homeric turn entails an intensification of the tone. This has been demonstrated convincingly for Philo's allusion to Homer's view of ambrosia in *Somn.* 2.249.[43] A parallel example is to be found in *Agr.* 24, where Philo subtly refers to *Il.* 5.587. In Homer, Sarpedon warns Hector that he should not be caught in an all-ensnaring net. Philo only takes over the adjective πάναγρα, isolated from its original context, in order to describe how the great majority of people are pursuing pleasure with all-capturing nets. Again, this is obviously more than just a fine *flosculum* for *ornatus's* sake. It also helps Philo's characterization of the ordinary people and intensifies the tone of his argument: they are really striving for every kind of pleasure.

The same dynamics can finally be found in *Ebr.* 103, where we find a sophisticated reference to the beginning of the famous catalogue of ships in book 2 of the *Iliad*. Homer declares that he cannot name the multitude of ordinary soldiers, "not even if he had ten tongues and ten mouths and a voice unwearying" (*Il.* 2.489). Philo for his part talks about the seductive power of the passions and adds that, even though each of these passions "should have a thousand tongues and mouths [μυρίοις στόμασι καὶ γλώτταις] with which to swell the war-shout [ὁμάδῳ], to use the poet's phrase, yet it could not confuse the ears of the perfect Sage." Here we may detect a double allusion to Homer. On the one hand, Philo uses the Homeric term ὅμαδος, and it is this use which explains the explicit reference κατὰ τοὺς ποιητάς (cf. its attributive position). On the other hand, the combination of στόμασι and γλώτταις recalls the above mentioned passage from the second book of the *Iliad*. But Philo strongly blows up the Homeric material: δέκα has become μυρίοις and he no longer deals with a list of ships but with war-cry. This reorientation is absolutely to the point, for it turns the passions into a horde of enemies who attack the sage amidst loud war-cries. This image obviously illustrates the danger of the passions much better and at the same time underscores the opposition between the turmoil of the passions and the unconquerable tranquillity of the sage. Here as well,

42 Thus Nieto Hernández, "Philo and Greek Poetry," 146–48.
43 See Ibid., 144–46.

Philo's use of Homer strongly intensifies the effect of his words and thus significantly contributes to his own position.

In all of these cases, then, typically Homeric turns or phrases prove to be relevant with regard to the content of Philo's arguments. They are not merely used for stylistic reasons but prove to be part and parcel of the argumentation. And this reflects the same careful reading of Homer that we also found above. Philo did not deal with Homer as a reservoir of possible *flosculi*, but as a storehouse of useful ideas that could be employed for his own purposes.

It may be added that Philo's usual omission of the original context sometimes leads to a new perspective. An interesting example is *Aet.* 132, where Philo defends the view that the world is everlasting.[44] His opponents—characterized as sophists—regard the unevenness (ἀνωμαλία) of the earth as an argument against its eternity. Philo replies by pointing to the trees, which shed their leaves in autumn and again bloom in spring, and then quotes *Il.* 6.147–148. These are famous lines from Glaucus's speech to Diomedes. The point of Glaucus's celebrated comparison "we are like the leaves" is, of course, the *mortality* of humankind.[45] Philo for his part introduces the verses into a completely different context, viz. a philosophical argument about *continuity*. Thus, while sticking to the literal meaning of the lines, he gives them an interesting turn.

4.4. Philo does not only omit the original context of the Homeric verses he quotes, but also "purges away" specific elements.

(1) Quite often, references to polytheism are strategically removed,[46] as in *Prov.* 2.16, where Philo leaves out a half verse that refers to the immortal gods (ἀθανάτοισι) or in *Conf.* 170, where he quotes, in support of his own monotheistic view, the Homeric verses that criticise πολυκοιρανίη ("the rule of many") and prefer the rule of one king (*Il.* 2.204–205). In Homer, these words are spoken by Odysseus who tries to control the soldiers and recommends them to listen to better men. He refers to one king who has received his power from Zeus himself. This addition, however, which adds a great deal to the persuasiveness of Odysseus's argument, is dropped by

[44] This is not Philo's real view; see David T. Runia,"Philo's De aeternitate mundi: The Problem of Its Interpretation," *VC* 35 (1981): 105–51, for a thorough discussion of what Philo is doing in *Aet.* 20–149.

[45] And so it was also understood by later authors; see, e.g., Plutarch, *Sera* 560C and *Suav. viv.* 1090B; cf. also (Ps.-?)Plutarch, *Cons. Apoll.* 104E.

[46] For Philo's criticism of polytheism, see esp. Karl-Gustav Sandelin, "The Danger of Idolatry According to Philo of Alexandria," *Temenos* 27 (1991): 109–50.

Philo, who corrects Homer in another way too. In his view, the saying "could be said with more justice of the world and of God than of cities and men." In other words, Philo takes over the basic ideal of one ruler which he finds in this Homeric passage, but entirely reorients it in light of his own monotheistic perspective.[47]

A similar strategy occurs in *Ios.* 265. Joseph there talks about the uncreated, eternal father, "who surveys all things and hears all things" (a verbatim quotation from Homer, *Il.* 3.277 = *Od.* 11.109 and 12.323). In Homer, these verses portray Helios and thus concern corporeal perception. By cleverly omitting the direct reference to Helios, Philo is able to connect the quotation with his own immaterial God and thus with mental perception. A similar emphasis on monotheism occurs in *Prov.* 2.15. Philo again points to one God who rules over the universe as a just king. Such a king is a father, and that is why Homer has called Zeus "father of gods and men." At first sight, this is quite an odd argument, since the quotation from Homer obviously implies a polytheistic perspective.[48] And yet, Philo mentions the lines with approval. In fact, they are interesting for him for at least two reasons. On the one hand, Homer characterizes his supreme deity as a father figure, and this is perfectly in line with Philo's own conception of God as a kind and caring father. On the other hand, Homer's phrase ascribes to Zeus a prominent position vis-à-vis the other gods. Such a perspective, albeit polytheistic, is not entirely irreconcilable with Philo's theological position[49] and can be regarded as a first step towards monotheism.[50]

In *QG* 4.8, Philo discusses the Scriptural passage where Abraham tells Sarah to mix three measures of wheat-flour (Gen 18:6). In his view, the choice for three measures is most natural, since everything is measured by three, as Homer knew as well. Philo explicitly quotes and approves Homer's position (*Il.* 15.189), which may again seem surprising, for the original context of the quotation is imbued with a polytheistic outlook. It actually concerns the division of power between Zeus, Poseidon, and Hades. As usual, Philo isolates the verse from its context, purifies it from every polytheistic taint, and then uses the general idea in order to explain a passage from Scripture.

47 Cf. Koskenniemi, "Philo and Greek Poets," 307.

48 It is perhaps no coincidence that the quotation is deleted from the text by Eusebius (*Praep. ev.* 8.14.3).

49 Philo also speaks of God as the God "not only of men but also of gods" (*Spec.* 1.307 and 2.165; *Mos.* 2.206; cf. Deut 10:17); Wolfson, *Philo,* 1:38–39 and 173–74.

50 Cf. also Marcel Simon, "Jupiter-Yahvé : Sur un essai de théologie pagano-juive," *Numen* 23 (1976): 40–66.

A final example is Philo's clever use of Homer in *Aet.* 37. He there argues that the nature of the universe desires the conservation of the All and therefore should be indestructible, as it prevails over everything. This idea of prevalence is further expressed by means of two verses from Homer (*Od.* 6.107–108), which deal with Artemis and her nymphs. What Homer says about the goddess and her companions is applied by Philo to the universe and its particular parts. In other words, it is Homer's idea of the relation between Artemis and her subordinate nymphs that is important for Philo: just as Artemis is superior, so is the universe. The reference to the goddess, however, is omitted and the idea is reoriented towards a general philosophical argument. This passage is one further telling illustration of Philo's outstanding familiarity with Homer. He here selects a core idea from a passing comparison that deals with a completely different topic—and that is not discussed in the scholia—and employs it for his own argumentative purposes.

(2) Next to the polytheistic context, the Homeric heroes also fade into the background, especially Agamemnon. In *Somn.* 2.144, for instance, Philo observes how many soldiers have bravely fought in the war and are then slaughtered "like oxen at the stall." The allusion to Agamemnon's fate is clear of course and is made even clearer by the reference to Homer (*Od.* 4.535 and 11.411). Yet Agamemnon himself is not mentioned and Philo prefers a more general perspective. To that purpose, he even slightly adapts the Homeric text, changing the singular βοῦν into the plural βόες. Thus we get a general story about people who "are shipwrecked in harbor itself" (*Somn.* 2.143).

In *QG.* 4.183, Agamemnon again disappears from sight. Philo argues that the passions should be ruled by a governor who has power as "both a goodly king and a warlike spearman." This is how Helen characterizes Agamemnon in *Il.* 3.179. Philo forgets about Agamemnon and uses this famous verse[51] in order to explain the deeper meaning of a Scriptural passage. Moreover, this is one of the rare cases where a verse from Homer is understood in an allegorical way: the king and spearman is none other than the mind. Whereas this passage at least preserves the idea of kingship, in *Her.* 189 even this idea is lost. Philo explains Moses's stipulation concerning the half of the didrachmon (Exod 30:15) by observing that every

[51] According to Plutarch (*Alex. fort.* 331CD), it was the favorite verse of Alexander the Great. Zosimus (3.34.4) says that the verse was used in the funeral inscription on Julian's tomb. It was also used in philosophical discussions, as appears, e.g., from Xenophon, *Mem.* 3.2.2 and *Symp.* 4.6; Ps.-Plutarch, *Plac. philos.* 881D.

number begins and ends with the unit. In this context, he quotes Nestor's words about Agamemnon (*Il.* 9.97): "with you I shall end and with you I shall begin." Nestor, however, also motivates his statement by underlining that Agamemnon is the ruler of many men and that he has received his kingly power from Zeus. This perspective has been dropped. In Philo's argument, the Homeric verses no longer focus on Agamemnon's distinguished position but throw light on the role of the unit. The Homeric king is replaced by elementary mathematics.

An analogous approach is followed regarding other Homeric heroes. In *Spec.* 2.6, for instance, Philo quotes Hector's words (*Il.* 6.266) and applies them to his own argument, without mentioning Hector by name. In *Somn.* 1.150, he characterizes the life of the practicer as a life "of alternate days" (ἑτερήμερος). This refers to *Od.* 11.303, where Homer deals with the Dioscuri who live one day and are dead one day. Yet in this case too, Philo does not mention the Dioscuri by name. He deals with the practicer, whose paradigm is Jacob rather than Castor and Polydeuces.

Here we also find the basic explanation of the above discussed strategy. The Homeric heroes are not really useful for Philo's purposes: they never function as paradigmatic figures whose behavior is worthy of imitation. That role is reserved for Abraham, Isaac and Jacob, and for so many other figures from Scripture. In *Prov.* 2.65, a few Homeric heroes are mentioned as prototypical examples of ephemeral power and beauty, and in *Contempl.* 9, Thersites is referred to as the classic example of ugliness. Especially illustrative is Philo's remark in *Congr.* 15 that the misery of the heroes can help to "despise the vain delusions of our empty imagination." This implies that they can to a certain extent be useful,[52] but that does not turn them into paradigmatic models of correct conduct.[53] Characteristically enough, the only time that the great Homeric heroes Patroclus and Ajax are mentioned in Philo, they turn out to be elephants (*Animal.* 59 and 89).

5. *Conclusion: Towards a More General Perspective*

The above analyses of specific passages have shown time and again that Homer's poetry plays a significant part in the presentation and elaboration of Philo's ideas. It is time now to broaden the perspective in an attempt to reach a better understanding of Philo's general evaluation of the relevance and importance of Homer.

52 See on this passage Niehoff, "Philo and Plutarch on Homer," 131.

53 That Philo's positive examples are all derived from Scripture is argued by Mendelson, *Secular Education in Philo of Alexandria*, 6–7.

5.1. Firstly, Philo steers in his Homer reception a middle course between two extreme positions. One extreme is mentioned at the outset of *On the Confusion of Tongues*. There Philo attacks some unnamed exegetes who connect the biblical story of the Tower of Babel with Homer's account of the Aloadae (*Od.* 11.315–316) and conclude that Scripture also contains mythical sections. This exegetical stance, which suggests an open-minded approach to Scripture, has received quite some attention in scholarly literature and therefore need not detain us here.[54] What is interesting for our focus is that these Jewish exegetes regard Homer's text as a myth that is on a level with some Scriptural passages. This position is rejected by Philo in radical terms: a clear dividing line should be established between Homer and Scripture.

Such a strict dividing line can be found in Plato, who banishes the poets from his ideal state. This is the other extreme, which is likewise rejected by Philo. He briefly presents the Platonic position in *On Providence* 2.34–39. His nephew Alexander there argues in a Platonic vein that all poems are full of impiety, that we are charmed by poetic language, and that the poets say nothing true about the gods (*vera de dis poetarum nemo dicit* [2.39]). Alexander's massive attack on the poets lacks any nuance and is countered by Philo, who appears as Alexander's interlocutor in this dialogue. Philo argues that the poets often do speak the truth, but that we have to search for the deeper meaning of their words (*Prov.* 2.40–41). In other terms, the poets can be defended against Plato's criticism by means of an allegorical reading. This is a traditional argument which, however, at best only partially reflects Philo's own position (cf. *supra* 4.1). We have seen indeed that Philo now and then indeed proposes allegorical interpretations of Homer, but such cases remain in the end rather exceptional. Thus, this passage from *Prov.* requires a complementary perspective. Nevertheless, it shows that the extreme Platonic position is no less criticized than that of Philo's fellow exegetes.

5.2. And thus we get a well-balanced position that both welcomes Homer and insists on the clear difference between Scripture and Homeric epics. The question remains, however, why Homer should be rescued at all. A straightforward rejection would have been much easier. Why did Philo,

[54] See esp. Niehoff, *Jewish Exegesis and Homeric Scholarship in Alexandria*, 77–86; cf. also Jean Pépin, *Mythe et allégorie: Les origines grecques et les contestations judéo-chrétiennes* (Paris: Études augustiniennes, 1976), 229–30; and, on Philo's reception of Homer's story of the Aloadae, Kamesar, "The *Logos Endiathetos* and the *Logos Prophorikos* in Allegorical Interpretation."

who endorsed the Platonic position on so many important issues, refuse to accept Plato's view of Homer? A first possible answer rests on the great respectability of Homer, who was widely regarded as the authority par excellence on so many aspects of human life. At first sight, this answer may seem odd and unconvincing in view of Philo's Jewish perspective. That could be the motivation of pagan authors, of course, but why would Philo share their view? Yet we have seen above that Philo and pagan authors were not so different in discovering connections between Homer's text and real life (*supra* 3.3) and we may here add that Philo repeatedly stresses Homer's authoritative position. He is characterized as the greatest and most famous of Greek poets (*Conf.* 4; *Mut.* 179; *Prov.* 2.15; cf. *Abr.* 10 and *QG* 4.2), whose fame is indeed spread over the whole world (*Prov.* 2.40). Philo, then, is apparently not indifferent to this aspect. Even more, such characterizations seem to suggest that Homer is introduced as a kind of *argumentum ex auctoritate*. It is an important source that cannot be neglected, not even by Jewish thinkers whose loyalty lies with Scripture.

Yet Homer's lasting relevance is not justified by his great fame alone: it also rests on the usefulness of his verses. This conviction already appears from Philo's defence of Homer against the Platonizing Alexander in *Prov.* 2.40 and is further elaborated in a well-known passage from *Somn.* (1.233). There Philo recalls an old story about the gods who went to the cities in human shape in order to observe the transgressions of men. The allusion is to *Od.* 17.485–487, and Philo's evaluation is particularly clear: the story is both false and useful (τάχα μὲν οὐκ ἀληθῶς, πάντως δὲ λυσιτελῶς καὶ συμφερόντως). Precisely the same evaluation returns in *Questions and Answers on Genesis* 4.2, where the story is used in a discussion of God's appearance to Abraham at Mamre.[55] Here too, Homer's story is regarded as false (because it reflects his polytheistic beliefs) yet useful (in that it throws light on the passage from Scripture).

It is important to see how nuanced Philo's position actually is. It has often been regarded as anti-Platonic,[56] but this is only half of the truth. As a matter of fact, Philo also echoes Plato's criticism that the story is false, and the importance of this point appears more clearly when we compare Philo's

[55] The (Armenian text of the) passage is discussed in detail in G. Bolognesi, "Postille sulla tradizione armena delle *Quaestiones et solutiones in Genesin* di Filone," *AGI* 55 (1970): 52–57.

[56] See, e.g., Adam Kamesar, "Philo, the Presence of 'Paideutic' Myth in the Pentateuch, and the 'Principles' or *Kephalaia* of Mosaic Discourse," *SPhiloA* 10 (1998): 34–65, esp. 41; Howard Jacobson, "A Philonic Rejection of Plato," *Mnemosyne* 57 (2004): 488; Niehoff, "Philo and Plutarch on Homer," 131–32. It is true indeed that Plato himself critically refers to the same passage in his *Republic* (2.380d1–381d4).

position with that of Plutarch. The latter mentions a philosophical tradition that connects these Homeric verses with Scipio the Younger, who was sent on an embassy and impersonated, as it were, the gods of the Homeric story.[57] This is an example of a strategy discussed above (*supra* 3.3), which consists in establishing a direct connection between Homer's poetry and concrete life. Thus, the old story acquires a new relevance. This, however, was a bridge too far for Philo: for him, the story is simply false, and in this, he fully agrees with Plato. Moreover, this conviction is far from unique in Philo's oeuvre. Sharp attacks on the deceptive fabrications of myth, the πλάσματα μύθου, often occur in his works.[58] Homer, then, is not above criticism,[59] but this criticism does not entail a total rejection. Here, Philo indeed parts company with Plato. In this passage from *On Dreams*, Philo distinguishes between two "principles": erudite readers of course understand that the story is false, but for less gifted readers, it contains some useful ideas that can contribute to their moral improvement and self-control.[60] And this, in fact, is confirmed by many of the above discussed passages, which illustrate in many different ways how useful Homer indeed can be.

And yet, this is not the whole story. For many passages discussed so far have also shown that Homer simply has it right. In other words, Homer is not used because he provides less talented readers with some useful moral advice, but because his position is perfectly in line with Scripture. In that respect, the well-known passage from *Somn.* 1.233 is as one-sided as Philo's defence of Homer in *Prov.* 2.40–41. Both passages deal with one aspect of the problem, but neither tells the whole truth. In probably the majority of the cases examined so far, Homer's position is both useful and true. He repeatedly appears as a source of erudition, of a rich παιδεία that reveals the truth.

An important passage in this respect is *Somn.* 2.260. In this passage Philo states that ideas die when they are set in undisciplined speech (ἐν ἀπαιδεύτῳ λόγῳ). This is characteristic of Thersites, who chatters unmeasured speech (ἀμετροεπεῖς; a reference to *Il.* 2.212). Such a speech is reckless (ἀκριτόμυθος, referring to *Il.* 2.246) and is nothing but a collection of useless

[57] See *Sayings of kings and commanders* 200E (attributed to Clitomachus) and *Philosophers and rulers* 777A (ascribed to Posidonius; = fr. 254 E.-K. or 125a Th.).

[58] Cf. *supra*, note 17.

[59] *Contra* Berthelot, "Philo and the Allegorical Interpretation of Homer in the Platonic Tradition," 157. We have already seen how Philo criticizes Homer in *Prob.* 31 (*supra*, 4.3) and *Conf.* 170 (*supra*, 4.4a).

[60] *Somn.* 1.233–237; the same position occurs in *Deus* 51–69; see Kamesar, "Philo, the Presence of 'Paideutic' Myth in the Pentateuch."

material (*Somn.* 2.275). Philo did not want to be such a Thersites. He always strived for a well-educated, well-ordered speech, both useful and true, and Homer could contribute to that end. From this perspective, the different pieces can finally be put together: Homer is appreciated by Philo as an important source of well-respected and useful traditional παιδεία that can be used to explain the truth of Scripture.

5.3. Such a παιδεία comes from the field of encyclical studies, the domain of Hagar. Philo's exegesis of the figure of Hagar, which is especially elaborated in his treatise *On the Preliminary Studies* but returns in many other works as well, has already received much attention in scholarly research.[61] In this view of Hagar, we find the basic interpretative key for a correct understanding of Philo's Homer reception. Philo really takes the field of Hagar seriously, yet he also gives it a well-defined place: the encyclical studies contribute to philosophy, which itself contributes to wisdom (*Congr.* 79). This is indeed the role that Homer plays in Philo's thinking. More in general, then, Philo's attitude towards the encyclical studies conditions his reception of Homer.

Firstly, it explains his preference for an intermediate position between the two extreme views taken by the anonymous Jewish exegetes and Plato. Hagar is a sojourner (*Congr.* 22): she stays in the city of virtue, which makes Plato's complete rejection too extreme. Yet she is not a full citizen but fundamentally remains a stranger. As a result, the Jewish exegetes, who exaggerate the similarities between Homer and Scripture, also commit a serious mistake. The position of Hagar requires a delicate balance, and this is precisely what we get in Philo's approach to Homer.

Secondly, it justifies Philo's excellent knowledge of Homer. Hagar can be appreciated; even more: we should marry her, although this marriage is not the end. Moreover, this does not imply that such a marriage is only for young people, and that we should abandon it as soon as we reach adulthood. Philo's frequent use of Homer was not confined to his youth, but permeates his whole oeuvre. He continued to use him even "on the threshold of old age," to use a Homeric expression which he quoted himself

61 *Leg.* 3.244–245; *Cher.* 3–10; *Sacr.* 43–44; *Post.* 130 and 137; *Fug.* 2 and 213; *Mut.* 255; *Somn.* 1.240; *QG* 3.19–25 and 35; cf. Alexandre, "La culture profane chez Philon"; Mendelson, *Secular Education in Philo of Alexandria;* C Kraus Reggiani, "'Enkyklios paidéia' e filosofia come possibili fasi dell'itinerario a Dio nell'allegoresi biblica di Filone Alessandrino," *Archivio di Filosofia* 53 (1985): 187–97; Koskenniemi, "Philo and Classical Education;" cf. also Bréhier, *Les idées philosophiques et religieuses de Philon d'Alexandrie,* 280–95; and Samuel Sandmel, *Philo's Place in Judaism: A Study of Conceptions of Abraham in Jewish Literature* (New York: KTAV, 1971), 153–58.

(*Somn.* 2.148). We have no reason to disbelieve him when he says himself that his ears were always greedy for παιδεία (*Plant.* 127). Hagar, then, remained important for him until the end of his life. If that is true, we may infer that we should in every stage of life go from Hagar to Sarah, or better, be married with Hagar while regarding Sarah as our true wife (*Congr.* 78).

Thirdly, it throws light on the relevance of Homer for Philo. We have seen that Homer is almost never used only for *ornatus*'s sake. After all, Hagar was no beauty model or belly dancer. She was a handmaiden who could do useful work for her mistress. Similarly, Homeric material can be very helpful for the interpretation of the meaning of Scripture.

Finally, it significantly conditions the picture of Homer that can be found in Philo's works. Philo's Homer is a *Homerus sui generis*. It is a Homer who voices the truth of a Platonically understood Scripture. Sometimes, this adds an interesting new dimension to Homer's text. At the same time, Philo only selects those passages which are relevant for his own purposes. In that sense, Philo's Homer is also a *Homerus dimidiatus*. There is no room for polytheism, nor for prominent heroes. Where fighting machines like Achilles and Diomedes are hardly mentioned, where the hotchpotch of all too human Olympians simply appears as τὸ θεῖον, and where the great Ajax makes his entrance as an elephant, the beating heart of Homer has lost its vital pulse.

Katholieke Universiteit
Leuven

The Studia Philonica Annual 29 (2017): 33–60

KNOWING GOD BY ANALOGY:
Philo of Alexandria against the Stoic God

SHARON WEISSER

Theology is undoubtedly one of the most essential constituents of Philo's thought. For Philo, God is the most perfect being, the one truly existent being,[1] and the cause of all that has come into being.[2] God's centrality is not only conspicuous in Philo's metaphysics but it also plays a fundamental role in his epistemology and ethics since, in his view, appropriate knowledge of God secures a happy life.

Many scholars have already pointed to the Platonic background that molded some fundamental tenets of Philo's notion of God, which is especially conspicuous in his treatment of God's utter transcendence.[3] While there is no doubt that Philo's Platonic and Middle Platonic indebtedness accounts for many important features of his views on God, in order to better appreciate Philo's theology, it is also necessary to situate it within the context of the Hellenistic discussions on God. The aim of this article, however, is not to assess the philosophical identity of Philo's views on God as compared to that of the Hellenistic schools of philosophy,[4] nor is it to

[1] Philo's texts abound with expressions referring to God as ὁ ὢν ὄντως ("the real Being"), τὸ δὲ πρὸς ἀλήθειαν ὂν ("the true Being"), πρὸς ἀλήθειαν θεός "(the true God"). See for example *Opif*. 172; *Spec*. 1. 308–309, 321, 332; *Post*. 166–167; *Mut*. 7; *Mos*. 2.67.

[2] With the exception of evils: *Agr*. 129; *Plant*. 127–129.

[3] There is a very large amount of literature on Philo's indebtedness to Plato or to contemporaneous Middle Platonist trends. I will only mention Mauro Bonazzi, "Towards Transcendence: Philo and the Renewal of Platonism in the Early Imperial Age," in *Philo of Alexandria and Post-Aristotelian Philosophy*, ed. Fancesca Alesse (Leiden: Brill, 2008), 233–51; John Dillon, "The Transcendence of God in Philo: Some Possible Sources," in *The Golden Chain: Studies in the development of Platonism and Christianity*, ed. John Dillon (Aldershot: Variorum, 1990), 1–8; see also Gregory E. Sterling, "'The Jewish Philosophy': Reading Moses via Hellenistic Philosophy according to Philo," in *Handbook to Philo*, ed. Torrey Seland (Grand Rapids: Eerdmans, 2014), esp. 137–41.

[4] If we want to situate Philo's treatment of God in relation to the three main schools of the Hellenistic period, it goes without saying that he is much closer to the Stoics than to the Epicureans' atheistic position. The Epicurean central cosmological tenet, according to which the world is not the product of an intelligent purposive creator but the result of the

provide a full list of the arguments proving God's existence endorsed by Philo and paralleled in Hellenistic debates. My aim is rather to focus on one specific argument that Philo recruits from the Hellenistic battery of proofs for the existence of god, which I will label "the human mind analogy." In its most basic form, the argument aims at proving God's existence by using an analogical inference leading from the human mind to God.

My contention is that the human mind analogy plays a fundamental role in Philo's epistemology. First, it offers a path to recognizing God's primacy and causality. Second, it is systematically used by Philo to combat a Stoicizing conception of God. Third, it may help us elucidate the origin of a key feature of his theology, namely, his description of God's nature as ungraspable (ἀκατάληπτος). The analysis of the human mind analogy not only shows Philo's readiness to endorse arguments proving God's existence devised—or at any rate largely developed—by the philosophers of the Hellenistic period, and mostly by the Stoics, but it furthermore shows that he is prepared to turn them against their very proponents. It appears thus that Philo did not passively absorb current theological tenets but took an active part in Hellenistic debates. This article's narrow focus on one argument should be seen therefore as part of a broader claim concerning the relevance of late Hellenistic theological discussions towards a better assessment of Philo's theology and, conversely, of Philo's views on God, for a more accurate picture of late Hellenistic debates on the subject. Before I proceed, a brief overview of the state of affairs of theology at the end of the Hellenistic period as well as a few words on the theme of God's ungraspability in Philo are apposite.

1. *Hellenistic Theological Debates*

Hellenistic theology is marked by an intense debate between the three dominant schools of the period: the Stoics, the Epicureans, and the Academic Skeptics. For the first generation of Stoic philosophers, theology belongs to the realm of physics and constitutes the last part of the philosophical curriculum (Plutarch, *Stoic. rep.* 1035B). For the Stoic philosophers, god is a bodily active principle that endows shapeless matter with form and design, and which is responsible for the generation of the world from

---

mechanical and fortuitous collision of atoms, is, for Philo, indefensible. As regards the Academic Skeptics, Philo's theocentric thought cannot accommodate raising doubts concerning God's existence. However, as we shall see, Philo's relationship to Academic skepticism on this topic is far more complex than that of a bold rejection.

within—for its organization, design, and structure. God is the cohesive factor that makes of the universe a unity, in which all parts share a mutual affinity. For the early Stoic philosophers, god could indifferently be called "Zeus," "Destiny," or "Providence." He was thought to be responsible for the intelligent planning of the universe, functioning as the causal nexus determining the way things are and will be. What is more, the Stoic philosophers appear to have devised many arguments proving god's existence. In the Hellenistic period, they appear virtually as the "heroes" of the arguments from design, that is, of arguments that infer from the observation of crafted objects or from the beauty and order of the world the existence of an intelligent creator. Further, since the founders of the school maintain that the main attributes of the divine include excellence, immeasurable longevity, superiority, and goodness, only the world, or its soul or mind, appeared to be entitled to these predicates. Thus for Zeno, Cleanthes, and Chrysippus, proving the existence of god often amounted to showing that the world is an ensouled being endowed with the most perfect rationality; in other words, that it is the most excellent, intelligent, wise, and long-lasting living organism. In addition to arguments from design, they devised multiple arguments aimed at demonstrating the world's highest rank in the scala of beings. Thus, the hierarchical ordering of nature, combined with the principle that the whole is more excellent than its parts, led the first Stoics to conclude that the nature of the world itself, which contains all that is, is by necessity of the most excellent and perfect kind.[5]

From the early Hellenistic period onwards, the Epicureans and the Skeptics challenged Stoic theology. Despite the scholarly debate concerning the physical reality of Epicurus's gods (that is, whether they are thought-constructs intended to emulate our ethical achievement or in fact possess real physical existence[6]), the gods as conceived by Epicurus stand—beyond doubt—in marked contrast to the gods of the Stoa. Admittedly, Epicurus seems to have agreed with the Stoics that the gods possess a bodily

[5] The Stoics can be considered as pantheists in the sense that god is one of the two constitutive principles of the world and is always present in matter but they also appear to be religious traditionalists as they adopted etymological reading of the names of the traditional gods and even engaged in allegory. See Jean-Baptiste Gourinat, "*Explicatio fabularum*: La place de l'allégorie dans l'interprétation stoïcienne de la mythologie," in *Allégorie des poètes, allégorie des philosophes*, ed. G. Dahan and R. Goulet (Paris: Vrin, 2005), 9–34.

[6] On this debate see the papers of David Konstan, "Epicurus on the Gods," and David Sedley "Theological Innatism," in *Epicurus and the Epicurean Tradition*, ed. Jeffrey Fish and Kirk R. Sanders (Cambridge: Cambridge University Press, 2011), 53–71 and 29–52 respectively.

constitution, albeit one composed of atoms, but the main difference with the Stoics is that Epicurus's gods do not interfere with the cosmos, nor do they care for human affairs. Accordingly, providence and divination have no place in Epicurus's theological system. From the perspective of ethics, fear of the gods was considered one of the main obstacles to the attainment of happiness. Since happiness and blessedness are incompatible with troubles and worries, men should see in the gods an object of emulation and reverence and should strive to imitate their perfect indifference.

Although assessing the position of the Academic Skeptic philosophers concerning the gods turns out to be more problematic, it is clear that the Academic philosophers were deeply involved in challenging Hellenistic dogmatic theology. As part of their assault on the Stoic theory of cognition, they confronted the Stoic proofs of the existence of the gods and tried to highlight the inconsistency of their theological propositions.[7]

As is always the case with Hellenistic philosophy, the broad outlines of the early Hellenistic debate presented above have been reconstructed by means of later sources—in this case, primarily the systematic expositions found in Sextus Empiricus (*Math.* 9.13–194 and *Pyr.* 3. 2–12), Cicero's *The Nature of the Gods* and to some extent in Philodemus's *On Piety* and *On the Gods* 3. It is important to note the numerous parallels and overlaps existing in the structure, sequence, and content of the arguments exposed in these

[7] On Hellenistic theology see Jaap Mansfeld, "Theology," in *The Cambridge History of Hellenistic Philosophy*, ed. Keimpe Algra et als. (Cambridge: Cambridge University Press, 1999), 452–78. For the Stoic proofs for the existence of god(s) see Myrto Dragona-Monachou, *The Stoic Arguments for the Existence and the Providence of the Gods* (Athens: National and Capodistrian University of Athens, 1976); P. A. Meijer, *Stoic Theology: Proofs for the Existence of the Cosmic God and of the Traditional Gods: Including a Commentary on Cleanthes' Hymn on Zeus* (Delft: Eburon, 2007); David Sedley, *Creationism and Its Critics in Antiquity* (Berkeley: University of California Press, 2007), esp. 205–38; Keimpe Algra, "Stoic theology," in *The Cambridge Companion to the Stoics*, ed. Brad Inwood (Cambridge: Cambridge University Press 2003), 153–79; Michael Frede, "La Théologie stoïcienne," in *Les Stoïciens*, ed. G. Romeyer-Dherbey and J.-B. Gourinat (Paris: Vrin, 2005), 213–32. On Epicurean theology, see for instance Jaap Mansfeld, "Aspects of Epicurean Theology," *Mnemosyne* 46 (1993): 172–210; Dirk Obbink, "'All Gods are True' in Epicurus," in *Traditions of Theology: Studies in Hellenistic Theology, Its Background and Its Aftermath*, ed. Dorothea Frede and André Laks (Leiden: Brill, 2002), 183–222. The evidences and secondary literature concerning Academic theology is more scarce and is found in various treatments of Ancient Skepticism. See for example Simo Knuuttuila and Sihvola Juha, "Ancient Scepticism and Philosophy of Religion," in *Ancient Scepticism and the Sceptical Tradition*, ed. Juha Sihvola (Helsinki: Philosophical Society of Finland, 2000), 125–44 and Anna Maria Ioppolo, "La critique de Carnéade sur la divination," in *Scepticisme et religion: Constantes et évolutions, de la philosophie hellénistique à la philosophie médiévale*, ed. Anne-Isabelle Bouton-Touboulic and Carlos Lévy (Turnhout: Brepols, 2016), 41–56.

texts. This, together with the testimony from the Aëtian doxography,[8] seems to indicate that by the end of the Hellenistic period, theological speculations underwent a process of systematization and standardization. Thus, it can be safely assumed that by Philo's time, there was a standard way of addressing theological issues, which not only included typical theological questions, worries, and points of view to be addressed, but also a series of topical arguments proving god's existence. Although Philo does not offer any systematic treatment comparable to what is found in the aforementioned works, he nevertheless displays a good acquaintance with the classic philosophical proofs for the existence of god and endorses them at multiple occasions in his exegesis of the Torah.[9]

2. *Theos ἀκατάληπτος*

The second preliminary remark concerns the important and striking feature of Philo's theology, that is, his qualification of God's nature as beyond the reach of human knowledge.[10] This characterization of God by Philo has given rise to many scholarly speculations concerning the origin of this idea or its role in the formation of negative theology.[11] Before attempting to find

[8] See Ps.Plutarch, *Plac.* 1.6–7, 880D–882A and Stob. *Ecl.* I 1.29b1–85; David T. Runia, "The Beginnings of the End: Philo of Alexandria and Hellenistic Theology," in *Traditions of Theology: Studies in Hellenistic Theology, Its Background and Its Aftermath*, ed. Dorothea Frede and André Laks (Leiden: Brill, 2002), 281–316.

[9] For instance, arguments from design appear frequently under his pen, e.g., *Spec.* 1. 33–35; *Leg.* 3.95–103; *Prov.* 1.33, 1.42–45, 1.72, and 2. 63; *Praem.* 42. Although the notes in the modern translations of Philo (in Loeb, Cerf, and now in the Philo of Alexandria Commentary Series) usually mention the presence of the classic philosophical proofs, there has been relatively little scholarly work on this topic. Harry Austryn Wolfson's chapter on Philo's use of the proofs (in his *Philo, Foundations of Religious Philosophy in Judaism, Christianity and Islam,* 2 vols. [Cambridge, MA.: Harvard University Press, 1947, reprint 1962, cit.], 2:73–93) is, to the best of my knowledge, a notable exception. Wolfson identifies three cosmological arguments, one teleological as well as a "nascent ontological argument." See also my forthcoming paper "Do We Have to Study the Torah? Philo of Alexandria and the Proofs for the Existence of God."

[10] See, for example, *Somn.* 1.63, 66–67, 230; *Mut.* 7–15; *Post.* 168–169; *Deo* 4; *Post.* 169; *Deus* 62; *Fug.* 161–165; *Leg.* 1.20.

[11] Many scholars have pointed to the Platonic origin of the idea of the unknowability of God (or of the name of God). David T. Runia (*Philo of Alexandria and the Timaeus of Plato* [Leiden: Brill, 1986], 111–13) points to the likely influence of Plato's *Timaeus* 28c (see also Cicero, *Nat. d.* 1.30 and Illaria Ramelli, "The Knowledge of God and the Dialectics of Apophatic Theology: Scripture and the Platonic Tradition" [paper presented at the Annual Meeting of the Society of Biblical Literature, San Antonio 2016]). John Dillon evokes the possibility that Plato's *Parmenides's* first hypothesis has influenced Alexandrian Platonism,

the possible origin of this idea, it is necessary first to attempt to explain it in light of Philo's own stance. Indeed, even if Philo endorses here a previous or current philosophical tenet, it is integrated into—and forms part of—a coherent theological position. As I have argued elsewhere, we may come to appreciate Philo's claim to the unknowability of God's substance if we begin by considering his complex and almost paradoxical approach to the question of apprehending God.[12] Philo indeed maintains both at the same time that God is the epistemological *telos*, the supreme object of knowledge that all should strive to reach, and that some of his features, such as his *ousia*,[13] his being, nature or deeds, are beyond the reach of human apprehension.[14] How to explain Philo's assertion that the supreme object of knowledge cannot in fact be known? The most obvious answer to this question is that by limiting the possibility for human beings to know God,

---

which has in turn influenced Philo (*The Middle Platonists, 80 B.C. to A.D. 220* [Ithaca, New York: Cornell University Press, 1997], 155 and see also David T. Runia, "Naming and Knowing: Themes in Philonic Theology with Special Reference to the 'De Mutatione nominum,'" in *Knowledge of God in the Graeco-Roman World*, ed. R. Van den Broek, T. Baarda, and J. Mansfeld [Leiden: Brill, 1988]; reprinted in Runia, *Exegesis and Philosophy: Studies on Philo of Alexandria* [Aldershot: Variorum, 1990], esp. 76–77). The idea that the supreme God is ineffable (ἄρρητος)—but can be grasped by the intellect—emerges in Alcinoos's *Did*. 10.3 and 10.4 (164.31–165.16) and is seen as a development of Eudorus's theology by John Dillon (*The Middle Platonists*, 127–28). Fransesca Calabi (*God's Acting, Man's Acting: Tradition and Philosophy in Philo of Alexandria* [Leiden: Brill, 2008], 39–56) defends the view that there is no incompatibility between Philo's claim that God's essence cannot be known and the various characterization of God in his works, since they express different ways in which human beings relate to God. Others have insisted on the biblical origin of this idea; see, for example, Martin Soskice, "Philo and Negative Theology," *Archivio di Filosofia* 70 (2008): 491–514. For the continuation of this motif in later Platonic and Christian sources see Illaria Ramelli, "The Divine as Inaccessible Object of Knowledge in Ancient Platonism," *Journal of the History of Ideas* 75 (2014): 167–88. The view that Philo is the inventor of this idea—defended first by Wolfson, *Philo*, 1:110–26, followed by Roberto Radice, "Observations on the Theory of the Ideas as the Thoughts of God in Philo of Alexandria," *SPhiloA* 3 (1991): 126–34—has been rejected by scholars (see for instance Runia, *Philo and the Timaeus*, 111). For the development of this theme in Middle Platonism, see for instance Jaap Mansfeld, "Compatible Alternatives, Middle Platonist Theology and the Xenophanes Reception," in *Knowledge of God in the Graeco-Roman World*, ed. R. Van den Broek, T. Baarda, and J. Mansfeld (Leiden: Brill, 1988), 92–117; Michael Frede, "Celsus, Philosophus Platonicus," *ANRW* 2.36.7: 5206–08.

12 See Weisser "Do We Have to Study the Torah? Philo of Alexandria and the Proofs for the Existence of God."

13 For a discussion of the meaning and use of the term *ousia* in Philo, see Charles A. Anderson, *Philo of Alexandria's Views of the Physical World* (Tübingen: Mohr Siebeck, 2011), 42–43 and appendix 1 at 195–98.

14 *Spec*. 1.20, 1.32, and 36–42; *Mut*. 10, 15, and 138; *Somn*. 67; *Det*. 89; *Post*. 15 and 169; *Deus* 62. In *Spec*. 1.46–50, it is the *ousia* of God's powers which is qualified as ἀκατάληπτος. Note the exceptions of *Ebr*. 108 and *Spec*. 1.20.

Philo aims to preserve God's supreme transcendence. In this view, God stands in such marked contrast to the created realm that he cannot be fully apprehended by creatures who are irreducibly bound to sensible reality. God's utmost transcendence and otherness thus preclude any boastful pretense to complete or secure knowledge. But this is a surprising claim, especially in light of Philo's strong Platonic commitments. If we take as a point of comparison Plato's epistemology as it emerges, for instance, in the fifth book of the *Republic* (476a–480a) and according to a standard scholarly approach, knowledge relates exclusively to the Forms that transcend the sensible particulars. More precisely, knowledge differs from belief and ignorance insofar as it applies to a different set of objects, namely the unchangeable, eternal, and intelligible Forms.[15] It is thus surprising to find under the pen of an author who drew so widely on Plato, the idea that it is precisely God's separateness from sensible reality that accounts for his being unknowable. Although Philo does not radically part company from Platonic epistemology—as he does maintain that knowledge of the transcendent forms belongs to a higher cognitive level[16]—he seems to commit himself to an additional claim, namely that if a human agent knows *x*'s true nature, *x* is in some sense ontologically limited. Thus Philo correlates between being the object of human cognitive grasping and being metaphysically limited. But God who is infinite and most perfect cannot be contained in any way. He cannot be defined by any names nor be circumscribed by any type of predication. It is in this sense, I presume, that God is, for Philo, beyond the reach of human comprehension.

Significantly, Philo found that the cognitive human limitation to fully comprehend God was adequately expressed in the adjective ἀκατάληπτος—"ungraspable."[17] From the Hellenistic period onwards, this term was clearly associated with the Academic Skeptics' idea that how things really are, is "ungraspable" (ἀκατάληπτος).[18] Given Philo's familiarity with some fundamental Academic tenets, it seems safe to assume that he knew the strong

[15] Against this standard two-worlds interpretation of Plato see Gail Fine, *Plato on Knowledge and Forms, Selected Essays* (Oxford: Clarendon Press, 2003), esp. 66–84.

[16] See for example, *Cher.* 97–98; *Spec.* 1.45–48.

[17] See note 10.

[18] See, for example, Sextus Empiricus, *Pyr.* 1.1.3; *Math.* 7.155; Eusebius, *Praep. ev.* 14.4.15; and Harald Thorsrud, "Arcesilaus and Carneades," in *The Cambridge Companion to Ancient Scepticism*, ed. Richard Bett (Cambridge: Cambridge University Press, 2010), 58–80. For a defense of the non-dogmatic status of this thesis see Gisela Striker, "On the Difference between the Pyrrhonists and the Academics," in Striker, *Essays in Hellenistic Philosophy and Ethics* (Cambridge: Cambridge University Press, 1996), 135–49.

Academic flavor of this term.[19] But Philo is not a Skeptic. Although he found the adjective ἀκατάληπτος suitable to describe the epistemic position in which every man stands in relation to God, he does not subscribe to the view that nothing can be said about God, nor to the view that for any argument concerning God's existence there is an equally powerful counter-argument. On the contrary, against the dangers of skepticism and therein of atheism concerning God's existence, Philo insists that we should all admit that God exists and that he is the first cause.[20] Appropriate knowledge of God's existence, of his causal primacy, is not only important on a theoretical level, but has a direct impact on our life and conduct. It is indeed crucial for Philo to connect the recognition of God's existence to the attainment of happiness. In his view, if we come to understand God's relation towards the created realm, we will come to appreciate the hierarchical ordering of the universe and we will accordingly align our motivations, goals, and activities. The transitory and impermanent objects of our desires will be replaced by desires for true and lasting goods, such as moral integrity, rationality or God. Thus, the proper understanding of God's causal primacy offers the prospect of articulating a comprehensive view of the universe and what is within its compass, which, in turn, allows us to lead a life in which our aspirations and desires are directed towards genuinely valuable ends.[21]

According to Runia, Philo's qualification of God's nature as beyond the reach of human knowledge marks the "end of Hellenistic theology."[22] In his view, Philo's theology marks a departure from the "directness" and confidence characterizing the theological approach of the Hellenistic period. Whereas the Hellenistic philosophers believed that it is possible to grasp

[19] See, for instance, *Leg.* 2.65. On Philo's relation to Skepticism see Carlos Lévy, "Le 'scepticisme' de Philon d'Alexandrie: Une influence de la Nouvelle Académie?," in *Hellenica et Judaica. Hommage à Valentin Nikiprowetzky*, ed. A. Caquot, M. Hadas-Lebel M., J. Riaud (Leuven: Peeters, 1986), 29–41; Lévy, "Deux problèmes doxographiques chez Philon d'Alexandrie: Posidonius et Enésidème," in *Philosophy and Doxography in the Imperial Age*, ed. Aldo Brancacci (Firenze: Leo S. Olschki, 2005), 79–102; Lévy "De l'époché sceptique à l'époché transcendantale: Philon d'Alexandrie fondateur du fidéisme," in *Scepticisme et religion: Constantes et évolutions, de la philosophie hellénistique à la philosophie médiévale*, ed. Anne-Isabelle Bouton-Touboulic and Carlos Lévy (Turnhout: Brepols Publishers, 2016), 57–73, and Karel Janácek, "Philon von Alexandreia und skeptische Tropen," *Eirene* 19 (1981): 83–97.

[20] *Spec.* 1.32–50; *Cher.* 125–127; *Praem.* 40; and see Gregory E. Sterling, "The First Theologian, The Originality of Philo of Alexandria," in *Renewing Tradition: Studies in Texts and Contexts in Honor of James W. Thompson*, ed. Mark W. Hamilton et al. (Eugene, OR.: Pickwick Publications, 2007), 145–62.

[21] See, for instance, *Det.* 86; *Migr.* 131; *Spec.* 1. 345 and 1.31; *Cher.* 129.

[22] Runia, "The Beginnings of the End," 281–316.

God's nature and essence—once God's existence has been acknowledged—Philo departs from this epistemological optimism by maintaining the unknowability of God's true being. For Runia, even the Academics' doubts concerning God's existence and their attacks on any dogmatic claim, possess a greater degree of directness than what is found in Philo. Runia explains God's unknowability in light of a fundamental principle of Philo's thought, according to which God adapts his beneficence to the level and capacity of the recipient. In developing this new kind of negative theology, Runia contends, Philo stands "at the interface of Hellenistic and later Greek philosophy."

3. *The Human Mind Analogy in Philosophical Sources*

With just this much background, we can now turn to the human mind analogy in philosophical sources. We know thanks to Sextus Empiricus that the mind analogy was part of the battery of proofs used by the dogmatic philosophers, that is by the Stoics, in order to show the origin of our concept of god:

> [But there are] others who say that the mind, being sharp and agile, came also to a presentation [ἔμφασις] of the universe by focusing on its own nature and assumed a surpassingly intellect-like power which is analogous to itself but divine in nature. (*Math.* 9.23, trans. R. Bett modified)

As I take it, the argument posits that we can draw an analogy between two domains—ourselves and the world—in order to conclude that god exists. Although the details of the inference are not provided, the Stoics appeared to have devised an argument, starting with the observation of one's own mind and concluding with the recognition of the existence of an intellectual power in this world, similar to that of one's own mind but of surpassing power.[23]

[23] The inference undoubtedly bears on the numerous similarities drawn by the Stoic philosophers between the individual soul and god (see, for example, Diogenes Laertius, *Lives* 7.138; Sextus Exmpiricus, *Math.* 9.76), but it furthermore probably rests on the idea that the human soul forms a part, is a fragment (ἀπόσπασμα), of the soul of the universe (Diogenes Laertius, *Lives* 7.143). Note that Philo is also ready to qualify the human rational soul as a "fragment" of the divine logos in *Opif.* 146 (see also *Leg.* 3.161) or of the divine soul (*Her.* 90). Furthermore, Philo often resorts to the notion of the human as a microcosm that can usefully be compared to the macrocosm that the universe is (*Plant.* 28; *Post.* 58; *Her.* 155). Of course, in Philo, the analogy from human mind will bear on a fundamental idea of his anthropology, that is, that the human mind was created after the image of God, that is according to the mind of God (as, for instance, in *Opif.* 69–71; *Her.* 83; see David T.

This analogy, as many of the arguments used by the Stoics in order to prove god's existence, in fact harken back to Socrates in Xenophon.[24] In the fourth book of the *Memorabilia*, Socrates puts forward the view that we can perceive God's activities and works in nature, despite his invisibility, in the same manner that we can perceive the ruling activity of our invisible soul (*Mem.* 4.3.13–14).[25] Likewise, *Mem.* 1.4.9 presents Socrates putting forward several arguments in order to persuade the impious Aristodemus that the gods exist and that they care for human affairs. To Aristodemus's objection that he was never able to see the gods in the same manner that he can observe the crafters of things in this world, Socrates replies that the invisibility of his own soul has never precluded him from recognizing its existence by observing its activity (1.4.8–9). A few paragraphs later, and in order to fend off Aristodemus's complaint that the gods do not take care of men, Socrates draws an analogy between the power of one's own mind governing the body and the even greater power of the intelligence of the universe (1.4.17).

Similarly, in the Pseudo-Aristotelian treatise *De Mundo*—a text better known in Philonic studies for representing a tradition that may have exerted influence upon Philo's notions of the powers of God[26]—the author claims that the invisibility of god should not constitute an impediment to our belief in his existence.

> For the soul whereby we live and dwell in houses and communities, though invisible, is yet seen in its operations; for by it the whole ordering of life has been discovered and organized and is held together [συνέχεται]—the ploughing and planting of the earth, the discovery of the arts, the use of law, the ordering of constitutions, the administration of home affairs and war outside our borders and peace. Thus, too, must we think of God, who in might is most powerful, in beauty most fair, in life immortal, in virtue supreme; for, though he is invisible to all mortal nature, yet is he seen in his very works. (*De Mundo* 399b12–22; trans.: E. S. Forster)

In both Xenophon and Pseudo-Aristotle, the rationale is plain. The reference to the human mind is used in order to fend off the complaint, whether implicit or explicit, that God's invisibility may obstruct our

---

Runia [intr., trans., and com.], Philo of Alexandria, *On the Creation of the Cosmos According to Moses*, PACS 1 [Leiden: Brill, 2001], 222–35).

24 Sedley, *Le Dieu cosmique*, vol. 2 of *La révélation d'Hermès Trismégiste*, 78–92 and 205–38.

25 See André-Jean Festugière, *La révélation d'Hermès Trismégiste; vol. 2: le Dieu cosmique* (Paris: J. Gabalda et Cie, 1949), 83–87. Festugière spots also the parallel argument in the *De mundo* 399a30–b22 as well as in Cicero, *Tusc.* 1.67–70.

26 A. P. Bos, "Philo of Alexandria: A Platonist in the Image and Likeness of Aristotle," *SPhiloA* 10 (1998): 66–86.

recognition of his existence. One remark is in order here. One may argue that although Socrates and Pseudo-Aristotle undoubtedly resort to an analogy between the human mind and God, it does not constitute *stricto sensu* an analogical argument. In other words, neither Socrates nor Pseudo-Aristotle suggest that there is a method of inducing God's existence from the observation of one's own mind. Rather they aim at alleviating reticence to attribute existence to an invisible being by resorting to the more familiar case of the invisible mind. Although it is true that neither author articulates an analogical argument in the strong sense of the term, both nevertheless assume that the existence of a non-perceptible entity can be inferred by the observation of its activity.[27] Thus, in Socrates's and Pseudo-Aristotle's view, just as we are ready to confer existence to our soul or mind by observing its causal efficacy, we must accept the existence of God, once we discern the visible effects of his activity in the world. Although this is not a full-fledged induction, it comes very close to positing an analogical argument, based on the similarity between the activity of the mind in man and that of God in the world.[28]

4. *The Role of the Human Mind Analogy in Philo*

4.1. *The Mind Analogy against Materialist Theology*

Turning now to the role of this argument in Philo, we observe that the mind analogy plays a crucial role in the interpretation of Abraham's journey. Surely, Abraham's journey is fundamental to Philo's epistemology, for the patriarch represents "the first person to hold the unshakable and firm judgment (ὑπόληψις) that there is one unique supreme cause, which takes care [προνοεῖ] of the world and of what is within its confine" (*Virt.* 216).[29] According to the allegorical reading endorsed by Philo, Abraham's successive departures symbolize the journey of a soul that gradually abandons its erroneous conception of God and seeks to reach the true God (*Abr.* 68).

More precisely, the human mind analogy appears in the context of Philo's interpretation of Abraham's departure from Chaldea. In his

[27] A principle also found in Plato, see for example *Leg.* 898d and adopted by Philo for instance in *Prov.* 1. 40–42 and 45.

[28] For some useful remarks concerning the difference between an analogy as (1) a rhetorical trope, (2) an appeal to a more familiar case with or without explanatory pretension or as (3) an induction, see Jonathan Barnes, *The Presocratic Philosophers* (London: Routledge, 1982), 40–42.

[29] See also *Praem.* 28–30 and *Gig.* 64.

writings, Philo often targets the Chaldean astronomy, or divinization of the stars. Predominantly Philo criticizes the fact that the Chaldeans assimilate God with the world or with its physical soul. Accordingly, Chaldea is for Philo the land of sense-perception as it represents a doctrine which grants existence to perceptible beings only. For Philo, the Chaldeans' crucial error originates in their failure to attribute causality to non-material entities:

> These people have formed the idea that this world is the only existing thing, or that itself is God, or that God is contained in it, as the soul of the universe. (*Migr.* 179)[30]

Abraham's departure from Chaldea represents for Philo a departure from the inquiries directed towards the sky and the discovery of the self. For Philo, through the story of Abraham, Moses urges those who endorse the Chaldean point of view to turn to knowledge of the self:

> Come down from the sky and when you get down, do not turn instead to the inquiry of the earth, the sea, the rivers, and of the kinds of plants and animals. But explore only yourselves and your own nature, and dwell in no other place than in yourselves. For by examining the things that concern your own dwelling, [and by observing] in yourselves that which governs and that which obeys, that which is animate and that which is inanimate, that which is rational and that which is irrational, that which is immortal and that which is mortal, that which is better and that which is worse, you will immediately gain the knowledge of God and of his works. For you will infer [λογιεῖσθε] that, in the same manner that there is a mind [νοῦς] in you, so there is one in the universe, and as yours has asserted its sovereignty and leadership over things in you and has brought each of the parts into subjection to himself, in a like manner the [mind] of the universe, being invested with the commandment, guides the universe by its plenipotentiary law and justice, taking care not only of those who are more worthy but also of those who are less obviously so. (*Migr.* 185–186)

The argument is straightforward. It proceeds to posit a correspondence between the ruling function of the mind over the body and the ruling function of God over the world, and it rests on the principle that like effects have like causes. The recognition of one's own mind governing the self leads to the apprehension of a mind-like entity governing the world, namely God. Formally, the argument can be spelled out as follow:

1. The human being exhibits governance of its parts.
2. The human governance of its parts is produced by the human mind.
3. The world exhibits governance of its parts.
4. Like effects have like causes.
5. Therefore the world is governed by a mindlike entity.

[30] Cf. *Abr.* 68–72, 78, *Migr.* 184; *Her.* 96–99; *Mut.* 16; *Ebr.* 94; *Congr.* 48–49; *Virt.* 212–213.

It is through this line of reasoning that Abraham and all those who endorse the Chaldeans' opinion will eventually correct their mistaken physical conception of God and of causation. However, it will be immediately noticed that the argument does not support the conclusion that God differs from the world or its soul. Indeed, in the absence of an explicit premise of a non-physical soul from which a similar non-physical God could be inferred, the argument does more to support the existence of a God contained in the cosmos as its soul than to refute any form of theological materialism. Indeed, so construed, the analogical inference from human mind to God can be easily used to support the idea that in the same manner that the human mind is contained in the body, God is contained in the world as its (physical) soul. This is probably the reason why the Stoics were eager to endorse the human mind analogy, as this conclusion is perfectly in line with their theological premises. It seems thus surprising that in our passage, Philo does not explicitly refer to the immateriality of the mind. Of course, one way to address this issue is to assume that he takes immateriality to be such a conspicuous feature of the mind that it hardly needs to be mentioned. We should note that the other instances of the human mind analogy in Philo make the immateriality of the soul an explicit premise. Thus, in the parallel passage in *De Abrahamo*, Philo is careful to mention the premise of the mind's immateriality, or rather of its invisibility:

> it is impossible that there is in yourself a mind [νοῦς] appointed as a ruler, which the whole community of the body obeys and to which each of the senses follows, and yet that the world—the most beautiful, the greatest and the most perfect work, of which everything else is a part—is deprived of a king who holds it together [τοῦ συνέχοντος] and rules over it with justice. (*Abr.* 74)

He immediately adds that we should not be surprised that the king is invisible, for our own mind is also invisible (*Abr.* 74). Philo goes on to say that it is by scrutinizing oneself that one comes to learn that the world is not the first God but the work of the first God and that the father of all, being himself without a shape [ἀειδὴς ὢν] makes visible the nature of all things (*Abr.* 75).

Similarly, in *On the Special Laws* (1.12–20), while interpreting the first commandment, Philo condemns the impiety of those who consider the sun, the moon and the other stars as gods and ascribe to them the causation of all events in the world. Philo strongly condemns them for mistaking the magistrates for the king, the horses for the charioteer; had these people learned to observe their own selves, they would have understood that in the same manner that the senses are the servitors of the human mind, sensible beings are the servants of that of the universe:

> It is indeed ridiculous to think that the mind in us, although it is extremely small and invisible, is the ruler of the organs of the senses, and that the greatest and most perfect [mind] of the universe is not by nature the king of kings, the invisible ruler of the visible beings. (*Spec*. 1.18)

Although the Chaldeans are not mentioned in this passage, the position condemned here closely echoes that ascribed to the Chaldeans insofar as the heart of the metaphysical error consists in considering causal interaction to be physical only.[31] This same line of interpretation is also maintained in the parallel passage of the *De Decalogo* (§§52–61), in which Philo condemns the inability to conceive of a cause beyond the perceptual realm and the resulting deification of the four elements, the planets, and the world. It is by means of the observation of one's own *invisible* soul that one can gain a notion of an *invisible* ruling God (*Decal*. 60). Note that in the last texts, Philo refers to the invisibility rather than to the immateriality of the soul. Still the point remains uncomplicated: it is our capacity to attribute causal efficacy to an entity that cannot be perceived by the senses—that is, to an immaterial entity—that lead us to infer God's immaterial existence. As such these arguments correspond to the analogies spelled out in Xenophon and in the *De Mundo*.

Going back to our text of the *De Migratione*, despite the absence of any precise reference to the immateriality of the mind, a rich argument is offered in support of the transcendence of God over the created realm. Philo explains that having learned to observe himself and to dwell in himself (this is symbolized by Abraham's sojourn in Haran), Abraham becomes able to gradually depart from his own abode—that is, from all the impressions (*phantasiai*) provided by sense-perception—and started acknowledging and contemplating the intelligible realm.[32] This new departure from sensible reality (Haran) provides new instruction on God.

> For you do not think that whereas your mind, having stripped itself of body, sense-perception and speech, is able, apart from these, to contemplate the beings, in their nakedness, and that the mind of the universe (τὸν δὲ τῶν ὅλων νοῦν), God, does not stand outside the whole material nature, and contains, and is not contained, and that he does not surpass it only by his thought, as is the case for man, but by his very essence (τῷ οὐσιώδει), as it befits to God. For our mind did not craft the body, this is the work of someone else, on which account it is contained in the body as in a vessel. But the mind of the universe (ὁ δὲ τῶν ὅλων νοῦς) has engendered all that is, and what crafts is better than what comes into existence, so that it could not be contained in what is inferior to him, apart

[31] Note that the idea of affinity (*sympatheia*) between the parts of the universe—a tenet that Philo generally attributes to the Chaldeans is also explicitly mentioned in this passage (*Spec*. 1.16).

[32] Cf. *Her*. 111.

> from the fact that it is not suitable for a father to be contained in his son but rather for his son to grow under the care of his father. And in this manner the mind, migrating gradually, will reach the father of piety and holiness. (*Migr.* 192–193)

This text works out a detailed argument for the immateriality and transcendence of God. In fact, upon close examination, it spells out the *differences* between the human mind and God, on account of which God cannot be thought to be contained in the world, as the mind analogy may lead one to suppose. This text assumes at the outset the validity of drawing a parallel between the human mind and God, but this time it aims to highlight their intrinsic differences. First Philo argues that once our mind becomes able to access by thought the immaterial and noetic realm, it becomes obvious that the most perfect being, the one who truly exists, is necessarily tied to the "truly existing" side of reality. What is important to notice here is that the analogy proceeds to posit a similar but *non-identical* capacity to transcend physical reality: one by thought (in the case of the human mind), the other by essence (in the case of God). Philo pursues the argument to the effect that God is not contained in the world by claiming that the superior is not contained in the inferior. But this premise could easily lend support to the idea that the mind (which is superior) is not contained in the body (which is inferior). For this reason, Philo carefully links two additional premises: (1) the mind did not craft the body and (2) the crafter/father is not contained in its work/his son. Together these premises show that whereas the human mind shares some critical similarities with God—which lends validity of the analogical inference from a directing mind in man to a mind-like entity directing the world, it differs from God in some crucial respects, namely in its ties to sensible reality and in its being contained in the body. By contrast, God transcends the universe and cannot be contained in it. Thus, it is the *limitation* of the analogical inference from mind to God that Philo wishes to stress in this passage. Read in this way, the argument surfaces as an explicit attempt to confront the divinization of the world or of its material soul that may be induced from the human mind analogy. It thus provides a much more articulate reply to those who consider God to be contained in the cosmos as its soul than the simple mention of an invisible mind.[33]

[33] Wolfson has pointed out the Stoic background of the human mind analogy, maintaining that the argument against the Chaldeans "is nothing but a vague restatement of a Stoic argument for the existence of God in the world from the existence of mind in man" (*Philo* 2:79). He furthermore argues that in order to show that God is not contained in the universe, Philo uses additional Stoic and Platonic arguments—from divination and from philosophic inspiration—which indicate that the human mind can occasionally experience existence apart from material body and that such a feature "must be true of

4.2. *Chaldean Stoics?*

Together these texts indicate that the human mind analogy is employed by Philo neither to target an atheistic position, nor any form of impiety, but rather to systematically attack one specific doctrine that, because of its failure to attribute causal efficacy to non-physical entities, mistakenly conceives of God as physical. Is Philo targeting a specific philosophical doctrine? Since most of the time he associates this error with that of the Chaldeans, the question boils down to whether Philo links the Chaldeans with one specific philosophical school. Without any doubt, in Philo's philosophical environment, it is the physics and cosmology of the Stoics that demonstrate the most similarities with the doctrine of the Chaldeans. However, in the absence of an explicit identification, one may wonder whether Philo targets Stoic physics under the guise of the Chaldeans or whether, as with other Roman authors, "Chaldeans" is broadly used to refer to adepts of astrology, characterized by a greater or lesser degree of philosophical sophistication.[34] Many scholars, such as Wolfson or Radice have spotted the Stoics behind Philo's portrayal of the Chaldeans' materialist theology.[35] Runia, however, has cast doubt on whether it is possible to identify one specific philosophical doctrine behind the Chaldeans, and argues that their doctrine differs from the immanentist theology of the Stoics on the ground that "there is not even a single logos pervading and ordering all things."[36]

In order to make the case for a deliberate attempt to assimilate the Chaldeans with the Stoics, one has to show that the doctrines Philo ascribes to the Chaldeans are *distinctively* Stoic and that they are explicitly associated with Stoicism in other contexts. First, let us briefly examine Philo's portrayal of the Chaldeans. Philo's Chaldeans are presented as astronomers, as astrologers, and as supporters of genethialogy. In their determinis-

---

God all the time" (ibid., 81). I believe however that Philo's strongest claim against theological immanentism is rather found in his emphasis of the dissimilarities between the two domains of the analogy.

34 See Cicero, *Div.* esp. 2.87–97; Sextus Empiricus, *Math.* 5 (*Against the Astrologers*) and Favorinus *apud* Gell. *NA* 14.1. Chan-Kok Wong ("Philo's Use of Chaldaioi," *SPhiloA* 4 [1992]: 10) has moreover pointed out that in keeping with current practice, Philo interchangeably uses the terms "astronomy," "astrology," and "mathematics."

35 Wolfson, *Philo,* 1:176–77 and 329–30 and 2:78. According to Roberto Radice ("Philo and Stoic Ethics. Reflections on the Idea of Freedom," in *Philo of Alexandria and Post-Aristotelian Philosophy*, ed. Fancesca Alesse [Leiden: Brill, 2008], 162–64), the Chaldean system is "prevailing(ly) Stoic." See also Peter Frick, *Divine Providence in Philo of Alexandria* (Tübingen: Mohr Siebeck, 1999), 122–23 and 126–27.

36 Runia, "The Beginnings of the End," 290.

tic system, fate and destiny are considered to be divine. Moreover, as we have seen, they are represented as endorsing a major metaphysical mistake, that is, that of confining existence and causality to sensible beings only. Because of this fundamental error, Philo contends, they are led to consider the world or the soul of the world as God, to divinize the stars and to attribute to them influence over human affairs. Note that despite his critical attitude towards the Chaldean doctrine, Philo does not reject the Chaldean position altogether. Astronomy is not in itself a bad occupation,[37] and Philo even recalls that Moses shares their idea of a mutual affinity or sympathy between the parts of the universe on account of the unity of the cosmos.[38]

There are some clear similarities between the Chaldeans' tenets and those of the Stoics. First is the Chaldeans' attribution of existence to physical entities only. Not only did the Stoics confine being to bodies but they furthermore defined "body" as what has the capacity to act or be acted upon. Thus, for the Stoics, not only is the soul a body, but virtue, impression, and truth are all thought to be corporeal insofar as they can bring about or be the recipient of causal interactions.[39] Strictly speaking, the Stoics better qualify as "corporealists" rather than as materialists, since their physics implies that unqualified matter does not actually exist as such in the universe.[40] Indeed, in the actual state of affairs, matter appears to always be pervaded by the active principle, which makes of it a qualified substance. It is on account of the specific through-and-through blending of the active and immanent bodily principle, that is god, with matter, the passive and causally inert substance, that the cosmos forms a unified whole, similar to a living organism and characterized by mutual sympathy of its parts:

[37] *Congr*. 50. For a more positive assessment of Philo's relationship to astrology see Alan Mendelson, *Secular Education in Philo of Alexandria* (Cincinnati: HUCA Press, 1982), 15–24; Emile Bréhier, *Les idées philosophiques et religieuses de Philon d'Alexandrie* (Paris: Vrin, 1925), esp. 164–70, and Kocku von Stuckrad, "Jewish and Christian Astrology in Late Antiquity—A New Approach," *Numen* 47 (2000): 1–40.

[38] The language chosen by Philo to expose this Mosaic tenet in *Migr*. 180 closely echoes the Stoic formulation of this idea, as found for example in Sextus Empiricus, *Math.* 9.78–80 (see also Cicero, *Nat. d.* 2.19), with the notable difference that in *Migr*. 180, Philo does not mention *phusis* as the cohesive factor that makes of the cosmos a unity. Note that *phusis* is however explicitly identified as the cohesive factor in *Aet*. 37.

[39] LS 45.

[40] Jean-Baptiste Gourinat, "The Stoics on Matter and Prime Matter, 'Corporealism' and the Imprint of Plato's *Timaeus*," in *God and Cosmos in Stoicism*, ed. Ricardo Salles (Oxford: Oxford University Press, 2009), 46–70; Eric Weil "Remarques sur le "matérialisme" des Stoïciens," in *L'aventure de l'esprit*, vol. 2 of *Mélanges Alexandre Koyré* (Paris: Hermann, 1964), 556–72, and Arius Didymus *apud* Stobaeus 2.7.5b.

> [Chrysippus] first assumes that the whole of substance is unified by a breath (*pneuma*) which pervades it all, and by which the universe is sustained and stabilized and made interactive [σύμπαθές] with itself. (Alexander, *De mixt.* 216, 14–218, 6 = LS 48C, trans.: A. Long and D. Sedley)

The second important parallel is the idea of cosmic sympathy advocated by the Chaldeans. The idea that the universe forms an almost organic unity, in which all parts mutually influence each other was undoubtedly a characteristic tenet of Stoic physics.[41] Third is the idea that destiny or fate are divine.[42] Fourth, and the most important point for our topic, is the fact that the Chaldeans equate God with the cosmos or with its physical soul. This was effectively the nucleus of the Stoics' view on god and, as we have seen, they maintained not only that god is the active corporeal principle pervading all matter, variously identified with fire or *pneuma*, but, like Philo's Chaldeans, they also identified it with the universe, or with its soul (ψυχή) or mind (νοῦς).[43] Note that this idea is moreover explicitly attributed to the Stoics by Philo. Indeed, in the *De Aeternitate Mundi*, in the course of his many attempts to pinpoint the inconsistency of the Stoic doctrine of conflagration, Philo not only mentions the Stoic divinization of the stars (another similarity with the Chaldeans) but he also recalls that they equate the world's soul with providence (*Aet.* 47)—another name of the Stoic god.[44] Later on in the same treatise, he explicitly refers to the Stoic doctrine of god as the soul of the world (*Aet.* 84).[45]

Are these parallels sufficient to posit a deliberate and consistent identification between the Chaldeans and the Stoics? First, we have to admit that not all Chaldean tenets are distinctively Stoic. Chaldean materialism is not nearly as sophisticated as the Stoics' conception of the conjunction of god with matter. In fact, it shares more affinity with the initial position held by the Giants in Plato's *Sophist* (246a–247c) than with the refined view of the

41 For the Stoic sympathy see Cicero, *Nat. d.* 2.19 and 39–40; Sextus Empiricus, *Math.* 9.79 and Susan Sauvé Meyer "Chain of Causes,What is Stoic Fate?," in *God and Cosmos in Stoicism*, ed. Ricardo Salles (Oxford: Oxford University Press, 2009), esp. 80–85.

42 Diogenes Laertius 7.134–135; Cicero, *Nat. d.* 1.39.

43 Cicero, *Nat. d.* 1.36–39. On the identification of god with the world or its soul, see, for example, Zeno's argument for the rationality, sentience, and intelligence of the cosmos in Sextus Empiricus, *Math.* 9.104; and Cicero, *Nat. d.* 2.20–22 and 1.39.

44 For the Stoics' identification of providence with God or Zeus, see Diogenes Laertius, *Lives* 7.136 and Cicero, *Nat. d.* 1.39.

45 Moreover, Philo shows awareness of the Stoic argument for the intelligence and animation of the cosmos (*Aet.* 94). What is more, in *Prov.* 1.45 he is ready to call providence the soul of the universe.

Stoics.[46] Second, by the end of the Hellenistic period, many Stoic tenets had made their way into astrological discussions and the idea of the sympathy of the parts of the cosmos, and its important upshot for any astrological doctrine that the stars exert influence upon the terrestrial realm, was prominently one of them.[47] Lastly, and most importantly, the Chaldeans are depicted as proponents of genethialogy which, as it has been shown by Long, was not adopted by the Stoics, despite their determinist outlook.[48] It seems thus that in spite of some important similarities, a complete identification between the two should be precluded.

When this is agreed, we should nonetheless pay heed to the fact that Philo's primary critique of the Chaldeans concerns the divinization of the world or of its soul.[49] Because Philo explicitly associates this view with that of the Stoics, and because the human mind analogy belongs to the Stoic battery of arguments, it seems legitimate to assume that he may have some form of Stoicizing target in his sights—or at least a theological point of view which could easily accommodate the Stoic one—when he points to a doctrine that considers the world or its soul to be divine.[50] When Philo enlists the human mind analogy in order to spell out a fundamental epistemic step in the search for an appropriate understanding of God, he probably knows that he is exploiting a topical argument of the doctrine he

[46] The Giants of Plato's *Sophist* first confine being to body. But they are then refuted by having to admit the premise that virtues are "beings" and that they are non-material. The new criterion of being, to which they adhere, is thus the capacity to act and to be acted upon. On the connection between Stoic corporealism and the Giants of Plato see, for example, A. A. Long and D. N. Sedley, *The Hellenistic Philosophers*, 2 vols. (Cambridge: Cambridge University Press, 1987), 1:274, and Katja M. Vogt, "Sons of the Earth: Are the Stoics Metaphysical Brutes?" *Phronesis* 54 (2009):136–54.

[47] Sextus Empirius, *Math.* 5.4; see note *ad loc* by Brigitte Pérez in Sextus Empiricus, *Contre les Professeurs*, intro., gloss., and notes P. Pellegrin, trans. Catherine Dalimier, Daniel Delattre and Joëlle Delattre (Paris: Seuil, 2002); cf. Cicero, *Div.* 2.33–34.

[48] The only Stoic philosopher who is reported to have adopted the Chaldean astrology is Diogenes of Babylon but it was immediately rejected by his student Posidonius; see Cicero, *Div.* 2.90.

[49] See for example, *Opif.* 7–9; *Migr.* 178–179, 184; *Abr.* 68–72; *Mut.* 16; *Virt.* 212–213.

[50] The fact Philo refers in a Stoic fashion to God as "the mind of the universe" in the analogical arguments may also indicate an attempt of adopting a Stoic argument in order to subvert it. We should note nonetheless that Philo endorses this expression in other occasions as, for instance, in *Opif.* 8 and 69. Another indication of the anti-Stoic background in which the human mind analogy was worked out is the context in which the analogy appears in *Decal.* 52–60. Philo targets in this passage those who consider the stars and the world to be divine. Among them are those who attribute to the elements the names of the Greek gods or identify the two hemispheres with the Dioscuri. In other words, they emerge clearly as people who endorse the Stoic reading of mythology. See Sextus Empiricus, *Math.* 9.37.

attacks. The analogy appears therefore as conscious opposition to a dominant theological view. Philo's procedure can reasonably be seen as an attempt to turn the tables against his opponents, by means of their own analogical weapons, and mostly by pointing out that the presence of shared features between the two domains of the analogy does not preclude fundamental dissimilarities between the human mind and God.

4.3. *Knowledge of the Self*

So far we have seen that the analogy supposes that a human being and the world exhibit some critical similarities, on the basis of which one further common feature may be inferred, namely that of being governed by a certain power. Thus fundamental to the mind analogy is the necessity of gaining knowledge of the self, as this constitutes the first step in achieving an appropriate apprehension of God. We therefore need to raise the question of the epistemic relation that we have with the two domains of the analogy: to our mind on the one hand, and to God on the other. Indeed, if we can reach knowledge of our own mind but not that of God's nature, it may seem that the type of cognition varies according to each domain of the analogy. It is then necessary to understand more precisely what is knowledge of the self, and on what grounds it is held to be a valid means for inferring the existence of a Being whose true nature is unknowable.

Some interpreters have argued that the specific piece of knowledge that is achieved by a thorough examination of the self refers to the nothingness of the created human being. Thus, according to Anderson, for instance, self-knowledge amounts to acknowledging the faultiness of sense-perception, which leads to the recognition of the "nothingness of the created being." This, in turn and by means of a dialectical opposition, begets knowledge of God.[51] Similarly, according to Courcelle, a human being's recognition of his own insignificance shatters his natural arrogance and leads him to understand that the divine power surpasses everything.[52] Without doubting the importance of the theme of man's nothingness in relation to God, it seems that it constitutes an incidental upshot of self-knowledge rather than its main object.

51 Anderson, *Philo of Alexandria's Views of the Physical World*, 69.

52 Pierre Courcelle, "Philon d'Alexandrie et le précepte delphique," in *Philomathes: Studies and Essays in the Humanities in Memory of P. Merlan*, ed. Robert G. Hamelton-Kelly (The Hague: Martinus Nijhoff, 1971), 248–49. He also notes the importance of the motif of self-knowledge for recognizing that the apprehension of God's true nature is beyond a human's cognitive ability. See also J.-G Kahn, "'Connais-toi toi même' à la manière de Philon," *Revue d'histoire et de philosophie religieuses* 53 (1973): 293–307.

First, it is important to observe that Philo's developments on self-knowledge figure consistently as the second stage of a two-steps process that starts with a departure from astronomical and physical inquiries (that is from Chaldea), as was the case with Abraham's journey. Assuredly, the most prominent representative of the Delphic maxim for Philo is Terah, who left Chaldea with his son Abraham to settle in Haran (*Somn.* 1.52). Terah is for the Hebrews what Socrates—who has devoted the major part of his life to knowledge of the self—is for the Greeks, with one notable difference: Socrates was a man but Terah is himself the very account (*logos*) of self-knowledge (*Somn.* 1.57–58). Here again, knowledge of the self is seen as a step that follows upon relinquishing vain inquiries into the heavens. Similarly, in *Migr.* 133–139, Philo firmly condemns the vanity and arrogance of the "seemingly-wise" men, who pretend to be able to accurately know not only what each thing is but also what causes them to be so, as if they attended the creation of the world. They are enjoined to leave the foolish investigations regarding the moon and the sun, and to learn instead to know themselves.

In *Somn.* 1.47–60, Philo offers a detailed exposition of what self-knowledge consists of: it starts with the examination of the organs of the sense, continues to sense-perception itself (*aisthēsis*) and finally turns to its mechanisms (*Somn.* 1.55).[53] In *Migr.* 137, knowledge of the self is described as the observation of what a human is in respect to body, soul, sensation, and *logos*, and as an examination of the functioning of the senses, of their activity and origin. Likewise, in *Fug.* 46, Gen. 27:44, which depicts Rebecca enjoining Jacob to momentarily dwell in Haran, is read as an appeal to

> learn the land of the senses, know yourself and your own parts [τὰ σαυτοῦ μέρη], what each [part] is, for which end it was made and how it naturally operates, and what it is which, being invisible, sets in motion and pulls the strings of the puppets in an invisible manner, whether it is the mind in you [εἴτε ὁ ἐν σοὶ νοῦς] or the mind of the universe [εἴτε ὁ τῶν συμπάντων].[54] (*Fug.* 46)

Without entering into the issue of the different topographies of the human soul that Philo offers throughout his oeuvre,[55] it seems clear that he commits himself to the idea that self-knowledge amounts to recognizing that

[53] Philo spells out a further step that consists in leaving sensible perception for the immaterial realm, but it was not undertaken by Terah.

[54] Note the occurrence of the human mind analogy; the mention of the puppets clearly recalls Plato *Leg.* 644d7–645c5. See also *Opif.* 117; *QG* 3.42; *Abr.* 73; *Fug.* 46.

[55] On the different models of the soul in Philo, see Grechten J. Reydams-Schils, "Philo of Alexandria on Stoic and Platonist Psycho-Physiology: The Socratic Higher Ground," in *Philo of Alexandria and Post-Aristotelian Philosophy*, ed. Fransesca Allesse (Leiden: Brill, 2008), 168–95.

the different parts forming the individual are all subject to one cohesive and directing principle.[56] In fact, Philo's plea to focus on sense-perception and its mechanism, which emerges prominently in the different treatments of self-knowledge, precisely fulfills this function. In effect, learning how sense-perception operates leads one to appreciate the distinctive ranking and role of the mind in the economy of the self. In Philo's view, sense-perception gives the mind access to the objects of the external world. However, neither the sense organs nor sense-perception constitute the ultimate agent of cognition. They are the messengers, as Philo sometimes calls them,[57] which present the mind with impressions coming from outside, but it is the mind that is ultimately responsible for cognition. Knowledge of the self thus amounts to the recognition of the cohesive function of the mind, of its superiority over the other parts of the self, and of its agency in apprehending sensible reality.

Does the treatment of self-knowledge lead us to assume that Philo is confident that we can gain knowledge of our own mind? If the answer is positive, the human mind analogy implies two very different types of cognition according to each domain: one that recognizes essence, in the case of a human, while the other acknowledges existence, in the case of God. As we shall see, Philo is in fact careful to assume an identical cognitive relation both with regard to the human mind and with regard to God. This, in turn, shows how the human mind analogy played a determinant role in Philo's elaboration of the idea of the ungraspability of God nature.

4.4. *From Ungraspable Self to Ungraspable God*

In the passage that offers the set-piece discussion of self-knowledge in *Somn.* 1.47–60, Philo stresses the importance of the injunction to know one's own mind or soul but adds that it is impossible to grasp (καταλαβεῖν) what the mind is (*Somn.* 1.56). In this remark, Philo explicitly connects his treatment of self-knowledge to a former discussion in the same treatise (1.14–40), in which he interprets the four wells dug by Abraham and Isaac in Gen. 1:25 as symbolizing the four elements composing the universe. Philo argues that men are shaped by the same number of basic constituents that make up the cosmos. *Prima facie,* the argument presented here looks like an occurrence of a well-known argument in support of the cosmic origin of the

[56] On the cohesive function of the mind, see, for instance, *Mut.* 111; *Deus* 42; *Opif.* 139 and 166; *Her.* 53; On the parallel connective function of God see, for instance, *Post.* 14; *Conf.* 136–137; *Fug.* 112; *Sac.* 40.

[57] *Somn.* 1.27.

human soul—an argument that has Socratic or even Presocratic pedigree[58] that emerges in Plato's *Philebus*[59] and is enlisted by the Stoics for proving the existence of god.[60] The classic argument sets out to show that since humans are composed of the basic cosmic constituents or stuffs that compose the universe, the human soul or mind necessarily originates from an external cosmic supply of soul or intelligence. In its classic version, such as it appears for instance in Xenophon, the argument posits that since we possess a small proportion of air and earth in ourselves deriving from the cosmic mass of earth and air, the existence of our personal mind entails that of a mind-like cosmic stuff from which it is derived. In Philo however, this classic argument is worked out for a different purpose, namely to show that the mind in us is ungraspable (ἀκατάληπτος). Philo does not argue that we are composed of the same basic stuffs that compose the world but rather that the fourth element both in the world—that is heaven (*Somn.* 1.15 and 20–24)—and in a human—that is the mind—is *akataleptic*.[61]

His point is, I take it, as follows: drawing an analogy between the world and a human is justified on the grounds that they share one critical similarity, namely that of being composed of four principal constituents. But just as the fourth constituent of the world, namely heaven, is *akataleptic*, so too the fourth element in us, namely the mind, is beyond the reach of human comprehension. Thus the critical similarity between a human and the world enables one to assume a further shared property. Here the shared property bears on the epistemic relation we stand in with respect to one corresponding item in both domains of the analogy.

Noticeably, Philo accounts for the ungraspable nature of heaven by providing a list of multiple contradictory opinions concerning its substance, nature and dimensions, and by exposing opposite views on the stars, their ensouled status, the illumination of the moon, and so forth. Similarly, it is by highlighting the *diaphoniai* concerning the substance, nature and location of the human mind (*Somn.* 1.30–33) that Philo sets out to show its

[58] Xenophon, *Mem.* 1.4.8–9; Diogenes of Apollonia B4, and Heraclitus B36 with the analysis of Gabor Betheg, "On the Physical Aspect of Heraclitus' Psychology," *Phronesis* 52 (2007): 3–32. See also *De mundo* 399a30–b22.

[59] *Phlb.* 29a–30d.

[60] As in Sextus Empiricus, *Math.* 9.92–94; Cicero, *Nat. d.* 2.18. Sedley, *Creationism and Its Critics in Antiquity*, esp. 212–25. Philo endorses some version of this classic argument in *Her.* 281–283 and *Aet.* 29.

[61] For a similar analogy between the human mind and the heaven, see *Her.* 232–233, and between the well-ordered soul of the wise and the heaven, see *Her.* 87–89. Note that this may come from the Stoic idea, maintained by Chrysippus and Posidonius, that the leading part (*hēgemonikon*) of the ensouled world is heaven (Diogenes Laertius, *Lives* 7.139–140).

ungraspability. For Philo, these multiple disagreements show that these issues are obscure (ἄδηλα), ungraspable (ἀκατάληπτα), based on conjecture and probabilities (στοχασμοῖς καὶ εἰκασίαις) and not on the truth. The doxographical character of this text has already been noticed by scholars, and notably by Wendland, Bréhier, Mansfeld and Runia. Whereas Wendland points to the *Vetusta Placita* as a possible source, Bréhier to Aenesidemus, and Mansfeld defends a Skeptical or Academic source combined with "mildly dogmatists arguments,"[62] Runia wishes to stress Philo's freedom in the adaptation of the material available to him.[63] Without denying Philo's independence, it seems nevertheless that the Academic orientation—and hence also origin—of this passage is attested on several grounds: the choice of the terminology (*akatalēptos, adēlos, stochasmos*), the use of the *diaphonia* for showing that the issue cannot be settled and, especially, the view that the nature of the mind is beyond the reach of human comprehension.[64]

The explicit connection between the discussion on the ungraspability of heaven and mind (*Somn*. 1.14–40) and that of self-knowledge (*Somn*. 1.52–55) suggests that Philo endorses the view that knowledge of the self not only amounts to discovering the distinctive position of the human mind but also to acknowledging its ungraspable nature. If this is the case, we can understand how the human mind analogy further supports the qualification of God as *akataleptic*, as the inapprehensibility of the human mind easily leads to inferring that of God. Further, as Mansfeld and Runia have noticed, it seems that in both these discussions, Philo relies on the same source of material.[65] Therefore, it can be reasonably assumed that the explicit connection between the *akataleptic* nature of the human mind and that of God was already at work in Philo's source(s).

Such an explicit connection is made in several places in Philo's corpus. Thus in *Leg*. 1.90–92, Philo interprets the fact that Adam, who symbolizes the mind, gives names to the other creatures at the exception of himself, as

[62] Jaap Mansfeld, "'Doxography and Dialectic: the Sitz im Leben of the 'Placita,'" *ANRW* 2.36.4: 3121.

[63] Paul Wendland, "Eine doxographische Quelle Philo's," *Sitzungsberichte der Königlich Preussischen Akademie der Wissenschaften zu Berlin* (1897): 1074–79. Bréhier, *Les idées philosophiques et religieuses*, 211–212; Mansfeld, "Doxography and Dialectic," esp. 3117–21; David T. Runia, "Philo of Alexandria and Hellenistic Doxography," in *Philo of Alexandria and Post-Aristotelian Philosophy*, ed. Francesca Alesse (Leiden: Brill, 2008), esp. 24–28.

[64] For the Pyrrhonian version of the *akataleptic* nature of the soul's claim against the dogmatic philosophers see Sextus Empiricus, *Pyr*. 2.31–32. For the Academic list of contrasting opinions concerning the substance of the soul, see the discussion in Cicero, *Acad. Pr*. 124, which follows upon the treatment of the gods.

[65] Mansfeld, "Doxography and Dialectic," esp. 3117–21; Runia, "Philo of Alexandria and Hellenistic Doxography," esp. 24–28.

an indication to the effect that the mind is able to conceive other things but cannot "grasp" (καταλαμβάνει) itself, just as the eye see all things but not itself. Note that here again, in order to shore up his claim, Philo mentions a *diairesis* exposing a checklist of questions concerning the substance of the mind: whether it is *pneuma*, blood, fire, air, or any other body, or whether it is corporeal or incorporeal. More importantly, Philo immediately connects the question of the substance of the soul to that of God:

> Also, are not those who inquire into the substance of God silly? For how these people who ignore the substance of their own soul, would know with precision that of the universe. Indeed, according to the [common] conception,[66] the soul of the universe is God. (*Leg.* 1.91)

The correspondence between our cognitive limitation concerning our own mind and that concerning God also emerges in the context of Philo's interpretation of the creation of humanity after the image and likeness of God (Gen 1:26). Since Philo takes the biblical term "image" to refer to the mind of the universe, it is in virtue of his mind that man resembles God:

> On that single mind of the universe, as on an archetype, the mind in each individual human being was modelled. In a sense it is a god of the person who carries it and bears it around as a divine image. For it would seem that the same rank that the great leader holds in the entire cosmos is held by the human mind in the human being. For it is itself invisible, yet it sees all things; its own substance is obscure [ἄδηλον], yet it comprehends [καταλαμβάνων] the substances of other things. (*Opif.* 69; trans. D. Runia, slightly modified)

Likewise in *Mut.* 10, Philo contends that the fact that the Being (τὸ ὄν) is ungraspable (ἀκατάληπτος) should come as no surprise given that our own mind is also unknowable (ἄγνωστος). To further support his claim, Philo adds that the obscurity (ἀδηλότης) of the soul has engendered countless disputes among the sophists, who have brought forward many opposite views.

Given that most of the texts that explicitly draw a parallel between the incomprehensibility of the human mind's nature and that of God take the *diaphoniai* concerning the mind to attest to its ungraspability, and since the collecting of disagreements (*diaphōnia*) was a distinctive Academic argumentative practice, it seems plausible to assume that the tradition on which Philo relies in these passages made explicit the analogy between an ungraspable human mind and an ungraspable god. This assumption may

66 I believe that by *ennoia*, Philo refers to "common notion" (*koinē ennoia*). Such a usage is commonly found in Plutarch; see Babut, *Plutarque, Sur les notions communes* (Paris: Belles Lettres, 2002), 122, n.3.

find confirmation from parallel arguments figuring in Cicero's first *Tusculan Disputation*—a text whose exposition of contradicting views on the mind (1.18ff) is so closely paralleled in Philo's *Somn*. 1.30–33 that it has lead scholars to posit a common source for both texts.[67]

4.5. *Parallels in Cicero's First Tusculan Disputation*

The most striking parallel to the analogy between the ungraspability of the human mind and that of God is found in Cicero's first *Tusculan Disputation*. In the course of the first book, in which Cicero attempts to refute the opinion that death is something bad, Marcus (Cicero) endorses the Platonic position of the eternity of the soul (*Tusc*. 1.49–55) upon the request of his interlocutor and as an *ad hoc* step in a vast attempt to show that fearing death is unwarranted. First, Marcus attacks the position of some philosophers who contend that the mind perishes with the body on the grounds that they cannot understand what the mind is without a body. On Marcus's view, their claim is unfounded since it is in fact harder and "more obscure" to understand what the mind is within a body: "as if they could understand what [the mind] is (*qualis sit*) in a body, what is its form, its size or its place" (*Tusc*. 1.50). According to Marcus, it is because of the extreme difficulty of understanding the nature and properties of the soul that some philosophers were led to deny its very existence. Cicero's point is to argue for the possibility of grasping some fact about the mind, just as it is possible to "grip with reasoning" (*cogitatione complecti*) something about god. This, Marcus adds, is the import of the Delphic maxim. The injunction to know oneself is an appeal to see the mind with the mind itself (*animo ipso animum videre*). Self-knowledge amounts thus to recognizing the mind's existence by means of its activity: "what is done by you, is done by your mind" (1.52). The mind does not know what itself is but it knows that it *is*.[68]

Later on in the same treatise when presenting the second argument for the eternity of the mind (1.56–76), Marcus draws an analogy between the intellectual human attributes and that of god in order to support the divine character of the human mind and hence its immortality. According to Marcus, some questions concerning the human mind, such as its seat, the kind of thing that it is, or its precise substance, cannot be settled.[69] What is

[67] Mansfeld, "Doxography and Dialectic," 3121–3137.

[68] This is, according to Marcus, the origin of Plato's famous argument for the eternity of the soul in the *Phaedrus* (245c–46a), which he quotes in this passage.

[69] He rejects however the possibility that the mind originates from the heart, the brain or the atoms (*Tusc*. 1.60), adopting thus a moderate skeptical attitude. Similarly, Philo rejects the corporeal view on the mind in *Somn*. 1.30.

important to recognize, however is that its origin—be it fiery, pneumatic or even from the fifth kind of nature—is divine (*Tusc.* 1.60 and 65). In the same manner that the eye sees all but itself, the mind cannot see itself nor capture its own shape (1.67). What the mind can perceive, however, is its capacity, memory, or motion. Marcus adds that in the same manner that the one who observes the beauty, regularity, and perfection of the natural world cannot cast doubt on the existence of a being who rules over—or has created—this perfect order, anyone noticing the activity of his mind necessarily concludes that it exists.

> Thus although you do not see the human mind [*mentem*], as you do not see god, nevertheless, you recognize god by his works, so you shall recognize the divine capacity of the mind by its memory of things, its invention, the swiftness of its motion and by all the beauty of its virtue. (*Tusc.* 1.70)

This is a fine example of an inverted design argument. Whereas arguments from design reach the conclusion of the existence of a purposive creator standing behind the order, organization, and beauty of the world, in this case, it is the existence of god that leads to infer that of the human mind. This is not the only case of a reversed design argument in this treatise. For example, the standard Stoic proof invoking Archimedes's sphere[70] is turned around to prove the existence of the divine *ingenium* in man (*Tusc.* 1.62–63). In fact, *Tusc.* 1. offers other standard theological arguments paralleled in the systematic expositions of Hellenistic theology in *On the Nature of the God* (and also in Sextus), such as the argument *e consensu omnium* concerning the existence of god (again, used to prove the existence of the human mind; 1.36) or the idea that gods are in fact deified men of old (1.29).[71]

Thus in addition to the parallel *diaphoniai* on the mind already detected by commentators, the first *Tusculan* shares with the Philonic texts that we have studied many structural and doctrinal similarities: the reference to the Delphic maxim, the moderate skepticism concerning the nature of the mind, the conspicuous theological background, the explicit link between the incomprehensibility of the human mind and the ungraspability of God's nature, as well as the view that whereas god's and the mind's substance is obscure, their existence cannot be doubted. All that, together with the Academic mold that has shaped the discussion of the *Tusculan Disputations*, not only in the genre—that of the *contra thesim disputare*[72]—

[70] Cicero, *Nat d.* 2.88; Sextus Empiricus, *Math.* 9.115.

[71] See, for example, Sextus Empiricus, *Math.* 9.60; Plutarch, *Comm. Not.* 1074F. Note that the *Tusculan Disputations* and *On the Nature of the Gods* correspond to the same period of Cicero's activity (July–December 45 BCE).

[72] *Tusc.* 2.9; see also 1.8 and 1.17.

but also in the philosophical position endorsed by Cicero, strengthens our claim of a common tradition with a strong Academic orientation for both Philo and Cicero. That this source may have explicitly posited the mind analogy in order to support the *akataleptic* claim concerning God's substance seems, in light of these elements, a reasonable assumption. That this source may also have attacked by the same token the theological arguments of the Stoics is a plausible assumption that the state of our evidence, nevertheless, does not allow us to affirm with any degree of certainty.

Of course, pointing to plausible influences does not amount to denying Philo's originality and independence in the adaptation of this argument. Even if Philo drew on previous Academic discussions in order to articulate his important notion of God's *akataleptic* substance, he ingeniously integrated it into his theological system in order to support the existence of God and to defend his utmost transcendence. What is more, as we have seen, the human mind analogy plays a fundamental role in his epistemology, as it constitutes the first step towards gaining appropriate knowledge of God. Finally, the dialectical setting in which the argument is laid out shows that Philo enlists it with the aim of combatting a contemporary dominant theological point of view that relied on this argument. This endorsement and "subversion" of the human mind analogy attest thus to Philo's involvement in the philosophical theological discussions of his time.[73]

Tel Aviv University

[73] This paper was presented at the annual meeting of the Society of Biblical Literature in San Antonio (2016). I wish to thank Ronald Cox for organizing the Philo seminar sessions as well as the participants and audience for their input.

The Studia Philonica Annual 29 (2017): 61–80

A NOOCENTRIC EXEGESIS
The Function of Allegory in Philo of Alexandria and Its Hermeneutical Implications

JEROME MOREAU

Much has already been written about allegory in Philo of Alexandria's works, as far as the history of allegorical interpretation, the typology or the cultural dimension[1] of this exegetical method are concerned, shedding light on these treatises and their place in the broader scope of Jewish exegesis or the history of philosophy. Nonetheless, much remains to be said, provided that the research is focused neither on general topics nor on a systematic typology, but starts from the texts themselves in their literary dimension and their complexity: conclusions may thus be drawn not only on allegory itself, as an autonomous object of research, but on its hermeneutical implications in Philo's exegesis.

If Philo's treatises truly are first and foremost a commentary on Scripture, as Valentin Nikiprowetzky stressed in a decisive way,[2] their coherence —and therefore the role of allegory—is to be found in a careful study of their composition and of the particular exegesis they deliver on each biblical verse or episode on which Philo chooses to comment. Reading these works this way, one may not only recognize the already well established place of allegory and its relationship with literal reading, or emphasize the way Philo uses other biblical verses to comment on his primary lemma: we may also understand in a new way the status of allegory as a tool, essential

[1] Among many other scholars, Jean Pépin may be the most prominent, in particular with "Remarques sur la théorie de l'exégèse allégorique chez Philon," in *Philon d'Alexandrie. Lyon. 11–15 septembre 1966*, ed. R. Arnaldez, J. Pouilloux, C. Mondésert (Paris: Éditions du CNRS, 1967), 131–67, and naturally his two books: *Mythe et allégorie: Les origines grecques et les contestations judéo-chrétiennes* (Paris: Études augustiniennes, 1976) and *La Tradition de l'allégorie de Philon d'Alexandrie à Dante, t. II, Études historiques* (Paris: Études augustiniennes, 1987). For the cultural dimension of allegory, see the disputable but rich hypotheses of David Dawson, *Allegorical Readers and Cultural Revision in Ancient Alexandria*, (Berkeley: University of California Press, 1992).

[2] Valentin Nikiprowetzky, *Le commentaire de l'Écriture chez Philon d'Alexandrie: Son caractère et sa portée; Observations philologiques*, ALGHJ 11 (Leiden: Brill, 1977).

and yet only a part of a larger project, both exegetical and philosophical. To put it more clearly: allegory is not the goal of the exegesis, it is only, yet deeply, linked to it, and most of the time it is a necessary path to reach it. It's all the more important to tell them apart from each other.

In fact, simply talking of "allegory" is not as clear as it may seem: this is already true for the notion throughout antiquity, but it is so even more when one tries to determine in each section of a treatise the method effectively used by Philo, and his purpose. A common definition of allegory in an exegetical context[3] is a reading which replaces the literal signification of a text with another one, hidden in the former but hinted at by some details—especially the most difficult or obscure ones—which can justify its authenticity. This definition is accurate, but may be too loose to grasp effectively the particular and various ways in which Philo uses allegory. One might also add that the allegorical reading introduces a Platonic separation between sensible and intelligible realities, the former being presented in the literal meaning, and the latter by the allegorical meaning. Closer to the truth as it is, this correlation is contradicted by several passages, preventing it from being a rule. Some of the clearest counter-examples are the passages where Philo comments on divine manifestations clearly stated by the biblical text, such as the theophany in Mamre (Gen 18)[4] or true signs of piety towards God from a human being.[5]

Two things cannot be denied: Philo seeks to justify and explain the difficulties of Scripture by using the long-known method of allegorical reading, and he tries to illustrate the eternal, that is, intelligible,[6] truths that Moses hid in the text of the law. Hence the idea that Philo's exegesis is a

[3] Allegory can refer both to a writing method (hiding more or less purposely the true content of a text) or to a reading method (seeing a text as a code that needs deciphering). The differences between these two meanings of allegory are often difficult to establish in a precise way, since allegorical readers may claim that allegory was intended while others don't need it to establish their interpretation. See, e.g., Robert Lamberton, "Allegory," in *The Classical Tradition*, ed. Anthony Grafton, Glenn W. Most, Salvatore Settis (Cambridge, MA: The Belknap Press of Harvard University Press, 2010), 34.

[4] See, e.g., *Abr.* 107–118, and our commentary below on *QG* 4.2.

[5] See Gen 15:6 and my article "Entre Écriture sainte et παιδεία: Le langage exégétique de Philon d'Alexandrie; Étude sur la πίστις d'Abraham dans le *Quis rerum divinarum heres sit*, 90–95," in *Philon d'Alexandrie: Un penseur à l'intersection des cultures gréco-romaine, orientale, juive et chrétienne*, ed. B. Decharneux et S. Inowlocki (Turnhout: Brepols, 2011), 241–263.

[6] In *Abr.* 50–55, Philo stresses the necessity to understand Abraham, Isaac, and Jacob as three virtues, whose nature is imperishable, so as to justify why God can name Himself by saying: "For this is my eternal name—the God of Abraham, the God of Isaac, the God of Jacob" (Exod 3:15), although the three patriarchs are human beings, and thus of a perishable nature.

twofold one, made of literal reading and sensible realities, on the one hand, and allegorical reading and intelligible realities, on the other hand. However, this general outline is more complex in its details than might first appear: it is not always possible to identify such a strict bipolarity, and more generally Philo develops several exegetical methods in different series of treatises which must be minutely taken into account before drawing overall conclusions.

This last point cannot be overemphasized. Is it possible to deal with allegory in the Exposition of the Law in the same way as in the *Quaestiones* or in the great Allegorical Commentary? The purpose of each kind of treatise is different and the specific use of allegory in each of them is one of the main differences between them. In the *De Abrahamo*, Philo comments on biblical chapters by first rewriting them, in what could be described as a literal reading of the story (or "rewritten Bible," as Peder Borgen put it),[7] and then interprets the whole of it in an allegorical way, in order to reveal its underlying intelligible meaning. In the *Quaestiones*, Philo usually comments on single verses, sometimes even less, both literally and allegorically,[8] but mostly allegorically, to solve difficulties of the text ("Why did he do that?," "What does it mean that…"). He may invoke other biblical verses to shed light on the lemma, but most of the time in a rather direct way. The exegesis of the great Allegorical Commentary is far more complex, so much so that the concept of allegory may not be enough to grasp its true nature. Allegory, as we shall see, appears as an obvious, if not the one and only, way to deal with Scripture, but it leads to a very thorough exegesis, with tens of paragraphs for only a few verses, and at the same time it tries to reach a more general teaching pertaining to the whole Law of Moses, with the use of many other biblical verses and a very thoughtful work on biblical and philosophical vocabulary. It is not enough to claim that the text "says something else," as the word "allegory" would refer to: it is a facet of a larger truth, entangled in a web of biblical and philosophical meanings. The traditional use of the word allegory may apply rather well to the two former kinds of treatises, but is insufficient for the latter—which happens to be, by far, the most frequent in Philo's works.

At this point, trying to define *the* allegorical reading of Philo may seem a foolish endeavour. As is often the case, getting out of this *aporia* implies

[7] See Peder Borgen, *Philo of Alexandria: An Exegete For His Time*, NovTSup 86 (Leiden: Brill, 1997), 46–79.

[8] We refer to David M. Hay, ed. *Both Literal and Allegorical: Studies in Philo of Alexandria's Questions and Answers on Genesis and Exodus*, BJS 232 (Atlanta: Scholars Press, 1991).

reversing the problem by going one step further: instead of starting from allegory itself, it may be much more profitable to look for the reason why Philo really needs allegory, apart from his indebtedness to the two traditions of Hellenistic Judaism and Middle Platonism. The general purpose of Philo's exegesis can be correctly identified only beyond the mere problem of allegory and its three main different ways in Philo's works. It seems to lie in what we could call a "noocentric" representation of Creation, of the law of nature as well as of the Law of Moses, and in the claim that they are identical. Whatever Philo's starting point or inspiration may have been, in the footsteps of Greek or Jewish allegorists, such as Aristobulus and the author of the *Letter of Aristeas to Philocrates*,[9] he developed a consistent *Weltanschauung* centered on an intellectual knowledge of the world through a chosen vocabulary rooted in the Law of Moses. Since God chose to reveal His will both through the words of Moses and through the laws of nature, only a well formed and pious intellect can grasp the true nature of Creation and answer its Creator in full consciousness. The widespread use of allegory ultimately appears as a consequence of this representation and cannot be explained merely by following a secular tradition in the study of Greek literature or even of Scripture.

This postulate is not a mere hypothesis. It can be established through the study of Philo's exegesis, especially in the great Allegorical Commentary, but also in some passages from the other treatises, which could be qualified as borderline cases. This is what we would like to illustrate with three texts taken from the three major commentary series, with a focus on Abraham, the biblical character who is granted the greatest place in each of them.[10] Unfortunately, the loss of some treatises or of some parts of the *Quaestiones* makes it impossible today to compare the three types of exegesis applied to a single biblical episode. Instead, we have decided to focus on three characteristic passages exemplifying the status and complexity of allegory in Philo's noocentric representation: the perilous trip to Egypt in *De Abrahamo*

[9] It is, of course, a necessity to take into account the development of an allegorical exegesis before Philo, in Hellenism as well as in Judaism, to establish the context of Philo's work and solve many problems which scholars may be faced with when reading his treatises. For instance, Philo has to be read as a Middle Platonist philosopher so as to understand the general purpose of his "allegory of the soul." But in the phenomenological point of view we would like to adopt, Philo's way cannot be explained only by referring to previous or parallel examples: it has a coherence which only partially matches that of other Greek or Jewish exegetes and which goes beyond a technical approach.

[10] Moses, who wrote the law and is the greatest wise man, is the most important character for Philo, but whereas there is a *Life of Moses*, the *Questions* and the great Allegorical Commentary do not deal with Exodus to the same extent, and by far, as they do with Genesis and episodes of the life of Abraham.

(89–106), on which Philo's allegorical commentary is a direct explanation of the literal meaning, rather than the introduction of a totally different kind of problem; the commentary on the Mamre theophany in the *Quaestiones in Genesim* (4.2), where Philo skillfully succeeds in doing without allegory to explain the biblical text; and the first part of the *De migratione Abrahami*, for two reasons: as we have said, the exegesis appears to be much more complex than a mere allegorical transposition of the biblical material, hinting at a deeper purpose, and the focalization on the intellect as a touchstone of the exegesis happens to be most obvious.[11]

1. *The Allegorical Explanation of the Literal Exposition in* De Abrahamo

In *De Abrahamo*, the first treatise of the Exposition of the Law, Philo comments on different episodes from the patriarch's life by developing for each of them a literal and then an allegorical explanation, with an almost perfect balance between the two readings and strong transitions between them or between episodes.[12] Though these two successive exegeses may appear at first as two different commentaries on a single episode, dealing with two different objects (the sensible realities in the literal explanation, and then the intelligible ones in the allegorical explanation), we would like to stress that these two readings are, in fact, deeply linked, whereas this is not always obvious depending on the episodes and their respective commentary. In general, the literal exposition may be considered as "rewritten Bible," that is, the retelling of a specific passage:[13] true as this is, we must keep in mind that Philo does not rewrite the biblical text for the sake of it. The literal exposition may come from the necessity to provide a significant lemma for his commentary, as he does in the two other kinds of treatises,

[11] We'd like to make clear that the order we are following is a logical one: we start from the clearest form of exegesis and the least analytical (each section of the *De Abrahamo* deals with a whole biblical episode), towards the most complex and analytical one, where dozens of paragraphs deal with only one biblical verse, while in the *Quaestiones* a single verse is commented on, most of the time, with only a few paragraphs at most, and without the rich overall composition of the allegorical treatises. We do not infer from this order any conclusion as to the chronology of Philo's works, but only assume that they reveal as a whole a single hermeneutical thought, even through different methods or periods of writing.

[12] *Abr.* 60, 68, 89, 99, 107, 119, 133, 147, etc.

[13] See Borgen, *Philo of Alexandria: An Exegete for His Time*; Gregory E. Sterling, "The Place of Genesis in the Commentaries of Philo," in *The Book of Genesis: Composition, Reception, and Interpretation*, ed. Craig A. Evans, Joel N. Lohr, and David L. Petersen, VTSup 152 (Leiden: Brill, 2012), 436.

although in that case the lemma would comprise several verses or even a chapter.[14] Instead of only alluding to it or copying it in its entirety, Philo chooses to rewrite it in such a way that he is able to explain what he regards as the overall meaning of an episode in a literal way, before giving an allegorical—and final—interpretation of it. In the literal exposition, he emphasizes some details and uses a specific vocabulary, so as to pave the way for that allegorical exegesis.

The commentary of the perilous trip of Abraham and Sarah to Egypt in order to escape a famine (*Abr.* 89–106), provides the clearest example of this overall coherence: the allegorical commentary does not introduce an "other meaning," as the word "allegory" would etymologically signify, but an explanation of the very problems which arise from the literal reading of the text. In this episode, the problem is the passivity and weakness of Abraham and the way God saves his marriage from the threat of Pharaoh. Indeed, though Philo first emphasizes the wisdom of the patriarch who chooses to leave to Egypt, with a careful explanation of the damages encountered by the cities of Syria and of the richness of Egypt thanks to the seasonal flooding of the Nile,[15] Abraham almost disappears from the narrative as soon as he arrives in Egypt. Philo even leaves out two embarrassing details from the Scripture: the plan to make the Egyptians believe that Sarah is his sister and the great gifts offered by Pharaoh to Abraham. They could have led the reader to wonder about Abraham's agreement about what happens to Sarah, or at least about his responsibility. The way Philo retells the story, Abraham is just a wise man who encounters an overwhelming danger and is "helpless, menaced as he was by the terror of stronger powers," thus leaving Sarah "at the mercy of a licentious and cruel-hearted despot," with "no one to protect her" (Abr. 95).[16] Sarah is not named yet, but her beauty is strongly underlined, so as to focus the narrative on the struggle between

[14] As we shall see, in the two other kinds of treatises, Philo can quote his lemma extensively because he only deals with short passages: one or two verses, a single sentence or even a few words. The scope of the exegesis in the Exposition of the Law is too wide and compels him to find another method in order to quote a chapter and at the same time begin his commentary.

[15] Philo closely follows the biblical text, Καὶ ἐγένετο λιμὸς ἐπὶ τῆς γῆς, καὶ κατέβη Αβραμ εἰς Αἴγυπτον παροικῆσαι ἐκεῖ, ὅτι ἐνίσχυσεν ὁ λιμὸς ἐπὶ τῆς γῆς ("And a famine occurred upon the land, and Abram went down to Egypt to reside there as an alien, for the famine prevailed upon the land" [Gen 12:10]—we quote biblical translations from the *New English Translation of the Septuagint*, ed. Albert Pietersma and Benjamin G. Wright [Oxford: Oxford University Press, 2009]), but he develops its content. The greater intelligibility it conveys to the narrative seems to help to emphasize Abraham's wise decision: he perfectly understands the situation and acts accordingly in the best possible way.

[16] For this passage, we quote Francis H. Colson's translation (PLCL VI).

a beautiful and helpless woman and a powerful but licentious king. Though the biblical narrative says close to nothing about her and her reactions,[17] Philo explains that she—and her husband, but only through her, it seems[18]—put their hope in God. Indeed, he eventually inflicts punishments on Pharaoh and his house through Sarah,[19] making the Pharaoh give up on his threat against Sarah and her marriage with Abraham.

In the allegorical development, Philo does not try to introduce a *different* explanation of the biblical narrative, which would only be a symbol of another reality, but he explains the *same* events in a deeper way. It is worth noting that Sarah's name finally appears in this allegorical explanation, in order to determine what Abraham and his wife stand for, that is, respectively the "good intellect" (σπουδαῖος νοῦς), a masculine name, and "virtue" (ἀρετή), a feminine name (*Abr.* 99). But Philo adds a personal tone to this first interpretation borrowed from "natural men" (φυσικοὶ ἄνδρες[20] [*Abr.* 99]), introducing the idea that the "bodily marriage" (*Abr.* 101), where the male has a masculine activity, and the female a feminine one, is the opposite of the "marriage made by wisdom" (*Abr.* 100), in which the virtue's function is "to sow good counsels and excellent words and to inculcate tenets truly profitable to life" (*Abr.* 101), that the intellect, or the "reasoning faculty" (λογισμός: *Abr.* 101)—another masculine name—only has to receive, passively. And this passivity, Philo concludes, "is its sole mean of preservation (σωτήριον)." Since Abraham is described as a wise man, this first allegorical transposition does not convey a new explanation so much as it explains why, in the biblical narrative—and even more in Philo's literal explanation—Abraham disappears and Sarah is the main character of the struggle, so that their marriage can be left "unharmed"

[17] The silence of Scripture could nevertheless be taken as an indication that neither Abraham nor Sarah rely on any natural mean to find an escape.

[18] He is just referred to by the words ἅμ' ἐκείνῳ ("together with him").

[19] Philo's exegesis can be based on the fact that God sends a punishment "because of Sara, Abram's wife" (περὶ Σαρας τῆς γυναικὸς Αβραμ [Gen 12:17]). The weak logical connection in Greek leaves the exegete to determine the precise reason for God's punishment (see *infra*). As a whole, and apart from its omission of Abraham's plan and of the many gifts he receives for Sarah, Philo's retelling of the episode is based on a careful reading of Scripture and the amplification of some important details. It is a rather faithful reading, although he chooses to emphasize some details more than others.

[20] To summarize in a few words a complex problem which is not directly relevant to our study, we can say that these men are those who study the real "nature" (φύσις) of things, a word that can mean the world as well as God (see Nikiprowetzky, *Le commentaire de l'Écriture chez Philon d'Alexandrie*, 127–28). These men probably are, in Philo's language, both philosophers and exegetes, the knowledge of nature and that of God's Law being in reality the same, as we will see again in our conclusion.

(σῷον [*Abr.* 90]), and Sarah's purity is "preserved" (διασῴζεται [*Abr.* 98]). For this reason the vocabulary in the allegorical development is the same as in the literal exposition.

This explanation is not an easy one: Philo goes as far as to say that language itself is deceptive, because in reality "the virtue is male … while thought is female" (*Abr.* 102). Not only does it contradict the common representations conveyed by language, but it also goes against the Stoic doctrine which regards the intellect as the directing part of the soul as, for instance, Aetius formulated it: Οἱ Στωϊκοί φασιν εἶναι τῆς ψυχῆς ἀνώτατον μέρος τὸ ἡγεμονικόν … καὶ τοῦτο λογισμὸν καλοῦσιν ("The Stoics say that the commanding-faculty is the soul's higher part. … They also call it the reasoning faculty" [4.21.1–4, *SVF* 2.836][21]). The true wisdom illustrated by Scripture is not that of the philosophers: the paradoxical weakness of Abraham can only be understood according to a higher wisdom, in which what is commonly thought of as masculine and prevailing, must be regarded as feminine, and vice versa.

That's why the real struggle is that of Sarah and the king, who is the opposite of Abraham and stands for "the mind which loves the body" (νοῦς φιλοσώματος [*Abr.* 103]). He acts as if he loved virtue, but only desires a "good repute" through a fake "fellowship," or "union" (κοινωνία [*Abr.* 103]) with virtue. This is precisely not just "*because of*" (περί [Gen 12:17]) this false marriage, but *through* it that he is chastised, since Philo explains that "the instruments of [the] tortures" the king receives are "the different parts of virtue," "for greediness is tortured by frugal contentment and lewdness by continence" (*Abr.* 104). The wicked mind suffers from the presence of virtue in the same way as the king suffers from taking Sarah in his home; or rather, we have to understand that these are only the two sides—the sensible one and the intelligible one—of a single reality. Scripture only tells of "great and grievous trials" (ἐτασμοῖς μεγάλοις καὶ πονηροῖς [Gen 12:17]). Philo chose in the literal exposition not to be too specific: the king's "body and soul" are filled "with all manner of scarce curable plagues," whose main effect is the eradication of "all appetite for pleasure" (*Abr.* 96). The physical and moral diseases all lead to a moral conversion: thus, the allegorical meaning is only another point of view explaining what happened during the events told by the biblical narrative, but through a focalization on the intellect and on virtue, now made visible.

To conclude his explanation, Philo returns to a detail previously left aside. Virtue, he says, does not even try to fight if she knows she isn't able

[21] We quote the translation from Anthony A. Long and David N. Sedley, eds., *The Hellenistic Philosophers*, 2 vols. (Cambridge: Cambridge University Press, 1990), 1:315.

to prevail. This refers, in the biblical text, to Abraham's plan to present Sarah as his sister, so as to escape the threat of Pharaoh. This detail, possibly revealing the weakness of the patriarch if presented in the literal exposition, is turned into a praise of virtue, i.e., of Sarah. If Abraham receives virtue's piece of advice not to try and fight, with a true hope that God will act against evil, then he is not to blame: he gives in to the highest of all virtues and lets his intellect be taught by God. To put it another way, he is a man of true faith and piety, who doesn't count on his own strength, but leaves his own salvation in the hands of God, as paradoxical as it may seem from the literal meaning of the episode. In a part of the treatise (*Abr.* 60–207) which is devoted to the illustration of Abraham's εὐσέβεια,[22] this probably applies not only to Sarah's and Abraham's faith in God at the precise time of the greatest danger, but rather to the whole attitude of Abraham who, though of a masculine nature, agrees to follow the advice of a feminine but supernatural virtue thanks to whom he acts in a righteous way, against any ordinary view.

This commentary illustrates the underlying anthropology of Philo's exegesis: he makes visible what is not explicit in the biblical text, by resorting to an allegorical explanation, which is, in this case, no more than the deeper explanation, at an intelligible level, of the facts of the biblical episode. There is a perfect symmetry and continuity between the two parts of the commentary, the literal and sensible one, and the allegorical and intelligible one. The focalization on Abraham's intellect is the key to this exegesis: it not only allows Philo to deal with facts and acts—or the lack thereof—, but to take into account their two dimensions, visible and invisible. Strikingly, Sarah's character is not dissolved into an abstraction, no more than Abraham yields to the intellect.

We can say for Philo's anthropology what George Boys-Stones stated about the link between allegory and cosmology "in later Platonist, or Platonist-influenced texts: that allegory is a mode of discourse peculiarly

[22] Philo introduces this first part very clearly: "We must now speak of the superior merits shewn by each separately, beginning with the first. Abraham, then, filled with zeal for piety, the highest and greatest of virtues, was eager to follow God and to be obedient to His commands" (λεκτέον δ' ἑξῆς, ἐν οἷς ἕκαστος ἰδίᾳ προήνεγκεν, ἀπὸ τοῦ πρώτου τὴν ἀρχὴν λαβόντας ἐκεῖνος τοίνυν εὐσεβείας, ἀρετῆς τῆς ἀνωτάτω καὶ μεγίστης, ζηλωτὴς γενόμενος ἐσπούδασεν ἕπεσθαι θεῷ καὶ καταπειθὴς εἶναι τοῖς προσταττομένοις ὑπ' αὐτοῦ [*Abr.* 60]) before stating that "the clearest proofs of his piety are those which the holy scriptures contain" (ἐναργέσταται δὲ τῆς εὐσεβείας ἀποδείξεις εἰσίν, ἃς περιέχουσιν αἱ ἱεραὶ γραφαί [*Abr.* 61]), and which he then illustrates through four biblical episodes. The second virtue is described at length at the beginning of the second part, as the "good and wise behaviour shown in his dealings with men" (τὴν πρὸς ἀνθρώπους αὐτοῦ δεξιότητα), which Philo calls elsewhere the "kindness" (φιλανθρωπία [*Abr.* 107, 109]).

adapted to philosophical accounts of the world, because it is a mode of discourse that in some senses shares its structure with the world as it reveals itself to a rational being."[23] Philo's allegory may well go even deeper, since it reveals the much closer relation between the acts of a man and his own intellect through a careful work on biblical and philosophical vocabulary.

That's why, in some cases where the intellect is explicitly or implicitly accounted for by Scripture, allegory may not be necessary to provide a satisfactory commentary according to Philo's standards, as we will now see.

2. *The Absence of Allegory in the Commentary on the Mamre Theophany as a Whole* (QG 4.2)

In the exegetical genre of the *Quaestiones*, Philo comments on the difficulties of Scripture in a more analytical way: each verse, each sentence, or even each important word may need an explanation. This may be a literal one, but in many *quaestiones* the allegorical explanation occupies the greater part and represents the final word of it, when it is not simply alone because the literal one would have been explicitly or implicitly discarded as obvious. Philo uses allegory in an expected way to introduce, behind a curious or even plain literal meaning, a teaching pertaining to intelligible realities, even if they relate only metaphorically to the letter of the biblical text. The commentary on the episode of the Mamre theophany (Gen 18:1–15) is all the more striking. In a way unparalleled in the *Quaestiones*, Philo announces as early as the second *quaestio* (out of nineteen) the general key of his understanding of the whole passage,[24] and he does so without needing allegory, even though he speaks not only of the sensible vision of three men, but also of the intelligible vision of God.

In the first *quaestio*, Philo stressed at length that Abraham's vision was imperfect and thus he was unable to receive a direct vision of God, in the same way that human eyes cannot contemplate the sun without being blinded very soon. This is a necessary introduction to his general interpretation of the main difficulty of the passage, the identity of Abraham's visitors.

23 George R. Boys-Stones, "The Stoics Two Types of Allegory," in *Metaphor, Allegory, and the Classical Tradition. Ancient Thought and Modern Revisions*, ed. George R. Boys-Stones (Oxford: Oxford University Press, 2003), 214.

24 Philo may follow the same general exegesis across several *quaestiones* pertaining to the same episode (see *QG* 3.18–25 on Gen 16:1–6), but he never announces beforehand the overall pattern and the several details in the whole text on which it is based as he does here.

Philo answers this major exegetical issue with a very skillful solution. Instead of choosing one vision against the other, the theophany or the visit of three men, or instead of trying to tell one from the other according to some details of the text, which is what one most usually encounters in Jewish exegesis at the time or afterwards,[25] Philo states that the vision is described in reality not as it could be perceived by a witness, or told by what we would call an omniscient narrator, but as Abraham thinks that he sees it. He attributes the double vision to the weakness of the patriarch's intellect, however pious or pure of heart he may have been as a wise man. Philo writes:

> With a single turning of the eyes the mind [26] apprehends a double appearance; the one was of God coming with His two highest powers ... and the other (appearance) was that of the strange men .... And being struck by either appearance, he was drawn towards seeing, now by one, now by the other. And he was not able to see just which of them was likely to be the true one.[27]

The key of this exegesis is twofold. First, Philo introduces the two Powers of God to explain how Abraham can see the One God in the three men appearing in front of him,[28] whereas he then speaks to God as to a single being,[29] and seems to eventually understand that there were no men.[30] But then, and perhaps more importantly, he needs to focalize his narrative on Abraham's intellect, an imperfect one, so as to explain why Abraham remains doubtful, knowing that a triple apparition can be that of God surrounded by the two Powers as well as that of human beings. Abraham's intellect is not explicitly present in the biblical narrative, but it appears

[25] See, e.g., the Targum for Gen 18:1–2 in the Neofiti 1 as well as in the Ps-Jonathan recensions, or the texts compiled by Louis Ginzberg, *The Legends of the Jews* (Philadelphia: Jewish Publication Society of America, 1909), 1.241.

[26] Probably νοῦς, even if the original text in Greek is lost.

[27] We quote Ralph Marcus's translation (PLCL, Suppl. 1:272).

[28] See our article "Outil exégétique ou enseignement métaphysique? Les puissances de Dieu dans les *Quaestiones in Genesim* (IV, 1–19)," in *Pouvoirs et puissances chez Philon d'Alexandrie*, ed. Francesca Calabi, Olivier Munnich, Gretchen Reydams-Schils, and Emmaneule Vimercati, Monothéisme et Philosophie (Leuven: Brepols, 2015), 203–207.

[29] From this point on in the *quaestio*, and thanks to the fact that the powers of God may or may not appear in a theophany, Philo moves one step forward and identifies in advance the different details in the whole episode which refer to a single being (God), and those which refer to three persons (the three human visitors). When Abraham speaks with one person, he believes he's speaking with God, and when he speaks with three persons, he believes he's speaking with three men.

[30] Philo proceeds in that matter accordingly to the biblical narrative, where only one person seems to be present from Gen 18:9 on.

useful and thus necessary to explain the joint presence of God and of men, and the eventual disappearing of the latter.

The main consequence of the combined use of these two tools is that Philo can do without allegory. And yet, at the end of the episode, commenting on Gen 18:16 ("Abraham was going along with them as he joined in escorting them"), Philo explains the identity of these beings with an almost commonplace distinction between the "literal meaning"—they are men, and a "deeper meaning"—they are "God and his Powers."[31] Doing without allegory in the *quaestio* 2 is thus a very deliberate choice, to explain the potential contradictions of a very difficult text by making all details coherent with each other.

This passage of the *Quaestiones* is one of the places where the foundation on which Philo's exegesis is generally built, and of which allegory is a consequence, appears directly, bare, so to speak, like an outcrop. The allegorical method reaches what we could call its "zero degree." This emphasizes the way the intellect acts as a primary focus for Philo's vision, even more deeply than the necessity to allegorize Scripture. If it belongs to the literal meaning, explicitly or implicitly, then allegory as a technical tool may become useless: no transposition is needed from one level to the other. The identity between the words or general meaning of Scripture and the intelligible realities which Philo wants to illustrate allows a direct expression of that deeper reality. In contrast, allegory is needed when that reality can't be reached directly through Scripture's words, because a new level of explanation is needed. It appears then as a way of elaborating on the biblical language and its metaphorical potentialities to reach invisible realities that would have remained hidden otherwise. To put it another way: in this passage, Philo's exegesis is neither literal nor allegorical, with all the traditional implications it may have, it is only intelligible. The complex theophany, indeed, through Philo's truly ingenious exegesis, can be explained by a direct focus on Abraham's intellect.

From these first two specific examples of Philonic exegesis, we have tried to illustrate how Philo's concern for the intellectual life explains the widespread use of allegory and its link to literal interpretation, but also why it may be missing even when an intelligible meaning is at stake. The focalization on the intellect explains the (mostly allegorical) exegesis in Philo's commentaries, not the other way around.[32] This must be kept in mind as we

31 *QG* 4.20 (PLCL, Suppl. 1:293).

32 Once again, we do not mean that Philo should not be studied as a milestone in the history of allegorical exegesis, after Jewish and philosophical precursors and in a specific Alexandrian environment, but that the coherence of his method must be found beyond the

move to a third kind of exegesis where the use of the word "allegory" is more likely to obfuscate rather than clarify Philo's exegesis.

3. *The Complexity of Allegory and the Intellect as a Hermeneutical Criterion in the* De migratione Abrahami

Though allegory appears as the main exegetical tool in the series of treatises commenting on the text of Genesis and known to scholars as the great Allegorical Commentary, it would be too bold an attempt to try and give it the same definition as in the other treatises: allegory is not a way to solve a problem, it appears as the only way to comment on a text, without the need to first explain the literal meaning of the text or its potential difficulties. At least that's what we can see from the beginning of the *De migratione Abrahami*.

After a direct quotation of the three verses (Gen 12:1–3) that are the object of the first 126 paragraphs, and without any kind of introduction, Philo begins at once its commentary by explaining how the first part of God's words to Abraham ("Depart out of thy land, and out of thy kindred, and out of thy father's house" [Gen 12:1]) apply to the "full salvation" (σωτηρίαν παντελῆ) that God wants to give to the "soul" (ψυχήν [*Migr.* 2]). Such a beginning makes clear that the allegorical reading is regarded by Philo as a perfectly natural and expected way of reading Scripture, no matter what may be the literal meaning, which is in fact completely left aside.[33] It may also indicate that the direct application of Scripture to the life of the soul is self-evident and needs no demonstration or justification whatsoever.[34] It leaves the reader to wonder how is it possible to speak of an allegorical meaning where there is no literal one. We could go nearly as far as to say that in the great Allegorical Commentary what we call

mere use of an allegorical reading of Scripture, even though he probably built his understanding of Scripture mostly as a result of the traditions of allegorical reading.

33 It is possible that the absence of any literal exposition, in contrast with the very didactic *De Abrahamo* where literal exposition as well as allegorical development are precisely circumscribed, characterizes an exegesis *ad intra*, for Jewish exegetes, already used to such an approach, whereas the *De Abrahamo* and more generally the Exposition of the Law would be apologetic works to present Jewish exegesis in a more convenient way for the Greeks who are not as familiar with Scripture. Whatever the case may be in this disputed matter, this does not seem to us to make any difference as far as Philo's hermeneutics are concerned.

34 One may suppose that Philo implicitly uses the same kind of method as in the *Quaestiones* but, as we shall see, no question can be precisely determined to account for the exegesis that follows, apart from a rather general "what does it mean that..."

"allegory" is in a way the "literal"—that is, immediate to a certain degree—meaning of the biblical text: Philo reads in—or through—Scripture the life of the intellect in search of God, almost as if he was only translating it, but it takes an elaborate exegesis to make it plainly visible.

We won't try to study the whole treatise, not even the whole commentary on the first verse: its length alone (52 paragraphs) is enough to grasp that this exegesis is far richer than that of the previous treatises. We will emphasize the first two parts and their teachings on the kind of exegetical method followed by Philo: the beginning of the commentary where allegory in its stricter meaning is developed, and the succession of biblical characters that follows, from Moses to Isaac, leading eventually to Philo himself.

From paragraphs 2 to 6, Philo's commentary is plain allegory: to each of the important words of the verse ("land,"[35] "kindred," "father's house"), he gives an allegorical[36] meaning (respectively: "body," "sense-perception," and "speech" [*Migr.* 2]). He then explains this transposition, rather quickly for kindred/sense-perception (*Migr.* 3), but in more detail for land/body (*Migr.* 3) and especially for father's house/speech (*Migr.* 3–6), where two words (father and house) and then their association require an explanation. Philo thus starts from the lower part of the world (the earth) and of a human being (the body), and then proceeds to its inner and higher part, the intellect, which is itself analogical of God and his Word, through which the world was created. This overall coherence and gradation from the creation to the Creator is not the only point worth noting: Philo's use of biblical quotations (Gen 3:19 and Gen 28:17)[37] to justify a transposition from a matter-of-fact meaning—respectively the earth and the father's house—to an intelligible one, means that allegory is not only a single transposition from one word or reality to another.

Philo's commentary shows that there is a web or a thread where all Scripture and all its allegorical meaning are interwoven, meaning that

[35] We quote here and below Francis H. Colson's and George H. Whitaker's translation (PLCL 4).

[36] Philo uses the word "symbol" (σύμβολον): in the *De Abrahamo*, this vocabulary applies not to the general method of allegorizing an episode, but to the specific transposition of one single reality to its allegorical counterpart (see, e.g., *Abr.* 52, 68, 72, 99).

[37] Such secondary lemmata are also part of the *Quaestiones*, as David Runia scrupulously showed (David T. Runia, "Secondary Texts in Philo's *Quaestiones*," in *Both Literal and Allegorical*, 47–79). However, beyond loose similarities, the secondary lemmata are part of a more complex method in the great Allegorical Commentary and can't be regarded as "wholly subordinate" (ibid., 66) to a main exegesis. They are quoted in an unexpected way, not so much to justify a previous interpretation as to create it: the "land" may mean the "body" only because the body is "earth" according to Moses in Gen 3:19.

allegory is not arbitrary but is grounded in Moses's words, whether directly —the link with Gen 3:19—or in a more complex way—the use of Gen 28:17. The key remains nonetheless a philosophical contemplation that justifies that the kindred, placed between the body and the uttered speech unveiled by the exegesis, may refer to sense-perception, without biblical proof. At this point of the commentary, this passage exemplifies what is commonly understood as Philo's allegorical method: Scripture can be read as an "allegory of the soul," meaning that its deeper meaning is the life of the intellect and the departure from sensible realities, but also that any part of it may shed light on any other verse. Allegory in itself is not enough if it is not supported by Scripture. To put it another way, the interpretation of a lemma is not a binary matter—the transposition of the literal meaning to another one—it involves a lemma, the intertextual reading of that verse (whether allegorically or not) and a philosophical point of view. Philo achieves this through careful work on the vocabulary, so as to merge the language of Scripture with the language of philosophy.[38]

This is further proved on a first level by the next two paragraphs (*Migr.* 7–8). Philo completes the allegorical transposition of the biblical verse by explaining the true meaning of the verb "to depart": it is not an absolute separation of the body and the soul—in a Platonic sense that could only mean death [39]—but it refers to the right distance kept by a king dominating his subjects (ὑπήκοοι, *Migr.* 8). Thus, he may come to know himself, as Moses teaches, saying "Give heed to thyself" (πρόσεχε σεαυτῷ [Exod 34:12]). This verse, very similar to the Socratic γνῶθι σεαυτόν, is thus seen, at the same time, as a strict equivalent to Gen 12:1, if read in the correct way, which is what we have to call allegory in a new manner. Scripture in itself has a philosophical meaning, and a coherent one: Philo does not only explain Scripture through Scripture,[40] he also explains Scripture through philosophy, and philosophy through Scripture, and allegory is the method through which they are brought to a common meaning.

[38] See, e.g., the various studies in *Philon d'Alexandrie et le langage de la philosophie, Actes du colloque international organisé par le Centre d'études sur la philosophie hellénistique et romaine de l'Université de Paris XII-Val de Marne, Créteil, Fontenay, Paris, 26–28 octobre 1995,* ed. Carlos Lévy (Turnhout: Brepols, 1998).

[39] The expression διαζεύχθητι κατὰ τὴν οὐσίαν is most likely a reference to Plato (see, e.g., *Phaed.* 88b8).

[40] This exegetical method common to Jews and Christians was already familiar among Alexandrian scholars who used to explain Homer through Homer: see e.g., Gilles Dorival, "Exégèse juive et exégèse chrétienne," in *Le commentaire entre tradition et innovation*, ed. Marie-Odile Goulet-Cazé (Paris: Vrin, 2000), 169–181.

Philo, however, does not stick to biblical or philosophical vocabulary. For instance, he works very minutely on the very important verb from the lemma: ἄπελθε, through various synonyms. He speaks first of a μετανάστασις ("migration," *Migr.* 2) before using the verb μετανίσταμαι ("to emigrate," *Migr.* 12). Neither of these words is biblical and nobody before Philo had ever used them with such a metaphorical meaning. In the paragraphs we just studied, Philo uses two other synonyms, διαζεύχθητι and ἀλλοτριώθητι, to make clear what kind of departure is dealt with in the lemma, i.e., a distinction more than a separation. We could even go as far as to say that the last imperative of paragraph 7, στῆθι, may refer to the very notion he introduced, the μετανάστασις, to make clear that the migration is not only a movement, but also a position or an attitude to keep strongly. This metaphorical language is central to Philo's method and may well define one of the greatest points of interest of his theology, i.e., the quest for a rational understanding and exposition of Scripture.

In the following paragraphs (*Migr.* 9–12), the commentary is raised to a higher level: though the allegorical reading of the verse may now be regarded as complete, Philo gives to this first transposition a new formulation through a triple exhortation to depart from each of the three elements previously explained. Not only does the contemplative exegesis give in to a paraenetic speech to reach its full extent, it also confirms the deep association made by Philo between Scripture and philosophy: each exhortation seems to have a double background, both biblical and philosophical, that adds to the first allegorical content. The image of the body and of desire as a prison (*Migr.* 9) is of course Platonic,[41] but it may also refer to Joseph's stay in prison.[42] The vocabulary of the loan made by the intellect of itself to the senses (*Migr.* 10–11) also carries a strong resonance with biblical prescriptions regarding lending and borrowing from other nations, which means for the Hebrews an alienation.[43] Finally, the development about the speech on the copies and the original realities (*Migr.* 12) conveys an obvious Platonic dimension,[44] as well as a probable inspiration from the prescrip-

[41] See *Phaed.* 82e.

[42] The word "jailer" (εἱρκτοφύλαξ), for instance, is only used by Philo in other passages in relation to Joseph's imprisonment: *Deus* 115; *Mut.* 173; *Ios.* 81, 84, 85, 123. The word "foul" (παμμίαρον) is also used, among other passages, to describe the evil accomplished by Joseph's jailers (*Ios.* 84).

[43] Deut 15:16; 28:12.

[44] The two main treatises are the *Cratylus*, for its inquiry on the relations between language and reality, and the seventh book of the *Republic*, for the allegory of the Cave and the subsequent development on ideas and their copies. In a way, Philo reads the *Cratylus* through the *Republic*, applied to the discussion on language.

tions against the idols, which Scripture similarly accuses of preventing the true knowledge as well of things—they are only "likenesses" (ὁμοιώματα; see Deut 4:16)—as of God—whose place they take.[45]

So far, it has already become impossible to reduce allegory to the mere transposition from sensible realities present in Scripture towards intelligible realities best expressed by a philosophical language. The literal meaning of the initial lemma does not appear as a problem and the true meaning of Scripture is at the same time biblical and philosophical, thanks to a precise work on the exegetic vocabulary.

In the following paragraphs, the very distinction between literal and allegorical commentary seems to become meaningless. Philo quotes several other biblical episodes about departures, starting from Moses and the archetypal Exodus from Egypt (13–15) and going backwards in time from Exodus to Genesis. He begins with Joseph (16–24), the example of an imperfect departure, linked to bodily realities as he was, but whose bones, i.e., the imperishable part of himself—as were his virtues—would eventually be brought back to his land. Then comes Jacob (25–28), an example of the efforts needed to make the departure in haste, as required in Exod 12:11, to reach the land promised to Abraham. Finally, Philo recalls Isaac, who never left his land but benefited from the greatest gift, life with God (*Migr.* 33). This backward succession thus leads back to Abraham and the promise made to him by God if he leaves his country.

Philo's real subject is the journey of the intellect towards God, be it from an almost direct reading of the text, akin to a literal one,[46] or from a metaphorical reading akin to an allegorical one.[47] The purpose is no more that of the *De Abrahamo* or the *Quaestiones*, where the method was as relevant as its result. Now, the Law of Moses as a whole is subsumed under the strongly unified focus of the intellect: Moses and the Hebrews, Joseph—in a partial way, because his virtue was not perfect—Jacob and Isaac are all

[45] Deut 4:15–8. See also Wis 13:2–5 for a contemporary reformulation of this attack against idols.

[46] In *Migr.* 13, in the first step of his new development, Philo speaks of the "wise man" (Abraham) to emphasize the way his parting from Lot (Gen 13:9) confirms the necessity for someone loving the incorporeal and incorruptible to flee from someone still attached to sensible realities. This is a literal reading provided that Philo does tell about a factual biblical event and human beings, but he introduces a philosophical focus that is at least implicit—if not completely missing—in Scripture.

[47] The bones of Joseph (*Migr.* 17) are a symbol of the part in his soul that resisted corruption. It is an allegorical reading, but among all that is recalled by Philo about Joseph (*Migr.* 17–24), some details refer to the biblical character as a human being, and others to a symbolic reading.

different facets of this fundamental reality which is relevant for Abraham as well as for the people whose father he is, the Jews.

The conclusion of this development is of the greatest importance regarding Philo's hermeneutics. He gives an example of his own experience in order to justify his reading of Scripture and he does so as a philosopher,[48] experiencing in his intellect what he recognizes in Scripture: the true fecundity of the intellect comes only from God, whereas the intellect may remain barren when it relies on its own strength. If reading and commenting on Scripture has a meaning and teaches something about each individual's life, this is, according to this whole development, in the intellect, which is thus the touchstone of all exegesis. The exodus that Philo lives as a Jew, faithful to the law of Moses, is that of the mind from sensible realities towards God, making him the follower of Moses and the patriarchs, or rather making him another facet of an eternal intellective reality.

4. *Conclusion*

Allegory is not arbitrary. It was already widespread enough in Alexandria among Greeks scholars as well as Jewish exegetes to be then used by Philo, but this should not hide the deeper coherence of Philo's thought. He does not only try to "save" Scripture by justifying difficult passages, illustrating their metaphorical meaning to prove the rationality of its prescriptions, nor does he only try to match biblical propositions with those of philosophy, with an apologetic purpose, as Aristobulus had done. The idea that the soul needs to ascend to its Creator, through stages revealed by God, represents the union at a deeper level of two revelations, or two laws, that of Moses and that of nature. Whatever may be the particular method used in different kinds of exegetical treatises, Philo seems to believe that the law of Moses in its entirety possess a deep and eternal truth, having been revealed by God himself to Moses, in the same way that creation is made according to eternal laws. More than any of the few predecessors still known to us, Philo tries to illustrate how much the law and creation are copies of each other: this purpose implies an exegesis of Scripture that takes into account the whole rational inquiry about creation and its laws conveyed by Greek culture, so as to allow the soul to know the world, to know itself and to reach its Creator as He prescribed it.

[48] By "the usual course of writing on philosophical tenets" (κατὰ τὴν συνήθη τῶν κατὰ φιλοσοφίαν δογμάτων γραφήν [*Migr.* 34]), Philo most probably refers to his exegesis, which is in his own view a method of philosophical research, as we tried to illustrate.

As Hindy Najman has clearly explained,[49] the idea that there could be a written copy of the law of nature, the idea of Scripture itself, is a true paradox. What appears to us as such was probably for Philo more of a challenge or a necessity: to conciliate two authorities, that of God's revealed law and that of reason. He does not try to solve the paradox, but on the contrary he builds on it, taking for granted that both philosophy and Scripture lead to the knowledge of the soul and of God, although he may not be able to justify it. Or rather, in the same way that Zeno's paradox on the impossibility of movement could be refuted (but not explained) just by walking, Philo's answer is his exegesis. The starting point remains the superior authority of Scripture, directly revealed by God, whereas the laws of nature have to be understood and formulated; but all of Scripture can be explained through Greek rationality.

To achieve this purpose, Philo needs two things. The first is a focus under which Scripture as well as philosophy can be subsumed: this is the intellect, through which alone the true nature of things can be known. The other is a language, a vocabulary. Thanks to the fact that Scripture has been translated in Greek, the language of the *paideia*, Philo is able to write this complex exegesis which relies for a great part on the means of language. It is true that in *De Abrahamo* or in the *Quaestiones* in general Philo illustrates how a biblical reality is the image of another; but in some particular passages, and especially in the great Allegorical Commentary, Philo is looking for what these two realities, taken together, can refer to. Scripture and philosophy are not only an allegorical translation of each other, but together, through the language of exegesis, they may refer to something more than each of them alone could do.[50]

There is a strong coherence between the focus on the intellect and the particular use of language made by Philo. Indeed, the truth reached by the intellect is not directly in the biblical events themselves nor in sensible creation, but in the knowledge of itself and of God that it perceives through them. In an analogical way, Scripture does not directly reveal its true meaning, whereas the language of philosophy is useful but imperfect, since philosophers don't have the full understanding that Moses has. In both cases, truth is reached through mediations, but beyond them, and language

49 Hindy Najman, "A Written Copy of the Law of Nature: An Unthinkable Paradox?," *SPhiloA* 15 (2003): 54–63.

50 In this matter, Anthony A. Long made very interesting remarks about the circularity of Philo's metaphor and its difference with the Stoic thought on language in his article "Allegory in Philo and Etymology in Stoicism: A Plea for Drawing Distinctions," *SPhiloA* 9 (1997): 198–210.

may be the precise way to try and reveal, metaphorically, the underlying coherence between law and creation.

We could compare Philo's exegesis to an arch. In some cases, the two pillars—Scripture and creation—may be regarded as identical, and they may be directly compared to each other. But Philo's final purpose is more elevated: in order to have these two pillars effectively unite with each other, he needs a keystone which is the intellect. It is reached thanks to language, acting as a complex scaffolding, allowing for the bending of the pillars into voussoirs progressively converging towards each other: nothing would be possible without it, but it is meant to eventually give in to the intellect, which relies on Scripture and creation, but is turned to the contemplation of God.

Lyons

The Studia Philonica Annual 29 (2017): 81–86

EXAMINING BLEMISHES
The Μωμοσκόποι and the Jerusalem Temple

YAKIR PAZ*

In his first book of *The Special Laws*, when describing the animals suitable for sacrifice, Philo notes (*Spec.* 1.166):

> All the animals must be perfect with no affliction troubling any part of their body, scathless throughout and free from defects [μώμων ἀμέτοχα]. In fact, so great is the forethought exercised not only by those who bring the sacrifices but also by those who consecrate them, that the most esteemed among the priests having been chosen according to their merit for the viewing of blemishes [οἱ δοκιμώτατοι τῶν ἱερέων ἀριστίνδην ἐπικριθέντες εἰς τὴν τῶν μώμων ἐπίσκεψιν[, examine them from the head to the extremities of the feet [ἀπὸ κεφαλῆς ἄχρι ποδῶν ἄκρων ἐρευνῶσιν[, both the visible parts and those which are concealed under the belly and thighs, for fear that some small blemish has passed unobserved.[1]

Philo's statement that all sacrificial animals must be unblemished is based on Lev 22:20–24. However, the appointment of designated priests to inspect the animals for blemishes (εἰς τὴν τῶν μώμων ἐπίσκεψιν) has no scriptural basis. The realistic depiction of these inspectors suggests rather that Philo is here describing contemporary practice at the Jerusalem Temple relying either on personal observation or hearsay.[2] In his allegorical treatise *On Cultivation* Philo explicitly mentions the title of these inspectors (*Agr.* 130):

* This short note is a product of my Hebrew annotated translation of Philo's *de Agricultura* under the editorship of Maren Niehoff (*The Writings of Philo of Alexandria*, vol. 4b [Jerusalem: Mosad Bialik, 2015], 95–144). I wish to thank Shlomo Naeh and Shraga Bar-On for their insightful comments.

[1] Translation PLCL, vol. 7, 193–95, modified.

[2] E. P. Sanders, *Judaism: Practice and Belief, 63BCE-66CE* (London: SCM Press, 1992), 85–86; Albert C. Geljon and David T. Runia, *Philo: On Cultivation. Introduction, Translation and Commentary*, PACS 4 (Leiden: Brill, 2013) 214; PLCL, vol. 7, 192–93 note c.

> For it is quite absurd to take care that priests are wholly sound in body and perfect, that the sacrificial animals have not even the very slightest blemish, and that inspectors [τινας διόπους][3] are appointed for this task—some call these 'defect-viewers' [οὓς ἔνιοι μωμοσκόπους ὀνομάζουσιν]—, that is, to supervise that the victims (τὰ ἱερεῖα) brought to the altar are without defect of damage [ἄμωμα καὶ ἀσινῆ], yet to permit the opinions in the souls of each person concerning God to be confused and not adjudicated by the standard of right reason.[4]

According to Philo, some (ἔνιοι) call these inspectors μωμοσκόποι, that is, defect viewers or examiners of blemishes. This is the only time in Philo's surviving oeuvre that this word appears. In fact, this is the first time this rare word is recorded at all in extant Greek literature. Albert Geljon and David Runia, in their recent comprehensive commentary of *On Cultivation*, have somewhat hesitantly suggested that this rare word might be a Philonic word.[5] However, the fact that Philo attributes this term to "some" (ἔνιοι) seems to indicate that he did not coin it.

It is clear though that μωμοσκόπος is of Jewish-Hellenistic provenance, since μῶμος is not used in classical Greek to denote sacrificial defects but rather "blame," "reproach," or "disgrace" and is even personified as Momus.[6] The use of μῶμος in a sacrificial context was introduced in the Septuagint, based on the striking similarity between the Greek μῶμος and the Hebrew מום (blemish).[7]

Besides this single occurrence in the Philonic corpus, the term is later recorded only four times in the writings of the church fathers[8] and is not to be found in extant Pagan literature. The earliest occurrence appears in Clement of Alexandria's *Stromata* (4.18.117), who notes that according to the law, there were blemish-examiners of the sacrificial victims (οἱ τῶν ἱερείων μωμοσκόποι). Although Clement was well versed in Philo's works, yet as Runia and Geljon state, "it is impossible to say whether there is a relationship between Philo's and Clement's passages."[9] Besides Clement,

[3] Geljon and Runia *(On Cultivation*, 81 n. 52) follow here Cohn's emendation of the difficult δεῖ ὅσους. The term δίοπος is used by Philo to describe Pinchas the priest in *Post.* 182.

[4] Translation Geljon and Runia, *On Cultivation*, 68.

[5] Geljon and Runia (*On Cultivation*, 215) refer to μωμοσκόπος as "the rare (and Philonic?) word." Further on verba philonica see ibid, 31, 118, 148, 177, 180 and David T. Runia, "Verba Philonica, ΑΓΑΛΜΑΤΟΦΟΡΕΙΝ, and the Authenticity of the *De Resurrectione* Attributed to Athenagoras," *VC* 46 (1992): 313–27.

[6] H. G. Liddell, R. Scott, and H. S. Jones, eds., *A Greek-English Lexicon* (Oxford: Clarendon, 1996), s.v. μῶμος.

[7] See e.g., F. Hauck, "μῶμος," *TDNT* 4: 829–30.

[8] Cf. G. W. H. Lampe, ed., *A Patristic Greek Lexicon* (Oxford: Clarendon, 1961), s.v. μωμοσκόπος.The word is also attested several times in late Byzantine authors.

[9] Geljon and Runia, *On Cultivation*, 214.

this word is later used twice by Cyril of Alexandria (*Hom. Pasch.* 4.6; *Mal.* 14) and once metaphorically by Theodoret (*Ep.* 16, 4.1077) to denote fault finders.

The cognate verb μωμοσκοπέω, which is not used by Philo, is slightly better attested among church fathers.[10] It is first documented in Clement of Rome's *First Epistle to the Corinthians* (41.2):

> Not in every place, brethren, are the daily sacrifices offered, or the peace-offerings, or the sin-offerings and the trespass-offerings, but in Jerusalem only. And even there they are not offered in any place, but only at the altar before the temple, that which is offered being first examined for blemishes [μωμοσκοπηθὲν τὸ προσφερόμενον] by the high priest and the ministers already mentioned.[11]

Here the verb μωμοσκοπέω is directly linked to the temple of Jerusalem.[12] This verb is also used figuratively[13] and later even denotes more generally "examining critically" or "criticizing."[14]

[10] The verb is mentioned twenty times (not including Byzantine authors). Most are recorded in Lampe, *A Patristic Greek Lexicon*, s.v. μωμοσκοπέω. Four of the references are also mentioned in Geljon and Runia, *On Cultivation*, 215.

[11] Translation after Philip Schaff, ed., *The Ante-Nicene Fathers 1: The Apostolic Fathers with Justin Martyr and Irenaeus*, (Grand Rapids, Mi.: Eerdmans, 1993), 27, modified.

[12] Cf. Cyril of Alexandria, *Ador.*15; *Mal.* 2.547, 567, 573, 574; Ps.-Macarius, *Sermones*, 7.2.1.

[13] E.g., Polycarp *Ep. Phil.* 4.3: γινωσκούσας, ὅτι εἰσὶ θυσιαστήριον θεοῦ καὶ ὅτι πάντα μωμοσκοπεῖται, καὶ λέληθεν αὐτὸν οὐδὲν οὔτε λογισμῶν οὔτε ἐννοιῶν οὔτε τι τῶν κρυπτῶν τῆς καρδίας: "Knowing that they (i.e., the widows) are God's altar and that all [sacrifices] are inspected for blemishes, and nothing escapes him neither the thoughts nor intents nor any of the secrets of the heart" (Translation after Schaff, *op. cit.* [n. 11] 43, modified). Cf. *Const. App.* 6.23.5; John Chrysostom, *Hom.* 20.2 in *Rom.* (9.657E); *Hom.* 17.4 in *Heb.* (12.170B); Ps.-Macarius, *Sermones*, 7.2.4. On this shift in meaning see Gerard J. M. Bartelink, "Zur Spiritualisierung eines Opferterminus," *Glotta* 39 (1960): 43–48.

[14] Lampe, *A Patristic Greek Lexicon*, s.v.μωμοσκοπέω E.g. Origin *Or.* 21.1; Gregory of Nyssa, *Ep.*18.9; *Hom. Opif.* 125d; Ephraem Syrius, *De divina gratia* 3.46d: μωμοσκοπήσατε δὲ τὰ σφάλματα τοῦ γράψαντος (K. G. Phrantzoles, ed., *Ὁσίου Ἐφραίμ τοῦ Σύρου ἔργα*, vol. 5, (Thessalonica: To Privoli tis Panaghias, 1994), 184; Marcus Eremita, *Disputatio cum quodam causidico*, 13.34: τοὺς διδασκάλους μωμοσκοπεῖ (G.-M. de Durand, ed., *Marc le Moine: Traités II*, SC 455 [Paris: Éditions du Cerf, 2000]). The use of μωμοσκόπος and μωμοσκοπέω in the sense of fault finder or critic was possibly also due to a "classical" understanding of μῶμος. This meaning is more common among Byzantine authors. So, for example, the following entry appears in the 13th century lexicon attributed to John Zonaras: Μωμοσκόπος. ὁ φιλόψογος. i.e., censorious, lover of faults (J. A. H. Tittmann, *Iohannis Zonarae lexicon ex tribus codicibus manuscriptis*, vol. 2 [Leipzig: Crusius, 1808; repr. Amsterdam: Hakkert, 1967], 1381). On the Byzantine use of the term see now the comprehensive study by Panagiotis A. Agapitos, "John Tzetzes and the Blemish Examiners: A Byzantine Teacher on Schedography, Everyday Language and Writerly Disposition," *Medioevo Greco* 17 (2017): 1–57. I wish to thank the author for sharing his article with me prior to its publication.

Even though some of these church fathers were well acquainted with Philo's writings,[15] their use of both the term and the verb does not seem to be dependent on Philo, further indicating that this was not a Philonic word. The term μωμοσκόπος though was probably introduced somewhat contemporaneous with Philo, as he attributes it to fellow Jews. Further indirect corroboration of this might be adduced from the fact that the author of the Letter of Aristeas seems unaware of this technical term when describing the priests who inspect sacrificial victims for blemishes (*Arist.* 93).[16]

Since μωμοσκόπος is part of a Jewish Hellenistic vocabulary directly linked to functionaries in the Jerusalem temple, it would seem appropriate to search for its origins in Hebrew sources.

In tannaitic literature the verb בק"ר (BQR) is used to refer to the blemish inspection of sacrificial victims. So, for example, in t. Sabb, 16:24 it is stated:[17]

> אין מבקרין את המומין ביום טוב ואין צריך לומ' בשבת. אם לבו ביום מבקרין את המומין בשבת ואין צריך לומ' ביום טוב.

> It is prohibited to examine the blemishes on the holyday and it goes without saying also on the Sabbath. If it is for the same day—they examine the blemishes on the Sabbath and it goes without saying also on the holyday.

The expression מבקרין את המומין (they examine the blemishes) is clearly equivalent to the verb μωμοσκοπέω.[18] An even earlier attestation to the role of these inspectors can be found in m. Tamid (3:4):[19]

> והשקו את התמיד בכוס של זהב אף על פי שהוא מבקר מבערב מבקרין אותו לאור האבוקות.

[15] See David T. Runia, *Philo in Early Christian Literature: A Survey*, CRINT 3.3 (Assen: Van Gorcum, 1993).

[16] Κατὰ πᾶν γὰρ ἐκλεγομένων οἷς ἐπιμελές ἐστιν ἀμώμητα καὶ τῇ παχύτητι διαφέροντα "For with respect to all of them, those whose charge it is to select the flawless and the ones with excessive fat." Translation: Benjamin G. Wright III, *The Letter of Aristeas*, CEJL (Berlin: de Gruyter, 2015), 204.

[17] All quotations from rabbinic literature are based on the versions in *Ma'agarim: The Historical Dictionary Project of the Academy of the Hebrew Language*, http://maagarim.hebrew-academy.org.il/Pages/PMain.aspx

[18] For further examples of the usage of the verb בק"ר to denote examination of sacrificial victims see, e.g., m. Arak. 2:5; Mek. RY 5 (16); Sipre Numbers 142 (188); t. Hag. 1:8; t. Hul. 2:8; t. Bek. 3:6. y. Hagiga 2:3 (78a).

[19] Most of this tractate is attributed to Shimon of Mitzpah from the first century CE. On the early dating of m. Tamid see further Jacob Epstein, *Prolegomena ad litteras Tannaiticas* (Jerusalem: Magnes, 1957) 27–31 [Hebrew].

> And they gave the daily sacrificial victim to drink from a golden chalice. Even though it had been examined the previous day, they examine it [again] by torch light.

However, it is only in amoraic sources that we find the technical term for these inspectors. As part of a list of various guilds which collect their wages from the Temple treasury (תרומת הלשכה),[20] the Palestinian Talmud preserves the following testimony attributed to R. Isaac bar Redifa (third–fourth century CE) in the name of R. Ami (third century):[21]

> רבי יצחק בר רדיפה בשם רבי אימי: מבקרי מומי קדשים נוטלין שכרן מתרומת הלשכה.

> R. Isaac bar Redifa said in the name of R. Ami: The examiners of offering blemishes would take their wages from the Temple treasury.

The term מבקרי מומי קדשים (examiners of offering blemishes) conspicuously resembles Clement of Alexandria's phrasing—οἱ τῶν ἱερείων μωμοσκόποι—discussed above. In the all but identical parallel in the Babylonian Talmud (b. Ketub. 106a), these inspectors are named מבקרי מומין שבירושלים ("the examiners of blemishes in Jerusalem"). Thus, מבקרי מומין is the official title of a professional guild at the temple.[22]

The striking similarity between the Hebrew and Greek term had already been noticed, in passing, by Yehoshua Amir. In his Hebrew translation of *Spec.* 1.166, he refers in a footnote to *Agr.* 130 and to the use there of μωμοσκόποι, "which," he briefly adds, "is identical to מבקרי מומים [*sic*] in rabbinic literature."[23] Indeed both terms refer, as we have seen, to specific priests in the Jerusalem temple. The terms, though, are not merely identical, as Amir had suggested, but rather the Greek μωμοσκόποι is most likely a calque of the Hebrew מבקרי מומין.

It would seem then that the term μωμοσκόπος was introduced sometime around the beginning of the first century CE by Hellenistic Jews, who were well-acquainted with the Jerusalem temple bureaucracy, in order to translate a technical term for a professional guild. They, however, did not simply use an existing Greek word but rather chose to coin a neologism.

[20] For a suggestion that at least part of this list represents changes in the temple bureaucracy which took place in the first decades of the 1st century CE see M. Beer, "Ha-Kitot u-Mahatzit ha-Shekel," *Tarbitz* 31 (1962): 298–99 [Hebrew], who attributes this change to the increasing influence of the Pharisees.

[21] y. Seqal. 4:2 (48a).

[22] In the sectarian compositions of the Dead Sea scrolls the term מבקר refers to the overseer. Cf., e.g., CD 9:18, 22; 13:7, 13, 16; 14:8, 13;15:8, 11; *Serek ha-Yahad* (1QS) 6:12, 20.

[23] Suzanne Daniel-Nataf ed., *The Writings of Philo of Alexandria*, vol. 2 (Jerusalem: Bialik Institute, 1991), 265 n. 237 [Hebrew].

Rabbinic literature thus provides us with the Hebrew origin of the term μωμοσκόπος. Philo, on the other hand, confirms the historicity of this rabbinic tradition and enriches it with a vivid, and possibly first-hand, description of the activity of these highly esteemed blemish-examiners, who seem to have had much in common with our modern-day critics.

Hebrew University, Jerusalem

The Studia Philonica Annual 29 (2017): 87–109

NOSTRE PHILON: PHILO AFTER TRENT*

ERIC J. DEMEUSE

The gaps in Philo of Alexandria's reception history are gradually being filled. David T. Runia's work on Philo in the church fathers and Philo in Byzantium brings the narrative up to 1500.[1] Joanna Weinberg has chronicled Jewish reception during the Renaissance,[2] and Cyril O'Regan and Benjamin Pollock launch us into the modern age with their works on Philo in Hegel and in Franz Rosenzweig respectively.[3] The forthcoming collection *The Reception of Philo of Alexandria* (ed. David Lincicum, Courtney Friesen and David Runia) promises to deepen our knowledge of Philo's legacy even further. One area that remains understudied, however, is the Christian use of Philo in the sixteenth century, and especially after the Council of Trent—an unfortunate oversight, since this century could arguably be called the beginning of modern Philo scholarship.

The sixteenth century witnessed a renaissance in Philonic studies rivaled only by developments from the nineteenth century onward.[4] Between

* I am especially indebted to Dr. Michael Cover and Dr. Ulrich Lehner for their guidance and insights on this article; to Stephen Calme, Sara Hulse, Jacob Kilgore, and Jodie Scordo for reading an early draft and offering comments; to Patrick and Catherine Timmis for reviewing my Latin translations; and to Nathaniel Peters for reviewing my French translations.

[1] David T. Runia, *Philo in Early Christian Literature: A Survey*, CRINT 3.3 (Assen: Van Gorcum; Minneapolis: Fortress, 1993); idem, "References to Philo from Josephus up to 1000 AD,' *SPhiloA* 6 (1994): 111–21; Runia, *Philo and the Church Fathers: A Collection of Papers* (Leiden: Brill, 1995); Runia, "Philo in Byzantium," *VC* 70 (2016): 259–81.

[2] Joanna Weinberg, "The Quest for Philo in Sixteenth-Century Jewish Historiography," in *Jewish History: Essays in Honor of Chimen Abramsky*, ed. Ada Rapoport-Albert and Steven J. Zipperstein (London: Peter Halban, 1988), 163–87.

[3] Cyril O'Regan, "Hegel's Retrieval of Philo: Constitution of a Christian Heretic," *SPhiloA* 20 (2008): 101–28; Benjamin Pollock, "Philosophy's Inquisitor: Franz Rosenzweig's Philo between Judaism, Paganism, and Christianity," *SPhiloA* 27 (2015): 111–27.

[4] See, in the nineteenth century, among others, the editions of C. E. Richter, *Philonis Iudei opera omnia*, 8 vols. (Leipzig: Schwickert, 1828–1830), Howard L. Goodhart and Erwin R. Goodenough, "A General Bibliography of Philo Judaeus," in Erwin R. Goodenough, *The Politics of Philo Judaeus: Practice and Theory: With a General Bibliography of Philo* (New Haven, CT: Yale University Press, 1938) (hereafter G-G), 191 (§413); L. Cohn and P. Wendland,

1520 and 1599, at least ten Greek "editions" and fourteen Latin translations of Philo of Alexandria's works were published—some individual treatises or pseudo-works, others selective collections or florilegium, still others complete for their time.[5] Added to these are the French, Italian, and English translations which made their way into circulation by mid-century.[6] One reason for this renewed interest in "Philo Judaeus," as he was called by Christian writers of the period, was the rise of renaissance humanism. In 1520, the Italian Dominican and biblical humanist Agosto Giustiniani (1470–1536) produced the first sixteenth-century Latin translation of Philo,[7] and other humanists from across the continent quickly followed suit.[8] The motivations for their work were manifold.[9] Many, like the French Hellenist

---

Philonis Alexandrini opera quae supersunt, 7 vols. (Berlin: Reimer, 1896–1930), the first three volumes were published in 1896, 1898, and 1899 respectively, G-G 194–95 (§431); J. B. Aucher, *Philonis Iudei sermones tres* (Venice: Typis Coenobii PP. Armenorum in Insula S. Lazari, 1822), and Aucher, *Philonis Iudei Paralipomena armena* (Venice, Typis Coenobii PP. Armenorum in Insula S. Lazari, 1826), G-G 197–98 (§§440–441).

[5] These numbers gathered from G-G 187–201 (§§388–397). Though G-G calls the ten Greek versions "editions," this term is used broadly to include volumes that could hardly pass for "editions" in the current sense of the word. A number of the Greek editions contain Latin translations. I did not include these translations in the "fourteen" above. I further do not include in the numbers above any later republications. Mireille Hadas-Lebel notes that "Philo was one of the first Greek authors to be published in the 16th century" (*Philo of Alexandria: A Thinker in the Jewish Diaspora,* trans. Robyn Fréchet [Leiden: Brill, 2012] 216–17).

[6] French: 1542 (Lyons; G-G §480) and 1575 (Paris; G-G §481); Italian: 1548, 1560, 1570, and 1574 (all Venice; G-G §§500–503); English: 1563 (London; G-G §466). The first German translation listed in G-G §487 is a 1778 rendering of *De vita Mosis.*

[7] Philo Judaeus, *Philonis Judaei Centum et duae quaestiones, et totidem responsiones morales super Genesim,* ed. and trans. Agosto Giustiniani (Paris: 1520). Giustiniani was perhaps best known for his *Octaplum Psalterium.* See Paul F. Grendler, "Italian Biblical Humanism and the Papacy, 1515–1535," in *Biblical Humanism and Scholasticism in the Age of Erasmus,* ed. Erika Rummel (Leiden: Brill, 2008), 233–40.

[8] Among the editors and translators of Philo were the renowned German jurist Johannes Sichard (1499–1552), the Bohemian classicist Sigismund Gelen (1495–1554), and the Englishman John Christopherson (d. 1558).

[9] Despite the rich exchange between Christian humanists and Jewish scholars during this period (Cardinal Tommaso de Vio Cajetan, for example, employed a Jewish Hebraeist to assist him in his translation of the scriptures from the "Hebrew truth." See his 1527 Proemium to the Psalter, translated by Allan K. Jenkins and Patrick Preston, *Biblical Scholarship and the Church: A Sixteenth Century Crisis of Authority* [Aldershot, England: Ashgate, 2007], 269), Joanna Weinberg has argued convincingly that Jews largely rediscovered Philo through Christians, not the other way around. As David Winston notes, one searches the Rabbinic writings in vain for an explicit reference to Philo, in "Philo and Rabbinic Literature," in *The Cambridge Companion to Philo,* ed. Adam Kamesar (Cambridge: Cambridge University Press, 2009), 231. And it was the Christian claim to Philo which prompted Azariah de' Rossi (1511–1578) "to counter the claims of those who associated Philo with the primitive Christian Church," Weinberg, "The Quest for Philo," 166.

Guillaume Budé (1468–1540), were intrigued by Philo's connection to Greek philosophy.[10] Fellow Frenchman Adrien Turnèbe (1512–1565), likewise fascinated with Philo's interweaving of "Jewish revelation and Greek philosophy,"[11] was also interested in Philo's depiction of the virtuous life.[12] Giustiniani struck a similarly Erasmian chord when he assured Louise of Savoy that Philo's *QG* "has nothing of disguise or vanity, and by simple words and without any rhetorical apparatus, can move the hearts of men," adding that she ought to ask her priest to explain Philo's "moral responses."[13] These new editions, as might be surmised from Giustiniani's praise, did little to alter the exalted status Philo enjoyed among Christians from the time of the church fathers. With some notable exceptions, Thomas Billings's nearly hundred-year old claim still generally holds true, that "up to the middle of the sixteenth century Philo was almost universally venerated by the Christian Church."[14] With new purposes for reading Philo and new critical tools for translating and expositing him this veneration took on variegated forms in the sixteenth century, such that we can delineate this century as a distinct period in Philo's reception history, and

[10] Budé, following Aldus Manutius, coupled (*agglutinandum*) the *De mundo* attributed to Philo with Aristotle's *De Mundo.* Budé is not persuaded that the work was actually written by Philo, and notes that the author, "whoever he was," seems to follow the philosophy of the Greeks more closely than that of the Hebrews: "Siquidem Philo (quisquis hic fuit qui librum de Mundo scripsit: nam inclytum illum Philonem, qui Platonem facundia aequavisse dicitur, nequaquam eum fuisse mihi persuadeo) disserendo de mundo, deque eius interitu aut aeternitate constituendo, non tam Hebraicae philosophiae alumnus, mea quidem sententia, quam Graecorum assectator esse viderique meditatus est." *Aristotelis philosophi nobilissimi de mundo libellus* (Paris: Ascensianis, 1526). On Budé, see the entry by M. de Moreira, "Guillaume Budé," in *The Catholic Encyclopedia* (New York: Robert Appleton Company, 1908), vol. 3:34. The *De mundo* was "attributed to Philo and first edited by Aldus Manutius in 1497 [G-G §387]... together with the works of Aristotle and Theophrastus [and] contains extracts from *Conf.*, *Virt.* d, *Plant.*, *Gig.*, *Immut.*, *Aet.*" (G-G 145).

[11] John Lewis, *Adrien Turnebe, 1512–1565: A Humanist Observed* (Geneva: Librairie Droz S.A., 1998), 168. On Turnèbe's Catholicism and the literature on this, see ibid., 318.

[12] See the introductory letter in *Philonis Iudaei de vita Mosis, lib. III, Adr. Turnebo interprete* (Paris: Turnebus, 1554).

[13] "Accipe itaque centum & duas in librum Geneseos quaestiones & argutissimas, nec minus morales responsiones, quas ubi tibi explicari iusseris sive publicis in concionibus, sive privatim, a sacerdotibus illis, qui animae tuae curam gerunt... Est siquidem farrago haec tota solida, firma, constans, dulcis, spiritalis, & amoena, nil habens aut fuci, aut vanitatis, & que verbis simplicibus, & sine aliquo rhetorico apparatu, possit movere corda hominum as psequenda [sic] omni studio caelestia & divina." Giustiniani, *Philonis Judaei*, dedicatory letter (all translations, unless otherwise noted, are my own).

[14] Thomas Henry Billings, *The Platonism of Philo Judaeus* (Chicago: University of Chicago Press, 1919), 4. Joanna Weinberg adopts Billings's chronology in her article "The Quest for Philo," 163. The "almost" here is important, especially given Augustine's famous criticism of Philo in the *Contra Faustum*. On this see part 3 below.

in many ways one of "revival." Not that Philo had necessarily fallen from grace and needed saving. Rather, as Runia has recently put it, after 1500 printed editions of Philo "begin to see the light of day and the contours of the modern study of his writings and thought gradually start to emerge."[15]

Yet just as the Aristotelian revival of the thirteenth century suffered condemnation by the Parisian Bishop Tempier in 1277, the Philonic revival of the sixteenth was not without its critics. Some detractors can be gleaned from the pages of Philo's defenders, though such opponents often go unnamed and their arguments un-nuanced.[16] There is, however, at least one instance of direct censure from ecclesiastical authorities. In 1582, ecclesiastical censors in Rome issued ninety condemnations against the *De republica Hebraeorum* of Italian humanist Carlo Sigonio, with thirteen of those condemnations specifically directed at Sigonio's use of Philo.[17] These thirteen vary in rationale, some lacking any reason—Censure 66 merely reads, "On page 331, he cites Josephus and Philo."[18] The majority accuse Sigonio of violating the decrees of the Council of Trent. Censure 4 reads:

> Various errors are stirred up if you do not grasp or interpret precisely the truths of the Scriptures exactly as the holy Council of Trent commands concerning the Vulgate Edition (session 4), where it enumerates all the books which should be considered approved under the penalty of anathema. But there neither Philo nor Josephus are enumerated, both of whom the life-giving Spirit of God does not enlighten.[19]

[15] Runia, "Philo in Byzantium," 260.

[16] See, for example, the French Franciscan André Thevet's life of Philo in *Pourtraits et Vies des Hommes Illustres* (Paris: Kervert et Chaudiere, 1584), fol. 84–85, discussed further below.

[17] William McCuaig, "The Tridentine Ruling on the Vulgate and Ecclesiastical Censorship in the 1580s," *Renaissance and Reformation* 18.3 (1994): 43. McCuaig notes that Sigonio's works were never put on the index of forbidden books.

[18] "Pag. 331. Citat Josephum, & Philonem." The censures against Carlo Sigonio, as well as Sigonio's replies, are compiled by Filippo Argelati in volume six of the former's *Opera Omnia* (Milan: 1737). McCuaig considers the censures as listed by Argelati "very defective." By McCuaig's description, however, the defect seems more one of omission in certain places than of distortion. Further, if McCuaig's critical edit of two of the censures reveals anything about the whole, then the bulk of the changes are accidental/grammatical rather than substantial. See McCuaig, "The Tridentine Ruling," 51–53. McCuaig does consider Argelati's edition of Sigonio's replies to be "fairly sound" and in any event the only text we have of them.

[19] "Primum varii errores excitantur, si Scripturae vera ad unguem non accipias, aut interpreteris, prout sacrum Concil. Trident. jubet de vulgata Editione sess. 4. ubi enumerat omnes libros, qui habendi sunt pro approbatis, sub anathematis poena. Ibi verò neque Philon, neque Josephus recensentur, quos non Spiritus Dei vivificus illustravit; sed occidens littera, & velamen eorum cordibus impositum, tenebris involvit," *Op. Omnia*, vol. 6, col. 1186. Related censures are as follows: Censure 33, where the censor rejects Sigonio's

The fourth session of Trent (8 April 1546) listed the canonical books, approved the Vulgate Edition of Scripture, and forbade any interpretation of the Scriptures contrary to that sense held by Holy Mother Church and "contrary to the unanimous teaching of the Fathers."[20] This last point the censors also flung at Sigonio when they suggested that he should consult the opinions of the holy doctors, not those of Philo.[21]

William McCuaig, remarking more broadly on all ninety censures which critique Sigonio's use of the Septuagint along with other historiographical and exegetical sources besides Philo, observes well that the censors "did not adhere to the strict construction of the Tridentine decree" but instead interpreted it dubiously to exclude "any sources for Judeo-Christian tradition except the Vulgate itself."[22] However, McCuaig draws a bold conclusion from this fact: "Indeed, [the censor's] was the dominant opinion until well into the seventeenth century. The voice of the censor is the authentic voice of the Counter Reformation."[23] It is this thesis that I want to challenge by investigating the reception and use of Philo after Trent. McCuaig's governing thesis is that "there was a fundamental conflict between the culture of the Italian Renaissance, which had vanished by the

---

use of 3 Esdras, "qui liber non est approbatus … & praeter rem Philone adduxit," ibid., col. 1208; Censure 48: "Citat Philonem, quasi authoritate sacrae Scripturae res hae apertius non comprobentur," ibid., col. 1217; Censure 54: "Videtur velle confirmare veritatem sacrae Scripturae verbis Philonis," ibid., col. 1220; Censure 67 again criticizes the citation of 3 Esdras, as well as Sigonio's altering of the words of Luke 10, "& deinde comprobat rem Philonis sententia," ibid., 1226; Censure 85: "Auctor veram non habet, & suam Josepho, Philone, & 3 Esdras comprobat, qui approbati non sunt," ibid., col. 1234.

[20] *Canons and Decrees of the Council of Trent*, trans. Rev. H.J. Schroeder, O.P. (St. Louis: Herder, 1941), 17–19. Contrary to popular belief, the Council did not disallow other versions of the Scriptures; see John W. O'Malley, *Trent: What Happened at the Council* (Cambridge, MA: Belknap, 2013), 96.

[21] Censure 10: "Atque ideo hic, qui rempublicam Hebraeorum informat, ex sacra scriptura et sanctis doctoribus decreta et instituta petere debebat, non a Josepho, Philone, etc…" edited text in McCuaig, "The Tridentine Ruling," 52. Related censures are as follows: Censure 1 notes Augustine's criticisms of Philo. This will be treated below; Censure 32: "Sabbatum durabat usque ad adventum Messiae, deinde abolebatur, ut alias omnes veteres coeremoniae, ut Sanctus Hieroymus [sic] epistola ad Augustinum, & Augustinus ad Hieronymum scripsit; & male Philonis nititur authoritate in referendis sacrificiis, qui error in sequendo Phylonem [*sic*] illi est peculiaris," *Op. Omnia*, vol. 6, col. 1207; Censure 46: "… hoc comprobare posset sententiis Doctorum, & Sanctorum interpretum, non Philonis" ibid., col. 1217; Censure 47: "Pag. 197. Ubi interponit verba sacrae Scripturae, deinde ut illa comprobet citat Philonem, & Josephum, quasi eorum authoritas gravior sit sacra scripturae, & sanctis Doctoribus, & Ecclesia Catholica" ibid.; Censure 77: "Primum cum non desint authoritates sacrae Scripturae, & Doctorum Sanctae Ecclesiae interpretationes, rejiciendus erat Joseph, & Philo," ibid., col. 1231.

[22] McCuaig, "The Tridentine Ruling," 51.

[23] Ibid.

end of the century, and the culture of the Counter Reformation."[24] Certainly there were tensions and discontinuities—we should only expect such given the religious and political upheavals of the reformations. Yet McCuaig's thesis fails to account sufficiently for the tensions already manifest in the first part of the century between humanists and ecclesiastical authorities,[25] as well as the continuities which persisted from renaissance humanism into early modern Catholicism.[26]

One instance of this continuity is the reception of Philo. Given McCuaig's thesis, we would expect efforts by post-Tridentine Catholics to distance themselves from association with Philo and evidence a growing suspicion toward the same. My thesis demonstrates, on the contrary, that Philo retained his exalted status among Christians during this period (part

[24] Ibid., 43. While some scholars have begun to chip away at this assessment in the decades following McCuaig's article, his overriding presumption regarding the disconnect between humanism and Tridentine Catholicism remains dominant. Adriano Prosperi, in his 2014 article on religion in the Italian Renaissance, offers a brief survey of recent developments on the Renaissance vs. Counter Reform question and concludes by summarizing: "one undisputed fact turns out to be decisive: the movement in sixteenth-century Italy from a period of extraordinary cultural and artistic plenitude to one of greatly diminished prestige, and indeed (according to some) of real and serious decline." "Religion," in *The Cambridge Companion to the Italian Renaissance*, ed. Michael Wyatt (Cambridge: Cambridge University Press, 2014), 277.

[25] Discussing Italian biblical humanism in the first part of the sixteenth century, Paul F. Grendler notes that despite some advocacy from Pope Clement VII, "papal support was individual and sporadic and never developed into a continuing or institutional program of biblical humanism." A number of Italian humanists even "spent much of their lives in France because of what they saw as limited opportunity to bring their scholarship to fruition in Italy." "Italian Biblical Humanism," 227–28. Yet not even France was immune to censure. Italian Dominican and Master General of the Order Cardinal Cajetan was heavily criticized by Ambrosius Catharinus and the theology faculty at Paris for certain exegetical moves and theological opinions. On this see I.-M. Vosté, "Cardinal Caietanus Sacrae Scripturae Interpres," *Ang* 11 (1934): 445–513; and Jenkins and Preston, *Biblical Scholarship and the Church*, 149–226, 267–300.

[26] In examining Catholic exegesis before and after the Fourth Session of the Council of Trent (1546), R. Gerald Hobbs "finds in Bellarmine both ruptures and continuities with the work of Italian Christian Hebraists." "Reading the Old Testament after Trent: Cardinal Robert Bellarmine and his Italian Predecessors on Psalm Four," *Reformation & Renaissance Review* 12 (2010): 207. Robert Aleksander Markys shows further continuities between the culture of renaissance humanism and post-Tridentine theology through the lens of Jesuit moral theology in *Saint Cicero and the Jesuits: The Influence of the Liberal Arts on the Adoption of Moral Probabilism* (Burlington, VT: Ashgate, 2008). I adopt the term "Early Modern Catholicism" from the work of John W. O'Malley, "Was Ignatius Loyola a Church Reformer? How to Look at early modern Catholicism," *CHR* 77 (1991): 177–93. The term depicts the milieu of mid to late sixteenth-century Catholicism more faithfully than either "Counter Reform" or "Catholic Reform." On a discussion of these terms see Robert Birely, *The Refashioning of Catholicism, 1450–1700* (Washington D.C.: CUA, 1999), 1–8.

I), and that defense of Philo even became a central feature of the Catholic defense of monastic vows (part 2). This survey does not suggest that Philo's works went uncriticized by Catholic exegetes (part 3). These criticisms, however, appear less an effort to avoid the stigma of a now unacceptable character, and more a genuine disagreement on interpretive points. And given the fact that church fathers were often criticized in the same breath, Philo could hardly have fallen far from grace. In short, it is Sigonio's response to his censors that sums up the general opinion of Philo after Trent: "We grant that there are bad things mixed with good (*mala bonis permixta*) in the works of Philo and Josephus ... But with respect to Philo, it would be excessive if I wished to produce each and every person who not only celebrated him, but even followed him ...."[27]

1. *The Philo Renaissance Continues*

A year after the closing of the Council of Trent in 1563, Roland Petrei sent his commentary on Philo's *De specialibus legibus* (Spec. 4c; G-G §395), coupled with letters between Quintus and Marcus Cicero, to a Parisian press, dedicating the work to Cardinal Odo Castilioneus.[28] Frédéric Morel published his own Latin edition of Philo's *De mutatione nominum* in Paris a few decades later,[29] and in 1575 the first French edition of *Les oeuvres de Philon Iuif* appeared.[30] In the dedication of this work, translator Pierre

[27] "Damus itaque in Philonis & Josephi operibus esse mala bonis permixta.... Quod vero Philonem respicit, nimius essem, si vellem singulos producere, qui ipsum non celebrarunt modo, verum etiam sequuti sunt....' Sigonio adds, '& num tota Reipublicae Hebraicae moles exinde labatur & concidat, quod Sigonius ad operis sui structuram duobus Hebraeorum praestantissimis viris utatur aliquando." *Op. Omnia*, vol. 6, col. 1179–80, *In censuram 1. responsio.*

[28] Roland Petrei, ed., *Epistolae duae, una: Q. Ciceronis ad M. Tullium: De petitione consulatus... His accesserunt eiusdem Petreii notae quoddam Προλεγόμενον Philonis, de officio iudicis* (Paris: Andream Wechelum, 1564).

[29] Frédéric Morel, ed., *Philonis Judaei liber singularis, quare quorundam in scripturis sacris mutata sint nomina. Ex interpretatione F. Morelli* (Paris: F. Morellum, 1593). His 1614 translation of Philo's *De septenario* (from *Spec.* 2) is dedicated to Ferdinand of Bavaria, Prince-elector archbishop of Cologne. Not to be confused with his father of the same name and profession, Morel (1558–1630) studied under Jacques Cujas and served as the king's printer. See Hugh James Rose, *A New General Biographical Dictionary*, vol. 10 (London: Richard Clay, 1853), 219.

[30] Pierre Bellier, trans., *Les Oeuvres de Philon Iuif, autheur tres-eloquent, et philosophe tres-grave* (Paris: Nicolas Chesnau, 1575). According to Didot, Bellier was "conseiller au Châtelet à Paris, et consecra tous ses loisirs à la traduction de Philon." *Nouvelle biographie générale*, vol. 5 (Paris: Firmin Didot Frères, 1866), col. 264. Both Didot and Rose recount that Bellier travelled to Rome in order to collect manuscripts on Philo from the Vatican library,

Bellier praises the "*grand et divin Philon,*" adding to the common proverb "Either Plato philonizes or Philo platonizes" that "As for me, it seems that just as the body is more excellent than the shadow which follows it, so also Philo is more excellent than Plato, because the former mounts the heights of divinity and there enters in, but the latter only approaches it, having drawn the greatest part of his divine opinions from the ancestors and precursors of Philo in a voyage that he made into Egypt."[31] Bellier conjectures that Plato imbibed his wisdom from the Mosaic font—the stock of Philo—and thus it is Plato who philonizes, not the other way around.[32] Here Bellier goes even beyond Jerome, who famously called Philo *Platonici sermonis imitator*.[33]

Following the example of St. Jerome, some scholars included Philo in their "lives of illustrious men," a popular genre during the renaissance and into early modernity. The French ecclesiastic André Thevet's *Pourtraits et Vies des Hommes Illustres* presents a telling depiction of Philo.[34] Perhaps best known among Philonists for its famous and enigmatic image of the Hellenistic Jew, Thevet's *Lives* hit the press in 1584. In the four pages dedicated to Philo, Thevet praises him as one who "has surpassed all the other philosophers, both ancient and modern," and has no difficulty "placing him in the ranks of the Ecclesiastical Doctors," since Jerome—never one to favor the Jews—placed him there.[35] But not all agree with Thevet:

> And when I hear anyone scoffing at our Philo (*nostre Philon*), I cannot resist laughing at their daydreams, and on the other hand condemning their malign and perverse nature, for they want to bring dishonor on Philo … [and] they

but found the library closed on account of Pius V's death. See Rose, *A New General Biographical Dictionary*, vol. 4, 44.

31 "Ou Platon philonize, our Philon platonize … Celà se dit communément: mais quant à moi, il me semble que, d'autant que le corps est plus excellent que l'ombre qui le suit, d'autant außi est Philon plus excellent que Platon: car celui là monte iusques au comble de la divinité, & y donne dedans, mais cetui ne fait qu'en approcher, aiant puisé la plus grande partie de ses divines sentences des ancestres & devanciers de Philon au voiage qu'il fit en Egipte," Bellier, *Les Oeuvres de Philon Iuif*, epistre.

32 Sigismund Gelen adopts a similar line of argumentation in his 1555 Latin translation of Philo's works. See Weinberg, "The Quest for Philo," 169.

33 Jerome, *Epistola* 22.35, in *PL* 22:421, ed. J.P. Migne (Paris: Garnier, 1845).

34 Formerly a Franciscan, Thevet obtained secularization in 1559. At the time of this publication, he served as both *Cosmographe du Roi* and *Aumosnier ordinaire* of Catherine de Medici. See Franz Obermeier, 'Thevet, André, OFM, später säkularisiert,' in *Biographisch-Bibliographisches Kirchenlexikon* (2003), vol. 22, col. 1348–58. bbkl.de.

35 "… il a surpassé tous les autres Philosophes tant anciens que modernes … De ma part, ie ne feroie point de difficulté de le mettre au rang des Docteurs Ecclesiastiques, puis que ie voy que ce grand & admirable docteur de l'Eglise sainct Hierosme a bien daigné l'y colloquer, qui n'estoit point souspeçonné de favoriser aux Iuifs." André Thevet, *Pourtraits et Vies des Hommes Illustres* (Paris: Kervert et Chaudiere, 1584), ch. 39, fol. 84–5.

want to make him a pagan because of the proverb which has made the comparison between him and Plato, that Philo platonizes, or that Plato philonizes. There they have drawn a consequence that Philo is contrary to the Christian religion, because he platonizes.[36]

Thevet's incredulity at such critics must be taken with a grain of salt. After all, Thevet includes Philo not in book 1 of the *Lives* alongside Pseudo-Dionysius, Origen, Gregory Nazianzen, and other Christians, but in book 2 among Pythagoras, Plato, Socrates, Plutarch, and other ancient pagans, with the exception of Eusebius who immediately follows Philo. Regardless, Thevet is emphatic that Philo does not oppose Christianity with his platonizing: "But would this be the reason," he writes, "to relegate Philo to the pagans, because he platonized? Very few people who have affection for Christianity could agree with this: otherwise, St. Augustine would be banished from the company of Christians, he who was so devoted to this divine philosopher."[37] At least in writing, though not necessarily in the overall structure of the *Lives,* the answer for Thevet is all too clear, and for him Philo remains among the revered writers in ecclesiastical history.

Of course, one could argue that these works—all from the presses of Paris—reflect in no way a *Tridentine* spirit, since the decrees of the Council were neither accepted nor promulgated in France right away.[38] Yet neither can it be shown that Philo flourished in France *on account of* this failed promulgation, especially given that the immediate publication of the conciliar decrees in Italy produced no hindrance to Philonic studies.[39] The Venice presses proved especially prolific in this regard. There, Veronese canon Petro Francisco Zino produced Latin editions of Philo's *De Iosepho*

[36] "Et quand i'entends railler aucuns de nostre Philon, ie ne puis me contenir de me rire de leurs resveries, & d'autre part condamner leur maligne & perverse nature, pour ce qu'ilz veullent tirer au des-honneur de Philon ... Ces contreroolleurs le veulent faire Payen, à cause du proverbe, qui a esté faict sur la comparaison de luy & de Platon, que Philon platonise, ou que Platon philonise: de là ilz tiré une consequence que Philon estoit contraire à la religion Chrestienne, puis qu'il platonisoit." Ibid., 85.

[37] "... seroit-ce la raison de releguer Philon au Paganisme, pae ce qu'il a platonisé? Bien peu de gens trouvera-on qui estás affectionnez à la Chrestienté, puissent l'accorder: autrement faudroit que sainct Augustin fust banny de la compaignie des Chrestiens, lequel a tellement esté addonné à ce divin Philosophe." Ibid., 85.

[38] Ulrich Lehner writes that the French kings "openly opposed the publication of the decrees of Council for a long time. As a consequence, generations of bishops and priests passed until the Council's decrees were accepted in France, and even then, only partially" (*On the Road to Vatican II: German Catholic Enlightenment and Reform of the Church* [Minneapolis: Fortress, 2016], 4).

[39] The first edition of the *Canones et decreta* appeared in 1564 in Rome by Paolo Manuzio.

and *De vita Mosis* in 1574 and 1575 respectively,[40] and the first Italian translations of the *De opificio mundi* (1570) and *De Iosepho* (1574) likewise appeared.[41] Only one work attributed to Philo was published in Rome—the *Liber Antiquitatum Biblicarum* in 1599—though this work was attributed by many at that time, as it is today, to "Pseudo-Philo."[42] Nevertheless, toward the turn of the century Rome gave rise to a crucial defender of Philo, the Italian Jesuit Robert Bellarmine.

Bellarmine, of course, was himself an ecclesiastical censor, a role he played most infamously in the Galileo affair. In McCuaig's book, *Carlo Sigonio,* the author implies that Bellarmine shared a similar mindset as that of Sigonio's censors.[43] R. Gerald Hobbs, however, suggests that the Cardinal faithfully implemented the Tridentine decree on the Vulgate according to a strict construction. "The Hebrew and Greek editions..." Bellarmine expresses, "are no less authentic than is the Vulgate Latin edition; on the contrary, they are more so, in that they are the springs, and the latter is the stream."[44] Hobbs helpfully curbs any facile conflation of Bellarmine's sentiment in this passage with that of earlier Italian humanists by noting the former's lack of enthusiasm for the Masoretic Hebrew when compared with the passion of the latter. Yet the point stands that Bellarmine did not interpret the decrees of Trent like Sigonio's censors—Hobbs even cites Sigonio's censors as "rivals [to Bellarmine's] understanding of Trent."[45]

[40] Petro Francisco Zino, ed., *Iosephi patriarchae vita a Philone Hebraeo graecè composita* (Venice: Christophorus Zanetus, 1574); Zino, *Example tria insignia naturae, legis, et gratiae, cùm in vita Iosephi patriarchae, & magni Mosis à Philone Hebraeo ...* (Venice: Bologninus Zalterius, 1575).

[41] M. Agostino Ferentilli, *Discorso universale di M. Agostino Ferentilli ... Aggiuntavi La Creatione del Mondo, descritta da Filone Hebreo* (Venice: Gabriel Giolito di Ferrarii, 1570); Petro Francisco Zino, *Il ritratto del vero e perfetto gentiluomo espresso da Filone Ebreo nella vita di Giuseppe Patriarca* (Venice: Giolito, 1574).

[42] *Historia Antiqua* (Bibliopolio Commeliniano, 1599). For a modern treatment of this work see Howard Jacobson, *A Commentary on Pseudo-Philo's* Liber antiquitatem biblicarum, *with Latin text and English translation,* 2 vols. (Leiden: Brill, 1996).

[43] "Together with learning, the art of controversy was cultivated in Gregorian Rome, where Roberto Bellarmino was active in the 1580s. Bellarmino was known for his rejection of the contributions of a Catholic scholar of the generation previous to his own, Sigonio's colleague Onofrio Panvinio. This mistrust of Onofrio Panvinio was shared by the author of the censures of Carlo Sigonio," William McCuaig, *Carlo Sigonio: The Changing World of the Late Renaissance* (Princeton: Princeton University Press, 1989), 290.

[44] In Xavier-Marie le Bachelet, *Bellarmin et la Bible Sixto-Clémentine: études et documents* (Paris: Beauchesne, 1911), 114–15, cited in Hobbs, "Reading the Old Testament After Trent," 230.

[45] Ibid., 232. Hobbs notes that "the understanding of Bellarmine would prevail in the long run."

Bellarmine's use of Philo, I suggest, proves a further buttress to Hobbs' thesis.

In volume 1 of his famous *De Controversiis christianae fidei*, Bellarmine critiques those who "falsely attribute too much purity to the Hebrew source" of the Scriptures. Yet he still defends that source despite its alloys, and refutes those who suppose that the Hebrew Scriptures were corrupted by the malice of the Jews (*malitia Judaeorum*).[46] Bellarmine praises the "incredible devotion of the Jews towards the sacred books" by invoking Philo's claim that the Jews did not change a letter of the law in over two thousand years, and that "any Jew would rather die a hundred times than allow the law to be changed in any way."[47] He further mines Philo along with the Church Fathers to defend the Septuagint, a twofold (literal and spiritual) interpretation of the scriptures, monarchy as the best form of governance, and the spiritual authority of the papacy.[48] The use of Philo to buttress these latter arguments seems to be widespread at the time, as Bellarmine's Spanish confrere Francisco Suárez also cites Philo's *De monarchia* (beginning at section 3 of his *Spec.* 1) alongside Justin, Athanasius, Jerome, and Cyprian.[49]

Bellarmine cites Philo other times, but the most informative appears in the Cardinal's *De scriptoribus ecclesiasticis*. In a genre akin to that employed by Jerome and Thevet, Bellarmine chronicles writers of the Church "who flourished to the praise of ecclesiastical wisdom ... from Moses as the first

[46] Robert Bellarmine, S.J., *Disputationum Roberti Bellarmini Politiani, S.J., S.R.E. Cardinalis, De controversiis christianae fidei adversus hujus temporis haereticos*, 4 vols (Ingolstadt: Adam Sartori, 1601). The first edition appeared between 1581 and 1593 in Ingolstadt. English translations from volume 1 of this work will be taken from Kenneth Baker, S.J., trans., *Controversies of the Christian Faith* (Ramsey, NJ: Keep the Faith, 2016).

[47] Bellarmine, *Controversies*, 107. Bellarmine invokes Philo here via Eusebius's *Praep. ev.* 8.2 [Baker's translation mistakenly reads 3.2, see *De Controversiis*, vol. 1, col. 88, C]. In 8.2, however, Eusebius quotes the *Letter of Aristeas*, which does not explicitly state that the language has been preserved without change. Bellarmine likely meant to cite the nearby *Praep. ev.* 8.6. There, Eusebius quotes Philo's *Hypoth.* 6.9, '... they held it all to come from God and after the lapse of many years, how many I cannot say exactly, but at any rate for more than two thousand, they have not changed a single word of what he wrote but would even endure to die a thousand deaths sooner than accept anything contrary to the laws and customs which he had ordained.' LCL 363, trans. F. H. Colson (Cambridge: Harvard, 1941), 420–21. Bellarmine misreads Philo's 'a thousand' as 'a hundred' (*centies*).

[48] Ibid., 117ff., 184, 618, 833. Bellarmine explicitly references *Mos.* 2 re: the LXX, and *De victimis* (*Spec.* 1.33ff.) re: the papacy, gleaning from the latter passage that in the Old Testament, "the high priest was greater than the king."

[49] Francisco Suárez, S.J., *Opera Omnia*, ed. M. André and C. Berton (Paris: Ludovicus Vivès, 1856–1878), vol. 12, *De fide theologica*, disp. 9, sec. 6, no. 8.

writer of the Church up to our age."[50] In addition to praising Philo's allegorical readings,[51] Bellarmine devotes an entire entry to *Philo Hebraeus*, "a man most learned by everyone's consensus." He lauds Philo for revering the Alexandrian Christians—something we will explore below—and for being a first (*primus*) expositor of the Old Testament.[52] Philo is thus praised for the precise reason Signonio's censors rebuke him: for his exegetical acumen, which Bellarmine elsewhere describes as "subtilissime."[53]

Bellarmine was no anomaly among Italian scholars in his high opinion of Philo. Fellow Jesuit and papal envoy Antonio Possevino writes that the works of Philo "excel in style, eloquence, gravity, piety, and truth."[54] And the Dominican Sixtus of Sienna, in his *Bibliotheca sancta* (first published in 1566), affirms Philo as one upon whom "all of the Christian fathers extend their praises" and who admirably and most clearly (*praeclarissime*) exposits the literal, moral, and allegorical senses of the divine Scriptures, excelling in the latter.[55] Sixtus goes on to devote five more columns to enumerating and

50 "… sapientiae Ecclesiasticae laude floruerunt." Robert Bellarmine, *De scriptoribus ecclesiasticis*, vol. 1 (Lyons: Horatius Cardon, 1613), preface. Cited in Christoph Bultmann, "Historical-Critical Inquiry," in *The Hebrew Bible: A Critical Companion*, ed. John Barton (Princeton: Princeton University Press, 2016), 433 [translation adjusted].

51 Bultmann, "Historical-Critical Inquiry," 434. Regarding the moral sense of Moses, Bellarmine writes: "… Philo Hebraeus, qui has allegorias subtilissimè explanavit." Bellarmine, *De scriptoribus*, 2.

52 "Philo Hebraeus, vir omnium consensu doctissimus … Et praeterea iure numeratur inter Scriptores Ecclesiasticos Testamenti veteris, quoniam scripturas divinas Testamenti veteris primus exposuit." Bellarmine's, *De scriptoribus*, 19.

53 Ibid., 2.

54 "Praeterea, quae legitima Philonis opera extant … quippe stylo, eloquentia, gravitate, pietate, veritate praestant" Antonio Possevino, *Bibliotheca selecta de ratione studiorum* (Cologne: Joannes Gymnicus, 1607 [first edition 1593]), book 16, sec. 4, ch. 1, E.

55 "Philo Iudaeus, patria Alexandrinus, Levitici sanguinis, in quem unum omnes sese Christianorum patrum laudes effundunt … Fuit praeterea ultrà quàm dici queat, admirabilis in divinis Scripturis exponendis, quas triplici sensu iuxta LXX editionem praeclarissimè explicavit, literali scilicet, morali, & praecipue allegorico, in quo quidem expositionis genere ita excelluit." Sixtus of Sienna, *Bibliotheca sancta* (Lyons: Sumptibus, 1593), book 4, p. 289. Sixtus of Sienna was raised Jewish and instructed in Rabbinic studies before he converted against the wishes of his parents, see John Warwick Montgomery, "Sixtus of Sienna and Roman Catholic Biblical Scholarship in the Reformation Period," *Archiv für Reformationgeschichte* 54 (1963): 220–21. However, it is difficult to ascertain whether this upbringing had any impact on his reception of Philo, since Winston writes that "If the Rabbis were aware of [Philo's] voluminous oeuvre and made occasional use of his teachings, the fact remains, nevertheless, that their attitude toward this Alexandrian Jewish sage was at best ambivalent." "Philo and Rabbinic Literature," 231. See also fn. 10 above. It is worth noting further that Markys thinks it likely that Possevino hailed from a family of converted Jews. See *Saint Cicero and the Jesuits*, 51, fn. 14.

describing Philo's "many and most noble volumes on the Old Testament."[56] Notably, Sigonio invokes Sixtus for support in his response to the censors.

Though this summary proves rather minimal and focuses only on select yet significant figures of the post-Tridentine age, it suffices to show that Sigonio's censors hardly tarnished the reputation of Philo among leading scholars and even ecclesiastical authorities. Rather, the chorus *Philo Iudaeus, vir disertissimus* resounded from the exegesis of Spanish Jesuit Alfonso Salmerón to the historiography of Italian Cardinal Cesare Baronio.[57] During this period, Philo even became a crucial component of the Catholic defense of monastic vows. Following the testimony of Eusebius, scholars such as Baronio and the Mainz Jesuit Nicholas Serarius argued that Philo's Therapeutae proved an ancient instantiation of Christian monasticism, and in this regard they readily employed Philo as a credible historiographical source *against* the Protestants. Philo thus became a crucial figure not only for classical historiography and exegesis, but also for early modern identity, though not, as I will argue, at the expense of critical inquiry.

2. *Philo against the Reformers*

Martin Luther's famous *De votis monasticis Martini Lutheri iudicium* of 1521 sparked numerous defenses of monastic vows by Catholic controversialists,[58] and already in 1530, Leuven theologian Jacob Latomus called Philo's Therapeutae to the Catholic defense.[59] It was Eusebius who first conflated Philo's Therapeutae, described in the *De vita contemplativa,* with early Christian ascetics, deeming them some of the "first heralds" of the gospel in Alexandria.[60] According to Jean Riaud, this attribution was adopted by all

56 "Scripsit autem in vetus Testamentum plurima & nobilissima volumina." Sixtus of Sienna, *Bibliotheca sancta,* bk. 4, p. 290.

57 Salmerón frequently uses this phrase in his *Comentarii in evangelicam historiam, & in Acta Apostolorum, in duodecim tomos distributi* (Madrid: Ludovico Sanchez, 1598), vol. 1, pp. 49, 59, 78, 156, etc. See also Cesare Baronio, *Annales Ecclesiastici* (Rome: Typographia Vaticana, 1588), vol. 1, p. 19, D.

58 Martin Luther, *D. Martin Luthers Werke: Kritische Gesamtausgabe* [hereafter WA] (Weimar: Hermann Boehlau, 1883–1983), 8:564–669; *Luthers Works* [hereafter LW] American Edition, ed. Jaroslav Pelikan and Helmut T. Lehman (St. Louis: Concordia Publishing House, 1955–1967), 44:243–400.

59 Jacob Latomus, *Libellus de fide et operibus, et de votis atque institutis monasticis* (Antwerp: 1530), as noted in Jan Machielsen, "Sacrificing Josephus to Save Philo: Cesare Baronio and the Jewish Origins of Christian Monasticism," *IJCT* 23.3 (2016): 240.

60 Eusebius, *Ecclesiastical History,* 2.17, LCL 153, trans. Kirsopp Lake (Cambridge: Harvard, 1926), 156–57.

the ecclesiastical writers of the first centuries and continued as the dominant opinion well into the sixteenth.[61] Yet another strand of thought intermingled with that of Eusebius. In the fourth century, a Latin translation of Philo's work circulated under the title *Liber de statu Essaeorum, id est Monachorum, qui temporibus Agrippae regis monasteria sibi fecerunt,* thus adding the Jewish sect of the Essenes into the mix, though not to the exclusion of Eusebius's theory.[62] A 1550 edition of *De vita contemplativa* was published under the same title.[63] During the course of the late sixteenth century, these two strands would, with the help of Josephus, be parsed in the throes of reformation controversy. Nevertheless, Philo was not simply commandeered for pro-papal polemics. Philo is certainly used to defend the antiquity of monastic practice; of this there is no doubt. Yet Josephus's account of the Jewish Essenes prompts variety among Catholic scholars, who consequently engage in a real historiographical effort and one not wholly dictated by confessional interests. This instance of Philonic reception thus evidences another place where the spirit of the "Counter-Reformation" did not necessarily trump that of the Renaissance.

Lutheran Matthias Flacius Illyricus and his fellow Centuriators of Magdeburg first challenged the traditional position of Eusebius.[64] In their *Ecclesiastica Historia* (originally published in 1559), the Centuriators note Eusebius's claim that Mark preached the gospel in Alexandria, yet "What Eusebius recalls from Philo concerning the Christians around Alexandria, it is more probable that he refers to the Essenes, the celebrated sect of the Jews, for the Christians did not yet have such practices."[65] The Centuriators maintain that the group described in Philo's *De vita contemplativa* is the

[61] Jean Riaud, "Les Thérapeutes d'Alexandrie dans la tradition et dans la recherche critique jusqu'aux découvertes de Qumran," in *Aufstieg und Niedergang der Römischen Welt,* pt. 2, vol. 20.2 (Berlin: de Gruyter, 1987), 1212. Notably, Pseudo-Dionysius, whose works enjoyed a revival in the sixteenth century, conflates the terms "monks" and "therapeutae." *The Ecclesiastical Hierarchy,* in *Pseudo-Dionysius: The Complete Works,* trans. Colm Luibheid (New York: Paulist Press, 1987), ch. 6, no. 1, p. 245.

[62] Runia, *Philo and the Church Fathers,* 32. Runia erroneously prints "fectrunt" which is a corruption of "fecerunt."

[63] See G-G, 199 (§448).

[64] Riaud, "Les Thérapeutes," 1215. On the Centuriators see Werner Elert, *The Theology and Philosophy of Life of Lutheranism Especially in the Sixteenth and Seventeenth Centuries,* vol. 1 of *The Structure of Lutheranism,* trans. Walter A. Hansen (St. Louis: Concordia, 1962), 485ff.

[65] "Scribit Eusebius lib. 2, cap. 16, Marcum primium in Aegyptum missum, ibique Evangelicam historiam a se compositam tradidisse, primumque ecclesias Alexandriae constituisse ... Quod autem Eusebius ex Philone commemorat de Christianis circa Alexandriam, id magis verisimile est de Essenia, Iudæorum celebri secta, referri. nondum enim Christiani talia exercitia habuerunt." *Ecclesiastica Historia* (Basel: Joannes Oporinus, 1562), vol. 1, col. 18, nos. 10–44.

Essenes, and since Josephus points to the existence of the Essenes before the time of Christ, they could not have been Christians.[66]

The Catholic response came swiftly but not uniformly. Cesare Baronio offers the most famous treatment in his 1588 *Annales ecclesiastici,* a direct response to the Centuriators own *Historia.*[67] Jan Machielsen has recently outlined Baronio's complex analysis of the Therapeutae, a word which Baronio does not use to describe the group. Rather, Baronio begins with the presumption that the group described in Philo's *De vita contemplativa* is not wholly distinct from the Essenes. Now he must try to prove that they were Christians. Faced with the attacks of the "novatores," as he calls his opponents, Baronio embarks on two strands of argument. First, he develops an argument from silence: the Essenes could not have existed before Christ, since nowhere in the Scriptures or even among pagan authors are the Essenes mentioned. Second, however, the testimony of Josephus concerning the existence of this sect before Christ must be reckoned with, and here Baronio concedes ground. He grants that even if the Essenes existed before Christ, they remain distinct from the group which Philo describes in *De vita contemplativa.* For Baronio, according to Machielsen, "Philo's Essenes had converted to Christianity but preserved those parts of their way of life which their new faith did not contradict."[68]

Francisco Suárez simplifies and strengthens Baronio's analysis by eliminating the first argument from silence and focusing on the second. In his *De statu religionis,* Suárez writes:

> Although it is probable that Philo speaks of Essene Christians, since he discusses those who began to profess a new way of perfection at that time, Josephus, however, seems to speak of Jews, for he shows them to be more ancient among the Jews, and he distinguishes them from the Pharisees and Sadducees, and he refers to certain teachings of theirs which are not consonant with the Christian religion ... Therefore, it is likely for the Essenes to have existed both before and after Christ, and many among them to have converted to the faith through the preaching of Mark in Alexandria, and to have preserved and perfected their moral way of living concerning the good itself in Christianity,

[66] Ibid., vol. 1, col. 236, nos. 1–12. Jewish scholar Azariah de' Rossi (1511–1578) adopts a similar line of argumentation against the Catholic appropriation of Philo, arguing contra Eusebius that "there is no reason to assume that [the Therapeutae] did not belong to the Essene sects," *The Light of the Eyes,* trans. Joanna Weinberg (New Haven: Yale University Press, 2001), 107.

[67] See Giuseppe Antonio Guazzelli, "Cesare Baronio and the Roman Catholic Vision of the Early Church," in *Sacred History: Uses of the Christian Past in the Renaissance World,* ed. Katherine Van Liere, et al. (Oxford: Oxford University Press, 2012), 52–71.

[68] Machielsen, "Sacrificing Josephus to Save Philo," 241–43.

> and thus indeed Philo speaks the truth about the Christians, yet not to the exclusion of the more ancient Essenes.[69]

Suárez here emphasizes and deepens the distinction between the two ancient groups. Like Baronio, he esteems the Essenes, though he does not deem them true religious (*non veri religiosi*), and he considers Philo's Therapeutae to be Christians and monks (*monachos*). Yet there is a subtle difference in Suárez's and Baronio's approach to this question. Whereas the latter thinks that Philo shows "manifestly enough" that he spoke of Christians,[70] the former seems less certain. In some places, the Spaniard indicatively asserts the existence of Essene monks and holds that Philo speaks of Christian converts.[71] In other places, however, his account is riddled with hypotheticals: it is *probable* that Philo speaks of Essene Christians;[72] it is *credible* that Essene Christians observed a higher way of profession according to Ecclesiastical custom.[73] Thus, Suárez's engagement with Josephus and other ancient authors (Porphyry, Epiphanius, Pliny, etc.) does not permit a fast and loose appropriation of Philo for the Catholic cause.

Other Catholic authors offer a variety of perspectives. Antonio Possevino facilely remarks: "Let the prudent reader join together Josephus with Philo, and he will discover that each one writes about the life of the same people. Indeed I remove only a few things that Josephus interweaves into his book from Jewish superstition."[74] Bellarmine maintains that Philo writes

[69] "At vero quanquam de Philone probabile sit loqui de Essenis Christianis, quia tractat de illis, qui novam perfectionis viam eo tempore profiteri coeperant, Josephus autem de Judaeis videtur loqui, nam antiquiores inter Judaeos illos esse significat, et a Pharisaeis et Sadducaeis illos distinguit, et quaedam eorum dogmata refert, quae cum Christiana religione non consonant ... Verisimile ergo est et ante et post Christum fuisse, et multos ex illis ad fidem conversos per Marci praedicationem Alexandriae, moralem vivendi modum de se bonum in Christianismo retinuisse et perfecisse, et ideo verum quidem esse Philonem de Christianis loqui, non tamen excludere antiquiores Essenos." *Op. Omnia*, vol. 15, bk. 3, ch. 1, no. 13.

[70] "Satis manifeste declarat, non nisi de Christianis esse locutum." Baronio, *Annales*, cited in Machielsen, "Sacrificing Josephus to Save Philo," 243.

[71] "Diximus autem supra, ex eodem Eusebio, lib. 2, Histor., c. 16, hos Essenos fuisse monachos," and "Unde licet Philo de Christianis loquatur ex Judaeis conversis ..." *Op. Omnia*, vol. 15, bk. 6, ch. 1, no. 3.

[72] See fn. 70 above.

[73] "Nihilominus per se credibile est Essenos Christianos, sicut antiquorum mores ad perfectionem Christianum transtulerunt et sublevarunt, ita altiorem modum professionis juxta Ecclesiasticum morem observasse." *Op. Omnia*, vol. 15, bk. 6, ch. 1, no. 3

[74] "Conserat prudens Lector Iosephum cum Philone, & utrumque eorumdem vitam scribere comperiet. Pauca quidem excipio, quae Iosephus ex Iudaica superstitione in suo libro interservit." *Bibliotheca selecta*, bk. 5, ch. 56, C. Possevino adds that the names "Essenes" finds its root in the name "Iesu": "Sed quoniam in Essaeorum nomen indicimus, placuit hoc obiter annotare: Essei sive Iessei primi exercitatores huius vitae Religiosae,

of Alexandrian Christians and not a sect of the Jews,[75] yet concerning Josephus he thinks both opinions probable: that Josephus and Philo speak of different groups and that both speak about Christians.[76] Thevet is even more ambivalent. He notes that some think Philo speaks of Christian monasteries, and others that Philo speaks of Essene conventicles. "What makes me enter into greater doubt," he writes, "is that Jean Tritheme writes that Philo the Jew offered great welcome to the disciples of St. Mark. To be able to draw from that that they were religious or Essenes, it is not at all clear to me." All that is evident, Thevet continues, is the affection and ardor with which Philo was moved for those who embrace the evangelical truth.[77]

By and large, however, almost all Catholic thinkers of the sixteenth century deemed Philo's Therapeutae to be the first manifestation of Christian monasticism.[78] Yet what Machielsen and the testimonies offered here reveal is that engagement with other ancient texts provoked nuance and disagreement on how this group came about and in what their relation to Judaism consisted. Between the facile conflation of the Essenes and Therapeutae in the Centuriators of Magdeburg, and the equally facile conflation

---

Epiphanio Auctore, à IESV nomine vocantur, à Iassa Hebraea voce, quae salutem et curationem significat, à cuius vocis significatione Therapeutarum Graecum in nomen impositum est, quo Monachos ab Apostolis vocatos testatur Dionysius. Idem ergo nomen Iesseus et Therapeuta à IESV nomine desumptum est, & utroque idem Religiosorum institutum significatur." Ibid.

75 "Philo scripsit librum insignem laudibus eorum Christianorum, qui sub Marco Evangelista in Aegypto vivebant; quem librum scriptum de laude Christianorum, non de secta aliqua Judaica, ut putant Centuriatores Cent. 1, lib. 2, cap. 3, col. 18, testatur" Bellarmine, *De controversiis,* vol. 2, *De notis Ecclesiae,* bk. 4, ch. 16, B; also "Philo scribit de primis illis Monachis, in lib. de vita contemplativa supplicum" Bellarmine, *De controversiis,* vol. 2, *De monachis,* bk. 2, ch. 39, A.

76 Bellarmine, *De controversiis,* vol. 2, bk. 2, ch. 5, cited in Machielsen, "Sacrificing Josephus to Save Philo," 241.

77 "Ce qui me faict entrer en plus grande doubte est que Iean Tritheme escrit, que Philon Iuif faisoit grand accueil aux disciples de sainct Marc de pouvoir de là tirer que ce fussent religieux ou Esseens, ie n'y vois aucune apparence. Seulement de cela me semble qu'on doit recueillir certain tesmoignage de l'affection & ardeur de zele, dont Philon estoit poussé à l'endrouct de ceux, qui embrassoient la verité Evangelique." *Pourtraits et Vies des Hommes Illustres,* ch. 39, fol. 85.

78 While this position was dominant among Catholics and largely rejected by Protestants, there were exceptions. For example, Anthony Grafton remarks that the Huguenot Joseph Scaliger (1540–1609) "found special cause for anger in those Protestants who, unlike Flacius, failed to see that the Essenes were Jews. J. J. Grynaeus' edition of Eusebius' *Ecclesiastical History,* for example, treated Eusebius as a complete guide to the early history of the Church, monastic Therapeutae and all—and had questioned, not Eusebius' identification of the Therapeutae as Christian monks, but his approval of the monastic life, of which Grynaeus did not think well." *Joseph Scaliger: A Study in the History of Classical Scholarship* (Oxford: Clarendon Press, 1993), 2:300–301.

of the Essenes, Therapeutae, and Christians in Possevino, there is a spectrum of opinions regarding Philo's *De vita contemplativa*. Further, Baronio, Bellarmine, Suárez, and others drove a wedge between the Essenes and the Therapeutae which had an enduring effect on scholarship,[79] as even today, though most deem the Therapeutae Jewish, many like Joan E. Taylor consider them a distinct community from that of the Essenes.[80] Thus, while Philo's Therapeutae certainly played a role in Early Modern confessional identity, this appropriation should not be deemed a violent misuse of Philo or a radical discontinuation with renaissance scholarship. Rather, these post-Tridentine scholars interwove ancient historiography and the weighty testimony of the fathers with that of Philo to give an account of that still mysterious sect on the banks of Lake Mareotis.

3. *Philo and the Scriptures: Mala Bonis Permixta*

The testimony of the fathers, of course, could not always be harmonized with that of Philo. The first censure against Sigonio notes that even if Philo was liberally educated and rivaled Plato in Greek eloquence, he did not have Christ, the end and focus of all Scripture.[81] The censor proceeds to cite Augustine's *Contra Faustum,* wherein the Doctor of Grace famously criticizes Philo's interpretation that the door of the ark of Noah is the lower parts of the body (*inferior corporis partes*): "It is no wonder, if he did not know the door, that he should wander from the doors; but if he had gone to Christ, the veil having been removed, he would have discovered the sacraments of the Church flowing from the side of Christ."[82] While many in

[79] Machielsen remarks that 'Not even [Huguenot Joseph] Scaliger was quite able to put them together again.' "Sacrificing Josephus to Save Philo," 245. Grafton writes that Scaliger "showed from Philo's own works that the religious community that the Alexandrian Jew Philo described was Jewish, like that of the Essenes described by Josephus." *Joseph Scaliger*, 2:299. Scaliger evidenced a complex and evolving relationship with Philo as an historiographical authority. While considering Philo "a marvelous writer and very much worth reading," Scaliger criticized Philo's ignorance of Hebrew, deeming him "more ignorant of [Hebrew and Syriac] than any Gaul or Scyth." He thus publicly dismissed Philo, in the words of Grafton, as having "no authority at all as a witness on Semitic languages and Hebrew traditions." *Joseph Scaliger*, 2:416 and 509–10.

[80] Joan E. Taylor, *Jewish Women Philosophers of First-Century Alexandria—Philo's "Therapeutae" Reconsidered* (Oxford: Oxford University Press, 2003), 12

[81] "Philo Judaeus tametsi liberaliter eruditus, eloquio graeco cum Platone certaverit, quae tamen interpretatus est, non ad Christum intelligendum, qui legis est finis, & totius Scripturae scopus retulit; in illum enim non crediderat…" *Op. Omnia*, vol. 6, col. 1177.

[82] "Nec mirum, si ostio non invento, sic aberraret à foribus; quod si ad Christum transisset, ablato velamine, Sacramenta Ecclesiae à Christi latere manentia invenisset."

the sixteenth century, like Sixtus of Sienna, praised Philo's exegetical acumen, others took issue with various interpretations made by the Hellenistic Jew. Yet, as will be shown, those exegetes who do disagree with Philo seem to be haunted neither by the censors nor even by Augustine.

Spanish exegete Benedict Pererius, S.J., provides a representative example of such critics. In his commentary on Genesis, published in Rome in the 1590s, Philo appears as an authoritative source whose opinions are frequently listed alongside the Church fathers, and Pererius has no problem calling him one of the "most learned of the Jews." But this does not prevent Pererius from taking issue with certain exegetical moves.[83] His strongest critique comes while discussing the creation of man. Regarding the words *Faciamus hominem,* Pererius writes:

> Philo, in his book *De opificio mundi,* affirms that "man," whose creation is described by these words, is not to be understood as sensible man, i.e., what we are, but as intelligible man, i.e., the idea and exemplar of man ... In which Philo certainly wanted to follow Plato's doctrine of Ideas; but he applies it to this place not only falsely, but even ignorantly, foolishly, and absurdly.[84]

Here Pererius displays his most vicious rhetoric toward Philo. But it is the exception, not the rule, as elsewhere his disagreements with Philo rarely approach these extremes.

In fact, Pererius often criticizes church fathers in the same breath as Philo. Earlier in his commentary, for example, Pererius thinks Philo's reason for God commencing the creation of animals on the fifth day—namely, that animate creatures differ from inanimate creatures in possessing five senses—is frivolous (*verum frivola est ratio*), since certain animals only have one sense, that of touch, and other more perfect animals have interior as well as exterior senses.[85] However, Pererius also refutes Augustine, who

---

Ibid. The text of Augustine reads: "Non mirum, si ostio non invento sic erravit. Quod si ad Christum transisset, ablato velamine, Sacramenta Ecclesiae manantia ex latere hominis illius invenisset." Augustine, *Contra Faustum* 12:39, in *PL* 42:275, ed. J. P. Migne (Paris: Garnier, 1865).

83 "Duo Iudaeorum doctissimi Philo & Iosephus," Benedict Pererius, S.J., *Commentarii et disputationes in Genesim* (Ingolstadt: David Sartorius, 1590), 1:121.

84 "Philo in lib. de Mundi opificio affirmat, hominem, cuius creatio his verbis describitur, non esse intelligendum hominem sensibilem, scilicet quales nos sumus; sed intelligibilem, hoc est, ideam & exemplar hominis ... In quo voluit quidem Philo Platonis doctrinam de Ideis sequi; verum quod ad hunc locum pertinet, non falso tantum, sed etiam inscienter, inepte & absurde." Ibid., 1:469.

85 "Philo tradit, propterea quinto die coepisse creationem animalium, quod animal sit animal propter sensum; quinque autem esse sensus, qui numerus congruit cum die quinto quo creari animalia coeperunt. Verum frivola est ratio: nam nec animal ut sit animal opus habet quinque sensibus, sed solo tactu, quo uno cum praedita sint quaedam animalia,

argued that God only created the fish causally and potentially on the fifth day. This Pererius deems hardly in accord with the narrative Moses offers.[86] Relatedly, Pererius also takes issue with Philo's stance that "six days" does not refer to an interval of time, but to the perfection of the world, since six is a perfect number.[87] He again couples Philo with Augustine, the latter arguing that the world was created at one point in time (*puncto temporis*). Pererius refutes both in favor of an understanding of creation little by little over six days (*paulatim et particulatim per sex dies*).[88] And though he exhibits significantly more reserve when dealing with Augustine, he still speaks rather strongly here: "the contrary opinion to that of Augustine, indeed I judge not only more probable, but even of certain and indubitable truth."[89] Thus in both instances, Philo is neither pitted against Augustine nor is he necessarily dethroned from his esteemed status among the ecclesiastical writers. Pererius recognizes the authority that Philo carries in the Christian tradition and deems it necessary to explain his opinions, even if in certain places he ultimately and strongly disagrees with them.

Plenty of exegetes, however, found much more to praise in Philo than did Pererius. As already mentioned, Sixtus of Sienna lauds Philo's threefold exegesis, and especially his allegories, and Alfonso Salmerón holds the Alexandrian in high esteem. In the seventeenth century, Spanish Jesuit Benito Fernandez frequently invokes the testimony of Philo in his Genesis commentary, often inserting lengthy quotations from Philo[90] and noting in

---

ceteris sensibus carent; & praeter quinque sensus externos, sunt alii sensus interiores in perfectis animalibus." Ibid., 1:180–1. For Philo's position, see *Opif.* 20.

[86] "S. Augustinus lib. 3, de Genesi ad literam cap. 4, existimat hoc die quinto non esse creatos pisces actu, sed tantummodo causaliter & potentialiter … Verum hoc minime concordat cum narratione Mosis." Ibid., 1:181.

[87] "Cum igitur Moses ait, Deum sex diebus absoluisse mundi fabricam, non est id, auctore Philone, ad intervalla sex dierum referendum, sed intelligendum est illo dierum numero significari mundi perfectionem quae per numeri senarii perfectionem designatur …" Ibid.,1:230. See Philo, *Leg.* 1.2.

[88] This literal reading is not unique to Pererius or even to Catholics at that time. Lutheran scholastic Johann Gerhard, generally sympathetic with Philo (see fn. 99 below), also rejects Philo's and Augustine's interpretations on the six days of creation in favor of fidelity to the letter, yet his rhetoric toward Philo is less heated than that of Pererius, see *On Creation and Angels*, in *Theological Commonplaces VIII*, trans. Richard J. Dinda, ed. Benjamin T.G. Mayes (St. Louis, Concordia, 2013), §21.

[89] "Verumtamen contrariam Augustino sententiam, equidem non modo probabiliorem iudico, sed etiam certae ac indubitatae veritatis censeo." Pererius, *Commentarii*, 1:231.

[90] See, inter alia, vol. 3, col. 305, 429, 653, 693, 1179, etc. He does this approvingly, and often merely adds a parenthetical "*scribit/adiungit/ait Philo*." Benito Fernandez, S.J., *Commentaria atque observationes morales in Genesim*, 3 vols. (Lyons: Horatius Cardon, 1618–1627). A brief note on Fernandez can be found in Augustine and Alois De Backer, S.J., *Bibliothéque des Éscrivains de la Compagnie de Jésus*, vol. 2 (Liège: L. Grandmont-Donders, 1834), 182.

the majority of places that Philo "speaks well" (*bene loquitur*) or "rightly" (*recte*) or "eloquently" (*eloquenter*) or "acutely" (*subtiliter*).[91] Philo's widespread use can be witnessed later in that century in the commentaries of exegetes like Cornelius Jansen and the Franciscan François Carrière.[92]

Taken together, these scholars saw in Philo's works what Sigonio saw, *mala bonis permixta,* bad things mixed with good things. Exegetes like Pererius found plenty to criticize in Philo, calling into doubt Billings's claim that it is not until 1644 and the work of French Jesuit Denys Petau that "we first find any objection raised to Philo's theological opinions."[93] Yet the overriding emphasis must be placed on the "good things," as exegetes continued to praise Philo's rhetorical eloquence and exegetical judgment, wrestling with him as they did with the church fathers. And here another important point arises. Philo's status as an ecclesiastical writer is not impinged by disagreement. In the late sixteenth century we witness both a great recovery of ancient sources as well as an increasing willingness to criticize and disagree with those same sources.[94] Pererius exemplifies this latter movement in his exegesis, but we can also find it in the works of Jesuit Gabriel Vásquez, who took little issue disagreeing with certain Fathers or ecclesiastical doctors so long as such disagreement did not jeopardize established church teaching.[95] The historical-consciousness and critical insight so indicative of the Renaissance continued, in many ways, after the Council of Trent. Thus when exegetes occasionally relegate Philo to the opposition, we must recall that he often finds himself among rather good company.

[91] See, inter alia, vol. 1, col. 661, 797, 1018, 1254; vol. 3, col. 846.

[92] See Cornelius Jansen, *Pentateuchus sive commentarius in quinque libros Moysis* (Louvain: Jacob Zegerius, 1641); and François Carrière, *Commentarius in universam scripturam* (Lyons: Horatius Boissat & Georgius Remeus, 1663).

[93] Billings, *The Platonism of Philo Judaeus,* 4. Regarding Billings's larger focus precisely on the "Platonism" of Philo, Pererius appears an especially noteworthy counter to Billings's claim that thinkers before Petau were "compelled by the tradition to regard Philo as a great, original thinker whose thoughts were in some sense authoritative," as the passages I cite above indicate that one of the areas the Pererius took issue with Philo was in his Platonizing of the biblical text.

[94] See Dominique Bertrand, "The Society of Jesus and the Church Fathers in the Sixteenth and Seventeenth Century"; and Jean-Louis Quantin, "The Fathers in Seventeenth Century Roman Catholic Theology," in *The Reception of the Church Fathers in the West: From the Carolingians to the Maurists,* ed. Irena Backus (Leiden: Brill, 1997), 2:889–950 and 951–986 respectively.

[95] On this see my forthcoming article, "Spanish Jesuits and 'the Greeks': Reception and Perception of the Eastern Church in Luis de Molina, Francisco Suárez, and Gabriel Vásquez," *JTS* (2017).

Conclusion

Through this brief survey of the Catholic reception of Philo after Trent, I have sought to curb McCuaig's claim that a censorial spirit of Trent overrode that of the Renaissance. The esteem which not only humanists but even ecclesiastical authorities like Bellarmine and Possevino held for Philo appears unaffected by the decision of Sigonio's Roman censors. Possevino even praises the great talent and historiographical works of Sigonio.[96] My analysis of Philonic reception coupled with other works like that of Hobbs suggests that Sigonio's censors were not "the authentic voice of the Counter Reformation," but rather a marginal cry. This is not to discount their role in the narrative of post-Tridentine scholarship and censorship; it is only to recognize that role with due proportion in light of all the currents of the age.

In like manner, the positive reception of Philo among Catholics must be seen within the broader currents of sixteenth-century Philonic reception. The Therapeutae controversy poignantly highlights the ways in which Catholic and Protestant uses of Philo were deeply intertwined and polemically—though not necessarily ahistorically—informed. Joanna Weinberg has shown how this Christian controversy even effected the Jewish scholar Azariah de' Rossi's (1511–1578) appropriation of Philo.[97] But the Therapeutae controversy is only one frame of this complex and interwoven plot. The new editions of Philo produced before and after the Council of Trent reached wide audiences, including de' Rossi. And Philo remained an exegetical source not only for Catholics but for Protestant theologians as well who often, like Pererius, listed the Alexandrian's opinions among those of the church fathers.[98] Much work remains to be done to disentangle these

[96] He lists Sigonio among "aliis insignibus Viris," adding "De Carlo Sigonio, qui magni ingenii dotibus viguit, ac de Republica literaria meritus est optime, quiq; historicos libros, praeter alios, nobis reliquit, plura dici hic possent." Possevino, *Bibliotheca selecta,* bk 16, sec. 3, ch. 43, p. 338.

[97] Weinberg, "The Quest for Philo," 166. The fact that de' Rossi felt the urgent need to respond to Catholic appropriations of Philo in 1573—ten years after the close of Trent—further bolsters my thesis that Philo remained a prominent source among Catholics.

[98] Lutheran scholastic Johann Gerhard (1582–1637), for example, would frequently invoke Philo as an authority to be reckoned with in his *Theological Commonplaces,* positively utilizing Philo's exegesis on the burning bush in *Mos.* 1.67 and praising Philo's beautiful exposition of man as a microcosm of creation in *Opif.*, see Gerhard, *On the Church,* in *Theological Commonplaces XXV*, trans. Richard J. Dinda, ed. Benjamin T.G. Mayes (St. Louis: Concordia, 2010), §27; and Gerhard, *On Creation and Angels,* §34. Some of Gerhard's forbears also esteemed Philo for various reasons. Martin Luther praised Philo as "one of the most learned and wisest men that the Jewish people have had since the prophets" (LW 35:341) and extensively used the *Breviarium temporum* as one of his primary

various trajectories and to discern the ways that they have effected our reception of Philo today.

One thing is certain from my small contribution to this effort: the identity of Philo remained as elusive in the sixteenth century as it is today. André Thevet's phrase—*nostre Philon*—proves as instructive as it is deceptive. On the one hand, it nicely sums up the opinion of most post-Tridentine Catholic thinkers, who claimed Philo as an ecclesiastical source whose authority most closely resembled that of a church father. Yet, on the other hand, Philo was not quite a church father or an ecclesiastical doctor — as the title *Iudaeus* suggests—and his widespread use across confessions and religions suggests that Catholic thinkers could hardly claim him as "ours." Rather, Philo proved both familiar and foreign to *all* groups involved, such that none could definitively make such a claim. Consequently, the sixteenth-century Philonic revival, taken as a whole insofar as such a thing is possible, further complicated Philo's enduring legacy for ensuing generations of scholars.

Marquette University,
Milwaukee, WI, USA

historiographical sources (WA 53:19). Melanchthon followed this latter judgment, deeming Philo's *Breviarium* useful for the study of history despite its shortcomings, see Philipp Melanchthon and Caspar Peucer, *Chronicon Carionis expositum et auctum multis et veteribus et recentibus historiis* (Frankfurt: Johannes Feyrabendt, 1594), preface, p. 127. The *Breviarium temporum* was spuriously but not deceitfully attributed to Philo by the late fifteenth-century Italian Dominican Annio of Viterbo (1432–1502) in his *Antiquitatum variarium*, vol. 17, bk. 14. By the latter part of the sixteenth century, most scholars did not attribute the work to Philo. Bellarmine, for example, writes in his *De scriptoribus* "Circumferetur nomine Philonis Braviarium temporum, sed ab omnibus reijcitur, ut etiam alii historici, qui cum eo Breviario simul editi sunt" p. 20. Nevertheless, the impact of this work especially on historiography cannot be dismissed. As Anthony Grafton observes, "At the origins of Renaissance chronology, as we have seen, stood Annius," *Joseph Scaliger*, 2:402. For more on the *Breviarium temporum*, see G-G, 319–20.

The Studia Philonica Annual 29 (2017): 111–14

SPECIAL SECTION

PHILO'S *DE PLANTATIONE*

INTRODUCTION

DAVID T. RUNIA

Since the beginning of the Philo of Alexandria seminar held at the Annual meeting of the Society of Biblical Literature for the first time in 1984,[1] it has been a frequent practice to focus a session on one of Philo's works. The first of these, which took place in November 1985, was devoted to the *Quaestiones in Genesin et Exodum* and was separately published as monograph in the Brown Judaic Series.[2] Since then another twenty-one sessions have been held along these lines, generally comprising three or four papers on the treatise in question.[3] From 1996 onwards, an important development took place. The previous year Gregory E. Sterling had announced the commencement of a projected series of critical commentaries on the major treatises of Philo.[4] Starting the following year, sessions were devoted to

[1] For a history of the Philo of Alexandria seminar see Gregory E. Sterling, "A History of the Philo of Alexandria Program Units in the Society of Biblical Literature," in *In the Spirit of Faith: Studies in Philo and Early Christianity in Honor of David Hay*, ed. David T. Runia and Gregory E. Sterling *[= SPhiloA 13 (2001)]*, BJS 332 (Providence RI: Scholars Press, 2001), 25–34. Subsequent years are covered by the News & Notes section of each volume of *SPhiloA*.

[2] David M. Hay, *Both Literal and Allegorical: Studies in Philo of Alexandria's Questions and Answers on Genesis and Exodus*, BJS 232 (Atlanta: Scholars Press 1991).

[3] The full list is: 1987 *De somniis*; 1990 *Hypothetica*; 1991 *De virtutibus*; 1996 *De opificio mundi*; 1997 *De vita contemplativa*; 1998 *De vita Moysis*; 1999 *Legum allegoriae*; 2000 *Quod deterius*; 2001 *Hypothetica*; 2002 *In Flaccum*; 2003 *De vita contemplativa*; 2005 *De virtutibus*; 2007 *De Abrahamo*; 2008 *De vita contemplativa*; 2009 *De agricultura*; 2010 *Legatio ad Gaium*; 2011 *De confusione linguarum*; 2012 *Legum allegoriae*; 2014 *De Decalogo*; 2015 *De plantatione*; 2016 *De mutatione nominum*.

[4] Gregory E. Sterling, "Announcement: Philo of Alexandria Commentary Series," *SPhiloA* 7 (1995): 161–68. The 2002 session on *In Flaccum* preceded the publication of the

works that were scheduled to appear in that series, which had received the name The Philo of Alexandria Commentary Series (PACS). The aim was to assist scholars preparing these commentaries. In 1996 the session discussed issues relating to the treatise *De opificio mundi,* and the Commentary appeared in 2001.[5] From 2006 onwards the papers of four of these sessions have been published as Special sections in the pages of this Annual.[6] The present Special section is the fifth in the series.

The treatise on which this section focuses, *De plantatione,* belongs to Philo's biblical commentary that is generally known under the title of the Allegorical Commentary.[7] In this, the longest of his works, Philo gives an allegorical exegesis of Gen 2–18. In general it is a verse by verse commentary, but not all texts are covered (and some of its component treatises are lost). The treatise preceding *De plantatione* is *De agricultura,* which commences a series of five treatises on the verses Gen 9:21–27, treating the new life that Noah and his sons commence after the great flood. But in these works the biblical figures hardly appear as persons. Following the allegorical method of interpreting scripture at its fullest and freest, Philo interprets their lives and actions in terms of the life of the soul.

A feature of the Philo of Alexandria Seminar sessions over the years has been a focus on the place of the treatises within the Philonic corpus and their structure, particularly in the case of allegorical treatises, but not only these. In his paper David T. Runia continues this practice, building on

---

second volume in the series, Pieter W. van der Horst, *Philo's Flaccus: The First Pogrom,* PACS 2 (Leiden: Brill, 2003).

5 David T. Runia, *Philo on the Creation of the Cosmos According to Moses,* PACS 1 (Leiden: Brill, 2001).

6 "Special Section: Philo's *De virtutibus,*" *SPhiloA* 18 (2006): 57–123 (preceding the publication of Walter T. Wilson, *Philo of Alexandria On Virtues: Introduction, Translation, and Commentary,* PACS 3 (Leiden: Brill, 2011); "Special Section: Philo's *De Abrahamo,*" *SPhiloA* 20 (2006): 129–65; "Special Section: Philo's *De Agricultura,*" *SPhiloA* 22 (2010): 83–138 (preceding the publication of Albert C. Geljon and David T. Runia, *Philo On Cultivation: Introduction, Translation and Commentary,* PACS 4 (Leiden: Brill, 2013); "Special Section: *De Decalogo;* Philo of Alexandria as Interpreter of the Ten Commandments," *SPhiloA* 27 (2015): 129–80. In 2010 a Special section was also published on the *Hypothetica* (*SPhiloA* 22 [2010]: 139–207), but these papers were not presented at the Annual Meeting of the Society of Biblical Literature.

7 This title has no foundation in the manuscripts, but has been in general use since the late nineteenth century. In Eusebius's catalogue it is called Νόμων ἱερῶν ἀλληγορία, *H.E.* 2.18.1. See further Jenny Morris, "The Jewish Philosopher Philo," in *The History of the Jewish People in the Age of Jesus Christ (175 B.C. – A.D. 135,* eds. Emil Schürer, Geza Vermes et al., vol. 3.2 (Edinburgh: T&T Clark, 1987), 830–40.

earlier work that he has done on this general topic.[8] It emerges that the place of *De plantatione* in the series of treatises is not as straightforward as it might seem, because of conflicting titles and the difficulties posed by the final part of the treatise where Philo departs briefly from his usual allegorical method. For the internal structure of the work Runia underlines the use of secondary (and even tertiary) biblical lemmata, which is more prominent in this series of treatises than anywhere else in the Commentary. Philo's citations and allusions to the biblical text form the backbone of the treatise. A future commentary on the work will have to start from this underlying structure, upon which Philo builds the splendid edifice of his allegories.

Philo's biblical citations are the main topic of James Royse's paper, but he approaches them from a different angle. During the past decades the Philo of Alexandria Seminar has been the beneficiary of his peerless knowledge of the Philonic manuscript tradition (including papyri). This is the fifth paper that he has devoted to various aspects of the Greek text of Philo's works.[9] For at least two reasons it is particularly difficult to establish what the original text of the biblical citations in *De plantatione* was. Although there is a solid manuscript tradition, the text has been corrupted in more places than usual. Moreover it appears that early in its transmission the biblical quotations were tampered with by a scribe making use of later translations that differed from the LXX on which Philo himself based texts that he cited or alluded to. Royse's observations, as well as his further comments on the treatise's text, will be invaluable for the translation and commentary which Albert Geljon and David Runia are preparing. They also remind Philo scholars, if such be needed, how important the philological basis is for the work of interpretation of Philo's works. Expertise in this field, requiring deep knowledge not only of Greek and other languages, but also the complexities of manuscript traditions, is very rare and we are most fortunate to be able to call on Royse's assistance.

The third article by Sami Yli-Karjanmaa takes as its starting point two passages in the opening chapter of *De plantatione* in which Philo, beginning with the text that Noah planted a vineyard, embarks on a free-flowing

[8] In earlier Special sections see "The Place of *De Abrahamo* in Philo's *Œuvre*," *SPhiloA* 20 (2008): 133–50; "The Structure of Philo's Allegorical Treatise *De Agricultura*," *SPhiloA* 22 (2010): 87–109.

[9] "The Text of Philo's *De virtutibus*," *SPhiloA* 18 (2006): 73–101; "The Text of Philo's *De Abrahamo*," *SPhiloA* 20 (2008): 151–65; "Some Observations on the Biblical Text in Philo's *De Agricultura*," *SPhiloA* 22 (2010) 111–29; J. R. Royse, "The Text of Philo's *De Decalogo* in Vaticanus gr. 316," *SPhiloA* 27 (2015): 133–42. He has also prepared a paper on textual aspects of *De mutatione nominum* which is so far unpublished.

allegorical reflection on the concept of planting interpreted in cosmological terms. The first relates to his description of the creatures that inhabit the various cosmic regions, the second to the make-up of the human being who dwells on the earth but, as a "heavenly plant" (Plato, *Tim.* 90a), is able to ascend to the heavens and even beyond. Yli-Karjanmaa notes that there are significant parallel passages in other treatises that can shed light on Philo's descriptions here. His article has the further aim of contributing to thinking on the methodological question of how we should interpret the text of Philonic treatise against the wider background of his system of thought. He argues that by reading a text together with significant parallel passages the result will be an enhanced understanding of Philo's thinking and message. In the case of this article too, the detailed interpretations put forward will be of considerable assistance for the preparation of the commentary on this intricate allegorical treatise.

Australian Catholic University
The University of Melbourne
Australia

The Studia Philonica Annual 29 (2017): 115–38

THE STRUCTURE OF PHILO'S *DE PLANTATIONE* AND ITS PLACE IN THE ALLEGORICAL COMMENTARY*

DAVID T. RUNIA

Introduction: The Riddles of the Allegorical Commentary

There was a time when Philo was above all known as an allegorist. He was widely admired, but also reviled for his interpretations of the Bible in terms of the history of the soul and its quest for knowledge of God.[1] In more recent times there has been a decline of interest in this part of the Philonic legacy. Modern scholars are generally more interested in what Philo can tell us about the beliefs and practices of the Judaism of his time than about the complexities of his ethical and theological interpretations of the scriptural text. It is one of the more important tasks of the Philo of Alexandria Commentary Series, I believe, to make these works more accessible to a broad circle of readers so that they can be recognised for the fascinating pieces of exegetical and philosophical literature that they are. So far a commentary has been published on only one allegorical treatise, *De agricultura*.[2] It is important that others soon follow. The present paper is based on work that Dr. Albert Geljon and I are doing in preparation for our commentary on *De plantatione*, the allegorical treatise which follows *De agricultura* in the generally accepted sequence of Philo's treatises.

* This paper was presented at the meeting of the Philo of Alexandria Seminar at the Annual Meeting of the Society of Biblical Literature in Atlanta in November 2015. I would particularly like to thank Dr. Albert Geljon for the fruitful collaboration that we are having on the current project of writing a commentary on *De plantatione*. Much in the present article is based on work we are doing together. I also thank the members of the Seminar for their constructive comments.

[1] Admired by church fathers such as Clement, Origen, Didymus the Blind, and (by implication) Ambrose; criticised by Theodore of Mopsuestia, Augustine, and (later) by the patriarch Photius. See David T. Runia, *Philo in Early Christian Literature: a Survey*, CRINT 3.3 (Assen: Van Gorcum, 1993).

[2] Albert C. Geljon and David T. Runia, *Philo On Cultivation: Introduction, Translation and Commentary*, PACS 4 (Leiden: Brill, 2013).

The Allegorical Commentary presents us with many difficult questions, some of which may prove impossible to answer. In the first place, what was its original extent? Even though it is by far the longest of Philo's three great biblical commentaries, we can be certain that it originally contained at least nine more books.[3] Did it start with an allegorical commentary on the first chapter of Genesis?[4] Were the gaps in the treatment of the continuous text of Genesis dealt with in writings that we have no inkling of?[5] Or was the Commentary as a whole divided into formal or informal clusters of treatises, with gaps in coverage to some degree analogous to what we find in the *Quaestiones*? In the second place, is there a unified and consistent method that Philo follows in composing his allegorical treatises, or did he develop and modify it as he went along? Should we in fact include in it at all the work *De somniis*, which seems to deviate in its method from the earlier treatises in the Allegorical Commentary? A related question is whether Philo devised a coherent overall conception for the entire Commentary, as he clearly did for the Exposition of the Law. How, indeed, did he intend this difficult work to be read and studied and in what context? Was it a deliberately esoteric work, composed for a select group of students who gathered together in what we might call a Philonic school?[6] And then there is the perennial question of how original Philo's work was in relation to his Alexandrian predecessors and contemporaries, but also in relation to the work of allegorists working in the Hellenic tradition.[7]

[3] For a listing of lost treatises see David T. Runia, "Confronting the Augean Stables: Royse's *Fragmenta Spuria Philonica*," *SPhiloA* 4 (1992): 78–86.

[4] On this question see the discussion in Gregory E. Sterling, "'Prolific in Expression and Broad in Thought': Internal References to Philo's Allegorical Commentary and Exposition of the Law," *Euphrosyne* 40 (2012): 55–76 at 63–64.

[5] See the analysis of the textual coverage in Jenny Morris, "The Jewish Philosopher Philo," in *The History of the Jewish People in the Age of Jesus Christ (175 B.C. – A.D. 135*, ed. Emil Schürer, Geza Vermes et al., vol. 3 part 2 (Edinburgh: T. & T. Clark, 1987), 809–89 at 830–40.

[6] Gregory E. Sterling, "'The School of Sacred Laws': the Social Setting of Philo's Treatises," *VC* 53 (1999: 148–64; Sterling, 'Philo's School: The Social Setting of Ancient Commentaries,' in *Sophisten in Hellenismus und Kaiserzeit: Orte, Methoden und Personnen der Bildungsvermittlung*, ed. Beatrice Wyss, Rainer Hirsch-Luipold and Solmeng-Jonas Hirschi, STAC 101 (Tübingen 2017), 123–42; Sterling, "The School of Moses in Alexandria: An Attempt to Reconstruct the School of Philo," in *Second Temple Jewish "Paideia" in Context*, eds. Gabriele Boccaccini and Jason Zurawski, BZNW 228 (Berlin: de Gruyter, 2017), 141–66.

[7] On Philo's predecessors see the studies of David M. Hay, "Philo's References to Other Allegorists," *SPhiloA* 6 (1979–1980): 41–75; "References to Other Exegetes," in *Both Literal and Allegorical: Studies in Philo of Alexandria's Questions and Answers on Genesis and Exodus*, ed. David M. Hay, BJS 232 [= *SPhiloA* 3] (Atlanta: Scholars Press), 81–97; Richard Goulet, *La philosophie de Moïse: Essai de réconstruction d'un commentaire philosophique préphilonien du Pentateuque*, Histoire des doctrines de l'Antiquité classique 11 (Paris: Vrin,

A Cluster of Five Treatises

Amidst all these questions, it is good to grasp hold of some facts which are beyond dispute. One of these is that the Commentary originally contained a cluster of at least five treatises giving an allegorical interpretation of the story of the life of Noah and his sons after the end of the flood, as described in Gen 9:21–27. Following the practice established from the beginning of the Commentary as it has come down to us, Philo begins the first of these treatises, *De agricultura,* with the quotation of the scriptural text, in this case Gen 9:20–21a. However, at the beginning of the next treatise, *De plantatione,* he deviates for the first time from this method and makes a reference to what he has done in the previous treatise. In the previous book, we read, he has discussed what is relevant on the art of cultivation in general and now he will turn to the specific art of viticulture (*Plant.* 1). He had in fact anticipated that he would write this treatise in his final words of that treatise at *Agr.* 181.

As Gregory Sterling has pointed out in a recent study of the internal cross-references in Philo's biblical commentaries,[8] the opening words of *Plant.* constitute a "secondary preface." They follow a well-established practice in the ancient world of introducing a new treatise written on a separate scroll but belonging to a larger work or series. The reader, when opening up the roll, could immediately identify the contents of the scroll and its particular place in the larger work. Many of Philo's treatises contain such secondary prefaces. It is also the case for the two following surviving treatises, *De ebrietate* and *De sobrietate*. The first of the treatises, *De agricultura,* is the only one to have an anticipatory concluding statement, as noted above. But there is a complication of which we must take note. At *Plant.* 139 Philo includes a transitional passage in which he summarizes what he has discussed in the book so far and introduces his next subject. This passage sits somewhat uncomfortably in relation to the beginning of the treatise and we will return to it below.

The relevant passages for the cluster of treatises can thus be set out as follows:[9]

Agr. 1 (the main biblical lemma, Gen 9:20–21a): "Καὶ ἤρξατο Νῶε ἄνθρωπος γεωργὸς γῆς εἶναι, καὶ ἐφύτευσεν ἀμπελῶνα, καὶ ἔπιε τοῦ οἴνου, καὶ ἐμεθύσθη ἐν τῷ οἴκῳ αὐτοῦ."

1987); Maren R. Niehoff, *Jewish Exegesis and Homeric Scholarship in Alexandria* (Cambridge: Cambridge University Press 2011), 77–129.

[8] Sterling, "Internal References," 60–62. I am much indebted to his excellent discussion of the series *Agr.–Sobr.*

[9] For translations of these texts see the appendix.

Agr. 181: τὰ δὲ περὶ τῆς φυτουργίας εἰρημένα αὐτοῦ λέγωμεν αὖθις.

Plant. 1: Ἐν μὲν τῷ προτέρῳ βιβλίῳ τὰ περὶ γεωργικῆς τέχνης γενικῆς, ὅσα καιρὸς ἦν, εἴπομεν, ἐν δὲ τούτῳ περὶ τῆς κατ' εἶδος ἀμπελουργικῆς, ὡς ἂν οἷόν τε ᾖ, ἀποδώσομεν. τὸν γὰρ δίκαιον οὐ γεωργὸν μόνον, ἀλλὰ καὶ ἰδίως ἀμπελουργὸν εἰσάγει φάσκων· "ἤρξατο Νῶε ἄνθρωπος εἶναι γεωργὸς γῆς καὶ ἐφύτευσεν ἀμπελῶνα" (Gen 9:20).

Plant. 139–141:[10] Περὶ μὲν οὖν γεωργίας τῆς πρεσβυτάτης καὶ ἱερωτάτης, ᾗ τὸ αἴτιον πρὸς τὸν κόσμον, τὸ παμφορώτατον φυτῶν, χρῆται, καὶ περὶ τῆς ἑπομένης, ἣν ὁ ἀστεῖος ἐπιτηδεύει, καὶ περὶ τῆς φερομένης τετράδος τὸ ἆθλον ἃ κατὰ προστάξεις καὶ ὑφηγήσεις νόμων συνεκροτεῖτο, ὡς οἷόν τε ἦν εἴπομεν. (140) τὴν δὲ τοῦ δικαίου Νῶε ἀμπελουργικήν, εἶδος γεωργικῆς οὖσαν, ἐπισκεψώμεθα. λέγεται γὰρ ὅτι "ἤρξατο Νῶε ἄνθρωπος εἶναι γεωργὸς γῆς· καὶ ἐφύτευσεν ἀμπελῶνα, καὶ ἔπιε τοῦ οἴνου, καὶ ἐμεθύσθη" (Gen 9:20–21a). (141) οὐκοῦν τὸ μέθης φυτὸν ἐξεργάζεται τεχνικῶς καὶ ἐπιστημόνως ὁ δίκαιος τῶν ἀφρόνων ἄτεχνον καὶ πλημμελῆ ποιουμένων αὐτοῦ τὴν ἐπιστασίαν, ὥστε ἀναγκαῖον τὰ προσήκοντα περὶ μέθης εἰπεῖν· εὐθὺς γὰρ εἰσόμεθα καὶ τὴν δύναμιν τοῦ παρέχοντος αὐτῇ τὰς ἀφορμὰς φυτοῦ. τὰ μὲν οὖν εἰρημένα τῷ νομοθέτῃ περὶ μέθης εἰσόμεθα ἐπ' ἀκριβείας αὖθις, νυνὶ δὲ ἐξερευνήσωμεν ὅσα καὶ τοῖς ἄλλοις ἔδοξεν.

Ebr. 1: τὰ μὲν τοῖς ἄλλοις φιλοσόφοις εἰρημένα περὶ μέθης, ὡς οἷόν τε ἦν, ἐν τῇ πρὸ ταύτης ὑπεμνήσαμεν βίβλῳ, νυνὶ δὲ ἐπισκεψώμεθα τίνα τῷ πάντα μεγάλῳ καὶ σοφῷ νομοθέτῃ περὶ αὐτῆς δοκεῖ.

Sobr. 1: τὰ περὶ μέθης καὶ τῆς ἑπομένης αὐτῇ γυμνότητος εἰρημένα τῷ νομοθέτῃ διεξεληλυθότες πρότερον ἀρξώμεθα τοῖς λεχθεῖσι τὸν ἑξῆς προσαρμόττειν λόγον· περίεστι τοίνυν ἐν τοῖς χρησμοῖς ἀκόλουθα τάδε (the main biblical lemma, Gen 9:24). "ἐξένηψε δὲ Νῶε ἀπὸ τοῦ οἴνου καὶ ἔγνω ὅσα ἐποίησεν αὐτῷ ὁ υἱὸς αὐτοῦ ὁ νεώτερος."

This collection of structural passages give rise to a number of questions of interpretation.

(1) The fact that *De agricultura* begins with the quotation of the text which will form the main biblical lemma of the three treatises that follow (and is cited a further two times in *De plantatione*) strongly suggests that this cluster of treatises belong together and were planned as a group. A more difficult question is whether the cluster ends with the final part of *De sobrietate* as it has been transmitted. I am inclined to think it does. The prayer of the σπουδαῖος to dwell in the houses of the one (Shem) who holds that what is noble is the only good (§68, based on Gen 9:27) is a fitting final theme. The final paragraph (§69) then makes an additional minor point drawn from the final line of the same biblical text. It is, however, a little unusual that Philo does not refer to the actual text and uses a different term (δοῦλος instead of παῖς). So we have to take into account that the final part may be mutilated. Moreover it should be noted that book 2 of the *Quaestiones in Genesim* asks a question of Gen 9:28 (not treated in *De sobrietate*) and then goes on to ask four more questions of Gen 10:1–8 (*QG*

[10] There are difficulties in the text of §139. We follow the suggestion of Colson and Whitaker, PLCL 3.285 to read τὸ ἆθλον ᾗ κατά κτλ.

2.78–82). So it remains possible that the treatise, which is of course unusually short,[11] continued with exegesis relating to all the names in Gen 10 and the cluster ended with some kind of transition to *De confusione linguarum*, which commences with a secondary preface which is completely unspecific and then proceeds to quote Gen 11:1–9. It is impossible to attain any degree of certainty on these matters.

(2) There are grounds for thinking that *De agricultura* and *De plantatione* are not separate treatises, but two books of a single work, analogous to *Legum allegoriae* with its three books or *De vita Moysis* with its two books.[12] Hints are provided in this direction by the transmitted title περὶ φυτουργίας Νῶε τὸ δεύτερον and the evidence supplied by Eusebius both in his catalogue in the *Historia ecclesiastica* and when citing from the books in the *Praeparatio evangelica*.[13] It very much looks like Philo himself is responsible for the confusion. At *Agr*. 181 he announces that he will speak περὶ τῆς φυτουργίας, but this subject is not mentioned in the opening words of *De plantatione* Then in the next section (§2) he speaks about the person who is going to give an exposition περὶ τῶν κατὰ μέρος φυτουργιῶν τε καὶ γεωργιῶν), but later at §139 he reverts to περὶ γεωργίας again. So it is possible that there were books α′ and β′ of Περὶ γεωργίας, as was apparently the case for *De ebrietate* (see no. 4 below), or they may have had separate titles. We cannot be certain. It is also worth noting that the two books could have been written on a single scroll (together they amount to seventy-five pages of C-W's Greek text, quite similar in combined length to longer treatises such as *Quis rerum divinarum heres sit* or *De specialibus legibus* 1). But, as Sterling suggests,[14] the fact that *De plantatione* has a secondary preface indicates that it was most likely written on a separate roll. Papyrus rolls could be tailor-made to the length of the treatise after it was copied out by glueing the sheets together. Only the total length could be a problem. If a book got much longer than seven metres, it became unwieldy and it was time to bring it to a close. Authors or copyists would have developed a sense of how big a pile of sheets a book of that length amounted to.

(3) We are not yet finished with the problems raised by the transitional passage at *Plant*. 139–141. In addition to the terminological issue already

[11] It is in fact the shortest of all Philonic treatises (about the same length as *De gigantibus*, but this work should not be regarded as a separate treatise, but rather as originally joined together with *Deus*).

[12] But note that *Legum allegoriae* originally had at least four books, as noted by Sterling, "Internal References," 64–65.

[13] I am indebted here to research on the treatise's title by Albert Geljon that will be published in our joint Commentary volume.

[14] Sterling, "Internal References," 60.

discussed above, there are two further points. Firstly the summary of the contents of *De plantatione* so far (i.e., §§1–138) has some oddities, which I will not discuss now. Secondly and more importantly, Philo says in §139 that he now wants to specifically discuss the subject of viticulture (he had said he would do this in §1, but then got distracted by his grand allegory on planting) and so he again quotes the main biblical lemma. But this means, he continues (§141), that because of its ethical implications (via allegory), it will be necessary to discuss the related subject of inebriation (περὶ μέθης). This is of course the title of *De ebrietate*. First, however, before examining what Moses says on the subject he will investigate what the philosophers think about it, and this topic takes up the rest of the book. Why did Philo not start a separate book at this point? After all, the subject matter of section §§142–177 fits in much better with *De ebrietate* than it does with *De plantatione*. The most obvious answer that comes to my mind is that he thought the contents of the book so far were a little on the short side for a decent scroll, so he should add another section of his commentary to it. There is another possibility, namely that he *did* start another book, that is, originally *Plant*. 139 was the beginning of *De ebrietate*.[15] The initial words of *De ebrietate* as we have it do not rule out this possibility, even if they do not contain a reference to a previous book or account as in *Plant*. 1 or *Sobr*. 1. However, the words of §§139–141 do not read like the beginning of a new book, not only because the summary of the previous book is rather long,[16] but especially because the title of the new book would not appear until the eleventh line. So I do not think this possibility is very likely.

(4) Lastly there is the problem of the lost other book of *De ebrietate*. We can be certain that there was another book. The opening words of *De sobrietate* indicate that the subjects of inebriation and nakedness had been discussed. The latter theme, obviously taking its starting-point from Noah's nakedness in the main biblical lemma, is not covered in *De ebrietate*. It is also very likely that the fourth meaning that Philo records Moses as associating with wine at *Ebr*. 4, "good humour and gladness," was discussed in the missing book. We return to this possibility later on in our paper.[17] The first three themes are covered in *De ebrietate* and the fifth is the

[15] It should be borne in mind that someone (Pantaenus?) may have had to rescue and re-edit Philo's writings after they had miraculously survived the "shipwreck" of Hellenistic-Jewish literature. See Runia *Philo in Early Christian Literature*, 22–23, Sterling, "Social Setting," 161–63.

[16] None of the secondary prefaces in the Allegorical Commentary discussed by Sterling, "Internal References," 62–63 are as detailed as this passage. However, some of those in the Exposition are quite lengthy and detailed.

[17] See below section 5 (6).

missing "nakedness." Eusebius and Jerome inform us that there were two books, as does the title in the ms. Laurentianus LXXXV 10. It surely seems very plausible that *De ebrietate* is the first of these two books and that the missing book covered what Philo had promised to discuss but is not contained in *De ebrietate.* The only snag is that the Oxyrhynchus papyrus dating back to the third century describes the extant book as book 2. I agree with Gregory Sterling that given our present knowledge this seems implausible, but the ancient scribe might have had access to evidence that we no longer have.[18] Long ago Adler suggested that the final part of *De plantatione* might be the missing first book of *De ebrietate* (he did not know about the papyrus).[19] This would mean that the missing subjects in the treatment of inebriation would have been found in a lost section of *De ebrietate* as we have it now. Adler's hypothesis certainly provides a solution if we are looking for a different first book of *De ebrietate* between the existing treatment of the biblical text in *De plantatione* and the beginning of the present *De ebrietate.* But the arguments he puts forward are not convincing. It seems quite unlikely that the arguments of the philosophers which commenced at *Plant.* 142 would have been of sufficient length to occupy an entire book, even if in the treatise's present state there is definitely some material missing.

Philo's Methods of Composition

We return now to the structure of the individual treatise, with a particular focus on *De plantatione* For this discussion we take our earlier work on the structure of Philo's allegorical treatises as the starting-point, and in particular our research on the structure of *De agricultura.*[20] We will take the basic features of our understanding of Philo's exegetical method in the Allegorical Commentary as given and not dwell further on its details except

18 Sterling, "Internal References," 62 n. 54. On the papyrus and its evidence see James R. Royse, "The Oxyrhynchus Papyrus of Philo," *Bulletin of the American Society of Papyrologists* 17 (1980): 155–65, at 160–61. The fragments preserved in the *Sacra Parallela,* which refer to both book 1 and 2 of *De ebrietate,* do not give any worthwhile clues regarding content: see Morris, "The Jewish Philosopher Philo," 837. The texts are printed in Paul Wendland, *Neu entdeckte Fragmente Philos: nebst einer Untersuchung über die ursprüngliche Gestalt der Schrift de sacrificiis Abelis et Caini* (Berlin: Georg Reimer, 1891), 22–25.

19 Maximilian Adler, *Studien zu Philon von Alexandreia* (Breslau: M. &. H. Marcus, 1929), 56.

20 See my article "The Structure of Philo's Allegorical Treatise *De Agricultura,*" *SPhiloA* 22 (2010): 87–109, which was preliminary to the Commentary on the treatise by Geljon and Runia, *Philo On Cultivation.*

to make a few additional points.[21] Its most important principle is the primacy of the biblical text. The structure that Philo constructs for a particular treatise is for the most part determined by his selection of biblical texts, in the first instance the main biblical lemma with which the treatise always commences, together with secondary lemmata that are linked to the main text through verbal and thematic association. These texts form the "skeleton" of the treatise and they point the way to an understanding of the allegorical thematics that Philo develops in the course of the treatise.

I would wish to defend the validity of this theory of how Philo composed his allegorical treatises and its value for understanding their structure. It is, I would emphasise, a purely *empirical* theory, based on observing how the treatises work and not on any preconceived notions about Philo's methods. In two respects it might be possible to add refinements. Firstly, there is the question of levels of textual exegesis. In my earlier articles I assumed the two levels of primary and secondary exegesis. In the meantime Gregory Sterling has pointed out that sometimes, also in *De agricultura,* Philo in fact also incorporates a tertiary level into his exegesis, that is, the citation of a secondary text leads by association to the citation of another text which is then given exegesis.[22] This tertiary level has already been incorporated into the structural analysis in the Commentary on *De agricultura.*[23] It is in fact particularly prominent in the three treatises which take the brief text of Gen 9:20–21 as their starting-point. We shall also include it in our analysis of *De plantatione* below.

Secondly, it may be worth looking a little further at the kinds of biblical text that Philo introduces as secondary and tertiary lemmata. These vary to a considerable degree, both in length and how they fulfil their structural role. The treatise contains a number of texts which Philo cites at some length and which determine the structure of quite long portions of the argument. Good examples of these are Exod 15:17–18 (§47, underpinning §§48–58), Gen 21:33 (§73, underpinning §§74–92), and Lev 19:23–25 (§95, underpinning §§96–138 with various other texts cited in the course of the

[21] Based on research in two articles published in the 1980's which has been further developed since then: "The Structure of Philo's Allegorical Treatises: A Review of Two Recent Studies and Some Additional Comments," *VC* 38 (1984): 209–56; "Further Observations on the Structure of Philo's Allegorical treatises," *VC* 41 (1987): 105–38; both articles reprinted in *Exegesis and Philosophy: Studies on Philo of Alexandria* (London: Variorum Reprints, 1990).

[22] Private communication as part of his editorial work for the Philo of Alexandria Commentary Series.

[23] See the structure published in Geljon and Runia, *Philo On Cultivation,* 11–15 and the list of cited texts at 16–17, with instances at §§51, 64, 107, 131, 145, 172.

exegesis). In other cases secondary or tertiary texts introduce shorter sequences of the argument, such as at §59 where the quite long text Deut 32:7–9 is followed only by a short explanation in §§60–61, before being succeeded by other texts linked through the theme of κλῆρος (Lev 16:8 in §61, Deut 10:9 and Num 18:20 in §63). Another method is to cite a brief secondary text, move to another text, then return to a continuation of the previous text. This occurs in §§32–45, when he first cites Gen 2:8, then moves to Ps 36:4, returns briefly to Gen 2:9 before linking this text with Gen 25:27. In all these cases the role of the first cited text is definitely structural. In most cases (though not all) the mode of transition is plainly inspired by verbal similarity (which of course does not exclude thematic continuity as well).

There are other cases where the secondary and tertiary texts appear to play less of a structural role. They are cited in order to illustrate a theme in the argument. A good example is the citation of the fundamental anthropological texts Gen 2:7 and 1:27 in §19. They serve to illustrate how Moses's doctrine of the human being differs from that of the philosophers. Similarly in §134 two texts are introduced to explain how Judah and Issaschar illustrate the numbers four and five in the secondary lemma Lev 19:24–25 cited for a second time in §132. These illustratory texts generally reveal a thematic rather than a verbal link with the biblical texts that they shed light upon. However, they may still be asked to play a structural role. In the case just noted above, both texts are further woven into the argument in §§135–136, before Philo cites two other texts and rounds off the chapter.

In analysing the different roles that secondary and tertiary texts play in determining the structure of the allegorical treatise, I have toyed with the idea of introducing further refinements, such as the distinction implied above between structural and illustratory texts. On the whole, however, it seems better to recognise that Philo has all manner of different ways of linking together and interweaving biblical passages and that the best way forward is to emphasise the flexibility of his technique within the parameters of his basic exegetical and allegorical method.

It is particularly the importance of the verbal linkages between the biblical texts that Philo uses in his allegorical treatises that strikes the reader once this method is discerned. Here we should especially observe the central role that the verbs φυτεύω and καταφυτεύω play in the texts selected for inclusion in *De plantatione*.[24] It is a remarkable fact that all the occurrences

[24] Here too I am indebted to research by Albert Geljon that will be incorporated in our Commentary.

of the two verbs in the first three books of the Pentateuch are utilised in the treatise:[25]

Gen 2:8, cited at §32: ἐφύτευσεν ὁ θεὸς παράδεισον ἐν Ἐδὲμ κατὰ ἀνατολάς, καὶ ἔθετο ἐκεῖ τὸν ἄνθρωπον ὃν ἔπλασεν.

Gen 9:20, cited at §1: ἤρξατο Νῶε ἄνθρωπος εἶναι γεωργὸς γῆς καὶ ἐφύτευσεν ἀμπελῶνα. At §140 he adds the words from v. 21 καὶ ἔπιε τοῦ οἴνου, καὶ ἐμεθύσθη.

Gen 21:33, cited at §73: φυτεῦσαι ἄρουραν ἐπὶ τῷ φρέατι τοῦ ὅρκου καὶ ἐπικαλέσαι τὸ ὄνομα κυρίου θεὸς αἰώνιος.

Exod 15:17, cited at §47: εἰσαγαγὼν καταφύτευσον αὐτοὺς εἰς ὄρος κληρονομίας σου, εἰς ἕτοιμον κατοικητήριόν σου ὃ κατειργάσω, κύριε, ἁγίασμα, κύριε, ὃ ἡτοίμασαν αἱ χεῖρές σου· κύριος βασιλεύων τὸν αἰῶνα καὶ ἐπ᾽ αἰῶνα καὶ ἔτι.

Lev 19:23, cited at §95: ὅταν εἰσέλθητε πρὸς τὴν γῆν, ἣν κύριος ὁ θεὸς ὑμῶν δίδωσιν ὑμῖν, καὶ καταφυτεύσητε πᾶν ξύλον βρώσεως, περικαθαριεῖτε τὴν ἀκαθαρσίαν αὐτοῦ· ὁ καρπὸς αὐτοῦ τρία ἔτη ἔσται ἀπερικάθαρτος, οὐ βρωθήσεται· τῷ δὲ ἔτει τῷ τετάρτῳ ἔσται πᾶς καρπὸς αὐτοῦ ἅγιος, αἰνετὸς τῷ κυρίῳ· τῷ δὲ ἔτει τῷ πέμπτῳ φάγεσθε τὸν καρπόν, πρόσθεμα ὑμῖν τὰ γεννήματα αὐτοῦ. ἐγώ εἰμι κύριος ὁ θεὸς ὑμῶν.

In addition, at §28 Philo cites a text containing the verb φυτεύω from outside the Pentateuch:[26]

Ps 93:9 (LXX): ὁ φυτεύων οὖς οὐκ ἀκούει; ὁ πλάσσων ὀφθαλμοὺς οὐκ ἐπιβλέψει.

The remaining occurrences of the two verbs in the Pentateuch are found in Deuteronomy and Philo does not cite these in *De plantatione*. However, he does cite three of these texts elsewhere in the Allegorical Commentary. One of them Deut 20:6, was in fact already cited in *Agr*. 148, and so in a sense anticipates the themes of the treatise that will be its sequel. The remaining two negative references to planting are alluded to in the Exposition of the Law as part of the discussion of curses in *De praemiis et poenis*.[27]

Without exception the six verses containing the word (κατα)φυτεύω, starting with the main biblical text, play key roles in the structure of the

[25] We cite the texts as found in Philo's text (there are some elements of paraphrase). The two verbs seem to be synonyms and Philo does not make any distinction between them.

[26] Note that there are nine instances of the two verbs in the Psalms, so Philo has been selective here.

[27] The texts are: Deut 6:11, cited in *Deus* 94, *Fug*. 175; Deut 16:21 cited in *Leg*. 1.48; Deut 20:6 cited in *Agr*. 148; Deut 28:30, 39, alluded to but not cited in *Praem*. 128.

treatise. This can be immediately seen if the structural analysis that we shall present below is consulted. In fact all the main sections of the work start with these texts (§1, §28, §73, §95, §140), to which can be added §47 within the long chapter §28–72). We shall return to these texts below.

In my previous paper on the structure of *De agricultura* I suggested that Philo must have studied the terms used in the Pentateuch for various activities and concepts very carefully and that he may have used some kind of concordance, unless he could draw on the resources of what was clearly a formidable memory.[28] I would like to add to this by making the further suggestion that he might have prepared a dossier of interlinked texts before composing his treatise. The linkages would be in many cases verbal, as we see in the striking example we have just studied, but they could also be thematic. Key biblical texts, such as those in the creation account might be included, but also texts that are quite obscure. In many cases the texts would have to be cited out of context. But for Philo this would not be a problem, for it is a basic assumption of his allegorical method that the Pentateuch constitutes an integrated network of meaning. A parallel case of a dossier of texts focusing on a particular topic, with emphasis on verbal linkages, can also be seen in the case of the following treatise *De ebrietate*, where the theme of planting gives way to that of wine (οἶνος) and inebriation (μέθη), both of which are contained in the main biblical lemma. Here too the major elements of the treatise's structure are all introduced by passages containing these terms or words based on them.[29]

The Structure of De Plantatione

It is now time to present the structure of the treatise, subdividing it into its separate structural and thematic elements in accordance with the method discussed above. The following abbreviations are used:

MBL = Main Biblical Lemma, the main biblical verse on which Philo comments.
SBL = Secondary Biblical Lemma, an additional biblical verse that is quoted to explain the MBL.

[28] Runia, "Structure," 96.

[29] See *Ebr*. 2 (Gen. 9:20–21); §14 (Deut 21:18–21, esp. οἰνοφλυγεῖ); §96 (Exod 32:17–19, esp. οἴνου); §127 (Lev 10:8–10, esp. οἶνον); §143 (1 Sam 1:11, esp. οἶνον καὶ μέθυσμα, cf. also v. 15 cited in §149); §166 (Gen 19:33, esp. οἶνον); §210 (Gen 39:1 etc., esp. ἀρχιοινοχόῳ); §222 (Deut 32:32–33, esp. οἶνος).

TBL = Tertiary Bibical Lemma, another biblical text that is quoted to explain a SBL.

MOT = Mode of Transition, the way in which the quoted verses are linked together. Note that a verbal MOT generally also entails a thematic transition, but not vice versa.

This structural analysis will form the basis of the divisions of our translation and the commentary based on it.

Philo of Alexandria
On planting (De plantatione)
Exegetical structure

Part 1: *On Planting (§§1–138)*

Chapter 1: God as planter (§§1–72)

Section A. The planting of the cosmos

(a) The planting of the greatest plant, the cosmos (§§1–10)

After treating the skill of cultivation we now turn to that of planting vines. God created the cosmos out of earth, water, air, and fire. There is no need to look for a corporeal base. God's eternal Word is the firm prop of the cosmos.

(b) The formation of plants and animals (§§11–16)

God created living animals, which are assigned to the four divisions of the cosmos. Those in the air include incorporeal souls. He also produced plants which always stand on the same place.

(c) The creation of the human being: citation of SBL Gen 2:7 and Gen 1:27 (MOT thematic) (§§17–22)

The human being is a heavenly plant. His soul has been inbreathed by the divine spirit and so the human being has been made after the image of God's Word. His body was made erect so that he looks up to heaven and towards God.

(d) Divine souls are called above: citation of SBL Lev 1:1 and Exod 31:2 (MOT thematic, but note the verbal link between Gen 2:7 and Gen 31:3 implicitly cited in §23) (§§23–27)

Those who long for wisdom are not focused on the body and earthly things but yearn for what is above in heaven. Examples are Moses and Bezalel, who are called upwards.

Section B. The creation of the human being, the microcosm (§§28–72)

(a) The trees in the human being: illustrated by SBL Ps 93:9 (MOT verbal φυτεύω) (§§28–31)

The senses and the powers in the body are like trees or shoots planted by God, as illustrated by the Psalmist.

(b) The planting of paradise, rejection of a literal reading: citation of SBL Gen 2:8 (MOT verbal φυτεύω, also ἔπλασεν) (§§32–35)
God plants a garden (paradise) in Eden, but a literal interpretation raises theological problems, so we must turn to allegory.

(c) The planting of paradise, allegorical reading: citation of TBL Ps 36:4 (MOT verbal), continuation of SBL Gen 2:9 (MOT thematic ξύλον), and TBL Gen 25:27 (MOT verbal ἄπλαστος) (§§36–45)
God has planted in the human soul a garden of virtues. The name Eden means "luxury," a symbol of a joyful soul that rejoices in the Lord as the psalmist says. Further details explained are its position towards the East, the fact that only the human being is placed there and not animals, and that it is the moulded man who was introduced there.

(d) Moses prays that Israel be planted in paradise: citation of SBL Exod 15:17–18 (MOT verbal καταφυτεύω) (§§46–58)
Moses prays that his people may be planted in the mountain of God's inheritance (κληρονομία) so that they can imitate God and lead a good life. This world is the mountain of God's inheritance because it is the possession and portion (κλῆρος) of its maker. God gives a portion since all things belong to him. The sacred band of wise souls is a special portion of God.

(e) The part that belongs to God: citation of TBL Deut 32:7–9 (MOT thematic, but note that μέρις recalls κλῆρος, κληρονομία) and TBL Lev 16:8 (MOT verbal διακληρόω) (§§59–61)
He who sees God is described as his portion and allotment/inheritance, whereas the sons of Adam are scattered. The former is symbolised by the goat that is assigned to the Lord on the Day of Atonement.

(f) The portion of the Levites: citation of TBL Deut 10:9 (MOT verbal μέρις, κλῆρος) and TBL Num 18:9 (MOT verbal (μέρις, κληροδοσία) (§§62–72)
The tribe of Levi, that is the purified mind, has the Lord as his portion, as stated in the two biblical texts. The name Levi means "He for me." To have the highest cause as one's allotment is the greatest honour of all, reserved for those who seek wisdom.

Chapter 2: Abraham as planter (§§73–93)

(a) Transition to new biblical text and outline of its interpretation: citation of SBL Gen 21:33 (MOT verbal φυτεύω) (§§73–74)
Transition to the practices illustrated by the allegory of planting. Quotation of another biblical verse with the verb φυτεύω. The wise Abraham imitates the planting by God. Brief outline of main components of the allegorical explanation: tree, plot of land, fruit.

(b) Explanation of "field": in SBL (§§75–77)
The field representing the tree measures ten thousand square cubits. This is the most complete and perfect number and symbolizes that God is the beginning and limit of all things.

(c) Explanation of "the well of the oath": in SBL, to which is added the citation of TBL Gen 26:32–33 (MOT verbal φρέαρ, ὅρκος) (§§78–84)
Those who investigate the nature of existing things resemble those who dig wells. Just as diggers of wells often do not find water, so researchers do not attain perfection of knowledge. The oath symbolizes the firm conviction of this fact, calling on God as witness.

(d) Explanation of "the name of the Lord, God of the ages": in SBL, to which is added the citation of TBL Gen 28:21 (MOT verbal κύριος, θεός) (§§85–92)
The two names representing the fruit of the tree refer to the two powers of He who IS: Lord indicating him as ruler, God of the ages as bestowing benefits, which he does continuously.

(e) Summary of allegorical exegesis of SBL Gen 21:33 (§93)
The summary didactically lists the main points explained (cf. §74).

Chapter 3: Human beings as planters (§§94–138)

(a) citation of the biblical text: SBL Lev 19:23–25 (MOT verbal καταφυτεύω) (§§94–95)
We, who are not yet perfect and are busy with our ordinary duties, also have to practise cultivation.

(b) Explanation of "entering of the land": SBL Lev 19:23 (§§96–98):
When the intellect has set out on the road of understanding it will cultivate trees that bring forth cultivated fruit, and will strive for freedom from passions, knowledge, and good things.

(c) Explanation of "cleansing the uncleanness": SBL Lev 19:23, to which is added the citation of TBL Gen 30:37 (MOT thematic) (§§99–112):
Harmful shoots that grow among the ordinary duties should be cut away, such as hypocrisy and dishonesty. Note the practiser Jacob, who stripped rods to the white bark by tearing away the green, that is he does away with what is harmful in the duties and reveals what is good.

(d) Explanation of "three years": SBL Lev 19:23 (§§113–116):
Three years refer to the three parts of time: past, present, and future. The fruit of instruction does not need cleansing and will last forever.

(e) Explanation of "the fourth year": SBL Lev 19:24 (§§117–131):
Scripture recognizes the special significance of the number four, for example in the physical world, in ethics and mathematics. The fruit of instruction is "praiseworthy" in that it teaches praise and thanksgiving to God, the importance of which is shown by an ancient story.

(f) Explanation of "the fifth year": SBL Lev 19:25, to which is added the quotation of TBL Gen 29:35 and Gen 30:18 (MOT thematic) (§§132–136):

The number five refers to the five senses which nourish the mind. Judah, the fourth son of Leah, means "confession of praise to the Lord" and Issachar, the fifth, means "reward". The cultivator receives a reward from the trees in the fifth year.

(g) Explanation of "I am the Lord your God": SBL Lev 19:25, to which is added the citation of TBL Hos 14:9–10 (MOT verbal καρπός) (§§137–138):

The fruit and the products belong to the One God. As the prophet states, the wise man who possesses the fruit of understanding will understand this.

Part 2: *May a Wise Person Get Drunk (§§139–177)*

Chapter 1: Introduction (§§139–148)

(a) Summary and repeated citation of the biblical text: MBL Gen 9:20–21 (§§139–140):

We have now dealt with the most ancient form of cultivation utilized by the first cause and other related aspects. We will now examine a species of cultivation, viticulture.

(b) Introduction of the theme of the inebriation of the wise person (§§141–142)

Noah cultivates the vine with knowledge and skill, but foolish persons do it in a unskillful way. We will later investigate what Moses said about drunkenness, now we discuss the opinion of the other philosophers on the question: will the wise man get drunk?

(c) Brief overview of two contrasting views of philosophers (§§143–148)

Some say that the drinking of wine befits a wise man, because his good sense will protect him from harmful results. Other say that a wise man should not drink wine, because he will no longer be able to control himself.

Chapter 2: The wise person may get drunk (§§149–174)

(a) Setting out the two positions of the argument (§§149–150a)

Our question clearly can be answered in two ways: the wise man will get drunk, or he will not get drunk. We start with proofs for the former position.

(b) First argument: "wine" and "drunkenness" are synonyms (§§150b–155)

There are homonyms and synonyms. "Drinking wine" and "getting drunk" are synonyms. Both words denote excessive indulgence in wine, which the wise man may wish to engage in for a variety of reasons.

(c) Second argument: in earlier times people drank wine in the right way (§§156–164)
In earlier times there was a more robust culture, in which wine was drunk with care and the appropriate decorum, as indicated by the etymology of the word μεθύειν as μετὰ τὸ θύειν describing the behaviour of the wise person. Nowadays people drink wine to excess with practices involving disgusting drinking contests.

(d) Third argument: wine provides relaxation (§§165–172)
Etymological argument: ἡ μέθη (drunkenness) is derived from μέθεσις (relaxation). Wine is the cause of relaxation for the soul. For Moses play and laughter belong to the goals of wisdom, as practised by Isaac (whose name means "laughter") and Rebecca (meaning "patience"). Wine intensifies natural impulses for good or for the opposite.

(e) Fourth (non-professional) argument: writers are positive about drinking wine (§§173–174)
A non-technical argument: many writers have written about drinking wine, but they do not report about its misuse and that it would be a bad thing for the wise person to do.

Chapter 3: Counter-argument: the wise person may not get drunk (§§175–177)

(a) Introducing the counter-argument: both points of view needed (§175)
It is also necessary to state the contrary position in the argument in order to reach a just verdict.

(b) First argument: no one confides in a drunkard (§§178–177)
No one will entrust a secret to a drunken man. But we should immediately state the opposed view. Absurd consequences for the wise person can be drawn from this argument.

End of treatise

Comments on the Treatise and Its Structure

The structure that I have presented, which will form the backbone of the commentary that is under preparation, gives rise to a number of comments.

(1) We have already noted that the treatise clearly consists of two parts, both of which start with the citation of the main biblical lemma, but which do not cohere well together. The title of the treatise in fact does not cover the subject matter of the second part at all. It would surely have been better if this part were joined up with the following treatise, since the common theme turns to wine and inebriation.

(2) In contrast to the treatise as a whole, the first part of the treatise taken on its own does have a tight and well thought through structure. To understand it fully, we have to return to the Pentateuchal use of the verbs of planting, φυτεύω and καταφυτεύω, which has already been discussed above. Not only is the activity described by the verbs important, but also who is performing that activity. There are four different subjects. The first is Noah in the main biblical lemma. Curiously, after this first mention, he disappears completely from the treatise, until briefly resurfacing at §140 when the second part of the work commences. On both occasions Philo gives him his scriptural epithet ὁ δίκαιος (Gen 6:9), but does nothing further with it. In *De agricultura* the status of Noah was important. In that treatise's second part Philo emphasises that he is a beginner and not strong enough spiritually to reach the final goal of full knowledge.

The second subject is God the planter. He is first depicted as planting the entire universe. Philo does not have a Pentateuchal text for this (the metaphor is not used in the creation account), so the section on cosmology (§§2–27) has to do without a text referring to God as planter (later at §48 he compensates for this through his allegorical identification of the "mountain" in Exod 15:17 as the cosmos). This changes when the formation of the human being is introduced, for after a brief discussion on Ps 93:9, which refers to God planting the senses, he can turn to the important text in the creation account when God plants a paradise, Gen 2:8, which provides plenty of rich allegorical material up to §45. Of course the sojourn of the soul in paradise comes to a sad end. The earthly mind Adam is removed and exiled (§46). But Moses prays that God will plant the people of vision on the mountain of his inheritance (Exod 15:17). So again God does the planting, if he responds to Moses's prayer, as he surely does. To have God as one's allotment (κλῆρος) is the greatest good that one can have (§72) and this rounds off the discussion of God's activity as planter rather nicely.

The third subject is the wise person Abraham, whose planting activity forms the core of the next cited text containing the verb φυτεύω at §73. The other two ancestors or patriarchs are also invoked (Isaac at §78, Jacob at §90). This is the stage that Noah had not yet reached in *De agricultura*. The wise understand that God is the source of all blessings. They trust in him and this makes them feel cheerful and safe (§§91–92). After this relatively short section we arrive at the fourth subject. This time it relates to the people of Israel as they enter the land which the Lord grants them (Lev 19:23), which Philo immediately converts into a first person plural, so it concerns those who have not yet attained perfection (just like Noah in *De agricultura*). This text about planting fruit provides a wealth of allegorical material sufficient to keep the exegete going until the end of the first part of the treatise at §138, ending with the themes of giving thanks, reward and recognition, and finally very briefly with the theme that the soul's fruits are the possession of God who is One.

(3) The correlation of the movement of the first part from God to us human beings who are not yet perfect with the subjects of the chief verbs φυτεύω and καταφυτεύω has given the treatise a tight and coherent structure, within which many ethical and spiritual themes can be elaborated in more or less detail. It is logical, therefore, to divide this first part into three chapters, corresponding to the three different subjects. However, this means that the first chapter, which takes up the entire section from §§2–72, is very long. This slab of text, however, clearly divides into two, a first part dealing with God as planter of the cosmos and all that it contains (§§2–27), the second treating God as planter of virtues in the human soul (§§28–72). So this has led me to divide this first chapter into two major sections, which makes them more manageable in size for the commentary and acknowledges that they represent two steps in the build-up of the argument.

(4) Long ago in my dissertation I gave the passage §§2–27 the title "Philo's phyto-cosmological excursus."[30] The label was intended to highlight that he here gives a compact presentation of an entire cosmology, patently based on the structure of Plato's *Timaeus* and the interpretations of its subsequent readers, which has been very creatively overlaid with the plant metaphor supplied by the subject of the treatise. (The two sources of Mosaic and Platonic metaphor neatly converge in the depiction of the human being as a "heavenly plant," duly utilized and attributed, though not by name, in §17.) In the different context of the exegetical structure of the work, it might well be argued that the word "excursus" is inappropriate, for we have seen that Philo integrates this passage quite tightly into the structure of the treatise. But it should also be noted that the section is not introduced by any biblical text and it gives a great deal of—admittedly fascinating—detail that is not of direct relevance for the main subject of the treatise, but in fact serves as background to the main themes.

(5) Turning now to the second part of the treatise, containing the arguments of the philosophers on whether the wise man will get drunk, it is immediately obvious that the kind of text that Philo presents here is totally different from his usual manner in the Allegorical Commentary. It resembles much more closely the style and content that we find in the philosophical treatises, and particularly (although the subject-matter is quite different) in the *De aeternitate mundi*. (It can also be compared with the

[30] David T. Runia, *Philo of Alexandria and the* Timaeus *of Plato*, 2nd ed., Philosophia Antiqua 44 (Leiden: Brill, 1986), 389–92.

famous section in *De ebrietate* when he draws on the tropes of of the Greek philosopher Aenesidemus as he explains the allegorical meaning of the names of the daughters of Noah (§§167–202). But it has to be said that there the philosophical material is much better integrated into the exegetical material than in the second part of *De plantatione*.) It has proved possible to divide it up into chapters and sections, as was done for Part 1, but these are generally much shorter than in the earlier part and apart from the introductory section they are wholly devoid of scriptural quotations, although there is a brief allusion to Moses and his depiction of Isaac and Rebecca in Gen 26:8 which is imported in §§168–169.

The main reason why this part of the treatise is so different is of course obvious. In putting forward the views of the philosophers on this subject, Philo has consulted an existing philosophical text (or possibly multiple texts) by an unknown author and has adapted it for use in the present context. The resemblance to *De aeternitate mundi* is not coincidental. Not only is he also in that treatise heavily dependent on philosophical sources, but in both cases he makes use of the same method of presentation. As I demonstrated in my analysis of that controversial treatise,[31] he uses the genre of the θέσις or *quaestio infinita*, a method of discussing a general question. That this is the genre is made quite clear by the way that Philo introduces it: προτείνεται δὲ οὕτως· εἰ μεθυσθήσεται ὁ σοφός (§142). The subject is put forward and arguments are produced in the affirmative and the negative. At the end of the treatise a decision may be made on which position and arguments are the stronger (usually it is the ones that are presented second), or the question may be left open.

The turning point between the two sets of arguments occurs at §175 where he says that in order to be judged victorious, it is also necessary to state those arguments which establish the opposed point of view. The term for "establish," κατασκευάζω, is exactly the same as that used at *Aet*. 20, when Philo introduces the long list of arguments defending the view that the cosmos is ungenerated and everlasting. It belongs to the technical vocabulary of the θέσις. This was already made clear when he commences the arguments in favour of the θέσις at §149.[32] However, only a single argument

31 David T. Runia, "Philo's *De aeternitate mundi*: The Problem of Its Interpretation," *VC* 35 (1981): 105–51. The study of this text in Hans von Arnim, *Quellenstudien zu Philo von Alexandria*, Philologische Untersuchungen 11 (Berlin: Weidmannsche Buchhandlung, 1888), 101–40, is flawed because, misled by the thematic similarities to Seneca *Ep*. 83, he interprets it as a Stoic ζήτημα.

32 Further examples of this use of the term at *Aet*. 12, 20, 56, 94, 113, 118, 124. Compare the use of the term by Theon Rhetor when describing the method of the θέσις; see *Progymn*. 121.1, 19, 123.8.

is put forward (§§176–177). This argument is then not allowed to stand on its own, as occurred in the case of the earlier arguments, but an opponent with a refutatory argument (φήσει δή τις ἐναντιούμενος) is immediately introduced. This argument forms the conclusion of the treatise.

There can hardly be any doubt that Philo did not intend the treatise to end in this way. Not only is the conclusion very abrupt and even anticlimactic, but it also runs contrary to the intent to present further arguments which he makes clear before introducing the opposing view, as indicated in the words "before we string together the other arguments in sequence" (§176). We can safely say that the final part of the treatise has been lost. How it would have ended is a matter of speculation. Philo may have been content to leave the question up in the air. He is often keen to show that the philosophers are in disagreement with each other.[33] Moses can supply the answer, and that will be revealed in the next treatise, *De ebrietate*.

(6) It might be argued that Philo will surely support the view that the wise person will get drunk, since is it not the case that this is what happens to Noah? This was the view that I took in my early article.[34] The situation, however, is more complicated. In the first instance, is Noah here a wise person? To be sure, the Bible calls him δίκαιος, "perfect (τέλειος) in his generation" and "well-pleasing to God" (Gen 6:8–9). Elsewhere Philo interprets these words as referring to the virtuous and (by implication) wise person.[35] But we recall that in *De agricultura* he was still a person making progress and had not yet reached the final goal.

It has already been remarked that it is noteworthy that in *De plantatione* the personage of Noah sinks wholly below the surface, only appearing twice when the main biblical lemma is cited.[36] In *De ebrietate* too he is scarcely mentioned (only once at §5). But in general terms the persons associated with getting drunk in the latter treatise do not come out of it at all well. It is associated with stupid chatter, complete insensibility, and insatiability (§4). These three themes take up the entire treatise. However, in the list of themes just alluded to two others are added, "good humour

[33] For example in *Ebr*. 199; *Her*. 246. On the sceptical background see Jaap Mansfeld, "Philosophy in the Service of Scripture: Philo's Exegetical Strategies," in *The Question of "Eclecticism": Studies in Later Greek Philosophy*, ed. John M. Dillon and Anthony A. Long, Hellenistic Culture and Society 3 (Berkeley: University of California Press, 1988), 70–102; repr. in Jaap Mansfeld, *Studies in Later Greek Philosophy and Gnosticism* (London: Variorum Reprints, 1989).

[34] Runia, "Philo's *De aeternitate mundi*," 114.

[35] *Deus* 118; *QG* 1.97.

[36] See above section 5 (2).

and gladness" (εὐθυμία καὶ εὐφροσύνη) and "nakedness" ((§4).[37] As we noted earlier,[38] it is very likely that these were the main themes of the missing second book of *De ebrietate*. The earlier of these themes will have allowed Philo to give the theme of inebriation a more positive twist, if indeed that was his wish. There are perhaps in *De plantatione* already some hints in this direction. Firstly, "good humour" is selected, together with "security" (ἀσφάλεια), as examples of what flows from having trust in God's love of humankind at §93, the final climactic words of the chapter which discusses the planting carried out by the wise person. Secondly, it is surely significant that, when presenting the philosophers' argument that wine produces relaxation in the soul, Philo adds the example of the εὐφροσύνη enjoyed together by Isaac and Rebecca (though it is not associated with drinking). If we are on the right track, then, despite the bad examples discussed in *Ebr.*, Philo would have ultimately agreed that the wise person can get drunk and that it can assist in producing joy and happiness for the soul. So he will not have been at all distressed if it proved to be the case that the philosophical arguments in favour of this position were stronger than those arguing the opposite view, whether or not he drew that conclusion at the end of our treatise.

Some Final Reflections

The Allegorical Commentary, with such a wealth of texts and themes, still has to yield many of its secrets. The central role of the biblical text, with its various layers and linkages, is one of them, or so I believe I have demonstrated. But it gives only a structure. The bare bones have to come to life when they are clothed with the allegorical themes that they summon up. I am conscious that much remains to be done, also in connection with this treatise that we have examined in the present article.

It is important to recognise that Philo uses a multiplicity of methods and techniques in this long work. Scholars such as Maximilian Adler have attempted to see a development in his method, and it is certainly the case that the final treatises that we have in the series, *De Somniis* 1–2, if indeed they belong in it, are very different from the first, *Legum allegoriae* 1–2.[39] Similarly the treatises in the cluster we have been studying have their own individual characteristics, among which the focus on a very brief single

37 Reading εὐθυμίας with the mss.

38 See above section 2 (4).

39 Adler, *Studien* (cited above n. 19)

main biblical text is surely the most striking. If there was development, it was not necessarily in a single direction as argued by Adler.[40] I would contend that Philo was very flexible in the various methods that he used and that these need to be further explored. For this the empirical approach that I am advocating is most suitable, because it starts off with only a very small number of assumptions and explores the text of the commentaries as they present themselves to the reader.

In closing I wish to draw attention to the performative aspect of the Philonic treatise.[41] The interpreter of scripture discerns and unfolds the themes that he believes are inherent in the texts that he has brought together. It is then the readers who "experience" these through the act of reading, as might have occurred under the gaze of the Master in Philo's school.[42] Ultimately that is what Philo wishes his readers to have, an experience that is both intellectual and spiritual, that will set the goal before them and then assist them in attaining it, a firm trust in and knowledge of God that will find expression in joy and thanksgiving.

Australian Catholic University
The University of Melbourne
Australia

40 See our remarks at Runia, "Structure," 90–91.
41 See Runia, "Further Observations," 129–130 (cited above n. 21).
42 See above n. 6 and text thereto.

APPENDIX
Translation of Passages Cited

The following is a translation of the biblical and transition passages cited above in section 2 of the paper.

> *Agr.* 1: (the main biblical lemma, Gen 9:20–21a) "And Noah began to be a human being* who cultivates the earth, and he planted a vineyard, and he drank from the wine, and he was drunk in his house."
>
> *Agr.* 181: "As for what has been said about his work as the planter (of a vineyard), let us discuss that on another occasion.
>
> *Plant.* 1: "In the previous book we discussed everything that was opportune in relation to the skill of cultivation in general. In this book we shall give an account, as best we are able, of the specific skill of viticulture. For he (Moses) introduces the just person not only as a cultivator, but also individually as viticulturist when he says: "Noah began to be a human being who cultivates the earth, and he planted a vineyard (Gen 9:20)."
>
> *Plant.* 139–141: "We have spoken as best we could about the most ancient and sacred form of cultivation which the Cause utilizes for the cosmos, the most fertile of plants, about the next kind of cultivation which the honourable person practices, and about the cultivation that wins the prize assigned to four and that was practised through the commands and injunctions of the laws. (§140) Let us now examine the viticulture practised by the just person Noah, which is a specific form of the skill of cultivation. For it is stated that "Noah began to be a human being who cultivates the earth, and he planted a vineyard, and he drank of the wine, and he became drunk (Gen 9:20–21a)." (§141) The just person, therefore, tends the plant of inebriation with skill and knowledge, whereas the foolish give it unskilled attention of the wrong kind. So it will be necessary for us to state what is fitting about the subject of inebriation, for we will then immediately also know the power of the plant that provides the means for it. What is said by the lawgiver on the subject of inebriation we shall deal with thoroughly on a later occasion. At the present moment let us examine the views of others."
>
> *Ebr.* 1: "The statements made by other philosophers on (the subject of) inebriation we have recorded as best we could in the book prior to this one. Let us now examine the views that the in all respects great and wise lawgiver has on it."

> *Sobr.* 1: "Having previously examined the statements made by the lawgiver on inebriation and the nakedness that followed upon it, let us now proceed by fitting the next topic to what has already been said. In the sacred oracles the words that follow are: "And Noah became sober from the wine and he realized what his younger son had done to him (Gen 9:24)."

* We translate ἄνθρωπος throughout either as "human being" or "person," but not as "man." The latter translation is reserved for the Greek ἀνήρ.

The Studia Philonica Annual 29 (2017): 139–58

THE TEXT OF PHILO'S *DE PLANTATIONE*[*]

JAMES R. ROYSE

The treatise *De plantatione* is reasonably well-attested within the Greek manuscript tradition, being found in MGHUF, of which Paul Wendland judges H to be the best.[1] Nevertheless, as David Runia observes, it is striking that so many conjectures have been made to this book.[2] (And I will add a few in this paper.) The apparatus of PCW reports on the earlier conjectures by Thomas Mangey as well as the conjectures by Leopold Cohn and by Wendland (who edited the book in PCW). Quite a few others are found in the subsequent translations into German, English, and French.[3] And one could add yet more from Markland's notes in his copy of Mangey's edition, as will be discussed later.

In this paper I will look at some of the more or less problematic places under several classifications.[4]

1. *Philo's Biblical Citations*

It is widely accepted that Philo knew his biblical text from the LXX translation.[5] Let us begin by looking at a few places where Dominique Barthélemy, in his very perceptive article, argued that readings derived from Aquila's Greek translation found their way into the manuscripts of

* Presented to the Philo of Alexandria Section at the annual meeting of the Society of Biblical Literature in Atlanta, November 23, 2015.

1 PCW 2:xxiii–xxv.

2 See the appendix, in which his results are presented.

3 I.e., PCH 4 (Heinemann), PLCL 3 (Colson and Whitaker), and PAPM 10 (Pouilloux).

4 Some of the textual issues found in PCW 2 are discussed by Wendland in his "Kritische und exegetische Bemerkungen zu Philo," *RhM*, N.F. 52 (1897): 465–504, at 496–504 for *De plantatione*.

5 On this vast subject let me cite merely Peter Katz, *Philo's Bible* (Cambridge: Cambridge University Press, 1950), as well as my own "21.4 Philo," in *The Hebrew Bible: Writings*, vol. 1.1C of *The Textual History of the Bible*, ed. A. Lange and E. Tov (Leiden: Brill, 2016), 741–46.

Philo.[6] Following the work of Peter Katz, Barthélemy identifies many such readings throughout the treatises of Philo, and explicitly discusses a few from *De plantatione*.

§29: Philo cites Ps 93:9 (94:9 MT), which is printed in PCW as: ἐν ὕμνοις λέγων ὧδε· "ὁ φυτεύων οὖς οὐκ ἀκούει; ὁ πλάσσων ὀφθαλμοὺς οὐκ ἐπιβλέψει." For the final two words the LXX has οὐ κατανοεῖ. The Hebrew verb is נָבַט, which Aquila translates by ἐπιβλέπω at five places.[7] Following Barthélemy one should edit οὐ κατανοεῖ against the manuscripts.[8] Moreover, where the LXX has τὸ οὖς and τὸν ὀφθαλμόν, Philo has the anarthrous οὖς and ὀφθαλμούς. The MT also has these nouns (both in the singular) without articles. Barthélemy notes that Aquila suppresses articles that are missing in Hebrew. Thus, it seems likely that Philo had the readings of the LXX, which have been replaced by the readings of Aquila.[9]

§47: The citation of Exod 15:17–18 has been retouched throughout. Katz had earlier discussed this passage at length.[10]

LXX	Aquila
καταφύτευσον G	καταφυτεύσεις ceteri
κληρονομίας Wendland (PCW)	κληροδοσίας codd.
εἰς ἕτοιμον κατοικητήριόν σου G	ἕδρασμα εἰς καθέδραν σου ceteri
ὃ ἡτοίμασαν αἱ G	ἥδρασαν ceteri
βασιλεύων G"H^{2}"	βασιλεύει MUF"H^{1}"
τὸν αἰῶνα καὶ ἐπ' αἰῶνα H (αἰώνων καὶ ἐπ' H in mg.)	τὸν αἰῶνα MGUF

The various readings assigned to Aquila represent the Hebrew text more literally than the LXX does. But in general Philo follows the LXX, and we have some confirmation that he read the LXX text for Exod 15:17–18. At *Congr*. 57 he reads καταφύτευσον without variation, and at *Plant*. 51 he cites

6 Dominique Barthélemy, "Est-ce Hoshaya Rabba qui censura le 'Commentaire Allégorique'?," in *Philon d'Alexandrie*, ed. Roger Arnaldez, et al. (Paris: Centre National de la Recherche Scientifique, 1967), 45–78, reprinted in his *Études d'histoire du texte de l'Ancien Testament* (Fribourg: Éditions universitaires, 1978), 140–73, and 390–91 (additional notes).

7 These are 1 Sam 2:32 (1 Reg 2:32 LXX: ἐπιβλέπω); Ps 10:14 (9:35 LXX: κατανοέω); 91:8 (90:8 LXX: κατανοέω); 102:20 (101:20 LXX: ἐπιβλέπω); Isa 63:15 (LXX: ἐπιστρέπω).

8 Barthélemy, "Hoshaya Rabba," 51 n. 7: "Ici encore, toute la tradition textuelle étant retouchée, Wendland a introduit à tort cette leçon dans son texte."

9 There is a complication at the second place. Instead of τὸν ὀφθαλμόν BS have ὀφθαλμούς, and R has τοὺς ὀφθαλμούς. Did Philo simply follow a text of the LXX that agreed with BS? Or is that reading in BS itself a revision to Aquila?

10 *Philo's Bible*, 34–36. See also Wendland, "Bemerkungen," 499.

βασιλεύων (without variation) and τὸν αἰῶνα καὶ ἐπ' αἰῶνα (MGUF, τῶν αἰώνων καὶ ἐπ' αἰῶνα HE). But the retouching continues in §54:

κληρονομίας UH	κληροδοσίας MGF

However, a different biblical text, Num 18:20, is cited at §63, which reads in all the manuscripts and in PCW: ἐγὼ μερίς σου καὶ κληροδοσία. Now, Mangey conjectured κληρονομία here, and this is surely correct. The LXX witnesses are unanimous in supporting κληρονομία,[11] and so the reading in the Philonic manuscripts is again a reading of Aquila, as Barthélemy notes, and Wendland should have restored κληρονομία as he did at §47.[12] Barthélemy finds another similar place where the retouching has occurred: *Her*. 162. At the citation of Deut 25:13–16 there, the Coptos Papyrus (Pap) reads ἐν κλήρῳ, with the LXX, while all the other manuscripts have κληροδοσίας. There Wendland had the testimony of Pap, which dates from the third-century,[13] to the true reading, in contrast to the retouched reading found in all the other manuscripts. At *Plant*. 63 we have no such early witness.

There is a further interesting reading at §47; namely, the first κύριε is found in G only, while MUFH have κυρίου. Almost all the LXX witnesses have κύριε.[14] The Hebrew has here the Tetragrammaton,[15] and Barthélemy states that this shows that the retoucher's text of Aquila preserved the Tetragrammaton rather than translating it.[16] That is, the retoucher saw the Tetragrammaton, and interpreted it (in Greek) as a genitive rather than a vocative. However, elsewhere I have argued that Philo's own biblical manuscripts would have written the Tetragrammaton instead of the translation κύριος that is now found in the bulk of our (much later) manuscripts of the LXX.[17] And I went on to suggest that this interpretation of the

11 A few read κληρονομίας or κλιρονομίαν.

12 Barthélemy, "Hoshaya Rabba," 50 n. 8: "Dans le deuxième cas [i.e., *Plant*. 63], Wendland, ne disposant pas de témoin non retouché, a eu tort de conserver cette leçon dont Mangey se défiait déjà." Indeed, Wendland, "Bemerkungen," 499 states: "§ 63 wird Mangeys Aenderung κληρονομία statt κληροδοσία durch die LXX und durch die Beobachtung der gleichen Korruptel in § 47 empfohlen."

13 On the importance of this codex for Philo's biblical citations in particular, see my "The Biblical Quotations in the Coptos Papyrus of Philo," *SPhiloA* 28 (2016): 49–76.

14 A few witnesses omit the word, and a few others omit κύριε ἁγίασμα; there is no support for κυρίου here, although one ms. (75) has that reading for the second κύριε.

15 But the second κύριε represents אֲדֹנָי (at least this is the MT).

16 Barthélemy, "Hoshaya Rabba," 54.

17 "Philo, Κύριος, and the Tetragrammaton," *SPhiloA* 3 (1991): 167–83. My argument there should be revisited; see the comments by Frank Shaw, *The Earliest Non-Mystical Jewish Use of Ιαω* (Leuven: Peeters, 2014), 169–70.

Tetragrammaton might have been Philo's own.[18] That is, Philo saw the Tetragrammaton in his copy of the LXX of Exodus, and interpreted it as a genitive, while (eventually) the LXX tradition interpreted it as a vocative. (See further below on *Plant.* 73.)

There are yet other places where Philo's biblical citations present textual problems.

§1 and §140: "ἤρξατο Νῶε ἄνθρωπος εἶναι γεωργὸς γῆς καὶ ἐφύτευσεν ἀμπελῶνα" (Gen 9:20). I have elsewhere discussed Philo's various citations of this verse, and concluded that Philo has inserted εἶναι as a stylistic addition.[19]

§19: PCW prints: "ἐνέπνευσε" γάρ φησιν "ὁ θεὸς εἰς τὸ πρόσωπον αὐτοῦ πνοὴν ζωῆς" (Gen 2:7). And the same placement of quotation marks is found in PLCL, PCH, and PAPM. The Göttingen LXX accordingly cites Philo as having here ἐνέπνευσε ὁ θεός for ἐνεφύσησεν, but correctly notes that he has the latter word at *Leg.* 1.31 and *Her.* 56. However, at *Her.* 56 PCW prints: "ἐνεφύσησε" γάρ φησιν "ὁ ποιητὴς τῶν ὅλων εἰς τὸ πρόσωπον αὐτοῦ πνοὴν ζωῆς, καὶ ἐγένετο ὁ ἄνθρωπος εἰς ψυχὴν ζῶσαν." Here PCH and PAPM follow PCW's placement of quotation marks, but PLCL correctly moves "the Maker of all" outside the quotation of Gen 2:7. In fact, the quotation marks are incorrectly placed in PCW at both *Plant.* 19 and *Her.* 56. These *should* be edited as:

> *Plant.* 19: ἐνέπνευσε γάρ φησιν ὁ θεὸς "εἰς τὸ πρόσωπον αὐτοῦ πνοὴν ζωῆς," κτλ.
> *Her.* 56: "ἐνεφύσησε" γάρ φησιν ὁ ποιητὴς τῶν ὅλων "εἰς τὸ πρόσωπον αὐτοῦ πνοὴν ζωῆς, καὶ ἐγένετο ὁ ἄνθρωπος εἰς ψυχὴν ζῶσαν."[20]

[18] "Philo, Κύριος, and the Tetragrammaton," 182.

[19] See my "Some Observations on the Biblical Text in Philo's *De agricultura*," *SPhiloA* 22 (2010): 112. The addition of εἶναι (not found in the LXX mss., and not supported by the Hebrew) before γεωργός is also found at *Agr.* 20 and 125, while at *Agr.* 1 Philo adds εἶναι after γῆς.

[20] Philo also quotes ἐνεφύσησε at *Opif.* 134; *Leg.* 3.161; *Det.* 80; *Somn.* 1.34; *QG* 2.59. Note that at *Leg.* 3.161 PCW also places the quotation marks incorrectly so as to include both γάρ and ὁ θεός in the citation. (Here PLCL and PAPM follow PCW; PCH correctly places "denn" outside the citation but incorrectly includes "Gott.") What *should* be edited at *Leg.* 3.161 is: "ἐνεφύσησε" γὰρ "εἰς τὸ πρόσωπον αὐτοῦ πνεῦμα ζωῆς" ὁ θεός, "καὶ ἐγένετο ὁ ἄνθρωπος εἰς ψυχὴν ζῶσαν."

A different issue is the presence of πνεῦμα ζωῆς here and at *Det.* 80 instead of πνοὴν ζωῆς, as found in all the LXX mss. and in Philo at *Opif.* 134; *Leg.* 1.31; *Plant.* 19; *Her.* 56; *Somn.* 1.34; *QG* 2.59 (this Greek fragment, found in Mangey 2:668, was identified by Aucher). The Göttingen LXX does not even cite πνεῦμα ζωῆς from the two passages in Philo, although Brooke and McLean do have the notation "Phil 2/7" (evidently ignoring *QG* 2.59, as does Herbert Edward Ryle, *Philo and Holy Scripture* [London: Macmillan, 1895], 8–9). I would *not* propose that one edit: "ἐνεφύσησε" γὰρ "εἰς τὸ πρόσωπον αὐτοῦ" πνεῦμα "ζωῆς" ὁ θεός, "καὶ

One must keep in mind that quotation marks were not available at the time of Philo, and that in modern editions they are the work of the editors.[21] We can of course reasonably presume that Philo made the conceptual distinction between a literal citation of the biblical text and a paraphrase, and between the actual words of the biblical text and his own introductory or clarificatory words. But all the evidence indicates that at his time the explicit marking of quotations would not have occurred.[22] Naturally, there is from time to time doubt about what Philo's biblical text was. But there is no reason to suppose that Philo thought that he was quoting Gen 2:7 either with the words ἐνέπνευσε, ὁ θεός, or with the words ὁ ποιητὴς τῶν ὅλων. At such places editors and translators have to make decisions about whether and where to place quotation marks, and those decisions should follow our best knowledge about what Philo would have considered to be the literal words of the biblical text.

§26: Philo here quotes "ἀνεκάλεσε Μωυσῆν" from Lev 1:1. Despite the fact that Philo explicitly ascribes the quotation to Leviticus, Mangey somehow overlooks the true source of the biblical quotation, and states on Λευιτικῇ

ἐγένετο ὁ ἄνθρωπος εἰς ψυχὴν ζῶσαν." Rather, either we suppose that Philo actually wrote πνεῦμα by mistake or deliberately as a stylistic "improvement," or we suppose that Philo consistently wrote πνοὴν ζωῆς everywhere and that πνεῦμα is a textual corruption. Certainly the latter hypothesis is suggested by Philo's explicit comment at *Leg.* 1.42 that the text uses "πνοήν but not πνεῦμα."

21 At best this work can be seen as reflecting later practice in mss. E.g., medieval mss. may indicate quotations by various devices such as the use of different ink. Within the tradition of Philonic mss., we see already in the third-century Pap the use of diples in the margin to indicate quotations, as noted by the editor, Vincent Scheil (*Deux traités de Philon*, Mémoires publiés par les membres de la Mission archéologique française au Caire 9:2 [Paris: Ernest Leroux, 1893], iv). But this usage seems not to be entirely consistent, and in any case does not have the precision of our quotation marks. At most the presence of diples would show that a citation is present on specific lines, but would not show precisely where the citation began and ended. Furthermore, it seems extremely unlikely that Philo himself would have used such a method. See further my comments and examples in "Composite Quotations in Philo of Alexandria," in *Jewish, Graeco-Roman, and Early Christian Uses*, vol. 1 of *Composite Citations in Antiquity*, ed. Sean A. Adams and Seth M. Ehorn (London: Bloomsbury T&T Clark, 2016), 74–91, especially 75–76, and additional references therein, as well as my "21.4 Philo," 743, and "The Biblical Quotations in the Coptos Papyrus of Philo," 53 n. 18.

22 Katz frequently comments on the need for more accuracy in the placing of quotation marks; see, e.g., *Philo's Bible*, 32, on PCW's text of *Agr.* 12, where the quotation marks give an incorrect impression of Philo's citation of Deut 20:20. (On this see also my "Some Observations on the Biblical Text in Philo's *De agricultura*," 115.) Valentin Nikiprowetzky, "Philo's Citations of and Allusions to the Bible in the *De gigantibus* and *Quod Deus*," in David Winston and John Dillon, *Two Treatises of Philo of Alexandria*, BJS 25 (Chico: Scholars Press, 1983) 105, also notes that quotation marks are frequently misplaced; see further his comments at 110, 112, 113, 117, 118.

(1:333 n. m): "Nescio annon Autor *σφάλματος μνημονικοῦ* sit reus, locus enim citatus exstat Exod. xix. 20." However, in fact Exod 19:20 reads *ἐκάλεσεν κύριος Μωυσῆν*. Thus, Mangey concludes that Philo's ms. read *ἀνεκάλεσεν* there, stating on the preceding *ἀνακεκλήσεται* (1:333 n. l): "In Exod. ix. 20. [sic, for xix. 20.] quo alluditur à Nostro, hodie scribitur *ἐκάλεσεν*. Atqui Philonem *ἀνεκάλεσεν* in suo Codice legisse, ex hoc loco constat." In fact, Philo seems not to cite Exod 19:20 anywhere, and given Philo's explicit reference there is no doubt that here he is citing Lev 1:1.

§32: "*ἐφύτευσεν ὁ θεὸς παράδεισον ἐν Ἐδὲμ κατὰ ἀνατολάς, καὶ ἔθετο ἐκεῖ τὸν ἄνθρωπον ὃν ἔπλασεν*" (Gen 2:8). The Göttingen LXX prints *κύριος ὁ θεός* for *ὁ θέος*, but Philo has *ὁ θεός* alone also at *Leg*. 1.41, 43; *Conf*. 61; *QG* 1.6 (as it seems).[23] The absence of *κύριος* is attested widely,[24] and so we can suppose that Philo was simply following the biblical text as known to him, which had *ὁ θεός* alone.

§73: In the Göttingen LXX Gen 21:33 reads: *καὶ ἐφύτευσεν Ἀβραὰμ ἄρουραν ἐπὶ τῷ φρέατι τοῦ ὅρκου, καὶ ἐπεκαλέσατο ἐκεῖ τὸ ὄνομα κυρίου θεὸς αἰώνιος*. (This is a fairly literal translation of the MT: וַיִּטַּע אֶשֶׁל בִּבְאֵר שָׁבַע וַיִּקְרָא־שָׁם בְּשֵׁם יְהוָה אֵל עוֹלָם. However, the Hebrew omits the name of Abraham, and this omission is found in family n of the LXX manuscripts. See also later on the final phrase.) Now, Philo cites the entire verse at §73, where the manuscripts present: *εὐθέως τοίνυν ὁ σοφὸς Ἀβραὰμ λέγεται φυτεῦσαι ἄρουραν ἐπὶ τῷ φρέατι τοῦ ὅρκου καὶ ἐπικαλέσαι τὸ ὄνομα κυρίου θεοῦ αἰωνίου*. (The only textual variation is that FH read Ἀβραὰμ.) Now, first of all it is clear that Philo has here shifted the construction so that instead of having a direct quotation (introduced as, for example, *λέγει· κτλ*.), we find indirect discourse: "Then at once the wise man Abraham is said to plant a hide of land at the well of the oath, and to invoke the name of the Lord God eternal."[25] Although the name of Abraham is moved forward, I suppose that Philo found it in his text of the LXX, and indeed that the only changes that he made were that move and the shift of the verbs from finite forms to infinitives.

[23] At *QG* 1.6, which is known only from the Armenian, "God" seems to be outside the quotation; nevertheless it still seems reasonable to think that Philo read merely "God" rather than "Lord God." The Göttingen LXX cites *Leg*. 1.41; *Plant*. 32; *Conf*. 61.

[24] John William Wevers, *Notes on the Greek Text of Genesis*, SBLSCSS 35 (Atlanta: Scholars Press, 1993), 25–26: "A popular tradition omits *κύριος* in line with the surrounding verses which both lack a rendering for MT's יהוה." By the way, where the other witnesses have *κύριος*, the earliest witness (907) has a paleo-Hebraic sign for the Tetragrammaton.

[25] I have here slightly modified the translation by Colson and Whitaker. Indeed, the three translations into English, French, and German seem to me not quite to capture the *oratio obliqua* of Philo's presentation.

However, that leaves us with the discrepancy at the end of the verse. Where the LXX (as printed, at least) has τὸ ὄνομα κυρίου θεὸς αἰώνιος, Philo's manuscripts have τὸ ὄνομα κυρίου θεοῦ αἰωνίου.[26] Mangey, following his conviction that Philo used the LXX,[27] simply emended the reading of the manuscripts to agree with the LXX.[28] While, as a general rule, I approve of this practice, there are here some complications.

What has happened (it seems) in the Philo manuscripts is that θεοῦ αἰωνίου is an assimilation to the genitive case found in the preceding word, κυρίου. That Philo wrote the nominative is confirmed by the citation at §85 (to be discussed immediately below) and the reference to θεὸς αἰώνιος at §89; at each of these places the nominative is transmitted uniformly.

On the other hand, the Loeb edition (PLCL) follows the manuscripts in printing κυρίου θεοῦ αἰωνίου. This departure from the text of PCW is noted, but no reason is given. At §85 the Loeb accepts the text of PCW: κυρίου θεὸς αἰώνιος. But the English is virtually the same at both places; at §73 we find "the Name of the Lord as God eternal," while at §85 there is "the Name of the Lord, as God eternal." This is remarkably similar to the French version (PAPM), which follows Wendland's Greek at both places and reads: "le nom du Seigneur comme Dieu éternel," and then "le nom du Seigneur comme le Dieu éternel." The subtle differences of a comma in the English and a definite article in the French seem to be simply the whims of the translators. On the other hand, the German version (PCH), also following PCW, has: "den Namen des Herrn ewiger Gott" at both places. At least this reflects the nominative case of θεὸς αἰώνιος, although I would think that the meaning would be clearer if "ewiger Gott" were placed in quotation marks as a name.

Now, let us turn to the later citation at §85. Here Philo makes a more straightforward direct citation: τίς οὖν ὁ καρπὸς αὐτοῦ, αὐτὸς ὑφηγήσεται· "ἐπεκάλεσε" γὰρ "τὸ ὄνομα κυρίου θεὸς αἰώνιος."[29] At least, this is the text as

26 Observe that (as usual) the LXX presents some textual variations. Here they seem to be very minor, but it is worth noting that θεου αιωνιου finds support from Arab "Arm^{ap}". Such sparse evidence is almost certainly the result of coincidental agreement in error rather than of some textual stream preserved in only a few places.

27 Mangey 1:43 n. b: "LXX Interpretes quos ubique sequitur Philo."

28 Mangey 1:340 n. s: "Melius θεὸς αἰώνιος. Ita Textus sacer & Philo ipse infra p. 226 [= Mangey 1:342 = *Plant.* 85]."

29 Wendland carefully places the quotation marks so as to remove from the quotation itself the conjunction γάρ, which of course relates the quotation to the context. Colson and Whitaker correspondingly place their "for" before the quotation proper (although they add an extraneous "'tis said"). However, Pouilloux places "en effet" (which must render γάρ) inside the quotation marks, while Heinemann places "nannte ja" (rendering ἐπεκάλεσε γὰρ) before his quotation marks. Both these latter readings fail to place the quotation marks

printed by Wendland. However, we see from the apparatus that the manuscripts read κύριος ὁ θεὸς αἰώνιος. Curiously enough, Mangey did not reconcile the two citations (despite referring at the first to the second). Rather, in his long note to the second he says on κύριος: "Textus κυρίου. Sed sic videtur Noster notanter scribere." He follows this with some citations illustrating Philo's frequent distinction between κύριος and θεός, but I do not see the relevance to the variation between κύριος and κυρίου.

Now, it would seem that at §85 the reading θεὸς αἰώνιος is assured by the unanimity of the manuscripts here and also at §89, as well as the overwhelming evidence in the LXX tradition (all except Arab "Arm^{ap}"). Furthermore, it is virtually certain that the article ὁ before θεὸς in the Philo manuscripts is a mere slip. It is not present at §73, and within the LXX tradition it is found only in the reading ὁ θεὸς ὁ αἰώνιος, which is found in "t^{-370}" (= six minuscules).[30]

A final comment on this issue. On my theory (noted earlier) that Philo's biblical manuscripts had the Tetragrammaton, Philo would have seen in his scroll of the LXX of Gen 21:33: ἐπεκάλεσε τὸ ὄνομα יהוה θεὸς αἰώνιος, or perhaps a similar text with the Tetragrammaton written in paleo-Hebraic letters.[31] Philo would then have had to make a decision about whether to render the Tetragrammaton as κύριος or κυρίου. Presumably his choice of κυρίου (if that is what he wrote) reflects the reading tradition that he was familiar with.[32] And it is this text with the genitive that he then comments on.

However, noting that the manuscripts of Philo read κύριος at §85, we see that there is another possibility, namely, that Philo interpreted the Tetragrammaton as a nominative and wrote τὸ ὄνομα κύριος θεὸς αἰώνιος at both §73 and §85. The tradition of the LXX understood the Tetragrammaton as a genitive, and so the manuscripts of Philo were altered to that "standard" reading at §73, but Philo's original nominative survived at §85.[33] (This, of

---

with the precision that Wendland as well as Colson and Whitaker do. Note that Mangey does not use quotation marks at all in his Greek. But he does mark quotations by italicizing the corresponding words in the Latin translation. And at this text we find "enim" (rendering γάρ) italicized inappropriately.

30 By the way, using the online images I can at least confirm that PCW correctly reports the readings of the two Florence manuscripts, Laurentianus pluteus 10.20 (M) and Laurentianus pluteus 85.10 (F), at these places.

31 More precisely, given the writing conventions of his time, Philo would have seen something like: ΕΠΕΚΑΛΕΣΕΤΟΟΝΟΜΑיהוהΘΕΟCΑΙΩΝΙΟC.

32 Again, what Philo actually wrote would have been: ΕΠΕΚΑΛΕCΕΤΟΟΝΟΜΑΚΥ-ΡΙΟΥΘΕΟCΑΙΩΝΙΟC.

33 This would accordingly be an example of the correct reading's finally gaining the victory, as John Wordsworth and Henry Julian White phrase it; see *Novum Testamentum Domini Nostri Iesu Christi Latine* (Oxford: Clarendon Press, 1889), 1:727–28.

course, requires emending the manuscripts to read κύριος at the former place, rather than emending to read κυρίου at the latter place.) Now, it seems to me that in fact the nominative would give a plausible sense (at least in Philo's eyes) at §85: Abraham invoked the name "Lord God eternal." Here we have the two titles ("Lord" and "God") of the two chief powers of God. Or perhaps, with an eye to what Philo says at §89, we should consider the names to be "Lord" and "God eternal." Of course, the addition of "eternal" to a name of God is unusual in any case; this is the unique place in the Pentateuch, and elsewhere there are only a few examples in Isaiah and Daniel. Philo attempts to explain this unusual usage at §89.[34]

Let me note also that the final words of the MT, בְּשֵׁם יְהוָה אֵל עוֹלָם, while usually rendered "on the name of the Lord God eternal" or the like, could be interpreted as "on the name of the Lord, God eternal," or "on the name, Lord God eternal." That is, there are three possibilities: (1) שֵׁם could be in the construct state, governing each of יְהוָה and אֵל: "name of the Lord (and of) God." (2) שֵׁם could be in the construct state, governing יְהוָה, and אֵל could be in apposition to יֵשׁ: "name of the Lord, God." (3) שֵׁם could be in the absolute state, and both יְהוָה and אֵל could be in apposition to it: "name, Lord God." (In any case, אֵל עוֹלָם is a construct chain: "God of the age" = "God eternal.")

Now, I do not suppose that Philo would have been cognizant of such matters, but the translators of the LXX would have been, and would have made their translation choice according to their interpretation.[35] Since they chose to write θεὸς αἰώνιος, as seems more or less certain, they clearly took אֵל as being in apposition to שֵׁם, rather than being governed by it. It might then be natural (although not necessary, of course) also to take the Tetragrammaton as in apposition. But, if they merely transcribed the Tetragrammaton here, there would have been no grammatical indication of that decision, and it would have been up to readers to choose whether to interpret the Greek equivalent as being nominative or genitive. The main line of the LXX tradition clearly chose the latter. But Philo (or some earlier tradition) could well have chosen the former.

[34] Unfortunately his explanation is obscure. Certainly at first Philo focuses on the divine beneficence that is indicated by the name θεός. However, at the end Philo unexpectedly shifts to κύριος. So perhaps "eternal" is taken as applying to both names. But as a result of the obscurity Colson and Whitaker suggest emending the text by inserting a negation (PLCL 3:258–59 n. a). On this see the response by Pouilloux (PAPM 10:64 n. 1).

[35] We should keep in mind that the translators, of course, would have seen an unpointed Hebrew text.

For what it is worth, I note that at Soṭah 10a–10b Gen 21:33 is cited, and it seems to me that the discussion takes אֵל עוֹלָם as being the name of the Lord.

§90: "καὶ ἔσται κύριος ἐμοὶ εἰς θεόν" (Gen 28:21). The LXX tradition is divided:

μοι κύριος	A M pm (Göttingen LXX)
κύριος μοι	D 961 rell (= MT)
κύριος εμοι	911 Philo Chrysostom
κύριος	54
κύριος μου	569 458

Philo's reading is also found in 911, from the late third century; so, it seems likely that Philo is here a witness to an ancient stream of LXX tradition.

§110: PCW prints: οὗτος γὰρ "ῥάβδους ἐλέπισε λεπίσματα λευκὰ περισύρων τὸ χλωρόν" (Gen 30:37). But here again the quotation marks are placed incorrectly. The Göttingen LXX has καὶ ἐλέπισεν αὐτὰς Ἰακὼβ λεπίσματα λευκὰ περισύρων τὸ χλωρόν, and cites Philo as having ῥάβδους ἐλέπισε for ἐλέπισεν αὐτάς.[36] However, rather than seeing a textual variation here, we should simply edit: οὗτος γὰρ ῥάβδους ἐλέπισε "λεπίσματα λευκὰ περισύρων τὸ χλωρόν." Or, perhaps we could print: οὗτος γὰρ ῥάβδους "ἐλέπισε ... λεπίσματα λευκὰ περισύρων τὸ χλωρόν." Naturally, Philo did not have ellipsis points at his disposal either, but often seems to have written with such a device in mind.[37]

§140: "... καὶ ἔπιε τοῦ οἴνου ..." (Gen 9:21). As discussed elsewhere, Philo has here (and also at *Agr.* 1 and *QG* 2.68) omitted ἐκ before τοῦ οἴνου, which is found in all the LXX manuscripts, and which reflects the Hebrew מִן.[38] Katz appropriately states that "πίνειν ἐκ was awkward Greek to Philo who set it right with a light touch."[39]

§169: PCW prints: τὸν Ἰσαὰκ εἶδε παίζοντα μετὰ Ῥεβέκκας τῆς γυναικὸς αὐτοῦ (Gen 26:8). Here PCW neglects quotation marks that would be appropriate. (PCH marks a quotation, but not PLCL or PAPM.) The Göttingen LXX has: εἶδεν τὸν Ἰσαὰκ παίζοντα μετὰ Ῥεβέκκας τῆς γυναικὸς αὐτοῦ, with only

36 It seems inconsistent that the Göttingen LXX notes that a Philo ms. (H) has ἐξέλπισε, but not that a correction made by the learned second hand of that ms. ("H^2"; see PCW 1:xi–xii) agrees with 71* in having λεπτά for λευκά.

37 See again my "Continued Quotations in Philo of Alexandria," 78–81.

38 "Some Observations on the Biblical Text in Philo's *De agricultura*," 113–15. Let me correct an observation at p. 114 n. 13 there: the Göttingen LXX mistakenly says that ἐκ is omitted in the apparatus of *Agr.* 1 (not of *Plant.* 140), whereas in fact it is omitted in the text of *Agr.* 1.

39 *Philo's Bible*, 32.

some minor variations. Rather than ignoring the verbatim citation here or considering that Philo has transposed the biblical text, one should edit: τὸν Ἰσαὰκ εἶδε "παίζοντα μετὰ Ῥεβέκκας τῆς γυναικὸς αὐτοῦ."

2. *Philo on an Ambiguity in the Biblical Text*

§113: Philo explicitly notes that Lev 19:23 is ambiguous (ἡ δὲ λέξις ἐστὶν ἀμφίβολος), since it can be divided into two clauses in two different ways. Maren R. Niehoff comments: "Philo is the first extant Bible scholar to have discussed a problem of punctuation, thus sharing another important concern of Homeric scholarship."[40] However, "punctuation" is not quite the correct term, since commas would not have been written. Thus, Colson and Whitaker's "the former punctuation" for τὸ πρότερον σημαινόμενον §114 should rather be "the former meaning," as we find in Heinemann's "Nach der ersten Bedeutung," Pouilloux's "Dans la première acception," and Niehoff's own על פי הפירוש הראשון.[41] Nevertheless, Philo was able to see that a sentence could be read in the two different ways that we now mark with different placements of a comma. Another example of ambiguity is found at *Mut.* 106–10, where Philo gives two interpretations of "Midian," namely as either ἐκκρίσεως ("of sifting," the genitive of ἔκκρισις) or ἐκ κρίσεως ("of judgment"). What Philo writes is edited as ἡ γὰρ προσηγορία τῆς Μαδιὰμ μεταληφθεῖσα ἐκ κρίσεως ὀνομάζεται, but this already takes the term in the second sense. The ambiguity becomes clearer when we note that Philo would have written ΕΚΚΡΙϹΕΩϹ, whether intended as one word or as two words, and the same format would have occurred in his onomastical source.[42]

40 *Jewish Exegesis and Homeric Scholarship in Alexandria* (Cambridge: Cambridge University Press, 2011), 139. See also the discussion in David Dawson, *Allegorical Readers and Cultural Revision in Ancient Alexandria* (Berkeley: University of California Press, 1992), 102–3.

41 I.e., "according to the first interpretation," rather than "punctuation." This is found in Maren R. Niehoff, ed., *Philo of Alexandria Writings*, vol. 4.2 (Jerusalem: The Bialik Institute and The Israel Academy of Sciences and Humanities, 2015), 191.

42 Lester L. Grabbe, *Etymology in Early Jewish Interpretation: The Hebrew Names in Philo*, BJS 115 (Atlanta: Scholars Press, 1988), 180. Although Grabbe quotes Philo's discussion at *Mut.* 106 and 110, he gives only ἐκ κρίσεως as Philo's meaning of the name "Midian." For another example of an ambiguity in Philo's onomastical source see my "21.4 Philo," 744.

3. *The Change of λόγος to νόμος*

At §8 and §10 editors have used Eusebius to emend Philo by writing λόγος and λόγου with Eusebius instead of νόμος and νόμου, which are read by all the Philo manuscripts. There is a similar change at *Deus* 57 where "UFL²" read νόμῳ for the λόγῳ of the other manuscripts.[43] Barthélemy attributes all three changes to the reviser of Philo's text who created the "aberrant text," even though at *Plant.* 8 and 10 this aberrant text has contaminated all the manuscripts. I note that already Mangey says of νόμος at *Plant.* 8: "Euseb. λόγος. & sic omnino rectius. Passim enim Philo rerum tum creationem tum conservationem λόγῳ tribuit." And at *Plant.* 10 he notes on νόμου: "Scribe iterum cum Eusebio λόγου, cui contextus certè fidem facit." At *Deus* 57 Mangey prints λόγῳ, with no report of manuscript variation, but he notes: "Λόγον esse rerum conditorem passim docet Philo." Note also *Plant.* 18–20, where Eusebius seems to preserve Philo's original words at several places where some or even all of the Philonic manuscripts have been corrupted.[44]

4. *Some Further Conjectures*

As I have discussed in an earlier article, the scholar Jeremiah Markland made many conjectures to the text of Philo, which are found as marginalia in his personal copies of the editions of Turnebus and Mangey, now preserved in the British Library.[45] These are occasionally reported in the apparatus of PCW. However, in looking over the pages of Markland's copy of Mangey's edition, I have noted that several of Markland's conjectures have found their way into the edition and even into the text of Cohn and Wendland, but without any attribution to Markland. At other places Markland's conjectures are confirmed by manuscripts cited in PCW (but not by Mangey). These and a few others of interest are:

§10: φωνῆς Mangey PCW : μούσης codd. Pouilloux, μουσικῆς Eusebius Colson.

§15: πρὸς τῷ codd. : πρὸ τοῦ Markland Wendland.
§16: ἀπειργάζετο R (Markland) : ἀνειργάζετο codd., εἰργάζετο E.
§29: ἑκάστην PCW Pouilloux : εἰς ἑκάστην Heinemann Colson.

[43] See Barthélemy, "Hoshaya Rabba," 56, on this, as well as my discussion in "The Text of Philo's *Legum Allegoriae*," *SPhiloA* 12 (2000): 20–21. (But my article incorrectly has "UFL2.").

[44] See Wendland, "Bemerkungen," 497.

[45] "Jeremiah Markland's Contribution to the Textual Criticism of Philo," *SPhiloA* 16 (2004): 50–60.

§41–42: This is a very difficult place. We have the following choices (at least): ὃ ἐπὶ λογικῶν μόνων τῶν ἀρετῶν ἐστιν. αἱ οὖν ἀσκήσεις τε καὶ χρήσεις ἐξαίρετον γέρας κτλ. codd. and PCW (Pouilloux om. οὖν per errorem) : ὅ ἐστιν, ἐπὶ τῶν λογικῶν μόνον ἀρετῶν. αἱ οὖν κτλ. Mangey (is μόνον an error for μόνων?): ὃ ἐπὶ λογικῶν μόνων [τῶν ἀρετῶν] ἔστιν <ἀκούειν>. αἱ οὖν κτλ. Cohn : ὃ ἐπὶ λογικῶν μόνων τῶν ἀρετῶν ἐστιν. αἱ γοῦν ἀρετῆς δεκτικαὶ φύσεις ἐξαίρετον γέρας κτλ. Wendland : ὅ ἐστιν, λογικῶν μόνον τῶν ἀρετῶν αἱ ἀσκήσεις τε καὶ χρήσεις. ἐξαίρετον γέρας κτλ. Colson (is μόνον an error for μόνων?).[46]

Markland comments on ὃ ... ἐστιν: "Non intelligo hoc; neque ea qua sequuntur, αἱ οὖν ἀσκήσεις τε καὶ χρήσεις." He continues with various suggestions. Wendland comments that the clause ὃ ... ἐστιν "lässt sich vielleicht ohne Aenderung halten, wenn man den Relativsatz als Erklärung des ἐκεῖ fasst."[47]

§43: τὰς ... ἀτιθάσους κἀξηγριωμένας κῆρας : Mangey (1:336 n. c) suggested θῆρας for κῆρας: "De bestiarum enim inductione in arcam agitur. Solenne enim Philoni affectus & vitia sub bestiarum ferarum specie exhibere." In the margin Markland adds: "Bene si legatur τοὺς – κἀξηγριωμένους."

§45: τιθέναι : τεθῆναι Markland Wendland.

§46: τοῦ θεοῦ κράτος αὐτοῦ καὶ τὰς ἵλεως καὶ ἡμέρους δυνάμεις codd. : τοῦ θεοῦ κράτος καὶ τὰς ἵλεως αὐτοῦ καὶ ἡμέρους δυνάμεις Markland : τοῦ θεοῦ κράτος καὶ τὰς ἵλεως καὶ ἡμέρους αὐτοῦ δυνάμεις Cohn.

§54: κληροδοτεῖν μὲν : κληροδοτεῖν μὲν <γὰρ> Markland Wendland.

§57: Mangey printed the reading of the mss., ἐκλογισταὶ ἀπὸ. Wendland emended this to ἐκλογισταὶ <τὰς> ἀπὸ, as found in the French edition.[48] But Cohn then suggested ἐκλογεῖς τὰς ἀπὸ (PCW 2:xxxiv), which Wendland approved,[49] and was adopted in the German and the Loeb. Indeed, the phrase ἐκλογεὺς (τῶν) φόρων is similarly found at *Spec.* 2.93; 3.159; *Legat.* 199. Philo's original text suffered two corruptions: the itacistic rendering of –EIC as –IC, and the change from TAC to TAI.

§58: ὁ ὀξυωπέστατα Markland Wendland : ὃς ὀξυωπέστατα MGUF : ὡς ὀξυωπέστατα H.

§62: τῇ <τοῦ> θεοφιλοῦς Wendland : τοῦ θεοφιλοῦς Markland : τῇ θεοφιλοῦς codd.

[46] See further Colson's extended note (PLCL 3:495).

[47] "Bemerkungen," 498.

[48] And also in *The Philo Index*. This passage also found its way into LSJ, where the word as found there is said to "= ἐκλογεύς."

[49] "Bemerkungen," 499.

§65–66: τοῦ θεοῦ. ὃ GUF Wendland : τοῦ θεοῦ ὁ MH : τῆς θεᾶς Mangey[50] : τοῦ θεοῦ. ὃ δὲ Markland : τοῦ θεοῦ. ὅπερ ὁ Cohn : τοῦθ' ὁ Heinemann Colson : τοῦ θεοῦ. Τοῦθ' ὁ Pouilloux.

Heinemann brings order to this passage by punctuating after *καταλαζονεύεσθαι*, and by seeing that τοῦ θεοῦ (which would have been written in earlier manuscripts as ΤΟΥΘ̅Υ̅), is a corruption from τοῦθ' (or ΤΟΥΘ'). Pouilloux has misunderstood what is in PCH and PLCL, and has conflated the reading τοῦ θεοῦ with the conjecture τοῦθ', rather than substituting the latter for the former.

§67: νῦν codd. : οὖν Markland Cohn.

§71: κτήματα τῶν Markland Wendland : κτημάτων MF : κτήματα GUH.

§86: καὶ : κἀν (PCW 2:150 l. 16) Markland Wendland. Note that there are several textual problems in the subsequent phrase, which is printed by Wendland as: ἥρμοττε γὰρ τὴν δύναμιν, καθ' ἣν ὁ ποιῶν εἰς γένεσιν ἄγων ἐτίθετο καὶ διεκοσμεῖτο, διὰ ταύτης καὶ [κατα]κληθῆναι. PCW has three textual notes. First, for the central phrase with the subject ὁ ποιῶν, Wendland conjectures ὁ ποιῶν <τὰ πάντα> εἰς γένεσιν ἄγων ἐτίθει τε καὶ διεκόσμει. And in his discussion he refers to several parallels that make the direct object explict.[51] The addition of τὰ πάντα seems plausible to me, but I would suggest that τὸ πᾶν, as found at *Abr.* 121, would be even more plausible, since its omission after ὁ ποιῶν seems easier (similar to a haplography). Further, the middle of διακοσμέω seems not to be used by Philo (although it goes back to Homer [see LSJ]).[52] Based on the parallels noted earlier, Wendland states that ἐτίθει τε καὶ διεκόσμει is "sicher … herzustellen."[53] Presumably the corruption from Wendland's conjectured original would have occurred when ἐτίθει τε was read as ἐτίθετο, and then this middle form occasioned the shift to διεκοσμεῖτο. For what it is worth, neither Mangey nor Markland hesitated over the construction of the mss., and Wendland's conjecture met with no approval in the Greek printed in PLCL and PAPM. On the other hand, PCH translates the relevant phrase: "der Schöpfer das All schuf, einsetzte und ordnete." The use of "das All" would correspond to Wendland's τὰ πάντα, and suggests that Heinemann was following Wendland's conjectures. On the

50 Mangey (1:339 n. m): "Quidni τῆς θεᾶς? scil. spectaculum." Presumably θέας was intended.

51 "Bemerkungen," 500: *Conf.* 137; *Migr.* 182; *Fug.* 97, as well as *Mut.* 29; *Abr.* 121; *Mos.* 2.99. One might also consider the parallels at *Deus* 56 (τὰ ἄλλα ἀγαγὼν εἰς γένεσιν) and *Migr.* 183 (τὰ μὴ ὄντα εἰς γένεσιν ἄγουσα), *QE* 2.64 (καθ' ἣν ἐποίει τὰ ὅλα θεός), *QE* 2.68.3 (καθ' ἣν ἔθηκε τὰ πάντα καὶ διεκόσμησεν ὁ τεχνίτης).

52 The passive occurs at, e.g., *Opif.* 47 and *Spec.* 2.151, and the active at, e.g., *Opif.* 53 and *QE* 2.68.3.

53 "Bemerkungen," 501.

other hand, Colson and Whitaker have "bringing the world into being," and Pouilloux has "en amenant le monde à l'être," although their Greek has nothing corresponding to "the world" or "le monde." So perhaps Heinemann has similarly just supplied the understood direct object, although "das All" is certainly closer to τὰ πάντα than are the phrases in English and French.

Second, Wendland follows H in printing ταύτης, noting that MGUF read τοῦτο. Mangey also printed ταύτης (as in the *editio princeps*), but in a note (1:342 n. g) states: "MSS. Vat. & Med. τοῦτο, & sic rectius." Despite looking at the accompanying Latin translation, I do not see what sense διὰ τοῦτο would make. Markland, though, conjectured τούτου, presumably taking the pronoun as referring to τὸ ὄνομα. But the reading ταύτης more plausibly, I believe, refers to ἡ πρόσρησις, which of course is understood in the ἡ μέν ... ἡ δέ construction; the noun itself occurs in the plural in the previous phrase. See further below on the translation.

Third, the verb καταχαλέω does not occur elsewhere in Philo, and both Cohn and Wendland made conjectures to remove it. Wendland records his own conjecture, ἐπικληθῆναι, but what Wendland prints is the conjecture of Cohn, namely to seclude the prefix and read simply κληθῆναι.[54] From a palaeographical perspective I find Cohn's emendation simpler and more plausible: the reading of the manuscripts arose as a kind of dittography of και as the similar κατα. Moreover, Philo seems not to use ἐπικαλέω within the context of "calling" the chief powers of God by their names, while καλέω is thus used (*Mut.* 29; *Abr.* 124; *QE* 2.68.3). However, in his discussion Wendland retracted both conjectures, saying: "An κατακληθῆναι 'anrufen' haben L. Cohn und ich wohl mit Unrecht Anstoss genommen." He then refers, not to uses of κατακαλέω, but to Philo's use of κατάκλησις at *Migr.* 56; *Mos.* 2.132; *Spec.* 4.40.[55] In any case, such uses seem to indicate that Philo would have found κατακαλέω appropriate in this context, and so there is no reason to emend the reading of the manuscripts.

A further conjecture was made by Markland: καταδηλουθῆναι. However, καταδηλόω seems not to be attested until after Philo, and in any case a form or compound of καλέω seems appropriate in this context.

[54] Nevertheless one finds κατακαλέω cited from this passage in Peder Borgen, Kåre Fuglseth, and Roald Skarsten, *The Philo Index* (Grand Rapids: Eerdmans; Leiden: Brill, 2000), while καλέω is not cited from this passage. Evidently Wendland's brackets around κατα were simply ignored. Of course, if one agrees with Wendland's subsequent view (discussed immediately below) that κατακληθῆναι should be retained, then the index has included the correct word here.

[55] The uses at *Virt.* 77 and *Praem.* 84 seem a little different.

Let me also make a comment on the translation of this sentence.[56] Colson and Whitaker's translation is: "For it was fitting that the Creator should be spoken of by a title coming to Him through that power in virtue of which, when bringing the world into being, he set and ordered it." However, my understanding of the Greek here (and of Philo's position generally) is that it is the power, not the Creator, that is given the title (i.e., "God"). I would thus render (with some adjustments to the stated English): "For it was fitting that the power, in virtue of which the Creator, when bringing the world into being, set and ordered it, also be called (or perhaps better, invoked) through that" (title, scil. προσρήσεως, i.e., the title of θεός). The same problem seems to affect the German and French translations. Note that κατά (as found in καθ' ἣν here) is frequently used in these contexts for expressing the relation between the Creator and his powers. Earlier in *Plant.* 86 we find καθ' ἣν ἄρχει and καθ' ἣν εὐεργετεῖ, where the subject of the verbs is τὸ ὄν. Exactly the same construction is found at, among other places, *QE* 2.64 and 2.68.3.[57]

On the other hand, Wendland states that the sense of this sentence is: "Es passt sich, dass durch die Schöpfungsgeschichte hindurch die θεὸς genannte δύναμις angerufen werde." He goes on to say explicitly that ταύτης refers to the preceding κοσμοποιίᾳ.[58]

§91: ὅθεν ὄντως MGHUF (ὄντων L) Pouilloux : ὅθεν τῶν ὄντως Mangey R : ὁ τῶν ὄντως Markland : τῶν ὄντως Colson. Colson incorrectly ascribes his conjecture to Mangey, apparently misinterpreting PCW's apparatus. Moreover, Mangey has a comma after ἀνελλιπῶς and a period after εὐδαιμονοῦσι. Markland changes the comma into a semicolon, which is what Wendland prints (without comment). Colson follows Mangey in having a comma after ἀνελλιπῶς, but then Colson puts a question mark after εὐδαιμονοῦσι, incorrectly attributing that as well to Mangey. Pouilloux follows the text of PCW (although he accepts Colson's characterization of Mangey's conjecture).

56 Colson and Whitaker say that this contains "an irregular construction." At PLCL 3:256 n. a they state: "τὴν δύναμιν ... διὰ ταύτης: an irregular construction for καθ' ἣν δύναμιν ... διὰ ταύτης." At first, I interpreted this as meaning that the regular construction would begin: ἥρμοττε γὰρ καθ' ἣν δύναμιν, καθ' ἣν ὁ ποιῶν κτλ. But this seems exceedingly awkward, and would hardly fit their translation. I now believe that they meant the regular construction to begin: ἥρμοττε γὰρ καθ' ἣν δύναμιν ὁ ποιῶν κτλ. But I do not understand how their translation would fit this Greek either.

57 See my note on the latter passage at "Philo of Alexandria, *Quaestiones in Exodum* 2.62–68: Critical Edition," *SPhiloA* 24 (2012): 60.

58 The German seems to me simply to ignore διὰ ταύτης. The French seems to take ταύτης as referring to δύναμιν, as it translates at the end "ce fut par elle aussi qu'il fût nommé." It is unclear to me what the grammatical status of τὴν δύναμιν would then be, and indeed the French seems to leave "la puissance" hanging.

§114: ταῦτα : ταύτῃ Markland Wendland

§118: ἀγαθὸν Turnebus : ἀπάτῃ codd., ἀγαθὸν φιλοσοφία Wendland, ἄκος ἀπάτης Colson-Whitaker. Markland conjectures: τὸ μέγιστον ψυχῆς κακὸν ἀπάτῃ ἀντίκειται.

§127: λόγος codd. : λόγος ὅς Markland Colson-Whitaker

§129: δὲ codd. N : δὴ Markland Wendland (in text)

§132: καὶ θαυμαστὸν ἡγεῖσθαι codd. : καὶ delendum Markland Wendland

§148: τὸν εὑρετήν MF (Markland) : τὴν ἀρετήν GUH Mangey

§148: Markland corrected Mangey's text to use initial capitals with Μαινόλην and Μαινάδας.[59] PCW also has small letters. It seems that the same correction should be made for Βάκχας.[60] All three words are proper names.

§160: χαίνοντες MGF (Markland) : χαίροντες UH.

§162: The construction σώματα καὶ ψυχὰς καθηράμενοι, τὰ μὲν λουτροῖς, τὰ δὲ νόμων καὶ παιδείας ὀρθῆς ῥεύμασι, is in fact ungrammatical. The first τά refers correctly to σώματα, but the second τά refers (or *should* refer) to ψυχάς.[61] Markland adjusts the grammar by proposing τὰς δὲ νόμων κτλ. Very close parallels are found at *Mos.* 1.301: τά τε σώματα καὶ τὰς ψυχὰς ἐπιδεδώκασι, τὰ μὲν ἡδοναῖς, τὰς δὲ τῷ παρανομεῖν καὶ ἀνοσιουργεῖν, and *Spec.* 2.214: σώματα καὶ ψυχὰς ἀναχέουσαι, τὰ μὲν τῷ ἁβροδιαίτῳ, τὰς δὲ τῷ φιλοσοφεῖν.[62] This change of τά to τάς seems to me to be one of the most convincing conjectures. Note further that Mangey (1:729) proposed to write σώματά τε, which Markland glossed with "Recte." This is plausible, but *Spec.* 2.214 counts against it.

§166: οὐδὲν MGUF : οὐδ' ἐν H : οὐδ' ἂν Markland Cohn (in PCW text)

[59] Actually, Mangey follows the *editio princeps* in reading μαινομένην instead of μαινόλην, which he cites from "MS. Vat."; see his comment at 1:351 n. i. Markland evidently found the latter reading preferable, but thought that it should be capitalized.

[60] This is spelled with a capital in LSJ.

[61] That is, this is not a construction where τὰ μέν ... τὰ δέ is used to mean, "on the one hand ... on the other hand," as in LSJ, s.v. ὁ, ἡ, τό, A.VIII.4; see Herbert Weir Smyth, *Greek Grammar* (rev. Gordon M. Messing (Cambridge: Harvard University Press, 1956), §1111.

[62] But both of these places have suffered textual corruption. At the first, instead of τὰ and τὰς GHP Barb. have τὰς and τὰ, while F has τὰς and τὰς, and K has τὰ and τὰ. F and K thus are both ungrammatical in different ways, but GHP Barb. simply transpose the references. At the second, the single manuscript (M) reads σῶμα, for which Cohn edited σώματα. The two earlier editors of this passage from M, Angelo Mai (ed., *Philonis Iudaei De cophini festo et de colendis parentibus cum brevi scripto de Iona* [Milan: Regiis Typis, 1818], 2) and Constantine Tischendorf, ed., *Philonea, inedita altera, altera nunc demum recte ex vetere scriptura eruta* [Leipzig: Giesecke and Devrient, 1868], 68) both read τὰς μὲν. However, in his note Cohn states that M appears to have τοῖς μὲν, but then he edits τὰ μὲν. Tischendorf does not remark upon the syntactical difficulty in his edited text (where τὰς must refer to σῶμα), but Mai notes that one might prefer to read τὸ μὲν (thus referring correctly to M's σῶμα) for τὰς μὲν. Surely Cohn's text is the best choice, as is his ἀναχέουσαι, which is Wendland's conjecture for M's ἀνασχοῦσαι.

§170: ἐμπρεπὲς Wendland : εὐπρεπὲς Clem., ἐμπρέπει codd. Mangey cites the passage from Clement in a note, and Markland there corrects εὐπρεπὲς to ἐμπ-. But he does not comment on the word in Philo's text.

§172: οἶδεν MGUF (Markland) : εἶδεν H (Mangey text)

§176: παρακατάθοιτο, <τῷ δὲ ἀστείῳ παρακατατίθεται> Wendland : παρακατάθοιτο, <τῷ δὲ ἀστείῳ εὐλόγως> Markland, παρακατάθοιτο, <τῷ δὲ σοφῷ παρακατατίθενται> von Arnim. Markland says "Argumentum claudicat," and refers to the final lines of *De plantatione*. In fact, as von Arnim notes,[63] Seneca (*Epistola* 83) cites the complete form of this argument from Zeno (SVF 229): "ebrio secretum sermonem nemo committit, viro autem bono committit; ergo vir bonus ebrius non erit." And from that von Arnim made his restoration. But I do not understand why von Arnim alters the occurrences of the verb and the adjective, which are both the same in Seneca. Thus, Wendland's form appears more justified. Moreover, von Arnim states of the text of Philo as found in the manuscripts: "Der Unsinn ist wohl nicht auf Textverderbnis, sondern auf Flüchtigkeit des Excerptors zurückzuführen."[64] But this seems unlikely to me. However negligent Philo (who was presumably the excerptor involved) might have been, he would have had the sense of the passage clearly in mind, while the two occurrences of very similar verb forms could have easily caused a scribe to skip a few words.

It is puzzling to me that Wendland would have failed to give Markland credit for so many of these conjectures. In working with the apparatus of PCW I have found the work of Cohn and Wendland to be meticulous, with very rare lapses. Of course, we might have here the phenomenon of great minds thinking alike, where Cohn or Wendland independently thought of a conjecture that had already occurred to Markland. But Cohn and Wendland were certainly aware that Markland had made conjectures, and the number of such places tempts me to think that perhaps there was some confusion in the notes of Cohn and Wendland, so that conjectures that they had found in Markland's copy of Mangey were somehow entered into their apparatus under their own names. In any case, these provide yet further examples of Markland's contributions to the text of Philo.

Claremont, CA

[63] Hans von Arnim, *Quellenstudien zu Philo von Alexandria* (Berlin: Weidmann, 1888), 135–36.

[64] Ibid., 135.

Additional Note

The Text of *De plantatione* in the Editio Maior of Cohn–Wendland

It is generally agreed that Philonic scholarship is fortunate in having a very good critical edition of his writings in Greek, prepared by Leopold Cohn and Paul Wendland and published in six volumes from 1896 to 1915, a period when German classical scholarship was at its zenith. It is well known that scholars in editing texts at this time made extensive use of emendations and conjectures in drawing up their texts—to a much greater degree than is the practice now when editors are more inclined to preserve the transmitted text whenever possible. Students of Philo's works are perhaps not always aware of the extent to which Cohn and especially the more radical Wendland modified the text transmitted in manuscripts (and in some cases papyri). The text of *De plantatione* in volume 2 of their text was prepared primarly by Wendland, but he received assistance from his co-editor Cohn, as is fully recognized on p. xxxi of the prolegomena to the volume.

In the following table I have added up the number of all the emendations that are included in Wendland's text, whether proposed by himself or other editors, and also of all the conjectures that he records in his apparatus criticus. This list also includes the ancient authors Clement and Eusebius, who cite Philo more or less verbatim (emendation in these cases means that the reading is included in the text, conjecture that it is not). In addition, I have added all the number of emendations proposed by Colson in his Loeb Classical Library text and also the number of textual problems discussed by translators of the treatise after Wendland's text was published. The conjectures noted for Markland are as listed by James Royse in the article above. In order to gauge the frequency of these modifications the text it is worth bearing in mind that the length of the treatise is 887 lines of text comprising 8900 words.

Editor	Emendations	Conjectures
Clement of Alexandria	4	0
Eusebius	13	17
Turnebus 1552	26	8
Mangey 1742	32	43
Markland		26
Wendland 1897	74	73
Cohn 1897	10	16
Other Critics Cited in PCW		
Ed. Tauchnitz	1	3
Von Arnim	2	3
Wilamovitz	1	
Osann	1	
Total	164	189

For the contribution of translators we count only those passages where they deviate from the text as established in PCW.

Heinemann German translation 1923	8 emendations
Colson English translation 1930	27 emendations
	44 passages discussed in notes
Pouilloux French translation 1963	7 passages discussed in notes
Radice Italian translation 1988	no passages discussed in notes
Coria Spanish translation 2010	7 passages discussed in notes
TOTAL	93 emendations and discussions

We thus have a total of 191 emendations, 188 conjectures, and 66 passages discussed, which amounts to a textual problem on average about every two and a half lines. It would in fact be a most worthwhile exercise to prepare a new edition of this text, but unfortunately this is not likely to happen in the foreseeable future. But at least it will be salutary for scholars to take into account the highly modified state of the text as it is available to us.

David T. Runia

The Studia Philonica Annual 29 (2017): 159–84

THE SIGNIFICANCE OF READING PHILONIC PARALLELS: EXAMPLES FROM THE *DE PLANTATIONE**

SAMI YLI-KARJANMAA

Introduction

In this article I discuss the question of how the exercise of reading together several Philonic passages can change our understanding of what the Alexandrian exegete wants to say. I take two examples from the *De plantatione*: the description of the creatures belonging to the cosmic regions at §§ 11–14, where my focus is on those of the air in §14, and the rich mixture of Philo's anthropological, ethical, and soteriological views that we find in §§ 17–25. For the former, the most important parallels are *Gig*. 6–18 and *Somn*. 1.133–141, but parts of *Conf.* 174–177 and *QG* 4.188 also clearly belong to the same series of more or less overlapping passages. For the latter, I mainly discuss *Plant*. 44; *Leg*. 1.31–38, 61; *Det*. 83–86 and *Her*. 54–64.[1]

My point of departure is that when Philo treats the same subject matter using similar vocabulary, he is giving expression to the same underlying set of ideas in each case, even though the subset of ideas explicitly expressed

* This essay is a revised version of the paper I delivered at the Society of Biblical Literature Annual Meeting in Atlanta in November 2015.

[1] These parallelisms have, to somewhat varying degrees, long been recognized. For the former case, see, e.g., Azariah ben Moses de' Rossi, *The Light of the Eyes: Azariah De' Rossi: Translated from the Hebrew with an Introduction and Annotations by Joanna Weinberg*, Yale Judaica Series 31 (New Haven: Yale University Press, 2001), 154–56; Thomas H. Billings, *The Platonism of Philo Judaeus* (Chicago: The University of Chicago Press, 1919), 28 n. 4; David T. Runia, *Philo of Alexandria and the* Timaeus *of Plato*, Philosophia Antiqua 44 (Leiden: Brill, 1986), 228–29; Anita Méasson, *Du Char Ailé de Zeus à l'Arche d'Alliance: Images et Mythes Platoniciens Chez Philon d'Alexandrie* (Paris: Études Augustiniennes, 1986), 281–93; and Wilfried Eisele, *Ein unerschütterliches Reich: Die mittelplatonische Umformung des Parusiegedankens im Hebräerbrief*, BZNW 116 (Berlin: de Gruyter, 2003), 196–227. For the latter (but not including all the parallels I discuss), see, e.g., Thomas H. Tobin, *The Creation of Man: Philo and the History of Interpretation* (Washington, DC: Catholic Biblical Association of America, 1983), esp. 87–93; Runia, *Philo and the* Timaeus, esp. 324–29 and Gregory E. Sterling, "'Wisdom among the Perfect:' Creation Traditions in Alexandrian Judaism and Corinthian Christianity," *NT* 37 (1995) 355–84, esp. 365, 375–76.

varies. Reading such passages together results in a better understanding of his thinking and his message.

The Souls of the Air

Inspired by Plato's account in the *Timaeus* (39e–40a) and possibly adapting some of its Platonist interpretations, Philo in *Plant.* 11–13 presents a division of the "plants" of the universe.[2] He begins with the distinction based on the capability of locomotion (§11). Those that possess that power he divides into the creatures of land, water, air, fire, and heaven (§12). After some remarks on these last, i.e., stars and planets, he states that the immobile kind is specifically called "plants." In *Plant.* 14 he then returns to two of the five regions, the earth and the air.[3] He wants to specify that each actually sustains two kinds of creatures.[4] As we will see, the human souls belong to both regions, to the air as discarnate (§14), to the earth as incarnate (§§17–25). The two "winged" kinds of beings in the air include two species: those that are sense-perceptible (the birds) and those that are not. The latter are further subdivided into those that enter bodies (the human souls, my main focus) and those that do not (the angels).

In what follows I first quote the parallel texts in *De plantatione*, *De somniis.*, and *De gigantibus* and then discuss the connections between these and certain other texts. I devote particular attention to features that I see as evidence that the Pythagorean–Platonic tenet of *reincarnation* is in Philo's mind not only in *Somn.* 1.138–139—which is his *locus classicus* on the subject—but also in the other texts.[5] Here, the links between the parallels and reading them together become an acute question.

The text in *De plantatione* goes:

> In the air He made the winged creatures perceived by senses, and other powers besides which are wholly beyond apprehension by sense. This is the host of the bodiless souls. Their array is made of companies that differ in kind. We are told

[2] φυτόν can also mean "creature" more generally.

[3] Philo's earlier description of the locations of earth, water, air, fire, and ether in relation to each other in *Plant.* 3 favors understanding these as cosmic regions rather than as elements. In *Gig.* 7 he calls the five (the fifth now being heaven) "primary elementary divisions (πρώτων καὶ στοιχειωδῶν μερῶν)," in *Somn.* 1.135 simply "parts of the universe (τὰ τοῦ κόσμου μέρη)."

[4] In PCW, §14 begins only after this statement.

[5] See Sami Yli-Karjanmaa, *Reincarnation in Philo of Alexandria*, SPhiloM 7 (Atlanta: Society of Biblical Literature, 2015). For the *De somniis.* passage and the history of its interpretation, see esp. 1, 9–13, 129–50.

> that some enter into mortal bodies, and quit them again at certain periods, while others, endowed with a diviner constitution, have no regard for any earthly quarter but exist on high nigh to the ethereal region itself. These are the purest souls of all whom the Greek philosophers call "heroes," but whom Moses, employing a well-chosen name, entitles "angels." (*Plant.* 14)[6]

In *De somniis*, in one of the interpretations he gives for the ascending and descending angels in Jacob's dream of the heavenly ladder (Gen 28:12), Philo writes,

> Of these souls [of the air] some, those that are closest to the earth and lovers of the body, are descending to be fast bound in mortal bodies, while others are ascending, having again been separated (from the body) according to the numbers and periods determined by nature. Of these last some, longing for the familiar and accustomed ways of mortal life, hurry back again, while others, pronouncing that life great folly, call the body a prison and a tomb but escaping from it as though from a dungeon or a grave are lifted up on light wings to the ether and range the heights for ever. Others there are of perfect purity and excellence ... that have never felt any craving after the things of earth ... These are called "daemons" by the other philosophers, but the sacred record is wont to call them "angels," employing an apter title. (*Somn.* 1.138–141)

I have argued elsewhere that this passage is not an isolated case but only the clearest manifestation of the fact that Philo endorsed the doctrine of reincarnation.[7] I have not found any serious attempt in scholarly literature to see *Somn.* 1.138–139 as something else than a description of reincarnation. Indeed, ever since Azariah de' Rossi's *The Light of the Eyes* (published in 1573–1575), it is this passage that has been the basis for seeing Philo as a proponent of the tenet.[8]

A third text probably also ultimately derived from, or influenced by, a common source is found in *De gigantibus*, where Philo is engaged in explaining the "angels" mentioned in the version of Gen 6:2 he had at

[6] The translations of both Philonic and other texts are those in the Loeb Classical Library (with occasional small changes), unless otherwise indicated; for *Gig.* I have used David Winston, *Philo of Alexandria: The Contemplative Life, The Giants, and Selections: Translation and Introduction* (London: SPCK, 1981). The text in *Plant.* 14 goes on to discuss the tasks of angels, and Philo's description here and those in *Gig.* 12, 16 and *Somn.* 1.141 are ultimately based on Plato, *Symp.* 202e.

[7] Yli-Karjanmaa, *Reincarnation in Philo.* My result was based on analyzing all available indirect and direct evidence bearing on the matter.

[8] See Rossi, *The Light,* 113, 156. Philo's attitude towards reincarnation has divided scholars in the twentieth and twenty-first centuries without ever having been the main subject of any study before mine. Debate between researchers has been almost non-existent. Earlier, during the seventeenth to nineteenth centuries there was a virtual consensus that Philo had appropriated the doctrine. See *Reincarnation in Philo,* 9–29.

hand.[9] He states (§6): "It is Moses' custom to give the name of 'angels' to those whom other philosophers call 'daemons,' souls that fly and hover in the air." A little later he says,

> Now some of the souls have descended into bodies, but others have never deigned to associate with any of the parts of earth ...[10] The former, however, descending into the body as though into a stream have sometimes been caught up in the violent rush of its raging waters and swallowed up, at other times, able to withstand the rapids, they have initially emerged at the surface and then soared back up to the place whence they had set out. These, then, are the souls of the genuine philosophers, who from first to last practice dying to the life in the body in order to obtain the portion of incorporeal and immortal life in the presence of the Uncreated and Immortal. But the souls that have been plunged into the surf below are the souls of the others who have had no regard for wisdom. They have surrendered themselves to unstable and chance concerns, none of which relate to our noblest part, the soul or mind, but all are related to that corpse which was our birth-fellow, the body. (*Gig.* 12–15)[11]

We can see that in addition to similarities, the accounts have many differences, for example, in *De gigantibus* two concepts that are in their original contexts linked with reincarnation, the image of the body as river and the practising of death, absent in the others, are added.[12]

We next turn to examining individual elements in *Plant.* 14. It is clearly the sparsest of these parallels. This can also be expressed by saying that—if it is accepted that each of the texts reflects the same scheme of the souls of the air—the *De plantatione* passage is the one for whose understanding the potential benefit of reading parallels is the greatest. The notion of there being *souls in the air* may in itself be regarded as a reincarnational feature. David Runia has commented in the context of *Somn.* 1.137 that seeing the

[9] The LXX as we have it speaks of the "sons" of God taking wives of the daughters of humans.

[10] What is omitted here is the description of the tasks of the angels as God's "ministers and helpers."

[11] For observations of Philo's exegetical technique in *Gig.De gigantibus*, see David T. Runia, "Further Observations on the Structure of Philo's Allegorical Treatises," *VChr* 41 (1987): 105–38, especially 133–34. For a further analysis with additional viewpoints regarding *Gig.* 6–18, see Sami Yli-Karjanmaa, "Philo of Alexandria," in *Brill's Companion to the Reception of Plato in Antiquity*, ed. Harold Tarrant et al. (Leiden: Brill, 2017), 115–129, 122–25.

[12] On the river metaphor, see Runia, *Philo and the* Timaeus, 260–62. See also Yli-Karjanmaa, *Reincarnation in Philo*, 114–17, 122–24 for the reincarnational contexts of both of these notions in Plato, and Philo's use of them. The differences between the parallels are further discussed below.

air as "a flourishing city, populated with immortal souls" whose number is astronomical[13]

> is an obvious attempt to systematize the doctrine of the *Timaeus* in relation to further data on demons and incorporeal souls in the *Symposium*, *Republic*, *Phaedrus* and *Epinomis*. The souls created by the demiurge are sown onto the planets *and* the earth (41e4–5, 42d4–5), so that it is natural to deduce that in the process of reincarnation there must be a continual procession of incorporeal souls in the air (cf. also *Phaed.* 81c–d).[14]

The idea may also draw on Pythagorean teachings. A similar notion is mentioned in Alexander Polyhistor's compendium of them (Diogenes Laertius 8.25–35): "The whole air is full of souls which are called genii or heroes (δαίμονάς τε καὶ ἥρωας); these are they who send men dreams and signs ..." (8.32).[15] Although these do not seem to be ordinary human souls and Alexander's description is thus only partly parallel to Philo's, it is worth noting that it is precisely "daemons" (*Gig.* 6; *Somn.* 1.141; *QG.* 4.188)[16] and "heroes" (*Plant.* 14) which Philo reports as the philosophers' names for angels.[17]

The Pythagorean idea that the soul is invisible (ἀόρατος) "just as the ether is invisible" (Diogenes Laertius 8.30) resembles Philo's "the air, too, must therefore be filled with living things, though they are invisible to us, since even the air itself is not visible to sense" (*Gig.* 8), even if the element mentioned is not the same. In *Plant.* 14 the souls' inapprehensibility by sense and in *Somn.* 1.136 their invisibility are mentioned.[18] Neither of these two passages says anything about the invisibility of the air, but based on the other features linking them with *De gigantibus* it would not seem sound

13 On this last point both Philo (*Somn.* 1.137) and also Alcinous (*Did.* 16.2) follow Plato (*Tim.* 41d).

14 Runia, *Philo and the* Timaeus, 254. Cf. Xenocrates who seems to have equated the air with Hades (fr. 213) which is compatible with the idea that souls reside in or travel through the air between incarnations.

15 See Méasson, *Du char ailé*, 275.

16 In the *QG* passage, the Armenian word is դեւք (*devkʻ*) which Marcus translates "divine beings." However, in a note he retranslates to Greek, οἱ δαίμονες, which accords with what G. Awatikʻean, X. Siwrmēlean, and M. Awgerean, *Նոր Բառգիրք Հայկազեան Լեզուի (Nor Baṙgirkʻ Haykazean Lezui)* [*New Dictionary of the Armenian Language*], 2 vols. (Venice: Mechitarist Press, 1836) (henceforth NBHL) gives for *devkʻ* (δαίμων, δαιμόνιον). The Old Latin translation of this passage has "daemones."

17 The identification of airborne souls with both daemons and heroes occurs, according to Augustine (*Civ.* 7.6), in the Middle Platonist Varro (d. 27 BCE) as well.

18 Another example of how a property may be assigned either to the ether or the air is the natural propensity to foster life (and the resultant necessity that the element in question has to have its own creatures): Aristotle (at Cicero, *Nat. d.* 2.42) opts for the ether, Philo, for the air (*Somn.* 1.137).

to think that it is *exclusively De gigantibus* that is drawing on a tradition similar to that recorded by Alexander. This is a noteworthy example of how a Philonic parallel with its tradition-historical links has an effect on how we view other passages in which the links are not equally manifest. This case also clearly exemplifies how Philo can sometimes leave part of the story untold without giving us any reason to assume that he has changed his mind or that the passages contradict each other.

Philo says in *Plant.* 14, "We are told that some enter into mortal bodies."[19] The first part, λόγος ἔχει, can be compared with "the old saying (ὁ παλαιὸς λόγος)" referring to Plato's *Timaeus* a little later in §17. Philo sometimes uses λόγος ἔχει for referring to the scriptures (see *Her.* 56), but here that is not the case; the pre-existence of souls is, at the literal level, not a notion that was present in Philo's Bible.[20] Instead, a Platonist (and thus reincarnational)[21] tradition is the likeliest source for Philo's εἰσκρίνεσθαι … σώμασι θνητοῖς—a source Alcinous too seems to be drawing on when writes in *Did.* 25.6: "It follows from the proposition that souls are immortal that they should enter into bodies (τὸ εἰσκρίνεσθαι αὐτὰς τοῖς σώμασι) … and that they should pass through many bodies both human and non-human … [perhaps because of] love of the body (διὰ φιλοσωματίαν)."[22]

[19] I pass by the statement, "Their array is made of companies that differ in kind." Azariah de' Rossi, who is the first author to mention Philo's endorsement of reincarnation (p. 113 in Weinberg's edition, section 1.4) criticizes Philo's views of the soul—not reincarnation but the idea that souls and angels do *not* differ in kind (Rossi, *The Light*, 157; section 1.6). He did not thus read *Plant.* carefully enough although he cites our passage (p. 155 Weinberg). His misunderstanding is understandable on the basis of *Gig.* 6, 16, although Philo ultimately ends up explaining that "bad" angels are really no angels at all but evil human souls. See David Winston and John Dillon, *Two Treatises of Philo of Alexandria: A Commentary on De Gigantibus and Quod Deus Sit Immutabilis* (Chico, CA: Scholars Press, 1983), 205 and Yli-Karjanmaa, "Philo of Alexandria," 124.

[20] It is present in later Jewish writings such as Wis 8:20; see David Winston, *The Wisdom of Solomon: A New Translation and Commentary*, First Yale University Press Impression, Anchor Yale Bible 43 (New Haven: Yale University Press, 2011), 25–32.

[21] This kind of underlining of the presence of reincarnation in Platonism may seem unnecessary. However, looking at approximately the last eighty years of research into Philo's views concerning the soul one can say that there has prevailed a noteworthy tendency to implicitly—i.e., without examining the question—assume Philo *rejected* this part of Platonist "dogma." See my *Reincarnation in Philo*, 17–18, 25–29.

[22] Tr. Dillon. I have omitted the other possible causes of incarnation which Alcinous mentions. For these, see John Dillon, *Alcinous: The Handbook of Platonism: Translation with an Introduction and Commentary*, Clarendon Later Ancient Philosophers (Oxford: Clarendon, 1993), 34, 155–58; David Winston, *Logos and Mystical Theology in Philo of Alexandria* (Cincinnati: Hebrew Union College Press, 1985), 35; Yli-Karjanmaa, *Reincarnation in Philo*, 44–52. Note that Philo's view of reincarnation could not accommodate human souls being born as animals, because it was his view that they do not possess the highest part of the soul.

There are several things to be noted. Philo seems to be one of the first authors to use the word εἰσκρίνω about the soul's entrance to the body.[23] This verb seems, in fact, to be connected to a noteworthy extent with the doctrine of reincarnation in later authors, both Christian and Neoplatonist.[24] Philo uses the verb to denote the entrance into the body in *Leg.* 1.32 as well; there the entity about to incarnate is the "earthly mind" one characteristic of which is that it is body-loving (1.33, from *Phaed.* 68b), just like the descending souls in *Somn.* 1.138 are "lovers of the body (φιλοσώματοι), descending to be fast bound in mortal bodies (ἐνδεθησόμεναι σώμασι θνητοῖς)."[25] This last expression, again, is paralleled in the "enter into mortal bodies (σώμασι θνητοῖς)" of *Plant.* 14. The notion of being "*bound* to a (mortal) body" is referred to several times by both Plato and Philo; for Plato, see, e.g., *Tim.* 44b: "So often as the soul is bound within a mortal body (εἰς σῶμα ἐνδεθῇ θνητόν) it becomes at the first irrational." In its Platonic contexts this expression can well be called reincarnational.[26]

De plantatione 14 is connected to *Somn.* 1.138 by the reference to time periods as well: souls quit their bodies "at certain fixed periods (κατά τινας ὡρισμένας περιόδους)" (*Plant.*) vs. "according to the numbers and periods determined by nature (κατὰ τοὺς ὑπὸ φύσεως ὁρισθέντας ἀριθμοὺς καὶ χρόνους)" (*Somn.*). Another parallel, particularly close to *De plantatione*, is found in *Her.* 282. In connection with death Philo states, "this debt [each of us] repays when the appointed time-cycles are completed (καθ' ὡρισμένας περιόδους καιρῶν ἐκτίνει τὸ δάνειον)." What is being referred to is the idea,

23 Another passage is *Somn.* 1.31 where Philo (rhetorically) asks, "At our birth, is [the mind] at once introduced into us from without (ἔξωθεν εἰσκρίνεται)?" As noted by Runia, "Philo and Hellenistic Doxography," in *Philo of Alexandria and Post-Aristotelian Philosophy*, ed. Francesca Alesse; SPhA 5 (Leiden: Brill, 2008), 13–54, 25, this has a loose parallel in Stobaeus (*Ecl.* 1.48.7): "Pythagoras, Anaxagoras, Plato, Xenocrates, and Cleanthes (said) the mind enters (εἰσκρίνεσθαι) from outside."

24 In addition to Alcinous, it (or the noun εἴσκρισις) is used in this sense, e.g., by Origen (*Comm. in Joann.* 6.14.85, *Cels.* 1.32), Epiphanius (*Panarion* 3.91.15), and Photius (*Bibl.* cod. 117, 92a25), as well as Plotinus (*Enn.* 4.3.9, 6.4.16) and Iamblichus (*De mysteriis* 1.8.36).

25 These souls can be identified with the reincarnating ones in 1.139 (see *Reincarnation in Philo*, 47), and there are also signs that with his "mind which is entering, but has not yet entered (εἰσκρινόμενον ... οὔπω δ' εἰσκεκριμένον), the body" in *Leg.* 1.32 Philo is, for some reason, referring to souls in the inter-incarnational state; see Sami Yli-Karjanmaa, "'Call Him Earth': On Philo's Allegorization of Adam in the *Legum Allegoriae*," in *Adam and Eve Story in the Hebrew Bible and in Ancient Jewish Writings Including the New Testament*, ed. Antti Laato and Lotta Valve, Studies in the Reception History of the Bible 7 (Turku: Åbo Akademi University; Winona Lake; Eisenbrauns, 2016), 272.

26 See Plato, *Tim.* 43a, 44d, 69e; *Phaed.* 81e, 92a; Philo, *Leg.* 2.22, 3.151; *Conf.* 92, 106, 177; *Her.* 274; *Mut.* 36; *Ios.* 264; *Spec.* 4.188; *Virt.* 74.

presented in *Tim.* 42e, that the portions of earth, water, air and fire, which constitute the physical body, are paid back at death.[27] Given the thoroughly reincarnational anthropology of the *Timaeus* this means, at *each* death. The reference to time periods is not, however, part of Plato's account. John Dillon has drawn attention to the fact that not only Philo but also Alcinous adds such a reference in a similar context at *Did.* 16.1: the gods "borrowed certain portions from primal matter for fixed periods (πρὸς ὡρισμένους χρόνους), with a view to returning them to it again."[28] Philo seems to be using a standard Middle Platonist formula for the duration of human life in all these cases (and some others).

The question of an author's intentions is always a tricky one. But we may ask: how would Philo's audience, if they were familiar with his interpretations of the dream about the ladder, have seen the accounts in *De plantatione* and *De gigantibus*? The parallelisms were surely no more difficult to notice in antiquity than they are now. Would Philo's hearers not have perceived the passages as referring to the same underlying pool of ideas about the journey of the soul? I think they would. With all its Platonic and Philonic links, *Plant.* 14 would have served to remind the audience, among other things, of the view that souls reincarnate until they denounce the bodily life and are ready to be saved.

Plant. *17–25: Protological Anthropology, Universal Soteriology, or Both?*

Between the two sections discussed in this paper Philo first deals with the species belonging to the earth (§15), the plants and animals.[29] He treats their different anatomy in Platonic terms (§16)—we are back in the *Timaeus* (91e–92a), in the concluding part of the dialogue where reincarnation plays a significant role. Humans make a somewhat unexpected reappearance in §17 when Philo moves from animals to the human constitution. Given the overall theme of the first part of *De plantatione* it comes as no surprise that

27 *Post.* 5 is similar, although more cosmological in idea and different in vocabulary. For a more detailed discussion of the notion of borrowing the elements as well as the references to periods of time in *De plantatione, Quis rerum divinarum heres sit* and *De somniis* and their background, see my *Reincarnation in Philo,* 117–19, 136–38.

28 Dillon, *Handbook of Platonism,* 137.

29 That land animals are presented paired with *plants* (which were already part of the first division at §§11, 13) is reminiscent of Apuleius's division of creatures: those of fire and air are followed by mortal kinds composed of both water and earth: plants and land creatures (*Dogm. Plat.* 204).

Philo wants to utilize the heavenly plant motif (90ab).[30] At §18 Philo wants to correct an anthropological error:

> Now while others, by asserting that our human mind is a portion of the ethereal nature, have claimed for the human being a kinship with the ether, our great Moses likened the rational class of soul to none of the created things. (*Plant.* 18) [31]

Philo himself is not innocent of advocating the view of the mind being a portion of the ether.[32] Thomas Tobin takes the corrective here as a criticism of "the Stoic conceptual framework used to interpret Gen 2:7."[33] However, the idea of *kinship* with the ether (συγγένεια ἀνθρώπου πρὸς αἰθέρα) is blameworthy too, or at least inferior to Moses's view. Thus Plato gets his share of censure; cf. the affirmation in *Tim.* 90a that the leading part of the soul raises the human body "up from earth towards our kinship in the heaven (πρὸς τὴν ἐν οὐρανῷ ξυγγένειαν)."[34] Once this is set straight, Philo puts his *Timaeus* scroll aside for a while, as it were, and returns to Genesis, now to 1:27 and 2:7. It is, in particular, his exegesis of these verses that I primarily discuss below.

So what is Moses's view more precisely?

> [He] averred [the rational class of soul] to be a genuine coinage of that divine and invisible "Spirit,"[35] signed and impressed by the seal of God, the stamp of

[30] For an analysis of the Timaean influences in *Plant.* 16–22, see Runia, *Philo and the* Timaeus, esp. 327–29, 347–48.

[31] The translation is based on the PLCL but adopts some of Tobin's (*Creation*, 91) corrections and introduces a few others. Worth mentioning is that I do not think Philo is referring to the rational *part* of the soul with τῆς λογικῆς ψυχῆς τὸ εἶδος. Cf. *Conf.* 176 (which is a clear parallel to *Plant.* 14 in many respects), where human souls are described as a reasoning (λογική), perishable species (εἶδος).

[32] Cf., e.g., *Leg.* 3.161 where the soul is described in virtually identical terms as "a portion of an ethereal nature." This kind of discrepancy is an example of such *differences* between parallels that should make a scholar fond of reading them together beware. The basic assumption of the passages telling (somewhat different parts of) the same story cannot then hold *in toto* and the limits of what can be read together need to be demarcated by analyzing what subjects the agreements and disagreements pertain to.

[33] Ibid. As for the history of the idea itself, cf. also Cicero, *Nat. d.* 1.27 where the notion that "the entire substance of the universe is penetrated and pervaded by a soul of which our souls are fragments" is ascribed to Pythagoras. See also Winston, *Logos*, 28–29, 64–65.

[34] This kinship is further discussed below, 160.

[35] I use quotation marks more than is customary in order to make a clearer distinction between what Philo is explaining and what his explanation is. The word πνεῦμα ("spirit," but also "wind" etc.) is a case in point. In its "spiritual" sense it is not a Philonic category. An analysis of all of its occurrences in the *Allegorical Commentary* leads to the conclusion that apart from the instances where it denotes a physical phenomenon or is related to the Stoic notion of cohesion, it always comes from the biblical text and is something Philo will

> which is the eternal Logos [τοῦ θείου καὶ ἀοράτου πνεύματος ἐκείνου δόκιμον εἶναι νόμισμα σημειωθὲν καὶ τυπωθὲν σφραγῖδι θεοῦ, ἧς ὁ χαρακτήρ ἐστιν ὁ ἀίδιος λόγος[. For "God inbreathed into his face a breath of life," so that it cannot but be that the one who receives is made in the likeness of the one who sends forth. Accordingly we also read that the human being is[36] "in accordance with the image of God." (*Plant.* 18–19)

The soul is, Philo says, a coinage *of* spirit, which is not a very precise description of the relationship between coinage and spirit. Regardless, it seems an impress is stamped on the soul whereby it receives the image of the Logos.[37] And this Philo takes to be described in Genesis *both* as the reception of the "breath of life" and being "in accordance with the image of God."[38]

Coming to the Philonic parallels, it is very interesting, first of all, to deal with *Plant.* 44 where Philo also discusses both Gen 1:27 and 2:7.[39] Philo begins by emphasizing the significance of details: "It is with deliberate care that the lawgiver says not of the human stamped 'after the image' but of the 'moulded' one that he was introduced into the garden."[40] The reason,

---

want to *explain* (away). For the details, and a critique of the use of this category in Philonic research, see my "Call Him Earth," 281–82.

36 γεγενῆσθαι; Whitaker: "has been made." For translating past tenses of γίγνομαι, see see LSJ, I.3 and II.

37 Cf. *Leg.* 3.95 where Philo speaks of an "image" (χαρακτήρ) which "God has stamped (ἐντετύπωκεν) on the soul as on a tested coin (νομίσματος δοκίμου τρόπον)." This character seems again to be the Logos (3.96, 104), although Philo is not quite explicit.

38 Sterling, "Wisdom," 365 sees the rationale for the connection between the "image" and the "breath" in Philo's contrast between Gen 2:7b–c and Lev 17:11a (discussed below). I do not agree, because the term "blood" (key in Lev) is not discussed in *De plantatione* On p. 365, primarily in connection with *Det.* 79–90 but apparently also referring to *Plant.* 18–19 he has just discussed, Sterling says that Philo takes both εἰκών and πνεῦμα as references to "the rational capacity of humanity," and (p. 375), based on *Plant.* 17–23, that "[t]he inbreathing of the θεῖον πνεῦμα is thus the anthropological basis for the reception of σοφία." I would agree with this, if it referred to reaching virtue and, ultimately, salvation. But Sterling seems to understand the "capacity" and "basis" in anthropological terms as the human mind (νοῦς; see 365, 375–76), which is quite problematic for the reason which *Leg.* 1.37, quoted on p. 375, makes clear: νοῦς is the *recipient* of the "breath."

39 A brief description of what happens in the second chapter of *Plant.* before §44 is in order. After some thoughts on the plants planted in the human being (§§28–31) Philo moves to a secondary lemma, Gen 2:8. He presents an interpretation which has close points of contact with his exegesis of the same verse in *Leg.* Cf. especially *Plant.* 32–42 with *Leg.* 1.43–47. In both, Philo takes a subsidiary lemma, Gen 6:19 in *Plant.* 43 and Deut 16:21 in *Leg.* 1.48–51, and even these have some common elements like the wildness (or the lack of it) of animals or plants. Note also the connections between §§33, 37 and 3.51–53, 253. These parallelisms should alert us to connections between Philo's exegeses of Gen 2:7 in the two treatises.

40 The reference is to Gen 2:8b. In *De plantatione* Philo does not launch into the kind of comparison between Gen 2:15 and 2:8b he presents in *Leg.* 1.53–55, building on the fact that

which Philo does not explicitly spell out, seems to be that the former already finds himself represented in Paradise:

> The human stamped with the "spirit" "in accordance with the image of God" [ὁ μὲν γὰρ τῷ κατὰ τὴν εἰκόνα θεοῦ χαραχθείς πνεύματι] differs not a whit, as it appears to me, from the tree that bears the fruit of immortal life. (*Plant.* 44)

Thus in both *Plant.* 18 and 44 the human (soul) receives a stamp, and this Philo sees described in both Gen 1:27 and 2:7. This much is quite obvious. The identification of the human after the image with the tree of life is somewhat surprising, but Philo kindly explains that "both are imperishable things (ἄφθαρτα) and have been accounted worthy of the most central and princely portion."[41]

What about the other human, then? "Nor does the 'moulded' human differ at all from the composite and more earthly (γεωδεστέρου) body" (§44). The key feature of both is having "no part in the unmoulded and simple nature (ἀπλάστου καὶ ἁπλῆς φύσεως ἀμέτοχος)." I find this statement strongly resonating with what I have called the *corporealization of the mind* defined as the mind's (or soul's) orientation towards, and its desire to experience, the world of matter in general and a physical body of its own in particular.[42] The concept is based on the Philonic notion of the mind becoming bodylike and earthly which is present in his interpretations of Gen 3:19 in *QG* 1.51 and *Leg.* 3.252–253. In the former, the first human is said to have "g[iven] himself wholly over to the earth," and in the latter he is "ranked with things earthlike and incohesive." For Philo, *this transformation* is the justification for God's words, "you are earth and into the earth you will depart" (Gen 3:19) and the explanation for the *aporia* (explicit in *QG* 1.51) that calling the first human "earth" ignores his inbreathed component: the soul, too, has become earthly and needs to return to earth—that is, reincarnate.[43]

Let us compare three expressions:

> In *Leg.* 1.31 the "heavenly human," who is "not moulded [οὐ πεπλάσθαι]," is "altogether without part in corruptible and terrestrial substance [γεώδους οὐσίας ἀμέτοχος]."

---

his text of v. 15 apparently read (like some LXX MSS. do) ἐποίησε instead of ἔπλασεν. The "made" human is in *Legum allegoriae.* interpreted as the one "after the image and archetype" (cf. Gen 1:26; 5:3). Nevertheless, Philo uses the same epithets in both treatises: the "moulded" (πεπλασμένος) human and the one "after the image" (κατ' εἰκόνα).

41 For the theme of centrality in a similar context, see *Leg.* 1.59–60 (cf. also 3.28–29).

42 I discuss corporealization as a potential cause of (re)incarnation in *Reincarnation in Philo*, 70–79.

43 In *Leg.* 3.252 Philo goes as far as to change the text of the LXX in order to usher in a reincarnational interpretation. See ibid., 76–77.

> In *Leg.* 3.252 the "foolish mind" which is "ranked with things earthly [γεώδεσι]" has been "'taken' (Gen 2:7) not from the sublime nature [τῆς μεταρσίου φύσεως] but from the more earthly matter [τῆς γεωδεστέρας ὕλης]."
>
> In *Plant.* 44 the human who is identified with the "more earthly [γεωδεστέρου] body" has "no part in the unmoulded and simple nature [ἀπλάστου καὶ ἁπλῆς φύσεως ἀμέτοχος]."

To fully appreciate the connections between these passages it is necessary to note a very important feature in both *Leg.* 1.31–32 and *Plant.* 44: Philo *connects Gen 1:27 with 2:7b and plays these against 2:7a* —the "image" and the "breath" against the "moulding" and the "earth."[44] I have argued elsewhere that Philo's famous "two types of humans"—the heavenly and the earthly—in *Leg.* 1.31–32 does not refer to Gen 1:27 and 2:7 as such but to the combination of 1:27 and 2:7b against 2:7a.[45] The rationale behind this splitting up of the human being of Gen 2:7 into two entities is that Philo's interpretation of the "breath of life" of Gen 2:7 in *Leg.* 1 is almost exclusively *universal* instead of *protological* (more specifically, it is soteriological).[46] In *Leg.* 1.31–32, God's act symbolized in the biblical text as the

44 Sterling ("Wisdom," 363) notes in *Opif.* 135 "a sharp distinction between Gen 2:7a which refers to the mortal nature of humanity and 2:7b which presents our immortal nature" and refers to *Opif.* 144; *Leg.* 1.33; *Det.* 83; *Her.* 55–57; *Spec.* 1.171; 4 123 as containing "similar statements." But I have seen no other references to this phenomenon in scholarly literature which I regard as the key to understanding *Leg.* 1.31–32 in particular. Gen 2:7 is naturally divided into three parts as follows: v. 7a: "And God moulded the human being, taking dust from the earth"; v. 7b: "and breathed into his face a breath of life"; v. 7c: "and the human being became a living soul." These are quoted by Philo three, eight, and five times, respectively (these are the figures for the quotations of entire sub-verses in Philo's surviving Greek *œuvre*). For a list of Philo's citations of and allusions to Gen 2:7 (51 in total) see ibid., 362 n. 22.

45 See Yli-Karjanmaa, "Call Him Earth," 292.

46 Steps in this direction in the interpretation of *Leg.* 1 have been taken in earlier research. See the references in Yli-Karjanmaa, *Reincarnation in Philo*, 36 n. 133. By universal as opposed to protological allegory I mean an interpretation of the biblical, protological narrative (in practice, the first chapters of Genesis) which does not take over its protological perspective. According to my observations, this is the dominant—although not exclusive—mode of Philo's exegesis in *Legum allegoriae.* Note the affinity between this distinction and the observation by David T. Runia, *On the Creation of the Cosmos According to Moses: Introduction, Translation, and Commentary*, PACS 1 (Atlanta: Society of Biblical Literature, 2001), 333–34 concerning the distinction in Philo "between a presentation as *history*, i.e., an account of the life of early mankind, and a presentation in terms of *actualization* and *idealization*, i.e. seeing Adam and Eve as types of human beings" (emphasis original). Cf. also the reference of Folker Siegert ("Philo and the New Testament," in *The Cambridge Companion to Philo*, ed. Adam Kamesar [Cambridge: Cambridge University Press, 2009], 175–209) at p. 184 to "mankind as it is in the present" in connection with *Leg.* 1.31–38.

"inbreathing" *converts* the "earthly" mind/human into a heavenly one. Compare the following expressions:

The heavenly human being (*Leg*. 1.31)	The earthly human being after receiving the breath of life (*Leg*. 1.32)
– κτ' εἰκόνα γεγονώς / οὐ πεπλάσθαι	– γίνεται, οὐκέτι πλάττεται[47] (νοερὰν καὶ ζῶσαν ὄντως)
– κατ' εἰκόνα τετυπῶσθαι	– οὐκ ἀδιατύπωτον (ἐτύπωσε in 1.38)
– φθαρτῆς καὶ γεώδους οὐσίας ἀμετοχος	– οὐκ ἀργόν[48]

As we have seen, Philo in *De plantatione* to an extent follows his exegesis of Gen 2:7–8 in *Leg*. 1 and at §44 splits Gen 2:7 into two parts as well, once more combining verse 7b with 1:27 and distinguishing these from verse 7a.[49] *Plant*. 18 too features this combination—but there 2:7a is absent.[50] In §§18–19 a key question demanding an answer is: is Philo being protological, telling us how the human being was *created*?[51] To answer this question we need to be clear on what it is that Philo says was inbreathed. To recall, his words were, "For 'God inbreathed into his face a breath of life,' so that it cannot but be that the one who receives is made in the likeness of the one who sends forth [ἀνάγκη πρὸς τὸν ἐκπέμποντα τὸν δεχόμενον

[47] Cf. also the characterization of the earthly human as "compacted out of incohesive matter [ὕλης] ... a 'moulded' work but not offspring [πλάσμα, αλλ' οὐ γέννημα] of the Artificer."

[48] Cf. *Mos*. 2.136, *Spec*. 1.21 and *Flacc*. 148, which show that ἀργός is a natural attribute of ὕλη.

[49] If we followed him further, we would find in §45–46 two other concepts used in the exegesis of Gen 2 in *Leg*. 1, ὁ μέσος νοῦς (*Leg*. 1.93, 95) and Adam as ὁ γήϊνος νοῦς (1.31, 90, 95). The latter is in my view a genuinely Philonic term for the "corporealized mind." See *Reincarnation in Philo*, 74–75.

[50] Its *exegesis* in *Leg*. 1 may, however, be hinted at a little later: The notion of *being compacted out of perishable matter* with the words ὕλη, φθαρτός, and πήγνυμι (within one line) appears only in *Plant*. 22 and *Leg*. 1.31 in the whole TLG. It seems that in *Leg*. the notion is still an elaboration of the biblical text rather than part of Philo's interpretation proper: he directly refers to the text of Gen 2:7a when he says Moses calls (κέκληκεν) *matter* "dust." Thus even though the actual allegorization of Gen 2:7a is in *Leg*. 1.31–32 framed in terms of the earthly human, "perishable matter" also refers to the physical human body. We thus come very close to the idea of the similarity between the body and the corporealized mind expressed more clearly in *Plant*. 44. Little wonder, then, that this entity has to hear God's words, "you are earth" (Gen 3:19).

[51] In stating that in *Plant*. 16–22 and *Det*. 79–90 "Philo looks at man as he is in his earthly existence" (in the same way as Plato is at the end of the *Timaeus* no longer dealing with protology) Runia seems to opt for a universal understanding (*Philo and the* Timaeus, 338). He continues that in those passages Philo "prefers to reconcile the two Mosaic texts, considering that also in this existence man's 'true self' is present, albeit dimly." This "dimming" of "the true self" corresponds to what I call corporealization.

ἀπεικονίσθαι]"—an elaboration of the soul's becoming "signed and impressed by the seal of God." Since the soul is thus the object of God's action, it must logically exist prior to the event described as "inbreathing." Philo's combined interpretation of Gen 1:27 and 2:7b in *Plant.* 18 *presupposes* the soul: it addresses neither its creation nor its coming together with the body.[52] It has to be regarded as universal, not protological.

It is illuminating to compare the text concerning sending and receiving just cited with two passages in *Legum allegoriae.* First, in 1.37 (exegesis of Gen 2:7) Philo makes a similar distinction between three factors: "that which inbreathes (τὸ ἐμπνέον) is God, that which receives (τὸ δεχόμενον) is the mind, that which is inbreathed (τὸ ἐμπνεόμενον) is the 'spirit' (πνεῦμα)."[53] I have argued that in *Leg.* this inbreathing, which enables the soul to "conceive of God" (1.38) is a salvific event granted to the soul, equivalent to its regaining its "own life" upon dying to the life of vice (1.107–108).[54] But what about *Plant.* 18–19: does Philo there too imply that the "breath" symbolizes a salvific event? *Plant.* 44 comes closer to *Leg.* 1.37, for the role of the spirit is more explicitly expressed. Let us compare three key expressions in the *De plantatione* passages:

- In §18 the soul is "signed and impressed [τυπωθέν] by the seal [σφραγῖδι] of God the stamp of which is the eternal Logos."
- In §44 we first have the human being "stamped [τυπωθέντα] 'after the image.'"
- Then, the same entity is said to have been "stamped with the 'spirit' [χαραχθεὶς πνεύματι] 'in accordance with the image of God.'"

In context, it is clear that the two expressions in §44 mean the same. Based on the identity between the Logos and the image of God in §§19–20 it seems §18 can also be taken as saying the same thing. It follows then that in the former expression the instrumental role of the "seal of God" is very similar to that of "spirit" in the latter one and that we can rather safely assume that

[52] An example *par excellence* of the use of undivided Gen 2:7 to denote the coming together of body and soul is *Leg.* 3.161. There are also passages where Philo uses Gen 2:7b only as evidence for the divine origin of the mind in a non-soteriological context. He states in *QG* 1.50, "the mind is a divine inbreathing" and calls the mind in *Somn.* 1.34 a divine fragment justifying this with the verse. This kind of interpretation can also be expressed in terms which are very similar to what we are discussing; cf. *Det.* 83 (discussed below), where the essence of the rational part of the soul is said to be "'spirit' [πνεῦμα] ... an impression [τύπον] and stamp [χαρακτῆρα] of the divine power [δυνάμεως] to which Moses gives the appropriate title of 'image.'"

[53] The similarity of the passages is such that Thomas Mangey in fact wanted to conjecture ἐμπνέοντα for ἐκπέμποντα at *Plant.* 19.

[54] See my "Call Him Earth," 266–81.

what is said about the "seal" in §18 can be taken as an *elaboration* of the more ambiguous "coinage of 'spirit'" used earlier in the same passage.[55] Thus the event whereby "the one who receives is made in the likeness of the one who sends forth" is one whereby *the soul receives the "image" of the Logos when God stamps it with "spirit."* This is in harmony with a soteriological interpretation of *Plant.* 18–19, but we need to read on before we can judge if that interpretation is to be preferred.

Before moving on to the second parallel in *Leg.* 1 we need to discuss a complication in *Plant.* 19. The italicized part in "it cannot but be that the one who receives *is made in the likeness* of the one who sends forth" translates a single word, ἀπεικονίσθαι, which is the middle/passive perfect infinitive (the only one for this verb in the whole TLG).[56] In Greek "the perfect denotes a completed action the effects of which still continue in the present."[57] It is very interesting to notice that the English (Yonge and PLCL), German (PCH) and French (PAPM) translations all use the *present* tense in rendering the verb.[58] They may, in fact, be right, and the perfect, wrong. First of all we may note that it would be difficult to make sense of "it cannot but be that the one who receives *has been made* in the likeness of the one who sends forth." For although the *effect* of having been made in the likeness of the sender is continuing at the moment of sending, the perfect tense unavoidably makes the *act* of making anterior to the act of the present-tense sending—thereby cancelling the causal relationship clearly implied by the logic of appealing to Gen 2:7b and the word ὥστε.[59] Fortunately, there seems to be an attractive way out of this dilemma. Eusebius quotes *Plant.* 18–20 (*Praep. ev.* 7.18.1–2), and in some Eusebian mss., as well as in the epitome *De mundo* (MS. E, see PCW 2.vii), the verb form in question is in the present tense, ἀπεικονίζεσθαι.[60] Wendland often follows Eusebius who, he notes, alone transmits the correct text, e.g., at §18 (see PCW 2.x). In my

[55] It is intriguing to note that in *Leg.* 3.95–96, another "numismatic" passage connected to Gen 1:27, the soul is said to receive a stamp like a tested coin (see above, n. 37), but now Exod 31:2–3 takes, as it were, the place of Gen 2:7b, although Philo does not explicitly mention the "divine spirit" of 31:3.

[56] For many of the observations mentioned below I am indebted to James R. Royse. The conclusions are mine.

[57] Herbert Weir Smyth, *Greek Grammar* (Harvard University Press: Cambridge MA, 1956), §1945 (henceforth HWS).

[58] This is also true for Sterling's translation, "is made in the image" ("Wisdom," 365).

[59] Note also that according to HWS §1865, although the infinitive does not have time of itself, it does express the stage of action, which for the perfect is that of *completion*. I.e., the action is *over*, only its effects continue.

[60] This is one of the thirteen occurrences of this verb form in the TLG.

view, we should opt for the present tense, the perfect being explicable as an accidental omission of two letters (Z and Σ not being altogether unlike).

The second parallel in *Leg.* 1 for the sending and receiving in *Plant.* 19 is 1.61, which in fact also bridges *Plant.* 19 and 44. Philo's primary lemma is Gen 2:9 which, in his view, tells us "what trees of virtue God plants in the soul" (1.56). It is worth highlighting that both planting the Paradise and breathing in the human face are, in Philo's view as expressed in *Leg.* 1, events whose essence is *God's action on the soul*. After some discussion of theoretical and practical arts and the extolling of virtue as best of them all (1.57–58) the tree of life is, because of its central position, identified with "virtue in the most comprehensive sense, which some term goodness" (1.59). Philo then notes that the biblical text does not reveal the location of the tree of knowing good and evil (1.60) and proceeds to declare that it is, "nominally (οὐσίᾳ) in [Paradise], but in effect (δυνάμει), outside" (1.61). To get to the points we are mainly interested in Philo needs a secondary lemma which, as he sees it, has a thematic connection with (the tree of) good and evil: "All this (πάντα ταῦτα) has come upon me!" cries Jacob in Gen 42:36. The link is that the human mind "is all-receptive and resembles wax that receives (δεχομένῳ) all impressions (τύπους) fair and ugly." Philo continues that whenever the soul

> receives [δέξηται] the stamp [χαρακτῆρα] of perfect virtue, it is [γέγονε][61] "the tree of life," but when (it receives) that of wickedness, it is "the tree of knowledge of good and evil." ... [Thus the mind which] has received [δεδεγμένον] [wickedness] is nominally in the "garden," for it has in it likewise the stamp [χαρακτήρ] of virtue properly belonging to the "garden." On the other hand, in effect it is not in it, because the impress [τύπος] of wickedness is alien to the divine "risings." (*Leg.* 1.61)

In *Leg.* 1 Philo ties *virtue* tightly together with the breath of life (1.34–35) as well as with Paradise with its tree of life and rivers (esp. 1.45–49, 54–66, 70–73, 88–89). It is difficult for me not to see the reception of the stamp of perfect virtue as referring to the same salvific act of God as the "breath of life" in Philo's exegesis. *Rejection* of virtue is, again, the essence of the Philonic notion of the death of the soul (1.105–108) from which the soul can recover to its own, true life—of virtue.[62] Concepts closely linked with virtue in *Leg.* are "heavenly wisdom" (1.43) and "the right principle" (*Leg.* 1.45–46, 92–93; 3.2, 80, 106, 147–148, 150, 168, 222, 251–252), and it is highly note-

[61] Whitaker: "shall have received ... straightway becomes."

[62] On this last point see Yli-Karjanmaa, *Reincarnation in Philo*, 64. For a more extensive treatment of all the issues in this paragraph, see my "Call Him Earth," 266–73.

worthy that the corporealization of the mind, that is, its becoming "earthly," involves forsaking both of these (3.252).

The question now is whether we should see the statement "the one who receives is made in the likeness of the one who sends forth" in *Plant.* 19 as a reference to the salvific event of the soul receiving the stamp of virtue. In my view this understanding is supported by reading §19 together with §44—which the striking image of being or becoming the "tree of life" connects to *Leg.* 1.61, and, through it, to Paradise, virtue and back to the "breath of life." We should add the fact that in Philo virtue is often almost a synonym for salvation.[63]

Let us now move on to *Plant.* 20. Philo posits a link, which is at least partially causal, between the soul's image-likeness and a series of notions related to *ascending*, starting here with the body:

> As a consequence, then, of the human soul having been made in the likeness (ἀπεικονισθείσης) (of and) after the image of the archetype, the Logos of the Cause, the body too—raised up towards the purest portion of the universe, the heaven—lifts up the eyes. (*Plant.* 20)

It seems Philo is moving towards a more protologically oriented discourse. I think this is because he has an aim. He will have wanted to end his excursus to Genesis—the end of which can be located at the words "the Logos of the Cause"—in a way that connects with the Timaean themes he was discussing before embarking on it: the gazing towards heaven and the implied erect posture of the human body, that is, its *design*. Against this background it is understandable that he now also speaks of the *soul's* original design, i.e., its being akin to the image of the Logos. He does this in fairly biblical terms, without blending in much allegory. He does narrow down the biblical act of creation to concern the soul only, and, as usual, interprets the "image" of Gen 1:27 in terms of the Platonic model–copy relationship. The purpose of the erect posture, Philo tells us, is "that by means of the visible [the soul] would clearly apprehend (καταλαμβάνηται) the unseen." The ascent motif continues as he in §21 refers to souls that are "drawn (ἀχθέντας)" by God. These statements open up new soteriological vistas to parallels in *Legum allegoriae*, *Quod deterius potiori insidiari soleat* and *Quis rerumdivinarum heres sit*, which we will now discuss before continuing further in *De plantatione*.

Philo brings up the notion of being *drawn up by God* in his exegesis of Gen 2:7 in *Leg.* 1.38 in a context which is seamlessly linked with his discus-

63 See, e.g., *Plant.* 37: the tree of life is called the "path [of the rational soul] to virtue, with life and immortality as its end." Cf. also *Post.* 31; *Abr.* 269; *QG* 1.51; 4.131.

sion in 1.37 of that which inbreathes, that which receives and that which is inbreathed. The purpose of "the union of the three," says Philo, is "that we may obtain (λάβωμεν) a conception (ἔννοιαν) of Him." He elaborates this as follows:

> For the human mind would never have ventured to soar so high as to grasp [ἀντιλαβέσθαι] the nature of God, had not God Himself drawn it up [ἀνέσπασεν] to Himself—so far as it was possible for the human mind to be drawn up—and stamped [ἐτύπωσε] it with according to the powers that are within the scope of its understanding. (*Leg*. 1.38)

Here the soul's being drawn up, its ascent and the ability to grasp the nature of God are presented as the consequences of the reception of both the "spirit" and the stamp by the mind. We again have here the combination of Gen 2:7b and 1:27.[64] Furthermore, the context which can with good reason be called soteriological.[65]

In *Quod deterius potiori insidiari soleat* the connection between the ability to know God and the joint interpretation of Gen 1:27 and 2:7b is explicit:

> It would be greatly to the advantage of the thing wrought should it obtain [λάβοι] a conception [ἔννοιαν] of Him who wrought it … He breathed into him from above [ἄνωθεν ἐνέπνει] of His own Deity. The invisible Deity stamped on the invisible soul the impress [τύπους] of itself to the end that not even the terrestrial region should be without a share in the image of God [εἰκόνος ἀμοιρήσῃ θεοῦ]. (*Det*. 86)

Here again, the inbreathing does not stand for the reception of the soul by the human being, or her creation.[66] Instead, the *soul is stamped* so that it shares the image of God. In a relevant statement a little earlier Philo says

64 The latter is often referred to by Philo using the terminology of stamping. See, e.g., *Opif*. 25, 71; *Leg*. 1.31; *Plant*. 20; *Her*. 231; *Mut*. 31.

65 Grasping God's nature and being drawn to him are, at the very least, highly conducive to salvation (understood as eternal, incorporeal existence in God's presence as in *Gig*. 14).

66 And yet Philo presents two very protological-looking statements in §§80, 83. In the first he says, "the essence [οὐσία] of soul is 'spirit,'" in the second, "the human soul [Moses] names 'spirit.'" Two things connect these two protologically geared statements. First, in both statements the aim is to distinguish the soul–"spirit" connection from the soul–"blood" connection of Lev 17:11, 14. The focus is on clearing their seeming contradiction. Second, both explicitly refer to the biblical text (φησίν … παριστάς, ὀνομάζει) thus indicating that Philo is moving closer to the *explanandum* than his *explanatio*, the latter being in both instances that the soul–"spirit" connection concerns the highest part of the soul. The word παριστάς in §80 can be thought of as introducing an *initial* explanation—"the essence of soul is 'spirit'"—needed to bring out the actual exegetical problem, the apparent contradiction with the Lev passage, more clearly. Note that now also Gen 2:7c, "and the human being became a living *soul*," as part of the problem, is quoted.

"spirit" is the essence of the rational power of the soul, "as it were, an impression (τύπον τινά) and stamp (χαρακτῆρα) of the divine power to which Moses gives the appropriate title of 'image'" (*Det.* 83). The details of the interpretation as "spirit" as the impression of the "image" come very close to *Plant.* 19, 44. Again, Gen 1:27 and 2:7b are interpreted jointly to mean a "greatly advantageous" (cf. *Det.* 86) event which facilitates the soul's orientation towards God and thus surely contributes to salvation.

Her. 54–64 presents us with a variation of this theme. Philo discusses the question of who can be the heir of divine and incorporeal things and answers, "one only is held worthy of these, the recipient of inspiration from above [ὁ καταπνευσθεὶς ἄνωθεν]" (§64). This statement operates at the universal level, not protological. That it refers to Gen 2:7b is clear based on §56, a passage parallel in thought to *Plant.* 18:

> On the other hand he did not make the substance [οὐσίαν] of the mind depend on anything created, but represented [εἰσήγαγεν] it as breathed down [καταπνευσθεῖσαν] by God. For the Maker of all, he says, "inbreathed into his face the breath of life, and the human being became a living soul"; just as we are also told that he was stamped [τυπωθῆναι] "in accordance with the image" of his Maker. (*Her.* 56)

The identification of the substance of mind with the "breath of life" comes juxtaposed with the connection made between blood and soul in Leviticus (§§54–55; Lev 17:11, 14).[67] Dealing as it does with the human constitution the identification is protological and it thus shows that Philo can use the combination of Gen 1:27 and 2:7b in such a context too. Philo's angle of approach is defined by verbal connections, one between his primary lemma, Gen 15:2 and the secondary one in Lev—"blood"—and another between the secondary and tertiary (Gen 2:7) lemmas—"soul."[68] There is a potential contradiction in the biblical texts involved, but—unlike in *Det.* 81—in *Quis rerum divinarum heres sit* Philo merely gives an explanation without raising an explicit *aporia*.[69]

At §57 Philo switches to the universal mode of exegesis. Very much like in *Leg.* 1.31 he states, "so the human kind is twofold."[70] The two classes are

[67] See previous note and also Runia, *Philo and the* Timaeus, 329.

[68] "Blood" is present in Gen 15:2 through Philo's interpretation of Damascus as the "blood of a sack," i.e., the blood-life of the body (§54).

[69] Philo's explanation differs a little from *Quod deterius potiori insidiari soleat* in that now "blood" becomes the substance of the *whole* soul.

[70] Other links with *Leg.* 1 are the term "earthly mind" as the epithet of Adam (§52; cf. 1.31–32, 90) and the offspring of sense-perception as "those who are in truth dead to the life of the soul" in distinction to "those who are really living" (§53; cf. *Leg.* 1.32 and the death of the soul in 1.105–108).

now described in terms of a distinction between the combinations Lev 17:11 and Gen 2:7a vs. Gen 1:27 and 2:7b:[71]

> that of those who live by the intellect, the divine "spirit," the other of those who live by "blood" and the pleasure of the flesh. This last is a "moulded clod of earth (πλάσμα γῆς)" the other is the faithful impress (ἐκμαγεῖον) of the divine "image." (*Her.* 57)

Insofar as this statement describes how the two kinds of people *live*, it is universal. There is, however, protology involved in the identification of the human intellect with the divine "spirit."[72] We thus have another example of the blending of the two modes of interpretation.

From the viewpoint of the soteriological interpretation of the combination of Gen 1:27 and 2:7b the main question is, are there signs of "traffic" between the two classes of humans? Or is it possible that "our piece of 'moulded clay' [which] has imperative need of God's help" (§58) in fact *fails* to get that help through which it becomes an impress of the "image"? I think there are such signs. The salvific role of the "breath" is in *Quis rerum divinarum heres sit* linked with the divine help symbolized by Eliezer (§58): Philo says, "the mass of blood … is quickened [ζωπυρεῖται] by the providence of God … since our race cannot of itself stand firmly established for a single day."[73] In §§63–64 (partly already quoted) he implies that the worthy inheriting soul is one that *stops* living its blood-life:

> Can he who desires the life of the blood and still [ἔτι] claims for his own the things of the senses become the heir of divine and incorporeal things? No; one alone is held worthy of these, the recipient of inspiration from above [ὁ καταπνευσθεὶς ἄνωθεν], of a portion heavenly and divine, the wholly purified mind which disregards not only the body, but that other section of the soul which is devoid of reason [ἄλογον] and steeped in "blood," aflame with seething passions and burning lusts. (*Her.* 63–64)

A little later in §68 Philo says the heir will not be "that intellect which abides in the prison of the body of its own free will, but that which released [λύθεις] from its fetters into liberty [ἐλευθερωθείς] has come forth [προεληλυθώς]

71 Sterling, "Wisdom," 365 n. 36 says Philo here argues that "Gen 2:7b-c (sic) presents two classes of humanity."

72 Or, perhaps, the "divine spirit." The placing of the quotation marks depends on whether one sees here an allusion to the "breath" (πνοή) of Gen 2:7b (both πνεῦμα and πνοή are cognate to πνέω; in, e.g., *Leg.* 3.161 πνεῦμα occurs in a quotation of Gen 2:7b) or to the "divine spirit" (πνεῦμα θεῖον) of Exod 31:3. The latter may also have been in Philo's mind; cf. *Her.* 53 where wisdom and knowledge are mentioned.

73 Cf. the interpretation of the angels on Jacob's ladder as God's *logoi* who "with their salvific breath may quicken into new life [σωτήριον πνέοντες ἀναζωῶσι] the soul which is still borne along in the body as in a river." (*Somn.* 1.147)

outside the prison walls."[74] Progress on the part of the intellect is an implied prerequisite of the inheritance; receiving the "inspiration from above" (§64) is connected to the liberation from the body.

Based on the texts discussed it seems likely that by writing what he does in *Plant.* 18–20 Philo wants to remind his audience not only of the divine origin of the mind but also of the actual possibility of receiving (quite possibly *again*, after losing it upon the death of the soul) God's salvific grace which he saw symbolized by the various biblical images and themes, and thereby gaining an apprehension of things divine, ultimately God.

In *Plant.* 22 Philo moves on to the theme of the flight of the soul:

> The strong yearning to perceive the Existent One gives [the eyes of the soul] wings to attain not only to the furthest region of the ether, but to overpass the very bounds of the entire universe and speed away toward the Uncreate. (*Plant.* 22)

This is a profoundly Platonic passage with the themes of wingedness, yearning and overpassing the bounds of the universe coming directly from the *Phaedrus*.[75] It is noteworthy that the thought comes close to two of Philo's most directly reincarnational passages. In *Somn.* 1.139 liberated souls "are lifted up on light wings to the ether," and in *QE* 2.40 "a holy soul is divinized by ascending not to the air or to the ether or to heaven [which is] higher than all but to [a region] above the heavens." In *QE* those whose desire for the divine is strong enough have their stay in the divine city sealed by God, but the fickle ones are drawn back to "Tartarus," by which Philo means the human body.[76] Similarly Philo in §23 says that those "who crave for wisdom and knowledge with insatiable persistence are said … to have been called upwards," and in §25 he states of the mind of the genuine philosopher that it is "borne upward insatiably enamoured of all holy happy natures that dwell on high."

74 Cf. *Somn.* 1.139 where the ideas of the body as a prison and the soul's voluntary entry to it occur. The idea of or self-induced prison terms fits reincarnation very well. Cf., e.g., *Phaed.* 82e: "the most dreadful thing about the imprisonment is the fact that it is caused by the lusts, so that the prisoner is the chief assistant in his own imprisonment."

75 See especially 245d–246a, 246c, 247d–248c, 249a, 251c–e. Furthermore, *Plant.* 24–25 contain a combination of Platonic reincarnational notions—pursuing philosophy correctly and the ascetic ideal of practising death (i.e., separation from the body and its needs)—which also appears in *Gig.* 14. The combination occurs thrice in the *Phaedo* (64a, 67e, 80e); the purpose of both practices is to allow the soul to depart pure so as to avoid a further incarnation (see, e.g., 80d–81e). In marked harmony with the ethos of the dialogue (e.g., 81b), in both *De plantatione* (§25) and *De gigantibus* (§15) the goods of the body are rejected. An additional commonality is that in both *Plant.* 22 and *Gig.* 14 God is called "uncreated" (ἀγενήτος; cf. *Phaedr.* 245d–246a).

76 Cf. *QG* 4.234. For *QE* 2.40 see my *Reincarnation in Philo*, 167–86.

It is worthwhile to pose the question, who is Philo actually speaking of in *Plant.* 17–25? The soul's orientation towards the heaven, ascent to God, craving for wisdom et cetera in §§20–25 are, in his thought, things that concern good souls only. It is *they* that can, in the Philonic way of thinking, experience the sort of ascent described. How far back in *De plantatione* can we assume this qualification to reach? Working our way backward, we can see that the soul's soaring "to the utmost height" (§24) is causally linked to the its "strong yearning to see the Existent" (§22) and "the attraction of the understanding" towards the same (§21), which, for its part is in a somewhat less precise manner coupled with the erect posture of the human body and our ability to lift our eyes towards the ether and the heaven (§§20–21). The erect posture, again, is linked with soul's being made in the likeness of the Logos (§20), which, finally, is identified with the reception of the "breath of life." A striking comparison can be made:

– In *Plant.* 18–25 we have the sequence	"breath" + "image" — erect posture — ascent
– In *Leg.* 1.31–32, 37–38, we find	"breath" + "image" ————————ascent

The beginning and the end are similar, but in *De plantatione* Philo's train has one more stop. Why is this? This is explained by his biblical lemma. The posture issue is directly linked with the heavenly plant motif—which Philo does not want to forego in a discussion concerning planting! Let Plato be quoted at some length:

> We declare that God has given to each of us, as his daemon, that kind [εἴδους] of soul which is housed in the top of our body and which raises us—seeing that we are not an earthly but a heavenly plant—up from earth towards our kinship in the heaven. And herein we speak most truly; for it is by suspending our head and root from that region whence the substance [γένεσις] of our soul first came [ἔφυ] that the Divine Power keeps upright our whole body. (*Tim.* 90a)

It in fact seems that although Philo, as is his custom, quotes sparsely from Plato and extensively from the Pentateuch, he makes his excursus to Gen 1:27 and 2:7b in *Plant.* 17–20 *in order to* partly support and partly criticize the Timaean notions quoted. Let us examine this more closely. The key statement comes right at the beginning of §18, immediately after the explicit reference to the heavenly plant motif in the *Timaeus* and just before to the references to Gen 2:7b and 1:27:

> Now while others, by asserting that our human mind is a particle of the ethereal substance, have claimed for the human being a kinship with the ether, our great Moses likened the fashion of the reasonable soul to no created thing … (*Plant.* 18)

Thus when Philo follows φυτὸν οὐκ ἐπίγειον ἀλλ' οὐράνιον in §17 with συγγένειαν ἀνθρώπῳ πρὸς αἰθέρα above, these correspond closely to Plato's πρὸς δὲ τὴν ἐν οὐρανῷ ξυγγένειαν ἀπὸ γῆς ἡμᾶς αἴρειν ὡς ὄντας φυτὸν οὐκ ἔγγειον ἀλλ' οὐράνιον (*Tim.* 90a).[77] This last idea fits Philo's exegesis perfectly, but he is critical toward Plato's formulation of the kinship. Runia seems to be right when he says that Philo is keen on demonstrating the human kinship with *God,* which is not precisely what Plato says.[78] The joint interpretation of Gen 1:27 and 2:7b in *Plant.* 18–19 does serve this demonstration, but it has also an important universal aspect to it.

Using the very useful (but still too little utilized) analyses, and concepts introduced to the research, of Philo's exegetical method by Runia, we can see that, in effect, *Timaeus* 90a–b acts as Philo's secondary lemma; mode of transition from Gen 9:20 is verbal, φυτόν.[79] This means that Gen 1:27 and 2:7b must in fact be seen as *tertiary*. The mode of transition from *Tim.* is strongly thematic, the divine origin and constitution of the human soul, but there are also common words (ψυχή, γῆ). From the viewpoint of analyzing Philo's exegetical method it is intriguing and indeed worth noting that, *regardless* of whether we see some kind of very general thematic link between Noah's vine-planting and the accounts of the human creation, their links with *Tim.* 90a–b are much more significant than with each other.

After the excursus to Gen 1:27 and 2:7b Philo makes the already quoted, but on a closer inspection surprising, statement in *Plant.* 20 where he posits a *causal* connection between the human image-likeness and the erect body with its upward-looking eyes. I cannot fathom the logic of this statement, but what is clear is that the said bodily features are very important for Philo—so much so that he wants to support them by a direct appeal to Gen 1:27. Moses thus gets the job of speaking for Plato!

77 Further commonalities include that both authors speak of the soul's highest part as ψυχῆς εἶδος (*Plant.* 18; *Tim.* 90a) and that Philo echoes Plato's reference to God's "keep[ing] upright (ὀρθοί) our whole body" (90a) with his statement that God "set high up (ἀνώρθωσεν)" the human eyes (§17); in both the context is the erect human posture.

78 Runia, *Philo and the* Timaeus, 341 n. 11: "it is possible that [Philo] is correcting an interpretation of the *Timaeus* which stresses the kinship of man to the heavenly beings at the expense of his kinship to the demiurgic creator." I think the referent is rather "the intellections and the revolutions of the Universe" (90c–d) than heavenly beings.

79 Secondary lemmas are used by Philo to interpret the primary ones (and tertiary sometimes to interpret the secondary). Philo moves between these using transitions which may be classified as based on a thematic or a verbal link he sees, or both. See David T. Runia, "The Structure of Philo's Allegorical Treatises: A Review of Two Recent Studies and Some Additional Comments," *VC* 38 (1984): 209–56; Runia, "Further Observations." For a recent application, see Albert C. Geljon and David T. Runia, *Philo of Alexandria: On Cultivation: Introduction, Translation and Commentary*, PACS 4 (Leiden: Brill, 2013).

Reflections and Conclusions

The discussion above aims to show that the notion of there being two species of souls in the air (*Plant.* 14) is, in Philo, part of a larger scheme that involves the journey of the human soul from its descent through reincarnation to its ascent, as well as the ever-unembodied angels and their tasks. The soul's journey with all its anthropological, ethical, and soteriological dimensions is, so this author believes, at the heart of the Philonic allegories concerning the soul, especially in the *Allegorical Commentary* but also the *Quaestiones*. In different contexts Philo exposes to view and discusses different parts of the journey and uses divergent illustrations. This does not, however, prevent his students from seeing the larger picture, although, together with Philo's habit of cultivating allusions of varying clarity, it does mean that they have to pay a lot of attention to the often very detailed links between the Philonic treatises.

The study of *Plant.* 14 with its parallels reveals the remarkable fact that Philo uses his scheme of the airy souls as an explanation of biblical verses that do not have much in common. This practice of Philo's (which is not limited to this scheme) represents, in my view, what William James has called *the law of dissociation by varying concomitants*: "What is associated now with one thing and now with another tends to become dissociated from either."[80] It would be forced to say that the scheme is inherently present in all the biblical texts Philo expounds, or even that Philo must have thought it was. It is my conviction that the further study of this phenomenon will enhance our understanding of not only individual passages in Philo's writings but, more importantly, his exegetical method and the fundamental question concerning the very different roles played by the biblical text—his *explanandum*—and the ideas presented as its *explanatio*.[81] Another intriguing issue deserving further study and related to Philo's method is his apparent use of the *Timaeus* as a secondary text through which to reach tertiary biblical lemmas in *Plant.* 17–18.

80 William James, *The Principles of Psychology*, 2 vols. (New York: Holt, 1890), 1:506.

81 Based on the observations in this essay we can see that the effect of the biblical text on the subject matter discussed in its exegesis varies widely. For example, the entire first part of *Plant.* (§§1–139) is really based on a single word in Gen 9:20, ἐφύτευσεν, whereas in *Somn.* 1.138–139 the biblical text to which the scheme is attached is broader: the upward and downward movement of angels between earth and heaven. It holds *a priori* that the narrower the biblical basis is, the fewer biblical constraints (things to be accounted for) there are and the larger freedom of maneuver Philo has with regard to the actual contents of his allegories. A systematic investigation of the extent to which Philo in practice avails himself of this freedom would be a worthwhile task.

In the case of the scheme of the souls of the air it seems that Philo's *explanatio* can be further divided into parts: On the one hand, we may think of the soul's journey from above to the world and the release from reincarnation and returning to God as the *interpretation proper*. On the other, what we find between this interpretation and the biblical text are various kinds of mostly Platonic/Platonist notions and images which Philo feels free to combine in different ways in his interpretations of different biblical verses (which do have their effect on his choice). These notions and images come, in a way, close to being mythical features, that is, narrative elements through which beliefs are expressed—for example, the image of the body as a river (*Gig.* 13) is precisely such a mytheme in its original context in the *Timaeus*.[82] These elements do not need to remain the same in different accounts (and they can even be incompatible with each other), because the beliefs that are conveyed are what counts.

As for *Plant.* 17–25, the observations made above concerning other Philonic passages containing allegorizations of the two descriptions of the creation of the human being suggest that Philo's primary orientation is not protological but universal.[83] Those allegorizations have given rise to different kinds of scholarly interpretations. There is no doubt that there are cases where, as Runia has stated, "the man κατ' εἰκόνα θεοῦ and the inbreathing of the divine πνεῦμα both refer to man's god-like part, the νοῦς or rational soul."[84] I would call this the protological interpretation, because it refers to the (original) design of the human soul. The other alternative is the universal interpretation, where being stamped with the "image" and receiving the "breath" of life both come to mean an action by God on the human soul or mind with greatly beneficial effects contributing to its salvation. That these biblical motifs receive a joint interpretation is based on Philo's dividing Gen 2:7 into parts: verse 7b(–c) belongs together with Gen 1:26–27 and refers, basically, to "heaven" while verse 7a refers to "earth." This distinction ultimately corresponds to the fundamental divide in the Platonic worldview, the noetic and the changeless vs. the material and the

82 For this definition of myth, see John Bowker, ed., *Oxford Concise Dictionary of World Religions* (Oxford: Oxford University Press, 2000), s. v. "myth."

83 I thus do not agree with Tobin who says that "the fact that [the interpretations of Gen 1:27 and 2:7] often appear together with their concepts and vocabulary combined (*Det.* 80–90; *Plant.* 14–27; *Mut.* 223; *O* 139, 146–146; *Spec.* 1.171) indicates they are referring to the same single *creation of man.*" (Tobin, *Creation*, 21, emphasis added.)

84 Runia, *Philo and the* Timaeus, 335. This statement is about Philo's exegesis of the creation accounts as *secondary* lemmas, and the examples Runia gives are *Det.* 80–86; *Plant.* 18–20; and *Her.* 56, all discussed above. I do not think that these passages can be meaningfully interpreted along these lines only. For examples of interpretations of Gen 2:7b of this kind, see above, n. 52.

ever-changing. At least within the *Allegorical Commentary*, the splitting up of Gen 2:7 is operative in both the running commentary in *Leg.* 1 and in many (but not all) treatments of the verse elsewhere. The human of Gen 1 is kept separate from the human of Gen 2:7a—but not from the human of verse 7b–c.[85]

The protological and universal interpretations of the accounts of the creation of the human being are not mutually exclusive. Philo accepts them both, but he also sometimes blends them so that his student may have difficulties following his train of thought: which does he mean? In *Plant.* 18–19 Philo in no way indicates he might not be discussing the general human situation (in distinction to the virtuous only), which speaks against a purely universal interpretation. On the other hand, pure protology is not possible either, because the soul is presupposed as the object of God's action. But do *all* souls receive the stamp of the Logos in §18? I do not think so, but regardless of one's answer, it is clear that there are these two interpretations and that the scholarly endeavor to understand Philo will benefit from taking both into account.

University of Helsinki

[85] Cf. Runia's view that in "*Opif.*, *Leg.* I–II and *QG* I Philo tends to keep the man of Gen. 1:27 separate from the man created in Gen. 2:7." He continues that in *Leg.* 1.31 "the attempt is *not* made to show that the mind created in Gen. 1:27 is the same as the rational part that is inbreathed in Gen. 2:7" (ibid., emphasis original.) These statements reflect an exclusively protological understanding of Philo's exegesis.

The Studia Philonica Annual 29 (2017): 185–228

BIBLIOGRAPHY SECTION

PHILO OF ALEXANDRIA
AN ANNOTATED BIBLIOGRAPHY 2014

D. T. RUNIA, M. ALESSO, E. BIRNBAUM, A. C. GELJON, H. M. KEIZER, J. LEONHARDT-BALZER, M. R. NIEHOFF, S. J. K. PEARCE, T. SELAND, S. WEISSER

2014[1]

E. ALBANO, *I silenzi delle sacre scritture: Limiti e possibilità di rivelazione del Logos negli scritti di Filone, Clemente e Origene*, Studia ephemeridis Augustinianum 138 (Rome 2014).

This extensive work (630 pages) is entitled 'The silences of the Holy Scriptures: Limits and possibilities of revelation of the Logos in the writings of Philo, Clement and Origen.' It investigates how the three Alexandrians have dealt with the 'silence of impossibility' (i.e., the impossibility to fully express divine reality in human words) and the 'silence of unveiling' (i.e. the need to hide, or only partially unveil, the deepest meaning of the text, protecting it from the unworthy) in their explanation of the Holy Scriptures. The first third of the book is dedicated to Philo (218 pages). It discusses in Chapter 1 the (rare) cases in which Philo reflects on things a Bible passage omits to say (*Plant.* 18–23; *Sobr.* 62; *Spec.* 3.168, 4.157; *Fug.* 60–61; *Det.* 177; *Her.* 22–29). Chapter 2 identifies how Philo expresses the difference between the θεῖος λόγος (divine word, of infinite nature) and the χρησμοί (human words) of Scripture. Chapters 3 and 4 focus on the difference in being (3) and in language (4) between God and human in Philo's thought. Chapters 5 and 6 investigate how Philo applies these principles in his interpretative work. Chapter 7 concludes that the central problem is that of the possibility of mediation between God and human. A form of mediation/incarnation identified by Philo is that of the νόμος ἔμψυχος. Philo's philosophical make-up leads him towards an ontological conception of inspired text that differs from the Hebrew view, in which text and divine word tend to coincide. (HMK)

[1] This bibliography has been prepared by the members of the International Philo Bibliography Project under the leadership of D. T. Runia (Melbourne). The principles on which the annotated bibliography is based have been outlined in *SPhiloA* 2 (1990) 141–142, and are largely based on those used to compile the 'mother works,' R-R, RRS and RRS2 (on the inclusion of works in languages outside the scholarly mainstream see esp. RRS2 xii). The division of the work this year is as follows: material in English (and Dutch) by D. T. Runia (DTR), E. Birnbaum (EB), A. C. Geljon (ACG) and S. J. K. Pearce (SJKP); in French by Sharon Weisser (SW); in Italian by H. M. Keizer (HMK); in German by J. Leonhardt-Balzer (JLB); in Spanish and Portuguese by M. Alesso; in Scandinavian languages (and by

M. Alesso, 'El concepto de dýnamis en la teología de Filón alejandrino y sus proyecciones en la Patrología,' in S. Filippi and M. Coria (edd.), *La identidad propia del pensamiento patrístico y medieval: ¿Unidad y pluralidad?* (Rosario 2014) 25–34.

The relationship between the Logos and power in Philo requires special attention in connection with the problem of divine transcendence: a highly significant plot is woven with symbolic ties that unite God with humanity through the scheme of the five powers. The article examines the problem especially in *Fug.*, but also compares the meaning of δύναμις in Philo with other philosophical expressions of his time, in order to corroborate the scope of the semantic conditions that the term develops in Hellenistic Judaism: in the fragments of Aristobulus (150 BCE) and in the treatise of an unknown author, *De mundo* by Ps.Aristotle, (ca. 100 BCE). Finally some developments of these ideas in patristic thought are analyzed. (MA)

E. S. Alexander, 'Ritual on the Threshold: Mezuzah and the Crafting of Domestic and Civic Space,' *Jewish Social Studies* 20 (2014) 100–130.

Situated on the threshold, the mezuzah may be connected to the inside or the outside of a house. This article explores the question of what role the mezuzah played in arbitrating the boundary between inside and outside and in giving meaning to space on either side of the boundary. In his discussion of the mezuzah, Philo assumes that Jews and non-Jews, men and women, adults and children, freemen and slaves all interact with the mezuzah in the public space, 'such that the mezuzah adds a distinctively Jewish moral and aesthetic presence to an already culturally and ethically diverse urban environment' (p. 100). The Tannaim, by contrast, focus on the mezuzah in the private, domestic setting, and its significance for the members of a Jewish household. Philo's comments in *Spec.* 4.142, in emphasizing the place of the mezuzah on the public side of the threshold, must be understood against the background of tensions over public space in early Roman Alexandria, as described in Philo's *Flacc.* His description of the mezuzah ritual 'stakes a claim for Jewish presence in the public spaces of a multicultural urban environment' (p. 107). (SJKP)

Scandinavian scholars) by T. Seland (TS); and in Hebrew and by Israeli scholars by M. R. Niehoff (MRN). This year too, assistance has been derived from the related bibliographical labours of L. Perrone (Bologna) and his team in the journal *Adamantius* (Studies on the Alexandrian tradition). Other scholars who have given assistance this year are Giovanni Benedetto, Cornelis den Hertog, and Jean Riaud. This year I once again owe much to my former Leiden colleague M. R. J. Hofstede, who laid a secure foundation for the bibliography through his extremely thorough electronic searches. However, the bibliography remains inevitably incomplete, because much work on Philo is tucked away in monographs and articles, the titles of which do not mention his name. Scholars are encouraged to get in touch with members of the team if they spot omissions or wish to have their own publications included (addresses below in 'Notes on Contributors'). In order to preserve continuity with previous years, the bibliography retains its own customary stylistic conventions and has not changed to those of the Society of Biblical Literature used in the remainder of the Annual.

F. Avemarie, 'Image of God and Image of Christ: Developments in Pauline and Ancient Jewish anthropology,' in J.-S. Rey (ed.), *The Dead Sea Scrolls and Pauline literature*, Studies on the Texts of the Desert of Judah 102 (Leiden 2014) 209–235.

Paul and Philo are compared in the context of the discussion of human beings as image of God in Paul. In Philo, based on LXX Gen 1:26–27, it is the Logos who is the immediate image of God, whereas the human being is merely a copy. Furthermore, there is the distinction between the intelligible, heavenly, and the corporeal human being. It is only the intelligible human being of Gen 1:27 who is called immortal. The corporeal human being of Gen 2:7 chose mortality (*Virt.* 205). Paul may have known this interpretation, but his reading of Christ as the image of God also has parallels in Palestinian Jewish traditions. (JLB)

M. Baretta, 'Filone, il *De vita Mosis* e le sue fonti,' *Studi Classici e Orientali* 60 (2014) 73–97.

This study of the sources of *Mos.* takes its starting point in 1.4 where Philo declares that he bases his biography on the 'sacred books' and the 'ancients of the nation,' thus indicating both written and oral tradition. The article reviews the various types of citations or references in the work. Regarding Scripture, there are quoted terms or expressions, free citations, and paraphrases. References to the oral tradition are much harder to establish; they may be identified where Philo uses φασί. Another category is that of Greek sources, especially Hellenistic-Jewish. In the final sentence of *Mos.* (2.292) Philo only mentions the Holy Scriptures as the basis of his account, thereby expressing which of his sources has for him the first and highest authority. (HMK)

P. C. Beentjes, 'Philo of Alexandria and Greek Ben Sira,' in G. G. Xeravits, J. Zsengellér and X. Szabó (edd.), *Canonicity, Setting, Wisdom in the Deuterocanonicals*, Deuterocanonical and Cognate Literature Studies 22 (Berlin 2014) 145–172.

This study by a prominent Ben Sira scholar examines the eleven Philonic texts listed in the supplement to the *Biblia Patristica* as a reference, echo, or allusion to passages from the Book of Ben Sira/Sirach. The author concludes that most of the correspondences given in the *Biblia Patristica* should be rejected and, for the most part, he confirms the negative conclusions of Herbert Ryle (1895) regarding Philo's knowledge of the Apocrypha. Among the texts under consideration, *Somn.* 1.50 offers a 'striking resemblance' to Sir 24:1. (SJKP)

W. Bejda, 'The City of Cain—the City of a Tyrant: The Political Aspect of the Cain Narrative in Josephus Flavius' *Antiquitates Judaicae*,' *Revue Biblique* 121 (2014) 283–297.

This paper offers an analysis of Cain's portrait in Josephus' *Antiquities* (1.52–62). It appears that Josephus adds many traits that turn the biblical killer into a full-blooded tyrant. His behavior can be compared with that of Herod the Great and the Roman emperors. Cain committed murder, just as Herod and the Roman rulers did. His name symbolizes 'grasping man,' which is interpreted to mean that he has a desire for sensual pleasures and is marked by ὕβρις. Cain is also pictured as 'teacher of wickedness.' The presentation of

Cain as a vile sophist-teacher seems to be dependent on Philo, who depicts Cain as such in *Post.* 35–38. The notion that Cain compels his subjects to live in the town that he ruled may be based on the actions of Dionysius the Elder, the tyrant of Syracuse. (ACG)

P. J. BEKKEN, 'Philo's Relevance for the Study of the New Testament,' in T. SELAND (ed.), *Reading Philo: A Handbook to Philo of Alexandria* (Grand Rapids, MI 2014) 226–267.

In this chapter, instead of proceeding from book to book in the New Testament, looking for similarities and parallels in Philo's works, the author has chosen a thematic approach. He surveys a vast range of topics and texts which show how a study of Philo is relevant for a New Testament student. The main sections of the chapter are: Scripture and exegesis; Beliefs, motifs, and metaphors; Jews' relation to non-Jews and pagan society; Inner-Jewish conflicts and punishments; and Historical information. (TS)

P. J. BEKKEN, *The Lawsuit Motif in John's Gospel from New Perspectives: Jesus Christ, Crucified Criminal and Emperor of the World*, Supplements to Novum Testamentum 158 (Leiden 2014).

This volume which contains an 'Introduction' (Chap. 1, pp. 1–19) and six extensive studies—all dealing with the Gospel of John—is included in this Philo bibliography because of its intensive use of texts from Philo of Alexandria. The studies as such are rather self-contained, but only one has been previously published. Chapter 2 (pp. 23–70), labelled 'The Jewish and Roman 'Trial',' argues that the attempts to have Jesus killed or arrested for certain crimes (breaking the Sabbath, blasphemy and seduction) inherent in John 5–10, could either be understood in light of Philo's writings (*Mos.* 2.213–220; *Spec.* 2.250–251; 1.54–57; 315–318) as legitimate, through extra-legal vigilante executions on the spot, or as regular processes in which the criminal is subjected to arrest, trial and execution. Chapter 3 (pp. 71–117), dealing with 'The Official Jewish and Roman Proceedings against Jesus in Light of Greco-Roman Protocols,' does not draw much on Philo's works, but focuses on an Egyptian papyrus located in Oslo, P.Oslo II,17, as evidence of provincial procedures of the Greco-Roman administration. In Chapter 4 (pp. 121–147), Bekken returns to a closer study of John 5 and 8 in light of Philo: 'The Debate about Valid Testimony in John 5:31–40; 8:12–20 and Philo, *Legum Allegoriae* 3:205–208.' This is a slightly revised version of a study published in 2008 (see *SPhiloA* vol. 23, p. 101) arguing that Philo's *Leg.* 3.205–208, supplemented with other Philonic texts, provide a relevant Jewish cultural background to the debate on valid testimony as reflected in John. John 5 is also in focus in the next chapter: 'The Reversal of the Accusation of Blasphemy: John 5:1–18 and 10:31–39 in a Jewish Context' (pp. 148–175). Next, Chapter 6 (pp. 179–210), is a study on 'The Divine Lawsuit Motif in John in Light of Philo's Treatise *De Iosepho*,' arguing that 'Philo's *De Iosepho* and John's Gospel both dramatize how a 'conspiracy' against the idealized protagonist is interpreted as a creative theodicy, in which the antagonists are seen to contribute toward the realization of God's plan' (p. 180). The seventh and final chapter breaks somewhat out of the judicial focus so prominent in the previous studies as it deals with 'The Theme of Jesus' Kingship in Negotiation with Jewish Hopes and the Roman Empire' (pp. 211–261). Here Bekken argues that Philo's eschatology as indicated by *Mos.* 1.288–291 and *Praem.* 93–97 provide a cultural context for Pilate's declaration of Jesus as the 'Man' in John 19:5, and that in the context of John's Gospel this serves as an ironic reversal of the mocking of a pseudo-Emperor, conveying the message that Jesus is the true king and 'Emperor' over against Caesar (p. 211). (TS)

K. Berthelot, 'Where May Canaanites Be Found? Canaanites, Phoenicians, and Others in Jewish Texts from the Hellenistic and Roman Period,' in K. Berthelot, J. E. David and M. Hirshman (edd.), *The Gift of the Land and the Fate of the Canaanites in Jewish Thought* (New York 2014) 253–274, esp. 261–263.

In this study of the ways in which the terms 'Canaan' and 'Canaanite' were used and understood by Jews in the Hellenistic and Roman periods, Philo is discussed as an example of an author who for these terms occasionally uses contemporary names—however inaccurate and anachronistic. Although the terms 'Canaan' and 'Canaanites' appear in some of his Pentateuchal interpretations, he also speaks of these people as 'Syrians' and Phoenicians' and calls the land of Canaan 'Syria,' 'Phoenicia,' 'Palestinian Syria,' 'Coele-syria,' and 'Palestine.' Philo's use of contemporary geographic designations when writing about Canaan may suggest that it did not matter to him to employ exact terminology. This impression, however, does not signify that he was indifferent to the land itself. Indeed he provides one of the few examples of the expression 'holy land' (*Legat.* 202), which is rare in both biblical and Second Temple sources. (EB)

E. Birnbaum, 'Philo's Relevance for the Study of Judaism,' in T. Seland (ed.), *Reading Philo: A Handbook to Philo of Alexandria* (Grand Rapids, MI 2014) 200–225.

A question much debated in connection with antiquity is whether one can refer to a 'common Judaism' with a core set of features or only a variety of Judaisms represented by different groups of Jews. To illustrate how Philo might shed light on this question, both specifically and on Jewish life in antiquity generally, the author considers evidence from his writings on the following topics: practices, beliefs and ideas, community institutions, the Bible and biblical interpretation, Jews and Jewish identity, Jews' interactions with and attitudes toward non-Jews and their culture, and historical events that pertain to Jews. While Philo has much in common with other Jews, 'he also displays important differences and distinctive features.' Instead of viewing him as representative or not representative of other Jews, we would do best 'to consider individual issues in all their complexity' (p. 225). Under the aforementioned topics, the chapter offers several examples of issues that merit further investigation. (EB)

E. Birnbaum, 'Philo at Yale,' *Adamantius* 20 (2014) 632–635.

This is a report on a conference that took place at Yale University, March 30–April 1, 2014. Entitled 'Philo's Readers: Affinities, Reception, Transmission, and Influence,' the conference focused on how Philo's works were received among later Jews, pagans, and Christians, ranging from Josephus in the first century CE to Franz Rosenzweig in the twentieth century. The report summarizes some 15 presentations and describes other conference-related activities. (EB)

P. Borgen, *The Gospel of John: More Light from Philo, Paul and Archaeology: The Scriptures, Tradition, Exposition, Settings, Meaning*, Novum Testamentum Supplements 154 (Leiden 2014).

Most of the chapters of this volume are reprints of studies originally published in various journals and books in the period of 1959–2010. Only two of these reprinted studies mention Philo in their title: 'The Gospel of John and Philo of Alexandria' (pp. 43–66, originally published in 2003, summarized in *SPhiloA* vol. 18, p. 174; and 'The Sabbath Controversy in John 5:1–18 and the Analogous Controversy Reflected in Philo's Writings' (pp. 179–191, originally published in *SPhiloA* vol. 3 (1991) pp. 209–221, summarized in vol. 6, p. 123. The volume also contains three other unpublished articles which refer more or less extensively to Philo and his writings. See the summaries below. See further the review by J. Leonhardt-Balzer in *SPhiloA* vol. 27, pp. 246–249. (TS)

P. Borgen, 'Philo—An Interpreter of the Laws of Moses,' in T. Seland (ed.), *Reading Philo: A Handbook to Philo of Alexandria* (Grand Rapids, MI 2014) 75–101.

This chapter is a slightly revised version of an earlier study by Borgen, published as 'Philo of Alexandria as Exegete,' in *A History of Biblical Interpretation. Volume 1: The Ancient Period.* Edited by A. J. Hauser and D. F. Watson (Grand Rapids 2003) 114–143, summarized in *SPhiloA* vol. 18, p. 147. The revisions consist mainly in deletion of some minor paragraphs. What is more regrettable is that the headlines are now printed in a way that does not differentiate between various levels, e.g., between level one and two of the headlines. The major sections, however, are still Philo's Expository Writings; Hermeneutical Presuppositions; Aspects of Philo's Exegesis; Philo as an Exegete in Context; Some Exegetical Approaches and Forms; and The Laws of Moses in the Alexandrian Context. (TS)

P. Borgen, 'Observations on God's Agent and Agency in John's Gospel Chapters 5–10: Agency and the Quest for the Historical Jesus,' in *The Gospel of John: More Light from Philo, Paul and Archaeology: The Scriptures, Tradition, Exposition, Settings, Meaning,* Novum Testamentum Supplements 154 (Leiden 2014) 193–218.

This previously unpublished chapter was originally read as a paper at the SBL Annual Meeting in Atlanta 2010, and to some extent elaborates somewhat further on issues of agents and agency dealt with in some of the other chapters included in this collection of articles, cf. above. The author asks: 'Is there a traditional structure form which holds all of John 5–10 together?' (p. 194). Borgen answers by stating that it appears that the basic structure inherent in these chapters is a story with subsequent judicial exchanges of views. The basic story is the healing of the paralytic (John 5:1–10), and the subsequent judicial exchanges cover the rest of the chapters 5:11–47; 7; 8:12–59; and (p. 194). Philo is briefly referred to several times as an exemplary witness of procedures or issues found in John; cf. p. 199 (*Dec.* 118–120, on a formulation parallel to John 5:23; *Conf.* 62–63, on relationship between father and son); p. 204 (*Spec.* 1.64–65, on reference to Deut 18:15–19); p. 205 (*Mos.* 1.148–159, on Moses as king); p. 210 (*Leg.* 3.205–207, on swearing); p. 211 (*QG* 4.144, on an envoy's report). (TS)

P. Borgen, 'Can Philo's *In Flaccum* and *Legatio ad Gaium* be of Help?,' in *The Gospel of John: More Light from Philo, Paul and Archaeology: The Scriptures, Tradition, Exposition, Settings, Meaning*, Novum Testamentum Supplements 154 (Leiden 2014) 241–260.

In this study, Borgen asks if Philo might have material which could be of help in providing parallels to the form and structure of a Gospel. Focusing on Philo's *Flacc.* and *Legat.* he compares these to the Gospel of John, and also to Mark. Hence Borgen deals with the following aspects: 1. Observations relative to opening sections; 2. The Scope; 3. The Law of Moses; 4. Crime reports; 5. Positive interpretations. Then he focuses on The Prologue of Philo's *Legatio ad Gaium*; The counterfeit God; Education; and The palinode. He suggests that his readings point to the conclusion that there is no room for understanding 'the Gospel of Mark as a model or frame for the form and structure of the Gospel of John' (p. 259). John seems in several cases to be closer to these works of Philo than to Mark. Concerning the relationship between Mark and John, Borgen suggests that there is no need to understand their relationship along a linear, historical time line. (TS)

P. Borgen, 'Summary: John, Archaeology, Philo, Paul, Other Jewish Sources. John's Independence of the Synoptics. Where My Journey of Research Has Lead Me,' in *The Gospel of John: More Light from Philo, Paul and Archaeology: The Scriptures, Tradition, Exposition, Settings, Meaning*, Novum Testamentum Supplements 154 (Leiden 2014) 241–260.

This chapter is not so much a summary of all the preceding chapters in the volume as a summary of the author's arguments for his view that the Gospel of John is independent of the Synoptic Gospels. In addition to drawing on the preceding chapters of this volume, Borgen also draws on some geographical and social information in the Gospel of John and archaeological findings that, when seen together, might strengthen his view that the Gospel of John is independent of the Synoptic Gospels. Then he summarizes the previous study on *Flacc.* and *Legat.*, arguing that John's kinship with aspects of Philo's *Legat.* supports his view that John's form and traditions are independent of Mark: 'The agreements between John and the Synoptic Gospels are better understood as agreements between John and synoptic-like traditions transmitted and interpreted independently of those three written gospels. Paul provides examples of such transmission and use' (p. 294). (TS)

F. E. Brenk, 'Philo and Plutarch on the Nature of God,' *The Studia Philonica Annual* 26 (2014) 79–92.

The article consists of a series of comparative reflections on the theology of Philo and Plutarch as interpreted in recent scholarship. The author emphasizes that religion involves worship and questions whether Greek philosophical religion as witnessed in Plutarch's thought is really monotheistic, given that the supreme god in Middle Platonism (much influenced by the *Timaeus*) is not the object of worship. Care needs to be taken in basing a monotheistic interpretation of Plutarch's theology on the speech of Ammonius in the *On the E at Delphi*, since there is some distance between his 'extreme views' (p. 85) and those of Plutarch himself. The role of 'Ammonius' is to explain the nature of God to educated persons acquainted with their religious traditions, just as Philo does. Plutarch himself, however, as a priest of Apollo has a vested interest in cult. So it may be concluded that 'worship of the traditional Apollo beside this God seemingly creates a contradiction between monotheism and polytheism, but only if our definition excludes worship of other gods, even when they are infinitely inferior to the real God. This puts Philo and Plutarch in a much closer relationship than just some sort of Alexandrian philosophical heritage. Both, on similar even if different paths, created theologies for their faiths, one essentially monotheistic, the other essentially polytheistic, theologies heavily inspired by Plato (p. 92).' (DTR)

L. Brisson, 'Alexandrie, berceau du néoplatonisme: Eudore, Philon, Ammonios et l'école d'Alexandrie,' in C. Méla and F. Möri (edd.), *Alexandrie la divine* (Geneva 2014) 354–363.

As part of a lavish catalogue in two volumes accompanying the exposition entitled 'Alexandrie la divine' held at the Fondation Bodmer in Geneva in 2014, the author places Philo in the context of the development of Alexandrian philosophy from the 1st cent. BCE onwards, in which Platonism and Pythagoreanism mingle together. 'It is this synthesis between Platonism and Pythagoreanism which constitutes the characteristic features of Philo's thought and which underpins his allegorical interpretations (p. 357).' For other articles in the work see the studies by Niehoff and Saudelli summarized below. (DTR)

J. Brumberg-Kraus, 'Contrasting Banquets: A Literary Commonplace in Philo's *On the Contemplative Life* and Other Greek and Roman Symposia,' in S. Marks and H. Taussig (edd.), *Meals in Early Judaism: Social Formation at the Table* (New York 2014) 139–162.

With one important difference, Philo's account of the meal of the Therapeutae belongs to a literary genre in which Greek and Roman symposia are described. Just as Philo presents the meal of the Therapeutae as superior when compared with other symposia such as those of Plato, Xenophon, the Cyclopes, and the Italians, so too do other examples of literary symposia (e.g., Athenaeus, *Deipnosophistae* 5.186–188; Mishnah Pesahim 10:8) include explicit or implicit comparisons where the symposium being described is considered to be better than others. Unlike other literary accounts, however, Philo eschews the dialogue form, in which some aspect of the meal gives rise to a discussion among participants who hold differing views. Instead, he tells how the leader of the Therapeutae discourses on a question related to Scripture and his lecture is met with complete accord and appreciation. In Bromberg-Kraus's view, Philo's portrayal of the group in this way is meant to convey his understanding of the ideal community as one that has no disagreements but is characterized by total unity and harmony among its members. (EB)

B. G. Bucur, 'Clement of Alexandria's Exegesis of Old Testament Theophanies,' *Phronema* 29 (2014) 61–79.

In the interpretation of the Old Testament theophanies (an understudied subject in biblical and patristic scholarship according to the author), Clement plays an important role because he initiates an approach which differs from some of his predecessors and contemporaries. He continues the 'noetic exegesis' of Philo (to use E. Osborn's characterization), as can be seen in his interpretation of the theophanies in Gen 18 and Is 6. The very act of reading the Scriptures is a transformative and mystagogical experience. (DTR)

F. CALABI, 'Le migrazioni di Abramo in Filone di Alessandria,' *Ricerche storico bibliche* 26 (2014) 251–267.

In Philo's interpretation of Abraham (in *Abr.* and *Migr.*), migration is a central theme, with various layers of meaning: migration away from home to the true home, from the corporeal to the intelligible, from the passions to virtue, from knowledge of the stars to self-knowledge to knowledge of God. The events of Abra(ha)m's life receive in Philo a precise significance as necessary steps on the way towards true knowledge. The article highlights where Philo's interpretation deviates from the biblical account or places different accents (e.g., remaining silent about Abraham's negotiating with God about the number of righteous in Sodom) and it confronts Philo's Abraham with the depictions of Hellenistic-Jewish literature. Philo's Abraham is an exemplary figure for the virtues and knowledge defined by Greek philosophy, as well as for his faith in God and for his obedience of the law of nature that coincides with Mosaic Law. (HMK)

A. CONWAY-JONES, *Gregory of Nyssa's Tabernacle Imagery in its Jewish and Christian Contexts*, Oxford Early Christian Studies (Oxford 2014).

This monograph examines Gregory of Nyssa's tabernacle imagery as set out in his *Life of Moses*. The major part of this study consists in a close reading of 2.162–201 (Chapters 6–14), which is subdivided into short sections. As part of the discussion on each section, the author investigates relevant passages in the works of the Alexandrian predecessors, Philo, Clement, and Origen. An important Philonic text within this discussion is the symbolic treatment of the tabernacle and the priestly vestments in *Mos.* 2.71–135. Gregory also follows Philo in his interpretation of the darkness in Exod 20:21 as a symbol of God's incomprehensibility. Just like his Alexandrian predecessors he weaves Platonic assumptions into the biblical account. He employs the heavenly and earthly tabernacles to lay out his own theological agenda, investigating themes as, for instance, God's incomprehensibility, the divinity of Christ, the incarnation, and living according to virtue. (ACG)

M. COVER, 'The Sun and the Chariot: the *Republic* and the *Phaedrus* as Sources for Rival Platonic Paradigms of Psychic Vision in Philo's Biblical Commentaries,' *The Studia Philonica Annual* 26 (2014) 151–167.

It seems that Philo makes contradictory statements about the content of contemplative vision which cannot be harmonized philosophically. Sometimes he denies that a direct vision of God is possible (*Praem.* 40–46), but he also suggests that a direct vision of God is the goal of Moses's mystical ascent (*Leg.* 3.100–101). The author focuses on the role of Platonic sources in the diversity of Philo's views of psychic vision. He investigates *Leg.* 3.100–101 and its background in the myth about the chariot soul in Plato's *Phaedrus*. First, he argues that Philo here offers the possibility of a direct vision of God. Second, he discusses echoes from Plato's *Phaedrus* in the text. Third, he deals with Neoplatonic interpretations of the *Phaedrus* myth. Finally, he discusses a counterexample to *Leg.* 3.100–101, found in *Mut.* 7–17, where Philo alludes to the *Phaedrus* myth as well, but does not admit a direct vision of God. It is concluded that 'Philo's statements on Moses's contemplative vision gain an exegetical coherence, when one considers: (a) the commentary series; (b) his Platonic intertexts; (c) the biblical figure that serves as contemplative paradigm; (d) the length of his biblical citation; and (e) the primary biblical lemma from Genesis to which the Moses exemplum is subordinated (p. 167).' The *Phaedrus* myth offers the possibility to see God directly. This idea seems to be in conflict with the apophatic emphasis elsewhere in Philo, but he does not completely eliminate this Platonic theme from his writings. (ACG)

M. R. D'ANGELO, 'Sexuality in Jewish Writings from 200 BCE to 200 CE,' in T. K. HUBBARD (ed.), *A Companion to Greek and Roman Sexualities* (Oxford 2014) 534–548.

The wide-ranging and quite detailed survey in this chapter addresses discourse about sex in Jewish writings from 200 BCE to 200 CE. Philo's own thought relating to sexuality is compactly presented on pp. 541–544. It is first noted how prevalent sexual and gendered imagery is in his work. Eros is regarded as a benevolent force, but its effect entails that pleasure needs to be controlled. Philo's identification of sexual bad practices is quite similar to that found in Roman writers, but the penalties that he prescribes, e.g., in *Hypoth.* 7.1, are far more extreme (involving death), exceeding in some cases what is prescribed in the Jewish law. The apologetic intent is clear: Jews must be shown to have superior mores. In his exposition of the sixth and tenth commandments in *Decal.* and *Spec.* Philo comes close to creating a realm of the sexual. In this material homoeroticism receives no more attention than other sexual crimes, but Philo's anxieties about it emerge elsewhere, in his accounts of the crime of Sodom (he is the first surviving interpreter to identify the crime as male-male sex) and his descriptions of banquets, esp. in *Contempl.* It may be concluded that for the most part sexual counsels in Jewish texts are conventional, but Philo is the great exception. His engagement with sexual and gendered imagery is extraordinary and it may be speculated that 'the idea of the lover of wisdom as producing spiritual children fixed his attention on the realities of sex and reproduction' (p. 546). (DTR)

F. DAMGAARD, 'Philo's Life of Moses as "Rewritten Bible",' in J. ZSENGELLÉR (ed.), *Rewritten Bible after Fifty Years: Texts, Terms, or Techniques? A Last Dialogue with Geza Vermes,* Supplements to the Journal for the Study of Judaism 166 (Leiden 2014) 233–248.

In the first part of the article the author argues that the first book of *Mos.* can be regarded as rewritten Bible. It rewrites a substantial part of the Bible, namely from Exodus 2 to Numbers 32. Exegesis is implicit rather than explicit. Philo makes also use of non-biblical oral traditions. In the second part the author discusses the editorial intention of *Mos.* Philo wishes to demonstrate to both Greek and Jewish readers that Moses embodies all the cardinal virtues. He constructs Moses's identity by dissociating him from Egypt and the Egyptians. The exodus of the Israelite people out of Egypt is interpreted as a migration of the soul towards virtue and the knowledge of God. This allegory is, however, implicit, and never stated explicitly. Furthermore, Philo gives the story a contemporary relevance by, presenting the exodus as a Jewish act of self-defence because of the Egyptian king's disregard for the civil rights of the Jews. Therefore Philo may also have a Roman readership in mind. Finally, the author claims that *Mos.* can be seen as a companion piece to *Flacc.* and *Legat.* (ACG)

J. DANIÉLOU, *Philo of Alexandria,* translated by James G. Colbert (Eugene, OR 2014).

An English translation of Cardinal Daniélou's classic work in the French language on Philo published in 1958 (R–R 5810). The translator's brief preface focuses on issues of reference and translation. It says virtually nothing about the context of the original work or the place of its author in Philonic scholarship. (DTR)

G. De Gregorio, 'Filone Alessandrino tra Massimo Planude e Giorgio Bullotes: A proposito dei codici Vindob. Suppl. gr. 50, Vat. Urb. gr. 125 e Laur. Plut. 10, 23,' in C. Brockmann (ed.), *Handschriften- und Textforschung heute. Zur Überlieferung der griechischen Literatur. Festschrift für Dieter Harlfinger aus Anlass seines 70. Geburtstages*, Serta Graeca 30 (Wiesbaden 2014) 177–230.

An in-depth analysis of a branch in the manuscript tradition of Philo's work, represented by Vindob. Suppl. gr. 50, Vat. Urb. gr. 125, and Laur. Plut. 10, 23. The Vienna manuscript is Byzantine, dates from the 11th century, contains *Mos.*, *De fortitudine* (which is part of *Virt.*), and *Ios.*, and shows textual interventions by the hand of Maximus Planudes (13th century). The Vatican manuscript is the work of the same Planudes (working in Byzantium), and contains *Spec.* 3, *Mos.*, and again *De fortitudine*. A descendant of Vat. Urb. gr. 125 is the Laurentian codex of which the copyist can be identified as Georgios Bullotes (early 14th century); it carries *Mos.*, *De fortitudine*, *Ios.*, and *Her.* The Laur. Plut. 10, 23 arrived in Florence in the 14th century and allows us to gain insight in the reception of Philo in Italian humanist circles. (HMK)

P. G. R. De Villiers, 'Union with the Transcendent God in Philo and John's Gospel,' *HTS Teologiese Studies/Theological Studies (South Africa, electronic publication)* 70.1 (2014) 1–8.

This article analyses the experience of divine presence within an intimate divine-human relationship, as conceptualised in Philo's writings, and compares this experience with mystical passages in John's Gospel. The article explains their understanding of God and how the union with a transcendent God is mediated. It investigates this union in terms of an underlying mystical pattern that existed in the first century CE and explains similarities of Philo's works with John's Gospel. Special attention is given to Philo's accounts because his own mystical experiences and views are relatively unknown in New Testament scholarship. The article pursues a discussion of Philo's understanding of the divine longing for union with humanity despite the divine transcendence, paying attention to the direct and indirect manner in which this union is mediated, and then concludes with an investigation of similar motifs in John's Gospel. (DTR; based on author's abstract)

B. Decharneux, 'The Carabas Affair (*in Flacc.* 36–39): An Incident Emblematic of Philo's Political Philosophy,' in P. J. Tomson and J. Schwartz (edd.), *Jews and Christians in the First and Second Centuries: How to Write Their History*, Compendia Rerum Iudaicarum ad Novum Testamentum 13 (Leiden 2014) 70–79.

The author briefly analyses the so-called 'Carabas Affair,' in which Philo describes the mock coronation of a madman names Carabas, carried out by the Alexandrian mob to denigrate the newly created Jewish monarch, Agrippa I, whose transit through Alexandria sparked violent reactions among some elements of the city's population (*Flacc.* 36–39). The narrative should be read as Philo's attempt to discredit the prefect Flaccus, under whose administration the protests against Agrippa were followed by a massive outbreak of violence directed against the city's Jews. Philo skilfully creates the impression that those who insulted Agrippa, the friend of Gaius, mocked the emperor himself. Flaccus is to be condemned for failing to prevent this. In this context, Philo's philosophical lesson is that the maintenance of social order is 'orchestrated by the divine' (p. 78). (SJKP)

J. DILLON, 'Pythagoreanism in the Academic Tradition: the Early Academy to Numenius,' in C. A. HUFFMANN (ed.), *A History of Pythagoreanism* (Cambridge 2014) 250–273, esp. 263–266.

For the revival of Pythagoreanism in the Platonist tradition it is necessary to examine developments in Alexandria in the second half of the first century BCE, and particular the role of Eudorus. The first discernible beneficiary of these developments is Philo, even though he is not properly speaking a Platonist. For Philo Pythagoras is a key figure, because he is the conduit for the transmission of the 'Mosaic' system of philosophy to the Greeks. Features of Philo's thought that may be identified as distinctively 'Pythagorean' are his system of first principles, his use of number-mysticism, and also aspects of his ethical theory, e.g. the way justice is linked to equality. Pythagorean influence even appears in the realm of logic, as seen in the order of Philo's listing of the categories in *Decal.* (DTR)

V. DOBRORUKA, *Second Temple Pseudepigraphy: A Cross-cultural Comparison of Apocalyptic Texts and Related Jewish literature*, Ekstasis: Religious Experience from Antiquity to the Middle Ages 4 (Berlin 2014), esp. 111–120.

A revised version of the author's Dphil thesis (University of Oxford, 2006), this monograph attempts to interpret the phenomenon of Second Temple period pseudepigraphy as a mystical experience, drawing on insights gained through a cross-cultural comparative study of automatic writing in modern Brazilian Kardecism. Within Chapter 5 ('Philo, Josephus and 4Ezra: the Main Testimonies for Inspired Writing during the Second Temple Period'), she offers a very brief examination of 67 Philonic texts (the majority of which belong to *Somn.* 1–2 and *Ios.*) that relate in various ways to mystical inspiration. Compared with other Second Temple sources under consideration, Philo emerges as the author who dwells most on causes, interpretation and uses of mystical experience. He is very careful to distinguish between different kinds of visionary experiences and, like Josephus, reflects a Greek educational background in offering sophisticated explanations of visionary experiences. (SJKP)

R. FELDMEIER, *Der Höchste: Studien zur hellenistischen Religionsgeschichte und zum biblischen Gottesglauben*, Wissenschaftliche Untersuchungen zum Neuen Testament 1.330 (Tübingen 2014).

The book is a collection of mainly previously published articles. There is nothing dedicated specifically to Philo, except one part of a previously unpublished chapter: 'Der oberste Gott als Vater: Die frühjüdische und frühchristliche Rede vom göttlichen Vater im Kontext stoischer und platonischer Kosmos-Theologie' (178–193, esp. 189–191). While the idea of God as father is not common in the Old Testament, in *Opif.* 21 Philo, following Plato, uses the term 'father and creator' in the philosophical sense. Following Stoic exegesis of Homer, he also uses the idea of the father to describe God as ruler of the world (*Opif.* 10). This idea of God as king and at the same time as father has consequences for the human approach to power (*Prov.* 2.15). The concept of God as father implies a special relationship to mankind (*Opif.* 77). The human body derives from God as creator, the human mind from God as father (*Opif.* 135). (JLB)

S. Fine, 'Caligula and the Jews: Some Historiographic Reflections Occasioned by Gaius in Polychrome,' in S. Fine (ed.), *Art, History, and the Historiography of Judaism in Roman Antiquity*, The Brill Reference Library of Judaism 34 (Leiden 2014) 51–62.

In recent years, research on polychromy has transformed the reconstruction and interpretation of classical art. In this thought-provoking article, the author reflects on the interpretative impact of the reconstructed colors of sculptures of Gaius Caligula (housed respectively at the NY Carlsberg Glyptotek, Copenhagen, and the Virginia Museum of Fine Arts) and how we should understand the relationship between Gaius and the Jews. Both Philo and Josephus deal with the Jews' encounters with Gaius 'from the perspective of colonized Jews, telling the 'Jewish' story in a way that was intended to curry sympathy from their Roman readers' (p. 55). The stories of Gaius' plan for an image of himself in the Jerusalem Temple, as narrated by Philo and Josephus, are rendered all the more striking by the polychrome, life-like statues of Gaius, 'which give us a sense of the material culture that our authors take for granted' (p. 56). To contemporary Jews the statue of Caligula would have represented the bald power of the imperial oppressor; the presence of a usurping 'divinity' in a place where only the invisible God of Israel was to hold court. Both Philo's account in *Legat.* and that produced later by Josephus attempt to show the emperor's policy as a transgression of Roman imperial norms, presenting Jews as loyally maintaining 'their side of a social contract that was enshrined in Roman law, custom, and habits' (p. 59), i.e. toleration of the traditional Jewish refusal to allow the use of images in the veneration of their rulers. (SJKP)

S. D. Fraade, 'Between Rewritten Bible and Allegorical Commentary: Philo's Interpretation of the Burning Bush,' in J. Zsengellér (ed.), *Rewritten Bible after Fifty Years: Texts, Terms, or Techniques? A Last Dialogue with Geza Vermes*, Supplements to the Journal for the Study of Judaism 166 (Leiden 2014) 221–232.

To show that lines cannot be drawn too sharply between the categories of 'rewritten Bible' and commentary, the author uses the example of Philo's treatment of the burning bush (Exod 3:1–6; . 2.65–69). After presenting the biblical passage in Hebrew, English, and Greek, Fraade identifies a number of issues raised by the passage which Philo addresses. These include Philo's emphasis that the divine image that Moses saw conveyed a message through a vision (rather than through hearing). Building on this notion of a silent message, Philo then explains the bush as symbolic of sufferers; the fire, of oppressors; and the angel, or messenger, of divine providence. Building further on this first symbolic level, Philo notes that the thorny bush is not only lowly but can itself cause harm through its thorns and is in fact protected and brightened by the fire. He then explains that all together, the image betokens the message, expressed in the second person, that the nation should take heart because its fame would eventually shine forth—a message that can be understood in relation to both the biblical nation and the Alexandrian Jews of Philo's own time. Finally, the fire teaches a lesson to the oppressors not to celebrate their own strength but rather to learn wisdom. By showing how Philo builds on his initial retelling of the biblical narrative, Fraade argues that the categories 'rewritten Bible' and '(allegorical) commentary' are 'intersecting partners in the multifaceted dynamics of ancient scriptural interpretation' (p. 231). (EB)

R. GISANA, 'Il ciclo di Abramo in 1Clemente ed Ebrei: Influssi giudaici o filoniani?,' *Ricerche Storico Bibliche* 26 (2014) 453–471, esp. 468–471.

A study of 1 Clement and its relationship with the Epistle to the Hebrews, focusing on the section dedicated to faith, in particular Abraham's (1 Clem. 3–20, esp. 10, and Heb 11). The evident similarities between the two epistles show that the author of 1 Clem. knew Heb well; however, 1 Clem. has its own approach, and the relationship between the two texts appears to be that of shared source material. The background of 1 Clem. is almost certainly Judaic. In fact, another text close to 1 Clem. is Jubilees, in particular with regard to the designation of Abraham as 'friend of God' (φίλος τοῦ θεοῦ, cf. Jub. 19.9), also found in James 2:23. Philo too (*Sobr.* 55–56) describes Abraham in this way, but his elaboration of its significance is quite different from that of 1 Clem. (HMK)

D. A. GIULEA, *Pre-Nicene Christology in Paschal Contexts: The Case of the Divine Noetic Anthropos*, Supplements to Vigiliae Christianae 123 (Leiden 2014).

This study, a revised Marquette University doctoral dissertation, re-examines the earliest texts relating to the feast of Easter in the light of Second Temple traditions, with a key emphasis on the role of the celestial or divine noetic Anthropos. Philo's evidence is discussed at two points. He sheds light on the roots of the 'divine Anthropos' tradition through his articulation of the two Adams, the one as noetic paradigm, the other as the historical and empirical figure, in both cases gravitating around the idea of the Image of God which is the Logos (pp. 56–60). Later in the study (pp. 273–283) Philo is studied as an important witness to the 'noetic turn' in Jewish thought. Using especially the opening chapters of *Opif.*, the author finds in Philo 'for the first time a coherently developed noetic ontology and a noetic epistemology' (p. 273). In addition, Philo reveals the use of mystery terminology, which is not just a metaphor but refers to the mystical, interior and noetic passage from the visible to the invisible. Philo's writings, together with the Hermetic texts, constitute 'a milestone of human culture,' because 'they represent the most ancient witnesses of the synthesis between the kabod theology and noetic epistemology' (p. 289). (DTR)

L. GUGLIELMO, 'Referenze e referenti di Ἐσσαῖοι ed Ἐσσηνοί in Filone alessandrino e Flavio Giuseppe: un'ipotesi di lavoro,' *Rivista Biblica* 62 (2014) 361–376.

This paper aims to show that in the works of Philo and Josephus the Greek names Ἐσσαῖοι and Ἐσσηνοί, translated into modern languages with the same term, Essenes, actually carry their own specific and discrete meanings. While Ἐσσαῖοι (in Philo and Josephus) is associated with γένος (lineage), Ἐσσηνοί (in Josephus, not found in Philo) is used with reference to mode of life and thought. Analysis of Philo's testimony, transmitted in Eusebius' *Praeparatio Evangelica* (8.1.1), allows us to deduce that the *Essei* were of a priestly lineage, while *Essenes* is a broader term including both *Essei* and laity. This laity adopted entirely or partially the customs of the *Essei*, sanctifying their lives in the way of the Nazirites. The study highlights the affinities between this interpretation and the hypothesis of M. Black (*The Scrolls and Christian Origins*, London 1961), according to which the Essenes were of priestly origins and their ancestors, the *Hasidim*, would have included the Nazirites. (HMK, based on the author's summary)

M. Hadas-Lebel, *Une histoire du Messie* (Paris 2014), esp. 136–138.

In this book, accessible to a wide audience, Hadas-Lebel examines the origin and developments of Jewish messianism, covering a period extending from the Bible up to the Talmud, with an additional chapter exploring messianic ideas from the Middle Ages up to the twentieth century. Philo is briefly treated in a chapter devoted to the Greek-speaking Jewish diaspora, in which the absence of messianism in the Septuagint and its meagre presence in the Third Sibylline book are also discussed. The author notes that neither Philo's treatment of the anointing of the priest—the only character described as 'anointed' in the Pentateuch, the source on which Philo focused his commentary—nor his interpretation of the ἄνθρωπος of Num 24:17 in *Praem.* 95 attest to a waiting for a personal Messiah or an expectation of eschatological redemption. For Philo, salvation comes from God only. (SW)

J. Hoblik, 'The Holy Logos in the Writings of Philo of Alexandria,' *Communio Viatorum* 56 (2014) 248–266.

The theme of the divine Logos in Philo enables an exploration of Philo's relationship both to Greek philosophy and the history of religious thought. The specific aspect of the theme that this article focuses on is the extent to which Philo's concept of the Logos has been influenced by the concept of 'the Holy.' It needs to be emphasized that Philo always speaks of God in personalist terms. Since God can only be referred to by means of improper speech, the character of the Logos can be said to correspond to the personality of God. The biblical background of the concept demonstrates the universal activity of the Logos, but because of Platonist influence creation no longer appears to be the direct work of God as described in Genesis. The article also explores the Logos's role as mediator and as the basic form of connection between God and humankind. It can be said that the Logos is something more than verbal utterance. Its dynamic nature can be inferred from its status as something between the interiority of God and his differentiated powers. It is thus holy power, but it only happens rarely that Philo calls the Logos 'holy' directly, perhaps because he calls the Torah the 'holy logos,' apparently because of the use of this term for the texts of the ancient mysteries. The holiness of the Logos is also seen in its connection with the High Priest and with its role in the symbolism of the ark placed in the Holy of Holies, as explained in the *QE*, esp. 2.53–68. Finally the article also reflects on the manifestation of the Logos in the burning bush in Exod 3, which 'creates and reveals an intersection between religion and philosophy.' (p. 265) (DTR)

G. Holtz, 'Von Alexandrien nach Jerusalem. Überlegungen zur Vermittlung philonisch-alexandrinischer Tradition an Paulus,' *Zeitschrift für die neutestamentliche Wissenschaft und die Kunde der älteren Kirche* 105 (2014) 228–263.

The article studies the modes in which Paul might have come into contact with Philonic ideas. The author argues that there are three main models used in scholarship to explain any similarities: direct 'literary dependence,' 'oral transmission of Philonic material … via Apollos and the Corinthians,' and a 'common background in Greek-speaking Judaism.' She compares the subject of human self-aggrandisement in Philo and Paul and finds similarities in the way human beings set themselves over God. Yet she finds no evidence for any of the three models in Paul, Philo, and other early Jewish sources. She suggests an explanation of her own, namely that there was a historically verifiable point of contact between Paul and Philonic thought in the Greek-speaking synagogues in Jerusalem or Antioch. (JLB)

P. W. van der Horst, *Studies in Ancient Judaism and Early Christianity*, Ancient Judaism and Early Christianity 87 (Leiden 2014).

This collection of essays by the renowned scholar of ancient Judaism and early Christianity contains two articles on Philo published in recent years: 'Two short notes on Philo' (2006, summarized in *SPhiloA* vol. 21, p. 85); and 'Philo and the problem of God's emotions' (2010, summarized in *SPhiloA* vol. 25, p. 182). Other articles also shed light on Philo and his world, including reflections on the meaning of the term φιλοσοφία in relation to Josephus' concept of a φιλοσοφία ἐπείσακτος in *Ant*. 18.9 (on Philo p. 58). (DTR)

J. Jae-chon, '알렉산드리아의 필로의 성경 주해 저술들과 알레고리의 성격' [Korean: The Biblical Exegetical Writings of Philo of Alexandria and the Nature of Allegory], *Canon&Culture (Korea)* 8.1 (2014) 85–108.

The article gives a general presentation on the role and methods of exegesis in Philo. It is argued that biblical interpretation pervades his religious and philosophical thought. The three categories of exegetical writings seem to be designed to suit the needs of specific groups of audience. Questions and Answers covers only parts of Genesis and Exodus, but they are formulated with the basic pedagogical format as well as simple responses. These features would work well with students at the elementary level. Under the Allegorical Commentary we have twenty treatises, most of which deal with the text of Genesis. These writings are structured with four-fold format: the first lemma, basic explication of the text, and secondary lemmas followed by figurative and allegorical meanings. The structure is featured with thorough and wide-ranging treatment of the text and is appropriate for the advanced students. Lastly, the Exposition of the Law deals with the entire Pentateuch, and while lacking in secondary lemmas, it features retelling of the biblical stories as well as literal and allegorical explications. Thus it might serve a wider audience, probably beyond the Jewish community. It does no justice to Philo to call him an allegorist. With some exceptions, Philo usually presents both literal and allegorical meanings, and appreciates the value of the former. Allegory is an indispensable tool for reaching the religious, philosophical truth, and can be justified by the thought-world in which Philo and his readers lived and operated. The portrayal of Moses as the supreme philosopher, prophet and priest lends additional support for his use of allegorical methods. For Philo, interpretation of the Bible is always a project for the benefit of the community to which he belongs and wants to serve. (DTR; based on author's abstract)

J. Joosten, 'Mixed blessings: the Biblical Notion of Blessings in the Works of Philo and Flavius Josephus,' in E. Bons, R. Brucker and J. Joosten (edd.), *The Reception of Septuagint Words in Jewish-Hellenistic and Christian Literature*, Wissenschaftliche Untersuchungen zum Neuen Testament 2.367 (Tübingen 2014) 105–115.

Philo uses the verb εὐλογέω to refer to the praise of God, a usage connected to LXX but also at home in secular Greek. From the evidence of passages where Philo depends on biblical texts containing εὐλογέω = Hebrew *brk*, 'to bless,' it is clear that he knows well the biblical usage of this verb (e.g., *QE* 2.18 on Exod 2:18). In the philosophical treatises, Philo shows sensitivity towards the Hebrew meaning of εὐλογέω by glossing the verb, or replacing it with εὔχομαι, 'to pray,' where the text refers to humans blessing other humans (e.g., *Mut*. 125; cf. Deut 33:1). In other contexts, the verb is identified with the transfer of benefits (*Somn.* 1.176) or the procurement of divine favor (*Migr.* 122). In many passages, however, 'the Hebrew meaning remains completely in the background and Philo draws out other meanings more consonant with non-biblical Greek, and with his own philosophical system' (p. 112). εὐλογέω is associated with ideas of honor and praise (e.g., *Migr.* 109–110); sound reasoning (e.g., *Leg.* 1.17); and eloquence and wise action (e.g., *Migr.* 70). In this usage, we see him 're-Hellenise' the Hebraizing Greek of LXX. In the same volume, R. Brucker ('A Sample Article: ᾄδω,' pp. 1–16) includes brief discussion of the verb ᾄδω in Philonic texts (pp. 9–11), while K. Berthelot ('The Notion of *Anathema* in Ancient Jewish Literature Written in Greek,' pp. 35–52) includes Philonic texts in relation to the words ἀνάθημα and ἀνατίθημι (pp. 47–50). (SJKP)

N. A. E. Kalospyros, 'Towards the Allegory of Idealized Oikos: Nuclear and Extended Family Versions, Succession and Inheritance Issues and Their Cognates in Philo Judaeus,' in B. Caseau-Chevallier (ed.), *Inheritance, Law and Religions in the Ancient and Mediaeval Worlds. Orient et occident*, Centre de Recherche d'Histoire et Civilisation de Byzance. Monographies 45 (Paris 2014) 117–138.

Part of a collection of studies on inheritance, law, and religions in the ancient and medieval world, this chapter forms one of four contributions to a section devoted to 'Kinship and Conflicts over Inheritance.' The focus in this chapter is on Philo's allegorical treatment of biblical texts dealing with marriage, parental relationships, and kinship in general. On the subject of succession and inheritance, Philo represents a distinctly more allegorical approach than that found in early rabbinic law: for Philo, according to the author, legitimate children are those who inherit the οἶκος of God; it is allegiance to God that 'transcends family ties and legitimates their subordination' (p. 137). Regarding Philo's understanding of the ideal 'family' or 'household,' the conclusion is reached that '... in Philonic philosophy *oikos* is a principal allegiance: the imprint of divine dwelling among men. In other words, he upgraded transcendentally the entity of family. This philosophical perception awaits allegorical application, in order to highlight the preference of the mental instead of the physical, the love of God instead of idolatry and other mundane bounds, and of divine priorities latent in the Pentateuch instead of literal readings easy to grasp' (p. 138). (SJKP)

D. Karadimas, 'Alexandria and the Second Sophistic,' *Electryone* 2 (2014) 14–36.

Alexandria was theoretically an ideal place to become a center of sophistic activity during the period of the Second Sophistic (middle of the last century BCE to the beginning of the first century CE). The fact is, however, that the centers of this cultural, educational, and intellectual activity were to be found in various cities of Asia Minor and Greece (e.g., Athens, Smyrna, Ephesus), while Alexandra is not mentioned among them. Philostratus, who gives a panoramic view of the sophistic movement of this period, does not include any sophists from Alexandria in his list, while the city itself is not mentioned at all. Moreover, Philostratus mentions four sophists from the neighboring Naucratis, and gives the impression of a certain sophistic activity there, but not in Alexandria. The questions that arise here are whether the sophistic movement had also developed in Alexandria and, if so, why Philostratus does not regard any of its sophists worthy of mention. The existing evidence (the Byzantine encyclopedia *Souda*, Dio Chrysostom, *Acta Alexandrinorum*, Philo (on Isidorus)) shows that there was a significant development of the sophistic culture in

Alexandria already from the early first century CE. As to the second question, the author maintains that there was a clear incompatibility between Philostratus' political ideas and the way he understood the role of the sophists, on the one hand, and the general tenets and practices of Alexandrians and Alexandrian sophists, on the other. This incompatibility, it is concluded, was the main reason for Philostratus' silence. (TS; based on the author's abstract).

M. Kister, 'The Fate of the Canaanites and the Despoliation of the Egyptians: Polemics among Jews, Pagans, Christians, and Gnostics—Motifs and Motives,' in K. Berthelot, J. E. David and M. Hirshman (edd.), *The Gift of the Land and the Fate of the Canaanites in Jewish Thought* (New York 2014) 66–111.

The author considers a range of Second Temple and rabbinic treatments of the Canaanites' loss of land to the Israelites and Israelites' despoliation of the Egyptians—two themes that share in common the Israelites' coming into possession of what is not originally theirs. Evidence from Philo is occasionally invoked in different ways. Like other Second Temple sources, he links the curse of Canaan (Gen 9:19) to the later loss of land (*QG* 2.65, p. 69). Philo's apologetic comments in *Hypoth*. 6.6–7 suggest that he may be responding to hostile accusations by Gentiles that the Jews were either cowards or robbers (pp. 77–78). Finally, his apologetic claims in *Mos*. 1.141–142 that the despoliation of the Egyptians served as payment or constituted a rightful act of war likewise suggest that he may be responding to outside criticism of the Jews, though we cannot know whether the Bible itself or some other source sparked this criticism (pp. 84–85). Kister observes that similar apologetic arguments are found in a variety of Jewish and even Christian sources spanning a thousand years and suggests that the arguments may have originated during Second Temple times in response to Gentile accusations against the Jews for illegally taking the property of others. (EB)

M. Klinghardt, 'The Ritual Dynamics of Inspiration: the Therapeutae's Dance,' in S. Marks and H. Taussig (edd.), *Meals in Early Judaism: Social Formation at the Table* (New York 2014) 139–162.

According to Philo's description of the all-night festival (παννυχίς) of the Therapeutae, the ritual moves from listening to the group's leader expound upon Scripture to the group's choral singing, their meal, and finally their dance (*Contempl*. 75–89). Since Philo presents the study of philosophy as the group's 'main occupation' (p. 140), a central question is how we might understand the tension between the physical act of dancing and the spiritual goal of seeing God. The author considers this question in relation to symposium accounts of Plato, whose symposium excludes song and dance, and Xenophon, for whom song and dance are key features that erotically arouse the participants. Also considered are statements by Hesiod about the inspiration provided by the dance of the muses, meal prayers in the *Didache*, and dance hymns in the *Acts of John*. In light of these comparisons, the dance of the Therapeutae appears to overcome dichotomies of individual and community, male and female, and body and mind. The group's dance facilitates inspiration and both are aspects of the same ritual practice. Since the aim of the practice is to gain a vision of the divine, whose content can hardly be communicated, Philo focuses on the group's ritual instead expressing their ideas. His account, in which he criticizes Greek and Roman symposia—even while adopting certain of their formal aspects—and in which he incorporates song and dance imagery from the Exodus reflects 'a kind of meal practice [in] early Judaism that both resists and integrates the imperial dominance in the larger society' (p. 154). (EB)

E. Koskenniemi, 'Philo and Classical Education,' in T. Seland (ed.), *Reading Philo: A Handbook to Philo of Alexandria* (Grand Rapids, MI 2014) 102–128.

This learned article on Philo's classical education divides into three main parts. The first part gives a wide-ranging sketch of the wider context of Greek education and the crucial role of the γυμνάσιον as it developed from the 5th century BCE onwards, first in Greece and then throughout the Eastern Mediterranean. In the second part the author moves to a discussion of the system of education in Alexandria. The scattered evidence does not allow an accurate presentation of educational institutions, but it is clear that the complex ethnic composition of the city was reflected in the functioning of the education system. It is not easy to determine which doors were open to Jews who wished to obtain a secular education. On the basis of the evidence of papyri and Claudius' famous letter, it may be concluded that Philo lived at a crucial time when the Jews' rights to secular education were in the process of change. The third part of the article puts forward the evidence that Philo's works provide. Texts such as *Congr.* and *Spec.* 2.229–230 tell us in general terms about the content of education, but not where it took place. Philo's works show him to have a deep knowledge both of Greek philosophy and Greek literature. For some of this knowledge he would have been indebted to the Alexandrian Jewish tradition which encouraged a positive attitude to Greek culture. Philo will have had his own library and people could have become acquainted with his learned treatises in the synagogue. However, times were changing with the advent of Roman rule and the rise of Greek nationalist sentiment. It seems that 'Philo was one of the last secularly trained Jews in Alexandria' (p. 128). (DTR)

J. Leonhardt-Balzer, 'Vorstellungen von der Gegenwart Gottes bei Philo von Alexandrien,' in B. Janowski and E. E. Popkes (edd.), *Das Geheimnis der Gegenwart Gottes: Zur Schechina-Vorstellung in Judentum und Christentum,* Wissenschaftliche Untersuchungen zum Neuen Testament 1.318 (Tübingen 2014) 103–118.

The chapter looks at ideas of the presence of God in Philo. The actual vision of God is inaccessible to human beings. The Logos is the divine in the sense that it is adjusted to human, spatial capacities, therefore he functions as God and is the place of God (*Somn.* 1.62–63). The Temple in Jerusalem is identified with the Logos as the place of God's presence (*Spec.* 1.67–70). In human beings the Logos is present in (but not identical to) the High Priest (*Somn.* 1.215), who at the same time represents creation (*Mos.* 2.133). Likewise, the wise person is a place of the presence of the Logos (*Somn.* 2.248). Yet the transcendent God is never described as dwelling on earth. Philo's language of dwelling is used for human habitation. Not God, but the wise dwells in in the desert sanctuary (*Leg.* 3.46), and Levi is the only tribe which represents the Logos who dwells in God (*Fug.* 102). The focus is not on the idea that God dwells on earth, but that the wise moves towards residence with God. (JLB)

D. Lincicum, 'Philo's Library,' *The Studia Philonica Annual* 26 (2014) 99–114.

The article builds on the author's index of Philo's non-biblical citations and allusions published in the previous volume of *The Studia Philonica Annual*, summarized in this bibliography at vol. 28 p. 410. Firstly, an analysis is presented of Philo's citations of and allusions by author. It is noted that it is difficult to prove literary knowledge by means of allusions, because these can be derived at second hand, a difficulty that can be illustrated by Philo's allusions to Herodotus. But there is also no doubt that he regarded certain authors as 'canonical,' such as various dramatists and philosophers. In fact it is striking that of the 133 collected citations just four authors make up well over half: Euripides, Heraclitus, Homer, and Plato. In the case of Aristotle, however, Philo often appears to allude to positions taken, but only mentions him four times at *Aet.* 10–18 and never cites him. Next, references to individual works are analyzed and here too there are a number of uncertainties and the results are more valuable for some authors than for others. The second half of the article then moves to reflections on how Philo might have accessed all these works and whether we can speak of his 'library.' There is a variety of potential sources for Philo's citations and more substantial allusions, as seen in the following list: lines committed to memory during the course of education; encounter with texts through performance; use of handbooks, e.g. for doxographical information; disputation and study in a house of prayer or a school; re-use of notes and excerpts; reading and revisiting continuous written texts. For access to written texts Philo may have made use of libraries in the city, e.g. the famous Alexandrian library and museum, but hints given in the text *Abr.* 22–23 suggest that he made use of his own library, allowing him to study away from the bustle of the city. So it is reasonable to conclude that he will have owned a modest philosophical library and possibly also copies of the literary works which he cited so freely. (DTR)

M. D. Litwa, 'The Deification of Moses in Philo of Alexandria,' *The Studia Philonica Annual* 26 (2014) 1–27.

Philo speaks about the deification of Moses in a variety of ways, illustrating the complexity of his theological thought. The article focuses primarily on his deification as seen in his ascent and death. The various stages are discussion in succession: Moses as philosopher-king; Moses as lawgiver; Moses as prophet and priest; his actual ascent; the vision of God that he receives; his final deification at death; and his burial (which does not contradict his deification). In Philo's thought it is possible to assert both a strong doctrine of monotheism and a realistic (ontological) form of deification without contradiction. According to the analysis presented in the article there are three fundamental theological ideas that underpin these assertions: (1) the recognition of different levels of divinity, in which a central role is reserved for the divine Logos; (2) the ability to participate in the deity, as illustrated by Moses; and (3) the notion of shareable and unshareable deity. Philo was able to present a form of deification that posed no threat to his primal God, the Existent. In fact Moses does not participate in the Existent at all, but rather in the Logos, the Mind of God. In being resolved into pure νοῦς, i.e., the realm of the Logos, Moses makes an enduring ascent to the divine realm and becomes divine himself. (DTR)

M. D. Litwa, Iesus Deus: *The Early Christian Depiction of Jesus as a Mediterranean God* (Minneapolis 2014), esp. 125–131.

In a monograph devoted to describing how early Christian writings, in their depiction of Jesus' life and ministry, made use not only of Jewish ideas but also of the wider Mediterranean understanding of deity, Philonic evidence is discussed in chapter 4 on 'Transfiguration as Epiphany,' which focuses primarily on the account of Jesus' transfiguration in the Gospel of Mark. It is to be agreed with recent commentators that the best background for understanding the Markan transfiguration is Moses's ascent up Mount Sinai, and particularly Philo's interpretation in which 'we learn that Moses the king is Moses the god' (p. 124). To be sure, the deified Moses becomes a different sort of god than the Existent, namely as a mediate deity. But there is also a process of 'noetification'; Moses becomes pure νοῦς, i.e., of the same nature as the Logos. This allows him to become immutable and have a vision of the Good. In addition, his body bore the marks of his deified mind, so that his radiant face is a sign of beauty as revealed in an epiphany. Philonic texts also illustrate the remark that is the culmination of the transfiguration, namely that Jesus is God's beloved son (Mark 9:7). In an excursus (pp. 137–138) it is argued that Philo acknowledges that human beings can be sons of God and that in the case of Moses he fulfils the type of the 'son of God (the Logos)' (p. 138). For both Mark and Jesus, the author concludes, neither Moses nor Jesus were revealed as gods in and of themselves, but rather as reflecting the light of a higher deity, in Philo's case the Logos. (DTR)

S. D. Mackie, 'The Passion of Eve and the Ecstasy of Hannah: Sense Perception, Passion, Mysticism, and Misogyny in Philo of Alexandria, *De ebrietate* 143–152,' *Journal of Biblical Literature* 133 (2014) 141–163.

Philo's approach to Hannah's prayer for a son (1 Samuel 1:9–28) in the Allegorical Commentary (*Ebr*. 143–152), an approach which involves (1) the deployment of particular philosophical teachings (Platonic sense perception, Stoic and Platonic psychological theories, and related dualistic models—sense perception and reason, physical and noetic spheres, mind and psyche, reason and unreason, passion and apathetic virtue), and (2) 'Greco-Roman mystical themes,' representing the profound spiritual experiences of Bacchic ecstasy, sober drunkenness, and contemplative ascent. In contrast with evidence for Philo's 'thoroughgoing androcentrism' (p. 142) and predominantly negative evaluation of women and association of negative values as characteristically feminine, it is argued that the treatment of the figure of Hannah in *Ebr*. 143–152 constitutes a rare and remarkable example of Philo's positive construction of 'the sensuous and passionate mystical praxis of an adept female mystic' (p. 141), amounting to 'what is surely the most emotional, embodied, and sensual *visio Dei* in the Philonic corpus' (p. 163). In his account of Philo's treatment of Hannah's 'passionate and ecstatic joy,' the author includes useful contextual discussion of ideas about the passions, 'psychosomatic kinesis,' joy and *eupatheia* in Plato, the Stoics, and Philo (pp. 146–154). In his divergences and adaptations of philosophical teachings, 'Philo appears to be walking a tightrope between his loyalties to Platonic and Stoic psychologies and theories of emotion, and his desire to portray Hannah as a passionate and ecstatic female mystic. In the end it appears his mystical agenda prevailed' (p. 154). (SJKP)

M. McGlynn, 'The Politeuma: Guardian of Civil Rights or Heavenly Commonwealth in Ptolemaic and Roman Egypt,' *Biblische Notizen* 161 (2014) 77–98.

In this study, the author's stated goal is to re-investigate the evidence for the πολίτευμα as a political body, and to ask for what particular rights were granted the Jewish communities under the Ptolemies and Romans. The author suggests there must have been several πολίτευμα in Alexandria and concludes: 'The formation of parallel politeumata made a way in which Jewish communities could maintain their position in relation to other communities around them, and could also guard what made them distinctively Jewish (p. 94).' (TS)

A. B. McGowan, 'The Food of the Therapeutae: A Thick Description,' in S. Marks and H. Taussig (edd.), *Meals in Early Judaism: Social Formation at the Table* (New York 2014) 129–138.

While Philo depicts the food and drink served at the meal of the Therapeutae as rather austere, the nature of what was eaten 'is a sign of robust and coherent ascetic sensibility, not of indifference' to material things (p. 129). In three separate accounts (*Contempl.* 37, 73–74, and 81–82) with somewhat different emphases, group members eat bread with salt and herbs, and water. As one description makes clear, the bread is leavened. Philo's accounts also provide different meanings for the food—as a reflection of 'ascetic moderation' to counter hunger and thirst (p. 132); as an avoidance of foods, such as wine, which stimulate desire; and as an indicator of cultic purity. This last meaning is somewhat complex since the food of the Therapeutae differs from the wine and meat of sacrificial victim, which the Temple priests consume, yet Philo presents this food as 'pure and holy in a way that invokes the holiness of sacrifice and Temple' (p. 134). (EB)

A. K. Moorthy, *A Seal of Faith: Rereading Paul on Circumcision, Torah, and the Gentile* (diss. Columbia University, New York 2014).

In this Columbia University dissertation, prepared under the supervision of John McGuckin, the question of Paul's understanding of circumcision is revisited. It is generally held that he dismissed the rite of circumcision for Gentiles. The dissertation, however, offers a different perspective. Through examination of relevant sources regarding the role of circumcision in conversion along with consideration of Philo of Alexandria's depiction of Abraham as an exemplar of and for the proselyte, the thesis is put forward that in Rom 4:11–12 Paul uses the example of Abraham in order to explain the value of circumcision for Jews as well as for Gentiles. It is to be argued, moreover, that Paul's objections to circumcision were not to the rite per se but rather to the notion that circumcision was necessary for entering the Abrahamic covenant and for receiving salvation in Christ. (DTR; based on the author's abstract)

C. Moreschini, 'Further Considerations on the Philosophical Background of *Contra Eunomium* III,' in J. Leemans and M. Cassin (edd.), *Gregory of Nyssa Contra Eunomium III: An English Translation with Commentary and Supporting Studies*, Supplements to Vigiliae Christianae 124 (Leiden 2014) 595–612, esp. 598–601.

In the context of studies on Book 3 of Gregory of Nyssa's *Contra Eunomium* the eminent Italian classicist cites the two passages in which Philo is named and makes brief comments. In the former, which deals with matter of style, Philo is not criticized. The latter does contain a polemic with Philo because Nicene theology does not accept that God reigns over his Son who has been generated and that divine power is separate from God. Finally he adds a comment on Gregory Nazianzus, namely that some of his doctrines are taken from Philo, including the interpretation of the trees in paradise. (DTR)

K. B. Neutel and M. R. Anderson, 'The First Cut is the Deepest: Masculinity and Circumcision in the First Century,' in P.-B. Smit and O. Creang (edd.), *Biblical Masculinities Foregrounded* (Sheffield 2014) 228–244.

This chapter considers male circumcision in the context of ancient ideas about masculinity and explores the extent to which connections were made by various groups—Greeks and Romans (focusing primarily on texts from Martial and Tacitus on 'masculinity and the male body'), Jews (Philo on 'male self-control as a Jewish defence'), and Christians (Paul and his 'mangled masculinity')—between masculinity and circumcision. Philo offers the most elaborate of Jewish apologies for the practice of circumcision, defending the practice against the understanding of circumcision as violating masculinity. At the same time, Philo's works show his near consistent acceptance of the conception of masculinity that underpins his contemporaries' arguments for the rejection of circumcision: the greater perfection and dominant nature of the male form vis à vis the female. In the case of circumcision, however, Philo deviates from this standard model of masculinity, e.g. in the defense of the restriction of circumcision to men (*QG* 3.47–48), on the grounds that it helps to check the libido, which is said to be greater in men than in women (contra Philo's much more frequently expressed view of women as associated especially with the senses and sexuality). In *Spec.* 1.1–11, Philo's connection between the exposed glans and the physical heart associates circumcision with the heart as the seat of rationality: the removal of the foreskin makes the male even more male, i.e. a creature of purely rational thought. As an apologist, Philo stresses that circumcision is a practice originating in piety and that leads to modesty, knowing that these masculine traits should win widespread admiration. (SJKP)

M. R. Niehoff, 'Les juifs d'Alexandrie à l'école de la critique textuelle des païen,' in C. Méla and F. Möri (edd.), *Alexandrie la divine* (Geneva 2014) 733–740.

As part of a lavish catalogue volume accompanying the exposition entitled 'Alexandrie la divine' held at the Fondation Bodmer in Geneva in 2014, the author summarizes here in French her research on Jewish exegesis and Homeric scholarship in Alexandria, arguing for close connections between Jewish and Greek interpreters. She analyses Philonic passages and identifies Philo's own methods as well as those of his colleagues. The article is accompanied by a fine photograph by F. Mori of the opening page of the text of *Deus* in the ms. Plut. 10, 20 from the Bibliotheca Laurentiana in Florence (p. 736).

M. R. Niehoff, 'Philo of Alexandria (Subject Area: Jewish Studies),' in *Oxford Bibliographies* (Oxford 2014).

Bibliography of Philonic studies presented using the distinctive method of the Oxford Bibliographies Online database (http://www.oxfordbibliographies.com). This bibliography was commissioned as part of the section on Jewish Studies. It aims at providing an overview of Philonic scholarship and continues to be updated. It deals with the following themes: Introductions; reference works and journals treating Philo; primary texts and translations; commentaries on Philo's works; Philo's life and historical circumstances; different series of his works; Philo's attitude towards Judaism; philosophy; mysticism; sexuality and gender; and his later reception in Judaism and Christianity. On this series of online bibliographies see also the note at *SPhiloA* vol. 27, p. 259. (MRN)

P. NIETO HERNÁNDEZ, 'Philo and Greek Poetry,' *The Studia Philonica Annual* 26 (2014) 135–149.

This beautifully crafted article examines Philo's attitudes to and use of Greek poetry. Like his favorite Greek philosopher Plato he has an ambivalent relationship to poetry. His own writing is often highly poetical, but he can also be negative and denounce the fictions that it promotes. There is no doubt, however, that he was seriously engaged with the Greek tradition and with Homeric poetry in particular. In the first part of the article the author briefly surveys Philo's views on archaic and classical poetry. He holds it in high esteem and regards it as an important source of moral education as seen in texts such as *Sacr*. 78 and *Prob*. 143. Only philosophy is held in higher esteem. Though aware of its limitations, the dominant attitude is one of 'respect and admiration for the Greek [literary] tradition as an excellent accomplishment of humankind' (p. 139). In the second part the author examines how Philo utilizes his extensive knowledge of Greek poetry. A particularly interesting example of how he cites a sizable portion of Homer's text is found at *Congr*. 16–17 where he actually indicates the location of the quoted lines in the thirteenth book of the Iliad (perhaps the first extant example of this practice) and it is plain that he stands in a long tradition of reflection on the 'milkeaters' mentioned there. The use of the term αἰνίττομαι reveals that Philo is launching an allegorical interpretation incorporating aspects of the Homeric text. Philo also often indicates that expressions are poetical and derived from the poets (usually Homer). His own language too can be highly poetic and two fascinating examples of this are examined in some detail: *Somn*. 2.249 (τὸ ἀμβρόσιον φάρμακον) and *Spec*. 1.74 (ἄχθος γῆς). There is still much research to be done on Philo's use of poetic quotes and allusions. He 'was a canny and subtle reader' and he himself … 'expected much of his cleverest readers' (p. 149). (DTR)

E. NODET, 'Le quartrième livre des Maccabées: D'une Judée oubliée à la philosophie pieuse,' in M.-F. BASLEZ and O. MUNNICH (edd.), *Le mémoire des persécutions: Autour des livres des Maccabées*, Collection de la Revue des Études juives 56 (Leuven 2014) 301–316.

Three aspects of 4 Maccabees are studied: (a) its erroneous attribution to Josephus resulting from the echo of a lost reference to 4 Macc still attested in the Slavonic Josephus; (b) the lack of interest for the Temple and the Hasmoneans, and (c) its philosophical stance. It is in this third respect that Philo is studied, together with Josephus and Stoicism. 4 Macc is a literal fiction promoting wisdom conceived in terms of a religious and practical piety. The idea that the Mosaic Law is in harmony with nature, also endorsed by Josephus and Philo, is in line with Stoicism. However, while one can doubt whether perfect harmony with god or the universe can be reached in Stoicism on account of the devastating effects of human passions, Josephus, Philo, and 4 Macc appeal to the universal value of biblical pedagogy. For Philo, the Bible secures direct access to God. Although Philo's perfect sage does not need any law, the ordinary man who lacks sufficient knowledge can discover the grace of God by his practical observance of the Mosaic Law. Both the pedagogical and universal relevance of biblical education show that 4 Macc, like Philo, mainly addresses proselytes. (SW)

S. Nordgaard Svendsen, 'Paul and the Provenance of the Law: The Case of Galatians 3,19–20,' *Zeitschrift für die neutestamentliche Wissenschaft und die Kunde der älteren Kirche* 105 (2014) 64–79.

In this essay, the author asks the question: What was, according to Paul's letter to the Galatians, the origin of the Jewish Law? His point of departure is Paul's statements in Gal 3:19–20, and his main hypothesis is that Paul thought about the genesis and passing of the law in much the same way as Philo of Alexandria thought about certain aspects of the origins of humanity. That is not to say that Nordgaard thinks Paul knew Philo, or that he was influenced by him indirectly, but that they both belonged to rather similar cultural milieus. Three different views are presented as prevalent among Pauline scholars on the origin of the Law as inherent in Gal 3:19–20: God as the origin of the Law and the angels as his intermediaries (the Law was given 'through' the angels); the angels as the authors and givers of the Law (διά = by); and thirdly, the inconsistency of Paul's statements. The author then sets forth a new proposal, drawing upon Philo's statements on the creation of humans in *Opif.* 69–75; *Conf.* 168–183; *Fug.* 68–72, and *Mut.* 30–32. Based on these passages, it is argued that, as God foresaw that it would not be appropriate for him to assume responsibility for the sins that humans would commit, he enlisted a group of others as collaborators in their creation. Hence, Paul was not inconsistent in his view; the Law had not been given by God, nor by angels opposed to his will, but 'the Law had been instituted by a group of angels whom God had commissioned for this task so that he himself could both have the Law, and also remain unblemished by its fundamental imperfection' (p. 79). (TS)

F. Oertelt, *Herrscherideal und Herrschaftskritik bei Philo von Alexandria: Eine Untersuchung am Beispiel seiner Josephsdarstellung in De Josepho und De somniis II*, Studies in Philo of Alexandria 8 (Leiden 2014).

The book provides an interpretation of the two treatises *Ios.* und *Somn.* 2 as contributions to political discourse. The ambivalent aspects of the biblical Joseph figure provide the opportunity to study the ideal ruler (shepherd, doctor, navigator) as well as the tyrant (passion driven, irrational) on different levels, using Hellenistic philosophy as well as the divine Torah. The tension between the two treatises, one seeing Joseph positively, the other critically, should not be removed and may constitute a conscious depiction of successful as well as tyrannical rule. The ambivalence of the Joseph figure enables Philo to develop a Torah-based theory of rule (guided by the divine spirit, pious, humane) which liberates political action from dependencies and opens universal directives for action and modes of control. See also the review by E. S. Gruen elsewhere in this volume. (JLB)

A. Paul, *Éros enchainé: Les chrétiens, la famille et le genre* (Paris 2014).

Motivated by the recent debates in France following the legalization of same-sex marriage, the author attempts to trace back the sources of the Christian sexual moral code. A broad spectrum of authors are discussed—including Plato, the Stoics, a variety of early Jewish texts, Paul and Clement of Alexandria—on various topics related to 'gender' such as the categories of male and female, the place of desire and pleasure, celibacy, the notion of a virginal birth, and the debate surrounding divorce in Jesus's days. Philo is presented as one of the main sources of influence on the formation of Christian sexual morality. The author's analysis is based on what he sees as the two foundational myths concerning *eros*: the discourse of Aristophanes in Plato's *Symposium*—which presents a natural equality between male and female—and that of the creation of the human being in Plato's *Timaeus*, in which the woman is radically inferior to man. By conceiving of woman as a degenerate form of masculinity and as representative of the 'erotic genre,' Philo is responsible for the historical victory of the *Timaeus*' model. Moreover, in establishing procreation as the unique goal of the union between man and woman (an idea labelled 'procreationism'), Philo—influenced on this point by Pythagorean trends—prefigures the rigorism of the early Christian sexual moral code. Philo's procreationism, which differs widely from the 'non-enchained' *eros* of Jesus and Paul, was later radicalized by Clement of Alexandria, who is seen as the true architect of an inhuman sexual code which still current in today's Catholic Church. (SW)

R. Polito, *Aenesidemus of Cnossus: Testimonia*, Cambridge Classical Texts and Commentaries 52 (Cambridge 2014).

Given that Philo is the first witness to the tropes of Aenesidemus, it is worth pointing out that the edition of his fragments contains only named references, so does not include the Philonic material which presents the tropes without reference to their author. There are, however, various references to Philo's evidence in the commentary. See the listings in the indices on pp. 385 and 391. (DTR)

V. Rabens, *The Holy Spirit and Ethics in Paul: Transformation and Empowering for Religious-Ethical Life*, 2nd ed. (Minneapolis 2014).

This work was originally published by Mohr Siebeck in 2010. The present volume is a Fortress Press edition that is identical to the second (revised) edition, published by Mohr Siebeck in 2013. The 2010 publication was, alas, overlooked in the 2010 Bibliography of *SPhiloA* vol. 25. There are, however, only minor changes in this new edition, and the original pagination is kept. The main question of the book 'is how Paul ... comprehends religious-ethical life to be empowered by the Spirit' (p. 1), that is, the 'enabling' work of the Spirit. In the first part of the study, the author examines what he calls 'the infusion-transformation approach' for the ethical work of the spirit. In the second part he develops an alternative approach to the ethical work of the Spirit, a model that is called 'relational' in that it suggests that it is primarily through deeper knowledge of, and in intimate relationship with, God, Jesus Christ and with the community of faith that people are transformed and empowered by the Spirit for religious-ethical life. Philo is dealt with in the first main part of this work on pp. 67–78. Here the author briefly investigates whether in Philo's view the Spirit is to be characterized as a material substance, and the result is negative. Philo did not think of the Spirit of God as being physical. Neither is it the case that Philo argues for the view that ethical life is enabled through the transformation of the inner nature of a person by the infusion of a material spirit and transformation of the person. Finally, on pp. 149–155 the subject of Philo and the issue of religious-ethical empowerment by the relational work of the Spirit is broached. This is strongly supported in Philo's works. Most of the Philonic texts dealt with in this study are to be found in these two sections. (TS)

V. Rabens, 'Pneuma and the Beholding of God: Reading Paul in the Context of Philonic Mystical Traditions,' in J. Frey and J. R. Levison (edd.), *The Holy Spirit, Inspiration, and the Cultures of Antiquity: Multidisciplinary Perspectives*, Ekstasis 5 (Berlin 2014) 293–329.

The present study is in many ways a brief presentation of the larger work presented above. The specific focus of the article is to investigate the role of *pneuma* in the context of the mystical theology of Philo and Paul, with a heavy emphasis on Paul; that is, it will 'uncover the work of the Spirit in the context of notions of mystical beholding of the divine' (p. 295). The claim is not so much that Paul is dependent on Philo, as that the writings of Philo can be seen as intertexts which formed part of the horizon of interpretation of Paul. Section 1 deals with 'Pneuma and the beholding of God in Philo' (pp. 299–304). Drawing upon Philonic passages such as *Migr.* 34–36; *Legat.* 45; *QE* 2.7; 2.29; *Mos.* 2.69; *Gig.* 54–55, the author concludes that a vision of God and a transformation of the human being are of great significance to Philo, and that both aspects are related to the work of the Spirit. Furthermore, there is also the ethical character of the transformation which is the result of the mystical spirit-enabled beholding of God. In the following two sections, the focus is primarily on Paul. While there are differences between the two, he finds that both Philo and Paul provide fascinating insights into early Jewish-Christian views of the work of the Spirit as enabling mystical beholding of and assimilation to the divine. (TS)

S. Radt, 'Philon *de Plantatione* 127–129: Ein übersehenes Testimonium zu Pindar fr. 31,' *Mnemosyne* 67 (2014) 646–647.

This very concise contribution points out that in *Plant.* 127–129 there is a reference to Pindar's hymn to Zeus fr. 31 which is earlier than all the fragments identified in the editions. (JLB)

T. Rajak, 'Philo's Knowledge of Hebrew: The Meaning of the Etymologies,' in J. K. Aitken and J. Carleton Paget (edd.), *The Jewish-Greek Tradition in Antiquity and the Byzantine Empire* (Cambridge 2014) 173–187.

Scholars have for many years been convinced that Philo did not have a working knowledge of the Hebrew language. The author regards this as an important question with many ramifications for our understanding of Alexandrian Judaism and Philo's place within it. She agrees that at present a definitive answer to the problem is unattainable. Nevertheless in this contribution she piles up a number of arguments in order to shed doubt on the existing consensus of opinion. The main focus must be on Philo's use of etymologies in his allegorical explanations of the Pentateuch, ably assembled and analyzed by Grabbe (RRS 8829). She gives a useful typology of the 166 etymologies of Hebrew names. Some are straightforward in translation terms, others are more far-fetched but still well within the conventions of such etymologizing. Some find widespread agreement in other sources, e.g. Josephus, while others differ strikingly from rabbinic intepretations, but agree with patristic etymologies. A few are unique to Philo, and some are also built upon the explanations found in scripture. There is every reason to suppose that Philo made use of word-lists (*onomastica*) that were available to him, although this fact does not necessarily entail that he did not know some Hebrew. On four occasions Grabbe thinks that Philo can be charged with gross ignorance, but on closer examination in each case alternative explanations are possible. If there is to be any hope of find positive proof of Philo operating with Hebrew it would have to be in the investigation of how his etymologies fit into his general allegorical system. If it appears that Hebrew etymologies are inextricable from the allegorical interpretation of a particular passage, it may be simpler to assume that the mind of the master was responsible for them, a capacious mind that might have had room for a decent knowledge of the original language. (DTR)

I. RAMELLI, 'Philo's Doctrine of Apokatastasis: Philosophical Sources, Exegetical Strategies, and Patristic Aftermath,' *The Studia Philonica Annual* 26 (2014) 29–55.

The concept of ἀποκατάστασις (re-establishment, restoration) has its origin in Greek thought where it can have an astronomical-cosmological meaning (as in the Stoic doctrine of the conflagration and rebirth of the cosmos) or a medical meaning in relation to the soul. Philo rejects the former but espouses the latter. His use of the concept is grounded in its use in scripture, where it occurs in a verbal form in the Septuagint on a number of occasions, including in the Pentateuch at Exod 14:26–27 and Lev 13:16. Philo takes up mainly the medical meaning, related to the illness of the soul and its recovery, occurring within the framework of spiritual pedagogy. A key text is *Her*. 293 where the noun is applied to the restoration of the soul to perfection. This occurs when the soul adheres to virtue, but the opposite leads to spiritual death. In speaking of the death of the soul, however, Philo appears to have postulated not just a spiritual death but also a substantial death of the rational soul. In *Praem*. he also speaks of the restoration of Israel, though he does not use the specific terminology of ἀποκατάστασις, but rather speaks of liberation (§164). Unlike in Paul, however, it is unclear how eschatological or universal the restoration of Israel described by Philo is. Throughout the article it is emphasized that Philo's doctrine of ἀποκατάστασις exerted a strong influence on the church fathers in the Alexandrian tradition, esp. Clement and Origen, but also later Gregory of Nyssa. A significant difference, however, is that Origen did not accept the death of the soul in substantial terms, but under the influence of the New Testament developed the doctrines of the resurrection of the body and universal salvation for all souls. (DTR)

I. RAMELLI, 'The Divine as Inaccessible Object of Knowledge in Ancient Platonism: A Common Philosophical Pattern across Religious Traditions,' *Journal of the History of Ideas* 75 (2014) 167–188.

The concept of the divine as an inaccessible object of human knowledge is prominent in a number of philosopher-theologians in the first four centuries CE. Notably these thinkers all belong to the the same philosophical tradition, that of Middle Platonism and Neoplatonism, but they come from three different religious traditions: Philo from Judaism, Plotinus from Greek religion, and Origen and Gregory of Nyssa from Christianity. All of them share a dialectic and tension between a declared apophaticism and the need for a discourse on the divine (θεολογία). This dialectic is clearly philosophical rather than religious. In the case of Philo, he is primarily an exegete, but philosophy offers him an indispensable framework for his exegesis. His contribution is seen above all in the principle, taken over by Origen and Gregory, that the divinity is unknowable in its essence, and thus also ineffable, but knowable through its activity. Divine revelation is the gnoseological factor that allows human beings to know something of the divinity, but as such it is subject to strict rules of interpretation centred on the hermeneutical tool of allegoresis. Key scriptural passages for Philo are Exod 20:21 and 33:20–23. A typical feature of Philo's exegesis is his use of the metaphor of blindness due to the excessive brightness of the divine essence, a theme which is followed by Gregory. The reflections of the four thinkers on the divine as an inaccessible epistemic object for human beings, which can nevertheless be experienced in a meta-cognitive way, is due to their common philosophical tradition, which provides them with a shared epistemological and ontological pattern of thought. (DTR)

M. J. REDDOCH, 'Cicero's *De Divinatione* and Philo of Alexandria's Criticism of Chaldean Astrology as a Form of Artificial Divination,' *Dionysius* 32 (2014) 54–70.

Philo appears to be influenced by a distinction found in Cicero's *De divinatione* between natural divination, inspired by the gods, and artificial divination, which arises from human observation of nature. Artificial divination, moreover, is based on a belief in cosmic sympathy (συμπάθεια), whereby correlations may be discerned between two apparently unconnected phenomena. Without using the term *sympatheia* specifically, Cicero includes a criticism of Chaldean astrology, which is based on this kind of approach. Although Philo does not specify the distinction between natural and artificial divination, he seems to recognize this distinction when he shows preference for types of natural divination like prophetic dreams and disapproval of types of artificial divination, such as those prohibited in Deut 18 and practiced by augurs, soothsayers, and others. Adopting the biblical prohibitions, Philo explains that the latter practitioners base their statements on observation of nature and ignore the real cause of natural phenomena, namely God. The same distinction underlies Philo's criticism of Chaldean astrology but his differs from the criticism in Cicero's work because he recognizes this astrology to be somewhat effective and portrays Moses as accepting the doctrine of συμπάθεια. Instead, Philo's objection is that the Chaldeans ignore the true God. Chaldea thus represents a place that must be left behind so that one may progress spiritually. (EB)

A. REINHARTZ, 'Philo's Exposition of the Law and Social History: Methodological Considerations,' in T. SELAND (ed.), *Reading Philo: A Handbook to Philo of Alexandria* (Grand Rapids, MI 2014) 180–199.

Defined as a 'preliminary attempt to address the question of whether it may be possible to draw social-historical data from Philo's exegetical discussions in the *Exposition*' (p. 181), this chapter deals with (1) the substantial methodological problems connected to such an approach; (2) the scholarly assumptions that would prevent or support the task; and (3) examples of Philo's scriptural interpretation related to family matters. This very useful study was originally published in the *Society of Biblical Literature 1993 Seminar Papers*, ed. Eugene H. Lovering Jr. (Atlanta 1993) 6–21 (RRS 9368). (SJKP)

J. RIAUD, 'Une communauté mystérieuse dans les environs d'Alexandrie aux alentours de l'ère chrétienne,' *Rivista di Storia e Letteratura religiosa* (2014) 2–50.

The first part of the paper surveys the vast history of scholarship on the authorship of *Contempl.* and on the reality and identity of the Therapeutae. The treatise fueled the controversy between the Catholics, who followed Eusebius's testimony according to which the Therapeutae were early Christians, and the Protestants, who defended their Jewish identity (Scaliger, 1583). Whereas nineteenth century scholars, such as Nicolas, argued for a second or third century forger, Philo's authorship was defended by Massebieau (1887), followed by Wendland and Conybeare. In the twentieth century, Nikiprowetzky argued against the widely held identification of the Therapeutae with the Essenes, which was predominant in the first half of the century. It was Hankius (1671) who first made the distinction between the Therapeutae and the Essenes, a thesis which was later established on a firmer footing by Edersheim (1887). Whereas Philo's authorship and the reality of the Therapeutae are widely acknowledged today, doubts concerning the historic accuracy of Philo's account have been variously addressed over time, ranging from a radical denial of their existence (i.e., Lagrange, 1931) and up to more recent studies highlighting the idealistic features of Philo's portrayal of the community. The second part of the paper presents the community, its members and its way of life. The Therapeutae are literate men and women of equal status, originating from the Alexandrian Jewish community's upper class who, having left their family and belongings, entered the community around the age of fifty in order to lead a modest and celibate life. Younger and older members—a distinction pertaining to the time spent in the community and not to the biological age—led a life devoted to contemplation, prayers, celebrations and allegorical reading of the Torah. This way of life was viewed as a form of continual and symbolic priesthood. Philo found the term θεραπευτής suitable to describe this community as it combines the idea of worship/ service with that of therapy (of body and soul). (SW)

J. Rist, 'Il 'Logos' nella Tarda Antichità,' *Acta Philosophica: Pontificia Universita della Santa Croce* 23 (2014) 43–54.

This paper presents a synthetic narrative of different concepts of *logos* in late antiquity. The Stoics distinguish between λόγος προφορικός and λόγος ἐνδιάθετος but consider the two on the same level and identify *logos* with propositional thought. In contrast, a more 'normal' (and Neoplatonic) understanding considers the *logos* of something inferior to that of which it is the *logos*. This difference is important if we are to grasp the path which Christian thought had to take to overcome subordinationism. The *logos* in Philo has both Platonic (subordinate) and Stoic (non-subordinate) features: Christians had to modify Philo's concept in order to apply it to the Son of God. The Christian *logos* concept has implications for cosmology (the universe is intelligible, built up from *logoi,* intelligible principles) and ethics (moral principles too are *logoi,* and they are attributes of God). The problems discussed in this paper indicate the importance of Pope Benedict's comments in his Regensburg address (the Christian faith agrees with reason and requires it) and shed light on how to understand them. (HMK, based on the author's abstract)

M. Rizzi, 'Philo, Clement, and Origen,' in *Bible Odyssey* (online project: Atlanta 2014), available at http://www.bibleodyssey.org/places/related-articles/philo-clement-and-origen.

Bible Odyssey is an online project of the Society of Biblical Literature, in which the world's leading scholars share the latest historical and literary research on key people, places, and passages of the Bible and readers are invited to explore the origins of the Bible and its history. The scholarship is presented in a non-sectarian way and consists of compact articles of less than a thousand words. Although there is no page exclusively dealing with Philo, in the present article he is placed in the context of the Alexandrian tradition of biblical interpretation which commences with the translation of the Septuagint and continues in the Patristic tradition. Links are made to related articles on Alexandria, Alexandria and allegory, and other relevant pages and a brief list of bibliographical items is included. (DTR)

M. Rodríguez Donís, 'El 'Theophrastus redivivus' y la eternidad del mundo,' *Endoxa: Series Filosoficas (Madrid)* 34 (2014) 425–461.

The anonymous author of the Latin manuscript *Theophrastus redivivus* (the second half of the seventeenth century) sets forth arguments about the eternity of the world taken from other philosophers such as Ocellus Lucanus and Philo of Alexandria. However, it must be borne in mind that the anonymus does not always express appropriately what the authors quoted by him attested, and this also occurs in the case of Philo. The author of the article bases his comments in relation to Philo's thoughts on the French translation of *Aet.* by J. Pouilloux and its Introduction by R. Arnaldez (Paris 1969). (MA)

J. M. Rogers, 'The Philonic and the Pauline: Hagar and Sarah in the Exegesis of Didymus the Blind,' *The Studia Philonica Annual* 26 (2014) 57–77.

In the early church two symbolic interpretations of Hagar and Sarah were current: Paul's interpretation of Hagar as the Jewish and Sarah as the Christian covenant (Gal 4:21–31), and the Philonic allegory of Hagar as the preliminary studies and Sarah as virtue or wisdom (*Congr.* 11, 20 etc). Clement of Alexandria and Origen follow the Philonic interpretation, but Didymus the Blind tries to combine the Philonic interpretation with Paul's allegory. In his reading he follows Philo to a great extent. He agrees with Philo's literal interpretation of Hagar and Sarah, and also offers Philo's allegorical explanation, referring twice to Philo by name. Didymus sets aside the Pauline explanation of Sarah in favor of the Philonic reading of Sarah as perfect virtue. He regards Hagar as a symbol of 'shadow,' ascribing this interpretation to Paul. In this way he can incorporate the Philonic theme of progressing through education (the shadow) in preparation for virtue. At the same time, Hagar, the shadow, represents the literal explanation, which has to be surpassed. (ACG)

D. Roth, 'Shared Interpretive Traditions of Joseph's 'σωφροσύνη' and 'Silence' in *De Iosepho* and the *Testament of Joseph,*' *Journal of the Jesus Movement in its Jewish Setting* 1 (2014) 54–68.

In the present study, the author considers the way in which *Ios.* shares common interpretative traditions concerning Joseph with the *Testament of Joseph*, a text used by early Christian communities. Two issues are singled out for a closer study: the self-control or chastity of Joseph and his keeping silent about the misdeeds of others. The aim is to highlight the shared interpretive context of Joseph traditions utilized in Second Temple Judaism and early Christianity. In these two texts, the issue of Joseph's self-control (σωφροσύνη) is directly connected to his confrontation with Potiphar's wife. However, the account in the Septuagint never utilizes this term. It turns out that the utilization of the traditions in the two texts studied here is not identical, but it may be noted that in both their similarities and differences these texts highlight a phenomenon evident in numerous other texts as well. (TS)

D. T. Runia, 'Philo in the Patristic Tradition: A List of Direct References,' in T. Seland (ed.), *Reading Philo: A Handbook to Philo of Alexandria* (Grand Rapids, MI 2014) 268–286.

As part of an introductory work to Philo (see below under the name of its editor, T. Seland) the list of references to Philo in the works of the Church fathers is presented, based on earlier research (RRS 3215, 9373, 9570). The list is prefaced by some brief remarks on why Philo's reception in early Christianity and the church fathers is important, focusing on the story of the survival of his writings and the influence that he exerted on Christian thought. (DTR)

D. T. RUNIA and G. E. STERLING (edd.), *The Studia Philonica Annual*, Vol. 26 (Atlanta 2014).

Volume 26 of the Journal dedicated to Philonic studies contains 4 articles, a Special Section on Philo's Hellenistic and Hellenistic-Jewish sources consisting of an introduction and 4 articles, the usual Bibliography (see the separate summary) and 8 Book reviews. The News and Notes section contains a notice in memory of Dieter Zeller (1939–2014), a long-serving contributor to the work of the Annual. The articles are summarised elsewhere in this bibliography. (DTR)

D. T. RUNIA, K. BERTHELOT, E. BIRNBAUM, A. C. GELJON, H. M. KEIZER, J. LEONHARDT BALZER, J. P. MARTÍN, M. R. NIEHOFF, S. J. K. PEARCE, T. SELAND, and S. WEISSER, 'Philo of Alexandria: An Annotated Bibliography 2011,' *The Studia Philonica Annual* 26 (2014) 169–216.

The yearly annotated bibliography of Philonic studies prepared by the members of the International Philo Bibliography Project covers the year 2011 (118 items), with addenda for the years 2002–2008 (8 items), and provisional lists for the years 2012–2014. (DTR)

M. L. SAMUEL, *Torah from Alexandria: Philo as a Biblical Commentator. Volume 1 Genesis* (New York 2014).

The present volume is the first in a projected series of five volumes. The purpose of the series, we read, is to make Philo's ideas intelligible for a modern reading audience (p. 33). The guiding idea behind this book thus seems to be that by gathering all sayings of Philo concerning particular passages in the Torah, one can create a kind of biblical commentary on these passages as taught by Philo from Alexandria. In the introduction to the present volume on Genesis (pp. 9–34), Samuel deals with several introductory topics, as for example the use of recreating Jewish life in Egypt; The Septuagint; Philo's sources; Philo's youth; Philo as a community leader; Philo's personal life and interests; Did Philo know Hebrew?; Philo's method of biblical interpretation; Philo's enduring relevance, and more. There then follows the exposition. The biblical text is given in bold text, most often verse for verse. A few times two or three verses are listed together, but more often a verse is split up into several parts. Then follow the comments from Philo, with the location in his works given in footnotes. Occasionally Samuel inserts a brief comment on the work of Philo quoted, or more often he may draw attention to similar views expressed in other Jewish works. The volume has a Subject Index (pp. 328–333); Primary Source Index (pp. 334–347); and a short Select Bibliography (pp. 348–349). (TS)

M. L. SAMUEL, *Torah from Alexandria: Philo as a Biblical Commentator. Volume 2 Exodus* (New York 2014).

The present volume is the second in a projected series of five volumes, the aim of which is explained in the previous summary. In the introduction to the present volume on Exodus (pp. 9–22), the author deals briefly with issues as for example evidence of Greek wisdom in rabbinic Judea; the unwritten laws and the rabbinic oral law; Philo combats anti-semitism, and other topics. Philo is said to have had not only a theoretical interest in Jewish Law but that he played an important role in determining Judaic Law in Alexandria. There then follows the exposition, which follows the same method as in the first volume, ending with indices and a brief Select Bibliography. (TS)

K.-G. SANDELIN, 'Philo as a Jew,' in T. SELAND (ed.), *Reading Philo: A Handbook to Philo of Alexandria* (Grand Rapids MI 2014) 19–46.

In the present study the author tries to illuminate Philo as a Jew from three sides: (1) What should be said in general terms of Philo as a Jew, i.e., how is Philo a Jew like any other Jews of his time (pp. 23–34). Here he briefly discusses issues such as 'Philo's view of God'; on the 'Bible and the Law'; and aspects of 'the Jewish way of life' (i.e. circumcision, Sabbath observance, dietary laws, sexuality, and marriage). (2) The second section (pp. 34–42) deals with 'Profile of Philo as a Jew: Student and Teacher of Wisdom' (wisdom and the word, the realm of wisdom, the realm of the word; the place of humans within the two realms), ending with a discussion on 'Philo's views on the ideal Jew.' (3) Finally, 'Philo and the other Jewish groups' (pp. 42–46) are discussed, of which he himself mentions two types: the Essenes and the Therapeutes. Philo does not mention the Pharisees or the Sadducees, but his views are briefly compared with what we know about these two Palestinian groups. According to the author, if we look for texts that represent views similar to Philo's, the Book of Wisdom comes close as so does the fourth book of Maccabees. (TS)

M. L. SATLOW, *How the Bible Became Holy* (New Haven 2014).

In this account of the gradual process whereby the Bible acquired authority, the main thesis is that '*Jews and Christians gave to the texts that constitute our Bible only very limited and specific kinds of authority until well into the third century CE and beyond*' (p. 3, his emphasis). Philo enters the picture in Chapter 9, 'The Septuagint: Alexandria, Third Century BCE–First Century CE.' The author considers it possible that the Greek translation of the Bible was commissioned for the Alexandrian Library by Ptolemaic authorities. Later, refugees from Judea at the time of the Maccabean revolt began to accord the Septuagint the status of an ancient, foundational text, similar to the role of the Homeric works for non-Jews, and knowledge of the Septuagint spread through productions for the theater and readings in the synagogue. Philo's writings attest to this central importance of the Septuagint by the first century CE. His aim was to demonstrate how 'the perfect, divine law' addressed the most basic issue of the meaning of life and he accomplished this aim by presenting the Pentateuch as 'the written expression of the very laws of nature' (p. 169). Through studying this text, one might receive guidance in suppressing the irrational part of the soul and progressing toward a life that would be in harmony with the universe. (EB)

L. SAUDELLI, 'Loi de Moïse et philosophie grecque: Le judaïsme Alexandrin,' in C. MÉLA and F. MÖRI (edd.), *Alexandrie la divine* (Geneva 2014) 726–731.

As part of a lavish catalogue volume accompanying the exposition entitled 'Alexandrie la divine' held at the Fondation Bodmer in Geneva in 2014, this chapter is a short notice on Alexandrian Judaism centered around the figures of Aristobulus, the Therapeutae and Philo of Alexandria. The author situates Philo's exegesis in the context of contemporary and multifaceted Middle Platonism. The various ways in which Philo conceives of God and of his relationship to the world, the relation of the human intellect to God and the importance of the theme of spiritual migration are explored. The article is accompanied by a magnificent photograph by F. Mori of the opening page of the text of *Opif.* in the ms. Plut. 10, 20 from the Bibliotheca Laurentiana in Florence (p. 727). (SW)

F. Schmidt, 'The Plain and Laughter: the Hermeneutical Function of the Sign in Philo of Alexandria,' in J. K. Aitken and J. Carleton Paget (edd.), *The Jewish-Greek Tradition in Antiquity and the Byzantine Empire* (Cambridge 2014) 188–199.

This article discusses the meaning of the word σημεῖον as indicating 'a manifest symbol of hidden reality.' This is the way it appears in *Det.* 1 (plain as a sign of contest) and in *Praem.* 31 (laughter as a sign of unseen joy). Philo follows the Stoic notion of sign, according to which a sign is something sayable and is the antecedent that reveals the consequent. He thus can use the notion of sign as an instrument to proceed from the literal statement of the text (the antecedent) to the allegorical meaning (the consequent). This instrument disappears, however, when he moves away from biblical statements, for example, when he explains ceremonial and ritual laws. The terms ἀφορμή and σύμβολον belong to the same conceptual configuration. With the term ἀφορμή Philo refers to a starting point of or a stimulus for allegorical interpretation. The word σύμβολον refers to the complementarity between the word and the hidden reality, the two halves of one object. (ACG)

T. Seland (ed.), *Reading Philo: A Handbook to Philo of Alexandria* (Grand Rapids, MI 2014).

This volume is designed as an introduction to Philo of Alexandria for students at the graduate and doctoral level. Its origins lie in Scandinavian research on Philo, but other scholars have also been invited to contribute. It comprises 11 chapters written by nine scholars. After a brief Introduction (pp. 3–16), written by T. Seland, there are five chapters dealing with 'Philo of Alexandria in context.' These are followed by another five chapters dealing with 'Why and How to Study Philo.' The volume concludes with a bibliography and comprehensive indices. Individual chapters are summarized in this bibliography under the name of their authors. See further the review by Kenneth Schenck in *SPhiloA* vol. 27, pp. 236–240. (TS)

T. Seland, 'Philo as a Citizen: Homo Politicus,' in T. Seland (ed.), *Reading Philo: A Handbook to Philo of Alexandria* (Grand Rapids, MI 2014) 47–74.

In this chapter, the author provides a description of Philo as a citizen in Alexandria of the Roman Empire. The main part of the essay is devoted to Philo's descriptions of Roman rule and his own activities as a politically active citizen. After some introductory comments on Philo's social location and his background as coming from a family of politicians, the chapter is divided into three main sections: recent studies on Philo and his politics (dealing with S. Tracy, E. R. Goodenough, S. Sandmel, and R. Barraclough); issues of political theory in Philo (Philo's views of Israel in the world, of himself as a cosmopolite, and of the Torah as the Law of Nature); and Philo as a practical politician as presented in his writings. Finally, he points out some major problems in interpreting Philo's narratives as well as other problems and prospects in understanding him as a politician. (TS)

T. Seland, 'Why Study Philo? How?,' in T. Seland (ed.), *Reading Philo: A Handbook to Philo of Alexandria* (Grand Rapids MI 2014) 157–179.

This chapter is a practical introduction in how to proceed when embarking on a study of Philo of Alexandria. Accordingly, it deals not only with where to begin among Philo's many writings, but also provides a presentation of available text editions, translations, indexes, and lexica, as well as how to read Philo on the computer, whether using programs containing his texts or by means of various searching resources, the Internet included. The chapter also lists and comments on bibliographies, reviews, and other handbooks as well as commentaries and introductions to Philo. (TS)

M. SHERIDAN, '"God is not as Man" (Num 23:19): The Theological Critique of the Scripture by Early Christian Writers,' *American Benedictine Review* 65 (2014) 242–256.

The author discusses how Origen treats texts in Scripture which provide difficulties, especially texts where God is presented as a human being (Deut 1:31, 8:5). These texts seem to be in contrast with the statement that God is not as a man (Num 23:19). Within this context the author also deals with Philo's critique of anthropomorphism. Philo argues that a statement as 'God is as a man' is said for the instruction of children. In his discussion of this matter Philo often employs the expression 'worthy of God' to avoid a literalist interpretation. In doing so, he stands in the tradition of philosophical interpretation of Homer, in which the term 'worthy of God' was used to find an acceptable interpretation of the Homeric epics. The term ἀνθρωποπαθής seems to be coined by Philo. Because human beings cannot escape their mortality, they attribute human passions to God. The terminology of ἀνθρωποπαθής was taken over by many Christian writers of the first centuries. (ACG)

F. SIEGERT, 'Die theoretischen Bewaltigung des Bösen bei Philon,' in F. JOURDAN and R. HIRSCH-LUIPOLD (edd.), *Die Würzel allen Übels: Vorstellungen über die Herkunft des Bösen und Schlechten in der Philosophie des 1.–4. Jahrhunderts*, Studien und Texte zu Antike und Christentum 91 (Tübingen 2014) 69–86.

The contribution studies Philo's thoughts on the topic of evil. First his background is outlined, then the biblical passages on temptation and testing used by Philo are mentioned. Philo's God cannot be the cause of evil. Evil, therefore, needs to be located not in theology, but in cosmology. This leads Philo to a Platonic idea of the good, for which the bad does not have an existence of its own, but is merely something which is less good. Philo also exhibits a Stoic idea of the non-good, according to which evil results from human decision. Philo derives moral evil from human desire. Regarding evil in history, Philo's idea of divine pronoia expresses the conviction that no evil will conquer Israel. This pronoia-concept, according to Siegert, cannot be derived from Philo's Logos theory, but appears as an attempt at containing historical evil and thus keeping it controlled within the order of the world. (JLB)

G. E. STERLING, 'Philo's Hellenistic and Hellenistic-Jewish Sources,' *The Studia Philonica Annual* 26 (2014) 93–97.

This brief article serves as an introduction to the special section of *The Studia Philonica Annual* on the subject of Philo's Hellenistic and Hellenistic Jewish sources consisting of four further articles by D. Lincicum, G. E. Sterling, P. Nieto Hernández and M. Cover summarized elsewhere in this bibliography. The author begins by briefly noting the praise for Philo's control of both Jewish and Hellenistic literature in Josephus and Eusebius. There can be no doubt of the extent of his knowledge of the scriptures and their interpretative tradition, and also of Greek philosophy and the liberal arts, but the nature of his indebtedness to these Greek traditions, especially in the domain of philosophy, is more difficult to assess. The purpose of the essays is to stimulate further research and discussion. (DTR)

G. E. Sterling, 'From the Thick Marshes of the Nile to the Throne of God: Moses in Ezekiel the Tragedian and Philo of Alexandria,' *The Studia Philonica Annual* 26 (2014) 115–133.

This article examines the relationship between Philo's *Mos.* and Ezekiel's *Exagoge*. Three areas are investigated: verbal parallels; exegetical traditions; and thematic similarities. It appears that there are 15 parallels between Philo and Ezekiel: some are common improvements or variations of the biblical text, but others are very striking. On this basis it can be concluded that Philo knew Ezekiel's *Exagoge*. The discussion of the exegetical traditions shows that there are a great number of exegetical agreements which are found across the entire story of Ezekiel. A significant thematic parallel is the presentation of Moses as having become divine. In his final conclusion the author states that 'Philo apparently liked a number of Ezekiel's turns of phrases and interpretive moves well enough that they become part of his own reading of the story of Exodus' (p. 133). (ACG)

G. E. Sterling, '"The Jewish Philosophy": Reading Moses via Hellenistic Philosophy according to Philo,' in T. Seland (ed.), *Reading Philo: A Handbook to Philo of Alexandria* (Grand Rapids, MI 2014) 129–154.

According to Sterling, it is impossible to read Philo's works without some understanding of his relationship to Hellenistic philosophical traditions: the presence of philosophy in Philo's writings is a given. He then sets forth Philo's views under three headings: 'Philo's predecessors' (Aristobulus, Pseudo-Aristeas; The Allegorists, pp. 131–136); 'An eclectic thinker' (Platonism; Stoicism; Aristotle and the Peripatetics; Neopythagoreans; other influential Philosophers, and opponents, pp. 137–148). Thirdly, he deals with 'The value of philosophy' (treating separately the commentaries; the philosophical treatises, pp. 148–153). Finally, It is argued that Philo was teaching in a kind of school and that Philo believed 'that Hellenistic philosophy—at least the traditions he accepted—and the Jewish faith came together at the most important juncture: the understanding of the divine' (p. 154). (TS)

G. E. Sterling, 'The People of the Covenant or the People of God: Exodus in Philo of Alexandria,' in T. B. Dozeman, C. A. Evans and J. N. Lohr (edd.), *The Book of Exodus: Composition, Reception, and Interpretation,* Vetus Testamentum Supplements 164 (Leiden 2014) 404–439.

The article focuses on Philo's understanding and reading of the book of Exodus. First, basing himself on frequency of citations and allusions to Exodus, the author concludes that for Philo Exodus is the most important book of the Pentateuch after Genesis. Secondly, the author examines how Philo understands Exodus. The frequency of references to each chapter of Exodus shows that Philo is keenly interested in Passover (Exod 12); the Decalogue (Exod 20); selections from the Book of Covenant (Exod 23); the Tabernacle (Exod 25); and the priesthood (Exod 28). It emerges that Philo interprets the cult of ancient Israel—the Passover, the Tabernacle, the priesthood—by spiritualizing and universalizing it. In the final part of the article there is a discussion of three of the Exodus verses to which Philo refers the most: Exod 3:14, where God makes himself known, a fundamental text for Philo's doctrine of God; Exod 21:13–14, which deal with unintentional and intentional murder; and Exod 20:17, the prohibition against coveting as the last of the Ten Commandments. The conclusion that for Philo Exodus was the second most important book of the Pentateuch may seem surprising because Philo lived in Egypt and Exodus narrates the exodus of the Jewish people out of Egypt. Furthermore, Exodus can be seen as a particularist text. Philo, however, could not ignore Exodus, which is important for Jewish identity. In reading Exodus, on the one hand he retells a great deal of it, on the other he moves from particular situations to a universal perspective. An appendix lists all the citations of and allusions to Exodus in the Allegorical Commentary and the Exposition of the Law. (ACG)

G. J. STEYN, 'Some Observations on Philo of Alexandria's Sensitivity to Strangers,' in J. KOK, T. NICKLAS, D. T. ROTH and C. M. HAYS (edd.), *Sensitivity to Outsiders: Exploring the Dynamic Relationship Between Mission and Ethics in the New Testament and Early Christianity*, Wissenschaftliche Untersuchungen zum Neuen Testament 2.364 (Tübingen 2014) 59–78.

In this chapter, Steyn argues that Philo's commentary on Scripture is directly influenced by the context of his own presence as a Jewish 'stranger' in Egypt as well as other factors (historical, theological, legal, philosophical, political and geographic influences). A brief examination of terms used for different kinds of 'strangers,' as designated in Philo's works, looks in particular at (1) temporary sojourners (ξένοι; see also the terms πάροικος and ἀλλότριον); and (2) resident aliens (προσήλυτοι; see also ἐπήλυτοι). Philo shows a positive attitude towards relationships with 'strangers.' The duty of respect towards 'strangers' is closely linked to his interpretation of Scripture, in which a positive concern for the 'stranger' is understood as required by God, the Protector of strangers (cf. *Mos.* 1.35–36). (SJKP)

G. J. STEYN, 'Reflections on the Reception of the LXX Pentateuch in Philo's De vita Mosis,' in W. KRAUS (ed.), *Die Septuaginta—Text, Wirkung, Rezeption. 4. Internationale Fachtagung veranstaltet von Septuaginta Deutsch (LXX.D), Wuppertal 19.-22. Juli 2012*, Wissenschaftliche Untersuchungen zum Neuen Testament 1.325 (Tübingen 2014) 363–380.

The article examines the explicit references to Scripture in *Mos.* and the relation between the terminology Philo ascribes to Scripture and the actual terminology in the LXX. It appears that the explicit reference to Scripture ('The sacred Scriptures say...') occurs almost exclusively in the second book of *Mos.* and particularly in the description of the Tabernacle (*Mos.* 2.56–143). The investigation of the references ends with the following conclusions. (1) Philo uses the Greek Pentateuch for his *Mos.* (2) In his explicit references to LXX terminology he sometimes employs synonymous terms which are more current. (3) Occasionally he explicitly refers to a LXX term which is absent in our LXX version. This may be the result of quoting from memory, or employing the oral tradition. (4) There exists a variety of terms to indicate the several screens and curtains which make up the structure of the Tabernacle and its courtyard. (ACG)

G. J. STEYN, 'Quotations from Scripture and the Compilation of Hebrews in an Oral World,' *Journal of Early Christian History* 4.1 (2014) 68–87.

The article interacts with the work of the South African scholar Pieter Botha, and particularly his monograph entitled *Orality and Literacy in Early Christianity* (2012). In order to do so it presents four 'scenarios' from the author's own research, the first two of which relate to Philo. The first draws attention to the fusion of oral and written traditions from the Pentateuch as perceived in Philo's *Mos.* 1.4, where he says that he is drawing on both the oral tradition from the elders in his society and the written tradition of the scriptures. The second relates to the Therapeutae who represent an example of an ascetic Jewish group that meditated allegorically on the laws, prophetic oracles and psalms. The main part of the article focuses on Hebrews. Its author not only draws on the pool of quotations in general circulation but also expands on them, which reflects his own first-hand familiarity with, personal study and exposition of the scriptures, a practice which finds parallels amongst Philo's Therapeutae. (DTR)

M. TARDIEU, 'Le paradis chaldaïque (fr. 107 et 165),' in A. LECERF, L. SAUDELLI and H. SENG (edd.), *Oracles chaldaïques Fragments et philosophie*, Bibliotheca Chaldaica 4 (Heidelberg 2014) 15–29.

The article provides an examination of fr. 107 of the *Chaldean Oracles*, which opposes the 'sacred paradise of piety,' characterized by virtue, wisdom, and good legislation, to deceitful astronomical calculations and mantic techniques. The oracle opposes the literal and non-symbolic sense of the term παράδεισος, which is a concrete territory made prosperous thanks to irrigation and plantation techniques, to a metaphorical usage of the term (and does not rely therefore on a Judeo-Christian understanding of the term). Tardieu takes up Kroll's original position—asserting that the association between paradise and virtue is due to the influence of Philo of Alexandria—but attempts to situate this influence in the Jewish context preceding Philo. The oracle's hostility towards 'the playthings' (τὰ ἀθύρματα), represented by astronomical speculations and technical mantics in their association with artisanal techniques, should be situated in the context of the Platonic Jewish philosophy of the Hellenistic period, as already attested in Ben Sira, which offers a similar opposition between astronomical amusements and paradise in a metaphorical sense. (SW)

H. TAUSSIG, 'The Pivotal Place of the Therapeutae in Understanding the Meals of Early Judaism,' in S. MARKS and H. TAUSSIG (edd.), *Meals in Early Judaism: Social Formation at the Table* (New York 2014) 117–128.

Introducing other chapters on Philo's description in *Contempl.* of the meal of the Therapeutae, this essay offers four reasons why this description is important for understanding meals in early Judaism generally. First, Philo's description is the most elaborate, sustained portrayal of a Jewish meal in antiquity. Second, evidence from Philo's description supports the view of the volume's contributors that 'early Jewish meals fit the main patterns of Greek and Roman meals' (p. 117). Third, this description confirms the integral relationship between Jewish meals and Jewish traditions. Finally, by illustrating a variety of social issues with which the group contended—such as the place of women, servants, and those who are spiritually advanced—Philo's description offers a concrete example of aspects of ritual theory. For other essays in the same volume on the meal of the Therapeutae, see also the summaries under A. B. McGowan, M. Klinghardt, and J. Brumberg-Kraus. (EB)

F. Timmers, 'Philo of Alexandria's Understanding of πνεύμα in *Deus* 33–50,' in J. Frey and J. R. Levison (edd.), *The Holy Spirit, Inspiration, and the Cultures of Antiquity: Multidisciplinary Perspectives*, Ekstasis 5 (Berlin 2014) 265–292.

In the introductory section, the author voices a certain reluctance to study Philo with reference to some of the ancient philosophical systems as we know them. Because of the risks associated with the concept of a philosophical school, which may result in light being shed primarily upon selective aspects of the ancient author's view, the author proposes to approach the ancient philosophical views along with those of Philo as an amalgam. Drawing from this analogy while analyzing Philo's views will mean, that one makes use of the taxonomy of philosophical schools to find a lead or where to look in order to understand certain terminology used by Philo, but the various phenomena should be studied on their own. Turning to *Deus* 33–50, it is argued that Philo describes four states that can govern physical bodies: cohesion, growth, life, and understanding. The author claims to find each of these states described in terms of πνεῦμα in Philo's works. But he also notes that these same four states appear as abilities of the mind (νοῦς) in *Leg*. 2.22. In sum, it is claimed that the diverse philosophical vocabulary that is encountered in Philo is a vocabulary shared by most educated people of his era. The modern taxonomy of philosophical schools helps us to know where to look to better understand this vocabulary. However, each particular concept should be carefully weighed on its own, without too quickly trying to understand it based on the modern perception of particular philosophical schools and their thoughts. (TS)

S. Torallas Tovar, 'Philo of Alexandria's Dream Classification,' *Archiv für religionsgeschichte* 15 (2014) 67–82.

The world of dream-theory and dream-interpretation in which Philo operated is marked by two kinds of dream classification. The one is five-fold and classifies dreams according to their form or manifestation, as found in Artemidorus and Macrobius. These are three kinds of predictive dreams (ὄνειρος, ὅραμα, χρηματισμός) and two kinds of non-predictive dreams (ἐνύπνιον, φάντασμα). Philo, however, makes use of the other, three-fold classification, which goes back to the Stoa and identified dreams according to their source and origin. It assumes that all dreams are ultimately God-sent, but their direct source varies, being either God, immortal souls or the soul of the dreamer. This classification provided Philo with a structure upon which he built his treatise *Somn*. The aim of this treatise was to comment on the dreams that occur in the book of Genesis in the strict order of their appearance. But in order to fulfil his aims he needed to expand the classification with other criteria which rank dreams in terms of their phenomenology and the clarity of the message they convey. While dreams sent by God are perfectly clear, those which have the soul as a source are obscure enough to require the intervention of a skilled interpreter. The obscurity or clarity of dreams depend on the perfection acquired by the soul of the dreamer. At this point a second three-fold classification complements the one on dreams, namely of types of lives or types of souls, which involves a gradation of the soul in its progress towards perfection, using as examples the characters appearing in scripture, mainly the Patriarchs. (DTR, partly based on the author's abstract)

S. C. Towers, 'An Analysis of Philo's Exegesis of the Sotah Ritual,' *Women in Judaism (electronic)* 11 (2014).

The author explores Philo's thinking about gender through an analysis of his comments on the Sotah ritual (Num 5:11–31) in *Spec.* 3.52–63 and *Leg.* 3.148–50 and their comparison with other ancient commentary on this text (in Josephus' *Antiquities*, Mishnah and Tosefta). Philo's distinctive treatment of the Sotah ritual, it is argued, tends to dismiss the central role of the Sotah, the wife accused of adultery, in the ritual; she is 'dissolved into body parts or subsumed into aspects of the male soul, reflecting Philo's preoccupation with purely male development.' Differences between the two Philonic passages are to be explained, the author argues, by the assumption of different intended audiences. In conclusion, it is proposed that 'Philo's writings on the Sotah ritual reveal a fundamental disregard for and disinterest in the female as spiritual being.' (SJKP)

A. Wypadlo, '"Seele" und "Seelenheil" im 1. Petrusbrief. Philonische Perspektiven auf eine alte Streitfrage,' *Theologische Revue* 110 (2014) 267–284.

Philo is used to decide the exegetical debate about whether in 1 Peter (esp. 1:3–12; 2:11) ψυχή refers to 'life' or the higher part of the human existence. The author points out that in the Middle Ages Philo was regarded as part of the Christian tradition. For Philo, the wise lives as a stranger in the world. The human ψυχή does not originate from this earth, but is from God (*Her.* 266–268). In this context the metaphor of rebirth plays an important part as part of the philosophical makeup of the time and is taken up in 1 Peter 1:18. Philo mentions the 'second birth' in *QE* 2.46 when referring to the liberation of the soul from material existence and its passions. He describes the soul as the higher (*Decal.* 134), pre-existing divine part of the human being, which is inserted into the human body (*Opif.* 135, 137), and which returns to God when the body dies (*Gig.* 13, *QG* 3.11, cf. *Mos.* 2.238; *Migr.* 2). (JLB)

B. Wyss, '„Vater Gott und seine Kinder und Frauen",' in F. Albrecht and R. Feldmeier (edd.), *The Divine Father: Religious and Philosophical Concepts of Divine Parenthood in Antiquity,* Themes in Biblical Narrative 18 (Leiden 2014) 165–179.

The Platonic father and creator (*Tim.* 28c) also plays a part in Philo, who uses the philosophical designation for God as 'father' no less often than other expressions such as ὁ ὤν and τὸ αἴτιον). The allegorical genre of Philo's writings means that the terminology of children is used metaphorically for functions of the soul. In the allegorical commentary the Logos is the first-born son of God (*Agr.* 51), while the cosmos is God's younger son, with ἐπιστήμη as the mother (*Ebr.* 30–31; *Deus* 31). The Logos is derived not from Greek mythology, but from the Old Testament idea of the word of God, although there are certain parallels to the Greek Hermes or the Egyptian Horus. Philo can also use the Greek concept of God (Zeus) as the father of the graces (*Migr.* 31; *Post.* 32) or of any good deed. God is also described as father of Sarah as virtue (*Her.* 62) and as wisdom/Sophia (*Fug.* 50–52). Yet sometimes Sophia also appears as mother of the cosmos (*Det.* 54, *Ebr.* 34), comparable to Hera or Isis. Yet Philo's perspective remains metaphorical. There is no mythological concept of a heavenly family in his writings. Isaac, whose name represents laughter, demonstrates that the purpose of God's begetting is human happiness in virtue (*Leg.* 3.219). (JLB)

J. YODER, *Representatives of Roman Rule. Roman Provincial Governors in Luke-Acts*, Beihefte zur Zeitschrift für die neutestamentliche Wissenschaft 209 (Berlin 2014).

The focus of this study is the political view of the Lukan works on the Romans as it comes to the fore in the characterization of Roman governors in the narratives as analyzed help of the method of 'narrative-rhetorical criticism.' Furthermore, in order to assess the rhetoric of Luke's narratives, the author also investigates contemporary narratives in which Roman governors play prominent roles. Hence, he also deals with Philo, who is studied primarily in chap. 2 entitled 'Narratives for Praise and Blame: Tacitus on Agricola, Philo on Flaccus. It is argued that *Flacc.* was written fairly soon after the death of Gaius, and was aimed at a non-Jewish readership, probably a Roman audience. As to genre, it should not be assigned to one particular genre. The work as a whole might have served more than one purpose and three are suggested: (1) to reassure readers that God's providential care is still extended over the Jews; (2) to use rhetoric as a way of incriminating Flaccus, and (3) to portray the Jews in general as good citizens of the empire. As to the picture of Flaccus inherent in the work, Yoder finds three examples of characterization of the governor Flaccus, one laudatory and two critical. In the more laudatory portrait, Philo describes Flaccus' good judgment and his interpersonal and administrative skills. But then the governor loses his prudence and confidence, falling victim to manipulation through his fear, vanity, hypocrisy, and negligence. Finally, Flaccus appears as malicious and cruel, abusing his authority in his eagerness to harm the Jews. It can be concluded that Philo has a generally positive view of Rome, but its governors can be incompetent and malicious or they can be competent and beneficial. If a governor is incompetent, it does not necessarily mean that Rome is to be blamed. Bad governors do not incur harsh criticism of Rome as such. (TS)

Extra items from before 2014

T. ALEKNIENE, 'La prière à l'Un dans le Traité 10 (V, 1) de Plotin et la tradition philosophique grecque,' in F. KARFÍK and E. SONG (edd.), *Plato Revived: Essays on Ancient Platonism in Honour of Dominic J. O'Meara*, Beiträge zur Altertumskunde 317 (Berlin 2013) 326–342.

In an examination of the prayer to the One in Plotinus *Enn.* 5.1 [10] against the background of the Greek philosophical tradition, the author notes that Plotinus follows above all the tradition of the Platonic dialogues, but deviates from them in a striking manner. Whereas the protagonists in the dialogues express their respect for the religious tradition, Plotinus insists on the personal character of his prayer. But it needs to be pointed out as well that there are a number of features of the prayer that are reminiscent of themes and expressions in the works of Philo, including the phrase γεγωνὸς φωνή and the formula μόνος πρὸς μόνον. These passages are sufficient to allow the conclusion that Plotinus probably read the works of the Jewish Platonist, to which he would have had easy access during his time in Alexandria. The essay has recently been republished in a volume of collected essays, T. Alekniene, *A l'approche du divin: dialogues de Platon et tradition platonicienne*, Vestigia 42 (Fribourg 2016). (DTR)

T. BÉNATOUÏL, *Faire usage: La pratique du stoïcisme* (Paris 2007), esp. 279–320.

This study examines the question how the Stoics employ the notion of use/usage (χρῆσις, χρᾶσθαι), and is divided into four parts: the use of nature; the use of reason; the use of virtue; and the use of indifferents. The final chapter of the last part discusses the drinking of wine as a model of good use, for which subject Philo is used as a source. In *Plant.* 142–172, where he uses the biblical text Gen 9:20–21 as his starting point ('Noah planted a vineyard, and he drank of the wine, and he became drunk'), Philo discusses the opinions of the philosophers regarding the question whether a wise man may be drunk. Although he does not refer to any philosopher by name, it is clear that his treatment reflects the discussion within Stoic circles. Philo reports the syllogism of Zeno which concludes that the wise person will not get drunk. He also refers to the view, usually attributed to Chrysippus, that a wise man may not drink wine and say foolish things. According to the opposite view a wise person may drink wine, without loosing his virtue. This view is generally attributed to Cleanthes. In his account Philo offers various arguments according to which a wise person may drink wine. In his discussion of these arguments, Bénatouïl involves the notion of the καθῆκον (what is proper in the circumstances). There may be circumstances in which it is fitting for a wise person to drink an excessive amount of wine. This view is not a development in later Stoicism, but may be attributed to Zeno and the first Stoics. (ACG)

C. BURNETT, 'Going through Hell; ΤΑΡΤΑΡΟΣ in Greco-Roman Culture, Second Temple Judaism, and Philo of Alexandria,' *Journal of Ancient Judaism* 4 (2013) 352–378.

Against the view that Second Temple period eschatology was influenced primarily or only by Persian/Iranian eschatology, the author argues that Second Temple Jewish writings show awareness of Greco-Roman mythological traditions. In much eschatological discourse among Jews of this period, the idea of the prison of Tartarus and the related myths of the Titans and Giants are of particular importance. The author offers a detailed discussion of relevant Greco-Roman traditions as context for the eschatology of Second Temple Jewish texts. Particular attention is paid to the works of Philo as an example of the impact of Greco-Roman traditions about Tartarus, Titans, and Giants; see pp. 374–377, with reference to *Praem.* 152; *Cher.* 78; *QG* 4.234) Philo's understanding of Tartarus 'suggests a strong dependence upon Greco-Roman culture,' distinct from any influence that might have been exerted by rare references to Tartarus in LXX. The influence of Greco-Roman myth may also be seen in Philo's treatment of the Giants of Genesis (Gen 6:1–4; cf. *Gig.* 58–59; *QG* 1.92). In this case, however, Philo tries to distance the Genesis tradition from the realm of Greco-Roman myth. (SJKP)

J. VON EHRENKROOK, 'The Afterlife in Philo and Josephus,' in J. H. ELLENS (ed.), *Heaven, Hell, and the Afterlife: Eternity in Judaism, Christianity, and Islam* (Santa Barbara 2013) 1.97–118.

In this short discussion of Philo's thoughts on the afterlife, his anthropology and the soul's immortality are treated. Prominent in Philo is the Platonic dualism between a material body and an immaterial soul. The human being is a borderline creature, mortal in respect of the body, immortal in respect of his soul. The soul is the essence of the human being and is entombed in the body as in a tomb. Death is seen as a liberation of the soul.

Upon death the soul is released from the body and returns to the divine realm. Philo makes a dinstinction between righteous and wicked souls and only the souls of the former are immortal. It is unclear whether Philo believes in a personal, individual beatic afterlife. (ACG)

C. DEN HERTOG, *The Other Face of God: I am that I am Reconsidered*, Hebrew Bible Monographs 32 (Sheffield 2012), esp. 155–165, 214–215.

This monograph undertakes to give a broadly based investigation into the meaning of the statement ascribed to God in Exod 3:14, 'I am that I am,' reaching the conclusion that the meaning of the statment is deliberately indefinite, which amounts to 'I may be who I may be.' The second half of the book focuses on the 'after-history' of the verse, since it has shaped subsequent understanding of how it should be interpreted right until our own time. Chapter 4 deals with the verse in the Septuagint and the influence of the Greek translation on later readers. The rendering ἐγώ εἰμι ὁ ὤν was generally understood in a highly philosophical way, and this influenced the way that the Hebrew text was understood as well, until it was disputed during the past two centuries. Naturally Philo's contribution is studied, since 'inasmuch as it is verifiable by the extant texts, it was Philo who first directly connected Exod. 3:14 and Greek philosophy, in particular that of Plato' (p. 214). First Philo's use of ὁ ὤν and related expressions—especially τὸ ὄν derived from Plato—is outlined. Then the various passages in which Philo reflects on the text are examined. It is clear that Philo depends completely on the Septuagint translation. It emerges that his interpretation is more diverse and nuanced that often assumed. 'Besides indicating the absence of a divine proper name, the divine statement points … to God's existence (in contrast with his essence), to the presence of truth on his side, or to the idea that (stable and lasting) Being belongs only to him.' He goes on to point out that only the last of these interpretations is clearly metaphysical in nature, the result of Philo's exploiting a possibility provided by the letter of the Greek translation. In a further discussion (p. 219) it is denied that the LXX translation was originally connected with Hellenistic philosophical thinking. It should not be thought, therefore, that there was a continuity between the translation and Philo's ontological-metaphysical interpretation. Finally he notes (p. 223) that Philo's emphasis on divine transcendence, which he links to the divine statement, in fact does even more justice to the Hebrew text than the Greek translation and its modern counterparts, because the Hebrew text points to God's otherness. There is, however, a problem with Philo's theology, namely his stratified model of the deity. (DTR)

M. D. LITWA, *We Are Being Transformed: Deification in Paul's Soteriology*, Beihefte zur Zeitschrift für die neutestamentliche Wissenschaft 187 (Berlin 2012), esp. 106–109.

The language of Paul's soteriology suggests a form of deification at work in his thought, which has Jewish roots, particularly in the treatment of Moses and his descent from Sinai. The best path into the interpretative traditions surrounding the glorified Moses is Philo. There follows a brief discussion of Philo's views, which have been further developed by the author in the article published in *SPhiloA* in 2014; see the summary above. (DTR)

S. PEARCE, 'Philo of Alexandria on the Second Commandment,' in S. PEARCE (ed.), *The Image and Its Prohibition in Jewish Antiquity*, Journal of Jewish Studies Supplement Series 2 (Oxford 2013) 49–76.

In his treatise *De Decalogo*, Philo gives the earliest known extended commentary on the Second Commandment, which deals with the prohibition of the making of images and their use in cultic practice (based on LXX Exod 20:2–6; Deut 5:6–10). Following a brief introduction to the LXX versions, this chapter offers an analysis of Philo's exposition of the prohibition in *Decal.* 66–81, focusing on the following topics: (1) The reason for the place of the prohibition in second place on the first table of the Decalogue. (2) The nature of what is prohibited, in which Philo emphasizes the shaping (μορφόω) of material substances into images; Philo's choice of terms to denote the prohibited images, familiar not from the LXX versions of the prohibition but from the realities of Philo's world (e.g. *ἀγάλματα, ξόανα, ἀφίδρυμα*), and which (it is argued) actualize the commandment for his readers; and the use of the term *χειρόκμητα*, the things 'wrought by hand,' which serves as a key term to define the nature of what is prohibited, drawing on the language of philosophical discourse about the divine origins of the cosmos. (3) The nature of the proscribed offence and why it is wrong, which Philo explains in terms of the spiritual destruction inflicted by idolatry and the specific example of Egyptian animal worship. (4) The positive purpose of the prohibition as a universal exhortation to honor 'the one God who truly exists' (*Decal.* 81)—for Philo, the Second Commandment opens up the road to the knowledge of God, a way that is open to all beings endowed with reason. By approaching the knowledge of God through the mind, and not through conceptions of God based on material things, human beings can become more like God, 'the unadulterated intellect of the cosmos' (*Opif.* 8). See also the review by H. Najman and S. Anderson elsewhere in this volume. (SJKP)

J. ZURAWSKI, 'Hell on Earth: Corporeal Existence as the Ultimate Punishment of the Wicked in Philo of Alexandria and the Wisdom of Solomon,' in J. H. ELLENS (ed.), *Heaven, Hell, and the Afterlife: Eternity in Judaism, Christianity, and Islam,* (Santa Barbara 2013) 1.193–226, esp. 194–207.

The death of the soul is an important aspect of Philo's worldview. Factors responsible for the psychic death are blasphemy, devotion to pleasure, and lack of education. Philo describes the death of the soul as a life without virtue, seeing it expressed by the odd phrase 'to die by death' (Gen 2:17, Exod 21:12 LXX). It consists of the destruction of virtue, and makes the soul a slave to the body. In answer to the question if there can be a return from death, the author argues that the soul which is dead cannot be cured, only one that is diseased can be cured. When Philo speaks about 'hell' he refers in a figurative way to the life trapped in the body on earth. Regarding the death of the soul, Philo deviates from Plato's concept of the soul's immortality. This is based on the explanation of the creation of human being described in Gen 2:7. (ACG)

The Studia Philonica Annual 29 (2017): 229–43

SUPPLEMENT

A Provisional Bibliography 2015–2017

The user of this supplemental Bibliography of the most recent articles on Philo is reminded that it will doubtless contain inaccuracies and red herrings because it is not in all cases based on autopsy. It is merely meant as a service to the reader. Scholars who are disappointed by omissions or are keen to have their own work on Philo listed are strongly encouraged to contact the Bibliography's compilers (addresses in the section 'Notes on Contributors').

2015

P. Adamson, 'To the Lighthouse: Philo of Alexandria,' in Idem, *Philosophy in the Hellenistic and Roman Worlds. A History of Philosophy without any Gaps Volume* 2 (Oxford 2015) 160–166.

M. Alesso, 'La complessità della teoria filoniana delle potenze nel *De fuga et inventione*,' in F. Calabi, O. Munnich, G. Reydams-Schils and E. Vimercati (edd.), *Pouvoir et puissances chez Philon d'Alexandrie*, Monothéismes et philosophie (Turnhout 2015) 191–202.

M. Alexandre Jr, 'Rhetorical Texture and Pattern in Philo's *De Decalogo*,' *The Studia Philonica Annual* 27 (2015) 155–180.

M. Alexandre Jr., 'Twofold Human Logos in Philo of Alexandria: The Power of Expressing Thought in Language,' in F. Calabi, O. Munnich, G. Reydams-Schils and E. Vimercati (edd.), *Pouvoir et puissances chez Philon d'Alexandrie*, Monothéismes et philosophie (Turnhout 2015) 37–59.

N. J. Andrade, 'The Jewish Tetragrammaton: Secrecy, Community, and Prestige among Greek-Writing Jews of the Early Roman Empire,' *Journal for the Study of Judaism* 46 (2015) 198–223.

J. M. G. Barclay, *Paul and the Gift* (Grand Rapids, MI 2015), esp. 212–238.

S. Bardet, 'La figure de Noé chez Philon d'Alexandrie et Flavius Josèphe,' *Revue d'Histoire de Religions* 232, no. 4 (2015) 545–565.

E. Birnbaum, 'The Bible's First War: Philo's Interpretation of the Struggle for Power in Genesis 14,' in F. Calabi, O. Munnich, G. Reydams-Schils and E. Vimercati (edd.), *Pouvoir et puissances chez Philon d'Alexandrie*, Monothéismes et philosophie (Turnhout 2015) 111–127.

R. Bloch, 'Leaving Home: Philo of Alexandria on the Exodus,' in T. E. Levy, T. Schneider and W. H. C. Propp (edd.), *Israel's Exodus in Transdisciplinary Perspective—Text, Archaeology, Culture, and Geoscience*,

Quantitative Methods in the Humanities and Social Sciences (Cham 2015) 357–364.

F. Calabi, O. Munnich, G. Reydams-Schils, and E. Vimercati, *Pouvoir et puissances chez Philon d'Alexandrie*, Monothéismes et philosophie (Turnhout 2015).

F. Calabi, 'Il potere regale di Dio e le sue crepe in Filone di Alessandria,' in F. Calabi, O. Munnich, G. Reydams-Schils and E. Vimercati (edd.), *Pouvoir et puissances chez Philon d'Alexandrie*, Monothéismes et philosophie (Turnhout 2015) 97–110.

F. Calabi, 'Intelletto e sensazione tra filosofia ed esegesi in Filone di Alexandria,' in E. Canone (ed.), *Anima–Corpos alla luce dell'etica: Antichi e moderni*, Lessico Intellettuale Europeo (Florence 2015) 83–96.

M. B. Cover, *Lifting the Veil: 2 Corinthians 3:7–18 in Light of Jewish Homiletic and Commentary Traditions*, Beihefte zur Zeitschrift für die neutestamentliche Wissenschaft 210 (Berlin 2015).

M. R. D'Angelo, 'Roman "Family Values" and the Apologetic Concerns of Philo and Paul: Reading the Sixth Commandment,' *New Testament Studies* 61 (2015) 194–215.

P. B. Decock, 'Philo of Alexandria: A Model for Early Christian 'Spiritual Readings' of the Scriptures,' *HTS Teologiese Studies/Theological Studies* (South Africa, electronic publication) 71.1 (2015) 1–8.

C. Delgado, 'Mimesis y arquetipo. Filón 'rescata' al poeta Platónico *Circe de clásicos y modernos* 19 (2015) 43–57.

P. Druille, 'Δικαιοσύνη en Filón de Alejandría: la 'justicia' en contexto judeo-helenístico,' *Circe de clásicos y modernos* 19 (2015) 41–56.

N. Ellis, *The Hermeneutics of Divine Testing*, Wissenschaftliche Untersuchungen zum Neuen Testament 2.396 (Tübingen 2015).

T. J. Farmer, 'Christ as Cosmic Priest: A Sociorhetorical Examination of the Crucifixion Scenes in the Gospel of John and Acts of John,' in V. K. Robbins and J. M. Potter (edd.), *Jesus and Mary Reimagined in Early Christian Literature*, Writings from the Greco-Roman World Supplement Series 6 (Atlanta 2015) 223–250.

M. Francis, *Borderline Bad: Philo of Alexandria on the Distinction between Voluntary and Involuntary Sin* (diss. University of Notre Dame 2015).

M. Francis, 'Wasted Seed and Sins of Intent: Sexual Ethics in *De Specialibus Legibus* 3.34–36 in the Case of Infertile Marriage,' *The Studia Philonica Annual* 27 (2015) 27–52.

C. J. P. Friesen, 'Hannah's 'Hard Day' and Hesiod's 'Two Roads': Poetic Wisdom in Philo's *De ebrietate*,' *Journal for the Study of Judaism* 45 (2015) 44–64.

C. J. P. FRIESEN, *Reading Dionysus: Euripides' Bacchae and the Cultural Contestations of Greeks, Jews, Romans, and Christians*, Studies and Texts in Antiquity and Judaism 95 (Tübingen 2015), esp. chapters 6 and 13.

J. GARROWAY, 'Philo on Moses,' *CCAR Journal: The Reform Jewish Quarterly* 62 (2015) 70–73.

K. GIBBONS, 'Moses, Stateman and Philosopher: The Philosophical Background of the Ideal of Assimilating to God and the Methodology of Clement of Alexandria's *Stromateis* 1,' *Vigiliae Christianae* 69 (2015) 157–185.

J. A. GLANCY, 'The Sexual Use of Slaves: A Response to Kyle Harper on Jewish and Christian *Porneia*,' *Journal of Biblical Literature* 134 (2015) 215–229, esp. 221–224.

M. L. GROSSMAN, 'Religious Experience and the Discipline of Imagination: Tanya Luhrmann meets Philo and the Dead Sea Scrolls,' *Dead Sea Discoveries* 22 (2015) 308–324.

A. DEN HEIJER, 'Cosmic Mothers in Philo of Alexandria and in Neopythagoreanism,' *The Studia Philonica Annual* 27 (2015) 53–70.

C. HEILIG, *Hidden Criticism? The Methodology and Plausibility of the Search for a Counter-Imperial Subtext in Paul*, Wissenschaftliche Untersuchungen zum Neuen Testament. 2.392 (Tübingen 2015).

O. KAISER, *Philo von Alexandrien: Denkender Glaube—eine Einführung*, Forschungen zur Religion und Literatur des Alten und Neuen Testaments 259 (Göttingen 2015).

O. KAISER, 'Metapher und Allegorie bei Philon von Alexandrien,' in M. WITTE and S. BEHNKE (edd.), *Deuterocanonical and Cognate Literature Yearbook 2014/2015: The Metaphorical Use of Language in Deuterocanonical and Cognate Literature* (Berlin 2014–2015) 299–330.

O. KAISER, 'Gesundheit und Krankheit bei Philo von Alexandrien,' *Medizin, Gesellschaft und Geschichte* 33 (2015) 9–34.

G. A. KEDDIE, 'Paul's Freedom and Moses' Veil: Moral Freedom and the Mosaic Law in 2 Corinthians 3.1–4.6 in Light of Philo,' *Journal for the Study of the New Testament* 37 (2015) 267–289.

N. KIEL, *Ps-Athenagoras De Resurrectione: Datierung und Kontextualisierung der dem Apologeten Athenagoras zugeschriebenen Auferstehungsschrift*, Supplements to Vigiliae Christianae 133 (Leiden 2015), esp. 430–440.

V. LAURAND, 'Puissance de la parole: Louer Dieu d'«une bouche que rien ne freine» (*Her.* 110),' in F. CALABI, O. MUNNICH, G. REYDAMS-SCHILS and E. VIMERCATI (edd.), *Pouvoir et puissances chez Philon d'Alexandrie*, Monothéismes et philosophie (Turnhout 2015) 61–77.

J. LEONHARDT-BALZER, 'Priests and Priesthood in Philo: Could He Have Done without Them?,' in D. R. SCHWARTZ and Z. WEISS (edd.), *Was 70 CE a Watershed in Jewish History? On Jews and Judaism before and after the*

Destruction of the Second Temple, Ancient Judaism and Early Christianity 78 (Leiden 2015) 127–153.

C. Lévy, 'Philon d'Alexandrie est-il inutisable pour connaître Énésidème,' *Philosophie antique* 15 (2015) 5–26.

C. Lévy, 'La dunamis philonienne et l'idée de puissance dans la pensée romaine de son époque,' in F. Calabi, O. Munnich, G. Reydams-Schils and E. Vimercati (edd.), *Pouvoir et puissances chez Philon d'Alexandrie,* Monothéismes et philosophie (Turnhout 2015) 159–174.

D. Lincicum, 'Philo of Alexandria and Romans 9:30–10:21,' in B. C. Blackwell, J. K. Goodrich and J. Maston (edd.), *Reading Romans in Context: Paul and Second Temple Judaism* (Grand Rapids, MI 2015) 122–128.

A. M. Mazzanti, 'La centralità del *logos* come componente antropologica in Filone di Alessandria: Natura e funzioni fra protologia e genesi della storia umana,' in F. Calabi, O. Munnich, G. Reydams-Schils and E. Vimercati (edd.), *Pouvoir et puissances chez Philon d'Alexandrie,* Monothéismes et philosophie (Turnhout 2015) 79–96.

O. McFarland, 'Philo of Alexandria and Romans 9:1–29: Grace, Mercy, and Reason,' in B. C. Blackwell, J. K. Goodrich and J. Maston (edd.), *Reading Romans in Context: Paul and Second Temple Judaism* (Grand Rapids, MI 2015) 115–121.

O. McFarland, 'Philo's Prepositional Metaphysics within Early Christian Debates about the Relation of Divine Nature and Agency,' *The Studia Philonica Annual* 27 (2015) 71–85.

S. Marculescu Badilita, 'Entre exégèse et réécriture biblique. Réflexions sur la figure de Noé chez Philon et Flavius Josèphe,' in S. Marculescu Badilita and L. Mellerin (edd.), *Le miel des Écritures. Cahiers de Biblindex I,* Cahiers de Biblia Patristica 15 (Turnhout 2015) 55–69.

K. Metzler, *Prokop von Gaza Eclogarum in libros historicos Veteris Testamenti epitome. Teil 1: Der Genesiskommentar,* Die griechischen christlichen Schriftsteller der ersten Jahrhunderte NF 22 (Berlin 2015).

J. Moreau, 'Outil exégétique ou enseignement métaphysique? Les puissances de Dieu dans les *Quaestiones in Genesim* (4.1–19),' in F. Calabi, O. Munnich, G. Reydams-Schils and E. Vimercati (edd.), *Pouvoir et puissances chez Philon d'Alexandrie,* Monothéismes et philosophie (Turnhout 2015) 203–217.

J. Moreau, 'Le travail de la citation et la méthode allégorique chez Philon d'Alexandrie,' in S. Marculescu Badilita and L. Mellerin (edd.), *Le miel des Écritures. Cahiers de Biblindex I,* Cahiers de Biblia Patristica 15 (Turnhout 2015) 29–53.

S. MORLET, 'Genèse 2,17: l'exégèse patristique,' in M. ARNOLD, G. DAHAN and A. NOBLESSE-ROCHER (edd.), *Genèse 2, 17: L'arbre de la connaissance du bien et du mal,* Études d'histoire de l'exégèse 9 (Paris 2015) 37–68.

O. MUNNICH, 'Les puissances divines dans les *Lois spéciales* de Philon,' in F. CALABI, O. MUNNICH, G. REYDAMS-SCHILS and E. VIMERCATI (edd.), *Pouvoir et puissances chez Philon d'Alexandrie,* Monothéismes et philosophie (Turnhout 2015) 219–243.

M. R. NIEHOFF (ed.), *Philo of Alexandria Writings. Vol. IV Part Two: Allegorical Exegesis and Philosophical Treatises* (Jerusalem 2015).

M. R. NIEHOFF, 'Accommodating the Political: Philo's King Metaphor,' *Deuterocanonical and Cognate Literature Yearbook* (2014–2015) 331–344.

M. R. NIEHOFF, ''The Power of Ares' in Philo's *Legatio*,' in F. CALABI, O. MUNNICH, G. REYDAMS-SCHILS and E. VIMERCATI (edd.), *Pouvoir et puissances chez Philon d'Alexandrie,* Monothéismes et philosophie (Turnhout 2015) 129–139.

M. R. NIEHOFF, 'Josephus and Philo in Rome,' in H. H. CHAPMAN and Z. RODGERS (edd.), *A Companion to Josephus* (New York 2015) 135–146.

M. R. NIEHOFF, 'Eusebius as a Reader of Philo,' *Adamantius* 21 (2015) 185–194.

M. R. NIEHOFF, 'Wie wird man ein Mediterraner Denker? Der Fall Philon von Alexandria,' in R. FABER and A. LICHTENBERGER (edd.), *Ein pluriverses Universum. Zivilisationen und Religionen im antiken Mittelmeerraum,* Mittelmeerstudien 7 (Paderborn 2015) 355–368.

C. S. O'BRIEN, *The Demiurge in Ancient Thought: Secondary Gods and Divine Mediators* (Cambridge 2015).

J. D. PARKER, *Moses and the Seventy Elders: Mosaic Authority in Numbers 11 and the Legend of the Septuagint* (diss. Durham University 2015).

S. PEARCE, 'Intermarriage and the Ancestors of the Jews: Philonic Perspectives,' *The Studia Philonica Annual* 27 (2015) 1–26.

S. PEARCE, 'Philo of Alexandria as Interpreter of the Ten Commandments: Introduction,' *The Studia Philonica Annual* 27 (2015) 129–131.

L. PEREZ, 'Οὐ μοιχεύσεις, «no cometerás adulterio»: El mandamiento bíblico explicado por Filón de Alejandría, *Emerita: Revista de Lingüística y Filología Clásica* 83 (2015) 87–109.

L. PERRONE, 'Doctrinal Tradition and Cultural Heritage in the Newly Discovered Homilies of Origen on the Psalms (Codex Monacensis Graecus 314),' *Phasis: Greek and Roman Studies (Ivane Javakhishvili Tbilisi State University)* 18 (2015) 191–212.

B. POLLOCK, 'Philosophy's Inquisitor: Franz Rosenzweig's Philo between Judaism, Paganism, and Christianity,' *The Studia Philonica Annual* 27 (2015) 111–127.

R. RADICE, 'Filosofia e allegoria in Filone di Alessandria. Questioni di metodo,' in F. CALABI, O. MUNNICH, G. REYDAMS-SCHILS and E. VIMERCATI (edd.), *Pouvoir et puissances chez Philon d'Alexandrie,* Monothéismes et philosophie (Turnhout 2015) 293–304.

G. REYDAMS-SCHILS, ''Unsociable sociability': Philo on the Active and the Contemplative Life,' in F. CALABI, O. MUNNICH, G. REYDAMS-SCHILS and E. VIMERCATI (edd.), *Pouvoir et puissances chez Philon d'Alexandrie,* Monothéismes et philosophie (Turnhout 2015) 305–318.

P. RICHARDSON, 'What Are the Spiritual Sacrifices of 1 Peter 2:5? Some Light from Philo of Alexandria,' *Evangelical Quarterly* 87 (2015) 3–17.

C. M. RIOS, 'Philo of Alexandria: An Introduction to the Jewish Exegete and His Intercultural Condition,' *Scriptural Exegesis* 114 (2015) 1–13.

J. J. RIPLEY, 'Killing as Piety?: Exploring Ideological Contexts Shaping the Gospel of John,' *Journal of Biblical Literature* 134 (2015) 605–635, esp. 614–617.

B. RITTER, *Judeans in the Greek Cities of the Roman Empire: Rights, Citizenship and Civil Discord,* Supplements to the Journal for the Study of Judaism 170 (Leiden 2015).

T. A. ROGERS, *The Representation of God in First Corinthians 8–10: Understanding Paul in the Context of Wisdom, Philo, and Josephus* (diss. Loyola University, Chicago 2015).

D. T. ROTH, 'Shared Interpretive Traditions of Joseph's 'σωφροσύνη' and 'Silence' in *De Iosepho* and the Testament of Joseph,' *Journal of the Jesus Movement in its Jewish Setting* 1 (2015) 54–68.

J. R. ROYSE, 'Composite Citations in Philo of Alexandria,' in S. A. ADAMS and S. M. EHORN (edd.), *Composite Citations in Antiquity: Jewish, Graeco-Roman, and Early Christian Uses,* Library of New Testament Studies 525 (London 2015) 74–91.

J. R. ROYSE, 'The Text of Philo's *De Decalogo* in Vaticanus gr. 316,' *The Studia Philonica Annual* 27 (2015) 133–142.

D. T. RUNIA, 'Cosmos, Logos, and Nomos: The Alexandrian Jewish and Christian Appropriation of the Genesis Creation Account,' in P. DERRON (ed.), *Cosmologies et cosmogonies dans la littérature antique,* Entretiens sur l'antiquité classique 61 (Vandœuvres-Geneva 2015) 179–209.

D. T. RUNIA, 'Philon von Alexandria,' in G. SCHÖLLGEN *et al.* (edd.), *Reallexikon für Antike und Christentum,* 27 (Stuttgart 2015) 605–627.

D. T. RUNIA, 'Philo of Alexandria on the Human Consequences of Divine Power,' in F. CALABI, O. MUNNICH, G. REYDAMS-SCHILS and E. VIMERCATI (edd.), *Pouvoir et Puissances chez Philon d'Alexandrie,* Monothéismes et philosophie 22 (Turnhout 2015) 245–256.

D. T. RUNIA and G. E. STERLING (edd.), *The Studia Philonica Annual*, 27 (Atlanta 2015).

D. T. RUNIA, K. BERTHELOT, E. BIRNBAUM, A. C. GELJON, H. M. KEIZER, J. LEONHARDT BALZER, J. P. MARTÍN, M. R. NIEHOFF, S. J. K. PEARCE, and T. SELAND, 'Philo of Alexandria: An Annotated Bibliography 2012,' *The Studia Philonica Annual* 27 (2015) 181–230.

J. RYU, *Knowledge of God in Philo of Alexandria*, Wissenschaftliche Untersuchungen zum Neuen Testament 2.405 (Tübingen 2015).

M. L. SAMUEL, *Torah from Alexandria: Philo as a Biblical Commentator. Volume 3: Leviticus* (New York 2015).

L. SAUDELLI, 'Filone e il concetto presocratico di 'potenze,'' in F. CALABI, O. MUNNICH, G. REYDAMS-SCHILS and E. Vimercati (edd.), *Pouvoir et puissances chez Philon d'Alexandrie*, Monothéismes et philosophie (Turnhout 2015) 319–334.

G. SCHIMANOWSKI, 'Religiöse Identität im Fokus: Selbstbeschreibungen und polemische Kontrastierung in Philos apologetischen Traktaten,' in N. FÖRSTER and J. C. DE VOS (edd.), *Juden und Christen unter römischer Herrschaft; Selbstwahrnehmung und Fremdwahrnehmung in den ersten beiden Jahrhunderten*, Schriften des Institutum Judaicum Delitzschianum 10 (Göttingen 2015) 141–163.

G. SCHÖLLGEN (ed.), *Reallexikon für Antike und Christentum* (Stuttgart 2015), Band 26 Nymphen–Pegasus.

R. J. Daly, Art. Opfer, 143–206, esp. 169–170 (sacrifice); C. Neuber, Art. Orakel, 206–350, esp. 3123–313 (oracle); A. Fürst, Art. Origenes, 460–567, esp. 490–491 (Origen); J.-C. Fredouille, Art. Paradoxon, 968–986, esp. 978–979 (paradox); B. Beer, Art. Parrhesia, 1014–1033, esp. 1023 (*parrhesia*); H. Buchinger, Art. Pascha, 1034–1075, esp. 1040–1042 (Easter). (DTR)

T. SELAND, 'Religious Offenses,' in B. A. STRAWN (ed.), *The Oxford Encyclopedia of Bible and Law Vol. 2: Mag-Wom* (Oxford 2015) 213–219.

G. SFAMENI GASPARRO, 'Filone et il potere di Roma: l'identità religiosa ebraica nell'*In Flaccum* e nella *Legatio ad Caium*,' in F. CALABI, O. MUNNICH, G. REYDAMS-SCHILS and E. VIMERCATI (edd.), *Pouvoir et puissances chez Philon d'Alexandrie*, Monothéismes et philosophie (Turnhout 2015) 141–158.

R. SOMOS, *Logic and Argumentation in Origen*, Adamantiana 7 (Münster 2015).

A. STANDHARTINGER, 'Philo im ethnografischen Diskurs: Beobachtungen zum literarischen Kontext von De Vita Contemplativa,' *Journal for the Study of Judaism* 46 (2015) 314–344.

E. STAROBINSKI-SAFRAN, 'La doctrine philonienne des puissances et la doctrine kabbalistique des sefirot. Essai de comparaison,' in F. CALABI, O. MUNNICH, G. REYDAMS-SCHILS and E. VIMERCATI (edd.), *Pouvoir et puissances chez Philon d'Alexandrie,* Monothéismes et philosophie (Turnhout 2015) 257–276.

G. E. STERLING, 'The Theft of Philosophy: Philo of Alexandria and Numenius of Apamea,' *The Studia Philonica Annual* 27 (2015) 53–70.

G. E. STERLING, 'When Virtue Is Impossible,' in F. CALABI, O. MUNNICH, G. REYDAMS-SCHILS and E. VIMERCATI (edd.), *Pouvoir et puissances chez Philon d'Alexandrie,* Monothéismes et philosophie (Turnhout 2015) 277–291.

G. J. STEYN, ''Dink voordat jy praat': Die krag van die tong by Philo en Jakobus [Afrikaans: 'Think before you speak': the power of the tongue in Philo and James],' *HTS Teologiese Studies/Theological Studies (South Africa, electronic publication)* 71(1) (2015) 1–7.

M. TARDIEU, 'Le paradis chaldaïque (fr. 107 et 165),' in A. LECERF, L. SAUDELLI and H. SENG (edd.), *Oracles chaldaïques Fragments et philosophie,* Bibliotheca Chaldaica 4 (Heidelberg 2014) 15–29.

A. TERIAN, 'The Armenian Textual Tradition of Philo's *De Decalogo,' The Studia Philonica Annual* 27 (2015) 143–153.

C. TERMINI, ''Il mio scettro è il libro *dell'Epinomide*' (*Spec.* 4.164): Monarchia divina d democrazia nello *speculum principis* di Filone di Alessandria,' in F. CALABI, O. MUNNICH, G. REYDAMS-SCHILS and E. VIMERCATI (edd.), *Pouvoir et puissances chez Philon d'Alexandrie,* Monothéismes et philosophie (Turnhout 2015) 175–190.

K. B. WELLS, *Grace and Agency in Paul and Second Temple Judaism: Interpreting the Transformation of the Heart,* Novum Testamentum Supplements 157 (Leiden 2015).

W. T. WILSON, 'Matthew, Philo, and Mercy for Animals (Matt 12,9–14),' *Biblica* 96 (2015) 201–222.

R. J. WILKINSON, *Tetragrammaton: Western Christians and the Hebrew Name of God. From the Beginnings to the Seventeenth Century,* Studies in the History of Christian Traditions 179 (Leiden 2015).

V. WITTKOWSKY, *Warum zitieren frühchristliche Autoren pagane Texte? Zur Entstehung und Ausformung einer literarischen Tradition,* Beihefte zur Zeitschrift für die neutestamentliche Wissenschaft 218 (Berlin 2015).

J. D. WORTHINGTON, 'Philo of Alexandria and Romans 5:12–21: Adam, Death, and Grace,' in B. C. BLACKWELL, J. K. GOODRICH and J. MASTON (edd.), *Reading Romans in Context: Paul and Second Temple Judaism* (Grand Rapids, MI 2015) 80–86.

L. WUIDAR, *L'uomo musicale nell'antico cristianesimo: Storia di una metafora tra Oriente e Occidente* (Brussels 2015), esp. 5–24.

B. WYSS, 'Philons Luxuskritik vor dem Hintergrund des aufblühenden Ostafrika- und Indienhandels,' in M. WASMUTH (ed.), *Handel als Medium von Kulturkontakt: Akten des Interdisziplinären altertumswissenschaftlichen Kolloquiums (Basel, 30.–31. Oktober 2009),* Orbis biblicus et orientalis 277 (Fribourg 2015) 119–142.

S. Yli-Karjanmaa, *Reincarnation in Philo of Alexandria,* Studia Philonica Monographs 7 (Atlanta 2015).

2016

Aa.vv., 'Philo Judaeus,' in *Columbia Electronic Encyclopedia,* 6th Edition, 2016.

T. Alekniene, *A l'approche du divin: dialogues de Platon et tradition platonicienne,* Vestigia 42 (Fribourg 2016).

T. Alekniene, 'Quelle est cette fuite? Le *Théétète* de Platon, Philon d'Alexandrie et l'invention de l'exégèse platonisante,' in T. Alekniene (ed.), *A l'approche du divin: dialogues de Platon et tradition platonicienne,* Vestigia 42 (Fribourg 2016) 271–320.

T. Alekniene, 'Le propos d'Héraclite: «Les cadavres sont plus vils que le fumier» (fr. 96 DK) chez les auteurs grecs anciens,' in T. Alekniene (ed.), *A l'approche du divin: dialogues de Platon et tradition platonicienne,* Vestigia 42 (Fribourg 2016) 271–320, esp. 329–333.

M. Alesso, 'Qué significa la divina providencia en la teología de Filón de Alejandría,' *Circe de clásicos y modernos* 20, no. 2 (2016) 113–129.

R. von Bendemann (ed.), *Philo von Alexandria—Über die Freiheit des Rechtschaffenen,* Kleine Bibliothek der antiken jüdischen und christlichen Literatur (Göttingen 2016).

E. Birnbaum, 'Some Particulars about Universalism,' in K. B. Stratton and A. Lieber (edd.), *Crossing Boundaries in Early Judaism and Christianity. Ambiguities, Complexities, and Half-Forgotten Adversaries: Essays in Honor of Alan F. Segal,* Journal for the Studies of Judaism Series 177 (Leiden 2016) 117–137.

E. Birnbaum, 'What in the Name of God led Philo to Interpret Abraham, Isaac, and Jacob as Learning, Nature, and Practice?,' in G. E. Sterling (ed.), *The Studia Philonica Annual Vol. 28 [= Studies in Philo in Honor of David Runia]* (Atlanta 2016) 273–296.

R. Bloch, 'Philo and Jeremiah in Egypt,' in H. Najman and K. Schmid (edd.), *Jeremiah's Scriptures,* Supplements to the Journal for the Study of Judaism 173 (Leiden 2016).

P. Borgen, 'Alternative Aims and Choices in Education: Analysis of Selected Texts,' in G. E. Sterling (ed.), *The Studia Philonica Annual Vol. 28 [= Studies in Philo in Honor of David Runia]* (Atlanta 2016) 257–271.

A.-I. Bouton-Touboulic and C. Lévy (edd.), *Scepticsme et religion: Constantes et évolutions, de la philosophie hellénistique à la philosophie médiévale*, Monothéismes et philosophie (Turnhout 2016).

J. M. Broderick, 'Custodian of Wisdom: The Marciana Reading Room and the Transcendent Knowledge of God,' *Studi Veneziani* 73 (2016) 15–94.

F. Calabi, '"It would not be Good that the Man should be Alone": Philo's Interpretation of Genesis 2:18 in *Legum Allegoriae*,' in G. E. Sterling (ed.), *The Studia Philonica Annual Vol. 28 [= Studies in Philo in Honor of David Runia]* (Atlanta 2016) 239–256.

V. Černušková, J. L. Kovacs and J. Plátová (edd.), *Clement's Biblical Exegesis: Proceedings of the Second Colloquium on Clement of Alexandria (Olomouc, May 29–31, 2014)*, Supplements to Vigiliae Christianae 139 (Leiden 2016).

M. B. Cover, 'Paulus als Yischmaelit? The Personification of Scripture as Interpretive Authority in Paul and the School of Rabbi Ishmael,' *Journal of Biblical Literature* 135 (2016) 617–637.

L. De Luca, 'Il serpente di bronzo secondo Filone Alesandrino in *Leg*. 2.79–81,' *Adamantius* 21 (2016) 173–184.

C. Delgado, 'Ecos del *Ión* platónico en los escritos de Filón de Alejandría,' *Emerita: Revista de Linguistica y Filologia Clasica* 84 (2016) 73–97.

C. Delgado, 'Una reminiscencia platónica en Filón de Alejandría (*R*. 2.377–9 en *Spec*. 1.28–30,' *Exemplaria Classica* 20 (2016) 117–131.

J. Dillon, 'Philo and the *Telos*: Some Reflections,' in G. E. Sterling (ed.), *The Studia Philonica Annual Vol. 28 [= Studies in Philo in Honor of David Runia]* (Atlanta 2016) 111–119.

P. Druille, 'Filón y las inscripciones griegas de los siglos II–I a.C.: la existencia de la 'gerousía' en Alejandría,' *Circe de clásicos y modernos* 20 (2016) 131–145.

C. J. P. Friesen, 'Dying Like a Woman: Euripides' Polyxena as Exemplum between Philo and Clement of Alexandria,' *Greek, Roman, and Byzantine Studies* 56 (2016) 623–645.

C. J. P. Friesen, 'Getting Samuel Sober: The 'Plus' of LXX 1 Sam 1:11 and Its Religious Afterlife in Philo and the Gospel of Luke,' *Journal of Theological Studies* 67 (2016) 453–475.

A. C. Geljon, 'Mag een wijze dronken worden? Philo van Alexandrië over dronkenschap' [Dutch: 'May a wise person become drunk? Philo of Alexandria on drunkenness],' *Hermeneus* 88 (2016) 111–115.

A. C. Geljon, 'Abraham in Egypt: Philo's Interpretation of Gen 12:10–12,' in G. E. Sterling (ed.), *The Studia Philonica Annual Vol. 28 [= Studies in Philo in Honor of David Runia]* (Atlanta 2016) 297–319.

A. van den Hoek and J. J. Hermann Jr., 'Chasing the Emperor: Philo in the *Horti* of Rome,' in G. E. Sterling (ed.), *The Studia Philonica Annual Vol. 28 [= Studies in Philo in Honor of David Runia]* (Atlanta 2016) 171–204.

S. Honigman, 'The Ptolemaic and Roman Definitions of Social Categories and the Evolution of Judean Communal Identity in Egypt,' in Y. Furstenberg (ed.), *Jewish and Christian Communal Identities in the Roman World*, Ancient Judaism and Early Christianity 92 (Leiden 2016) 25–74, esp. 64–70.

T. Iacono, *Filone di Alessandria, De sobrietate, introduzione, traduzione e commento* (M.A. thesis University of Padua 2016).

A. Kamesar, 'ΔΗΛΩΣΙΣ and ΑΛΗΘΕΙΑ: The Septuagint, Philo, and Some Late Rhetorical Texts,' in P. F. Beatrice and B. Pouderon (edd.), *Pascha Nostrum Christus: Essays in Honour of Raniero Cantalamessa* (Paris 2016) 17–26.

A. Kamesar, 'Philo and Ps.Longinus: a Case of Sublimity in Genesis 4,' in G. E. Sterling (ed.), *The Studia Philonica Annual Vol. 28 [= Studies in Philo in Honor of David Runia]* (Atlanta 2016) 229–238.

A. Kirsch, *The People and the Books: 18 Classics of Jewish Literature* (New York 2016).

S. Kottek and H. Paavilainen, 'Embryology in the Works of Philo,' *Korot* 23 (2015–2016) 99–107.

J. Leonhardt-Balzer, 'Philo and the Garden of Eden: An Exegete, his Text and his Tools,' in S. Kreuzer, M. Meiser and M. Sigismund (edd.), *Die Septuaginta—Orte und Intentionen. 5. Internationale Fachtagung veranstaltet von Septuaginta Deutch (LXX.D), Wuppertal 24.–27. Juli 2014*, Wissenschaftliche Untersuchungen zum Neuen Testament 361 (Tübingen 2016) 244–257.

C. Lévy, 'De l'epochè sdeptique à l'epochè transcendentale: Philon d'Alexandrie fondateur du fidéisme,' in A.-I. Bouton-Touboulic and C. Lévy (edd.), *Scepticsme et religion: Constantes et évolutions, de la philosophie hellénistique à la philosophie médiévale*, Monothéismes et philosophie (Turnhout 2016) 57–73.

C. Lévy, 'Philon d'Alexandrie face à l'altérité. Le problème des sagesses barbares,' in S. H. Aufrère (ed.), *Alexandrie la divine. Sagesses barbares: Échanges et réappropriation dans l'espace culturel gréco-romain* (Geneva 2016) 313–338.

C. Lévy, 'Continuity and Dissimilarity in Middle Platonism: Philo and Plutarch about the Epicurean *ataraxia*,' in G. E. Sterling (ed.), *The Studia Philonica Annual Vol. 28 [= Studies in Philo in Honor of David Runia]* (Atlanta 2016) 121–136.

C. MARKSCHIES, *Gottes Körper: Jüdische, christliche und pagane Gottesvorstellungen in der Antike* (München 2016), esp. 63–66.

J. P. MARTÍN (ed.), *Filón de Alejandría Obras Completas Volumen IV* (Madrid 2016).

O. W. MCFARLAND, *God and Grace in Philo and Paul*, Novum Testamentum Supplements 164 (Leiden 2016).

K. METZLER, *Prokop von Gaza Der Genesiskommentar: Aus den „Eclogarum in libros historicos Veteris Testamenti epitome" übersetzt und mit Anmerkungen versehen*, Die griechischen christlichen Schriftsteller der ersten Jahrhunderte N.F. 23 (Berlin 2016).

M. R. NIEHOFF, 'Justin's *Timaeus* in Light of Philo's,' in G. E. STERLING (ed.), *The Studia Philonica Annual Vol. 28 [= Studies in Philo in Honor of David Runia]* (Atlanta 2016) 375–392.

C. NOUGUÉ and L. MONTEIRO DUTRÁ, *Fílon de Alexandria: Da Criação do Mundo e outros escritos* (São Paulo 2016).

A. PAUL, *Croire aujourd'hui dans la résurrection* (Paris 2016), esp. 60–64.

S. PEARCE, 'Notes on Philo's Use of the Terms ἔθνος and λαός,' in G. E. STERLING (ed.), *The Studia Philonica Annual Vol. 28 [= Studies in Philo in Honor of David Runia]* (Atlanta 2016) 205–226.

I. L. E. RAMELLI 'The Mysteries of Scripture: Allegorical Exegesis and the Heritage of Stoicism, Philo and Pantaenus,' in V. ČERNUŠKOVÁ, J. L. KOVACS and J. PLÁTOVÁ (edd.), *Clement's Biblical Exegesis: Proceedings of the Second Colloquium on Clement of Alexandria (Olomouc, May 29–31, 2014)*, Supplements to Vigiliae Christianae 139 (Leiden 2016) 80–110.

I. L. E. RAMELLI 'Hebrews and Philo on ΥΠΟΣΤΑΣΙΣ: Interlocking Trajectories?,' in P. F. BEATRICE and B. POUDERON (edd.), *Pascha Nostrum Christus: Essays in Honour of Raniero Cantalamessa* (Paris 2016) 27–49.

I. L. E. RAMELLI *Social Justice and the Legitimacy of Slavery: The Role of Philosophical Asceticism from Ancient Judaism to Late Antiquity*, Oxford Early Christian Studies (Oxford 2016).

M. RIZZI, 'The Bible in Alexandria: Clement between Philo and Origen,' in V. ČERNUŠKOVÁ, J. L. KOVACS and J. PLÁTOVÁ (edd.), *Clement's Biblical Exegesis: Proceedings of the Second Colloquium on Clement of Alexandria (Olomouc, May 29–31, 2014)*, Supplements to Vigiliae Christianae 139 (Leiden 2016) 111–126.

J. R. ROYSE, 'The Biblical Quotations in the Coptos Papyrus of Philo,' in G. E. STERLING (ed.), *The Studia Philonica Annual Vol. 28 [= Studies in Philo in Honor of David Runia]* (Atlanta 2016) 49–76.

D. T. RUNIA, 'Philo in Byzantium: An Exploration,' *Vigiliae Christianae* 70 (2016) 259–281.

D. T. RUNIA, 'Art. Philo Alexandrinus,' in R. DODARO, C. MAYER and C. MÜLLER (edd.), *Augustinus-Lexicon* (Basel 2016) 716–719.

D. T. RUNIA, 'La receptíon del *Fedón* de Platón en Filón de Alejandría (translated by M. ALESSO),' *Circe de clásicos y modernos* 20, no. 2 (2016) 91–112.

D. T. RUNIA, M. ALESSO, K. BERTHELOT, E. BIRNBAUM, A. C. GELJON, H. M. KEIZER, J. LEONHARDT BALZER, M. R. NIEHOFF, S. J. K. PEARCE, and T. SELAND, 'Philo of Alexandria: An Annotated Bibliography 2013,' *The Studia Philonica Annual* 27 (2016) 393–448.

G. SCHÖLLGEN (ed.), *Reallexikon für Antike und Christentum* (Stuttgart 2016), Band 27 Pelagius–Porträt (= Lieferungen 210–217).

A. Felber, Art. Pflanzung, 532–544 (esp. 536–537 (planting); D. T. Runia, Art. Philon von Alexandreia, 605–627; J. Zachhuber, Art. Physis, 744–781, esp. 756–759 (nature); M. Erler, Art. Platonismus, 837–955, esp. 866–868 (Platonism).

T. SELAND, 'The Expository Use of the Balaam Figure in Philo's *De vita Moysis*,' in G. E. STERLING (ed.), *The Studia Philonica Annual Vol. 28 [= Studies in Philo in Honor of David Runia]* (Atlanta 2016) 321–348.

M. SPINELLI, 'O conceito grego da 'egkýklios paideía' e sua difusão no período helenístico,' *Hybris, Revista de Filosofía* 7 (2016) 31–58, esp. 44–46.

G. E. STERLING (ed.), *The Studia Philonica Annual [= Studies in Philo in Honor of David Runia]*, Vol. 28 (Atlanta 2016).

G. E. STERLING, 'A Soaring Mind: The Career of David T. Runia,' in G. E. STERLING (ed.), *The Studia Philonica Annual Vol. 28 [= Studies in Philo in Honor of David Runia]* (Atlanta 2016) 3–13.

G. E. STERLING, 'David T. Runia: A Bibliography of his Publications, 1979–2016,' in G. E. STERLING (ed.), *The Studia Philonica Annual Vol. 28 [= Studies in Philo in Honor of David Runia]* (Atlanta 2016) 15–45.

G. E. STERLING, 'When East and West Meet: Eastern Religions and Western Philosophy in Philo of Alexandria and Plutarch of Chaeronea,' in G. E. STERLING (ed.), *The Studia Philonica Annual Vol. 28 [= Studies in Philo in Honor of David Runia]* (Atlanta 2016) 137–150.

A. TERIAN, 'Philonis *De visione trium angelorum ad Abraham*: A New Translation of the Mistitled *De Deo*,' in G. E. STERLING (ed.), *The Studia Philonica Annual Vol. 28 [= Studies in Philo in Honor of David Runia]* (Atlanta 2016) 77–107.

T. H. TOBIN S.J., 'Reconfiguring Eschatological Imagery: The Examples of Philo of Alexandria and Paul of Tarsus,' in G. E. STERLING (ed.), *The Studia Philonica Annual Vol. 28 [= Studies in Philo in Honor of David Runia]* (Atlanta 2016) 351–374.

N. VALIM DE SENA, 'Violência, monumentalidade e poder: o conflito alexandrino de 38 d.C.,' *Romanitas, Revista de Estudos Grecolatinos* 7 (2016) 69–87.

A. Villeneuve, *Nuptial Symbolism in Second Temple Writings, the New Testament and Rabbinic Literature: Divine Marriage at Key Moments of Salvation History*, Ancient Judaism and Early Christianity 92 (Leiden 2016).

S. Yli-Karjanmaa, "Call Him Earth:' On Philo's Allegorization of Adam in the *Legum allegoriae*,' in A. Laato and L. Valve (edd.), *The Adam and Eve Story in the Hebrew Bible and in Ancient Jewish Writings Including the New Testament*, Studies in the Reception History of the Bible 7 (Turku 2016) 253–293.

2017

T. Alekniene, 'Le parent comique du monastère: À propos du *De vita contemplativa* de Philon d'Alexandria,' in A. Van den Kerchove and L. G. Soares Santoprete (edd.), *Gnose et manichéisme: Entre les oasis d'Égypte et la route de la soie; Hommage à Jean-Daniel Dubois*, Bibliothèque de l'École des hautes études sciences religieuses 176 (Turnhout 2017) 647–668.

P. Church, *Hebrews and the Temple: Attitudes to the Temple in Second Temple Judaism and in Hebrews*, Novum Testamentum Supplements 171 (Leiden 2017).

P. W. van der Horst, *150 Book Reviews (Ancient Judaism, Early Christianity, and Hellenism)* (posted online at Academia.edu 2017).

B. Lang, 'Jesus among the Philosophers: The Cynic Connection Explored and Affirmed, with a Note on Philo's Jewish-Cynic Philosophy,' in A. Klostergaard Petersen and G. H. van Kooten (edd.), *Religio-Philosophical Discourses in the Mediterranean World: From Plato, through Jesus to Late Antiquity*, Ancient Philosophy & Religion 1 (Leiden 2017) 187–218, esp. 212–218.

B. Lang, *Philo von Alexandria: Das Leben des Politikers oder Über Joseph. Eine philosophishe Erzählung*, Kleine Bibliothek der antiken jüdischen und christlichen Literatur (Göttingen 2017).

C. Lévy, 'From Cicero to Philo of Alexandria: Ascending and Descending Axes in the Interpretation of Stoicism and Platonism,' in T. Engberg-Pedersen (ed.), *From Stoicism to Platonism: The Development of Philosophy, 100 BCE to 100 CE*, (Cambridge 2017) 179–197.

K. Martin Hogan, 'Would Philo Have Recognized Qumran Musar as Paideia?,' in M. Goff and E. Wasserman (edd.), *Pedagogy in Ancient Judaism and Early Christianity*. Early Judaism and Its Literature (Atlanta 2017) 81–100.

H. M. van Praag, *Slecht zicht: Een hommage aan de twijfel* [Dutch: Bad sight: homage to doubt] (Eindhoven 2017).

T. L. Putthoff, *Ontological Aspects of Early Jewish Anthropology: The Malleable Self and the Presence of God*, The Brill Reference Library of Judaism 53 (Leiden 2017).

D. T. Runia, 'From Stoicism to Platonism: The Difficult Case of Philo's *De Providentia* I,' in T. Engberg-Pedersen (ed.), *From Stoicism to Platonism: the Development of Philosophy, 100 BCE to 100 CE* (Cambridge 2017) 159–178.

D. T. Runia, 'Synesius of Cyrene's Homily 1 and the Alexandrian Exegetical Tradition,' in E. Minchin and H. Jackson (edd.), *Text and the Material World, Essays in Honour of Graeme Clarke*, Studies in Mediterranean Archaeology 185 (Uppsala 2017) 329–338.

G. Schöllgen *et al.* (edd.), *Reallexikon für Antike und Christentum* (Stuttgart 2017), Lieferungen 220–221.

J. C. Thom, Art. Pythagoras, 496–522, esp. 508 (Pythagoras); C. Ritter, Art. Rachel und Lea, 625–637, esp. 627–628 (Rachel and Lea). (DTR)

G. E. Sterling, 'Philo's School: The Social Setting of Ancient Commentaries,' in B. Wyss, R. Hirsch-Luipold and S.-J. Hirschi (edd.), *Sophisten in Hellenismus und Kaiserzeit: Orte, Methoden und Personen der Bildungsvermittlung*, Studien und Texte zu Antike und Christentum 101 (Tübingen 2017) 123–142.

G. E. Sterling, 'The School of Moses in Alexandria: An Attempt to Reconstruct the School of Philo,' in G. Boccaccini and J. Zurawski (edd.), *Second Temple Jewish "Paideia" in Context*, Beihefte zur Zeitschrift für die neutestamentliche Wissenschaft 228 (Berlin 2017) 141–166.

J. M. Zurawski, ' Mosaic Torah as Encyclical Paideia: Reading Paul's Allegory of Hagar and Sarah in Light of Philo of Alexandria's,' in M. Goff and E. Wasserman (edd.), *Pedagogy in Ancient Judaism and Early Christianity. Early Judaism and Its Literature* (Atlanta 2017) 283–308.

The Studia Philonica Annual 29 (2017): 245–64

BOOK REVIEW SECTION

FRIEDERIKE OERTELT, *Herrscherideal und Herrschaftskritik bei Philo von Alexandria: Eine Untersuchung am Beispiel seiner Josephsdarstellung in* De Josepho *und* De Somniis II. Studies in Philo of Alexandria, vol. 8. Leiden: Brill, 2014. xvii + 362 pages. Hardcover. ISBN 978900427039. Price $202, €152.

This work began as a dissertation at Marburg, under the direction of Angela Standhartinger, and is now a welcome addition to the growing number of recent volumes devoted to studies in Philo that have enriched the field.

Friederike Oertelt addresses a topic that has long puzzled scholars, one that has received many answers but no satisfactory explanation. Why did Philo treat the biblical figure of Joseph with such favorable attention in the *De Josepho* and with such disparagement and disapproval in the *De Somnis* II? Oertelt does not exactly provide a resolution. But she approaches the question at another level. Her concern is not to reconcile the differences between the two texts or to account for the shift in tone and meaning, as others have, by the passage of time, a change of mind, contrasting audiences, or different objectives in each treatise. Instead, she finds Joseph to be almost an incidental figure, the main episodes of his life to be useful means of conveying lessons, both positive and negative, that advance Philo's larger goal of establishing the characteristics of the ideal statesman. In that way the two treatises, though ostensibly very different, actually contribute to the same purpose, the development of Philo's philosophy of model leadership.

Oertelt develops her case systematically and scrupulously. An introductory chapter sets out the issue of Philo's dual portrait of Joseph, the various scholarly interpretations of it, and their limitations. Her aim is to transcend the discussion of Philo on statesmen and tyrants and to gain a fuller appreciation of his own insights into political systems and the range of activity possible under them. This is an ambitious aim, which she fulfills only in limited fashion. Oertelt supplies useful background for the study. She sketches the portrait of Joseph in Genesis and the variations it undergoes in several Second Temple texts, like the *Wisdom of Solomon*, the *Testaments of the Twelve Patriarchs*, *Jubilees*, *4 Maccabees*, Artapanus, and *Joseph and Aseneth*. Although Oertelt seeks to place Philo's treatment of Joseph in a

Hellenistic Jewish tradition, it is not clear that any of these texts actually influenced that treatment. She herself claims that Philo's interest in power structures and different political forms distinguishes him from most Hellenistic Jewish authors. She asks the very pointed question of whether Philo's regular resort to allegory represents assimilation to the prevalent Hellenic culture or an apologetic thrust in defense of Judaism. Unfortunately, apart from a very brief resumé of current scholarship, she does not pursue that important question. Her principal thesis is that Philo participated in a contemporary discourse on authority occurring in the context of the early Roman Empire. That may well be true. But the book neglects to fill in that context in any substantial fashion.

Oertelt does provide a helpful summary of the metaphorical motifs of the ruler as shepherd, physician, and steersman as they appeared in earlier literature. And she rightly observes that Philo departs from his predecessors by putting less emphasis on guidance by the ruler than on his appeals to the laws of the nation, i.e., essentially the laws of Moses. In a parallel discussion, Oertelt recognizes Philo's debt to Hellenistic philosophy, particularly Stoicism, in its identification of natural law and human reason, but notes, quite significantly, that Philo abandons standard Greek political theory centered upon the image of the lawgiver and stresses instead God-given law as equivalent to the universal law of nature which alone should determine the statesman's governance of his flock.

In pursuit of her thesis, Oertelt explores Philo's interpretation of the biblical narrative of struggle between Joseph and his brothers. She sees it as a parable of social life and political activity. Joseph's behavior is judged quite differently in the two treatises, but Philo's purpose, according to Oertelt, has the broader aim of assessing the statesman's appropriate relation to features like jealousy, ambition, and retaliation in both texts.

The story of Joseph and Potiphar's wife further serves this wider purpose. The attempted seduction of the Israelite youth by the Egyptian temptress, as Philo presents it, has, in Oertelt's view, significant political implications. Philo sees Potiphar's wife as emblematic of the irrational desires of the masses that need to be resisted by the temperate and steadfast statesman. That analysis seems quite sound, especially in light of Philo's disdain of mob rule expressed elsewhere. But Oertelt may go too far in seeing this as an echo of Augustan propaganda against the wicked wiles of Cleopatra and the dereliction of duty by Antony. She presses her case still further in interpreting the confrontation between Joseph and Frau Potiphar as resistance to assimilation and refusal to succumb to the alien culture of Egypt which would entail an abandonment of Jewish values and traditions. This goes well beyond Philo's text which stresses Joseph's adherence to

Jewish laws on sexual behavior and the issue of his duty toward his benefactor Potiphar—not a wholesale divide between the nations.

Oertelt is perhaps too prone to see Philo as echoing Roman concepts in describing the positive attributes of Joseph. She reckons allusions to the Israelite's reverence for God as resonating with Roman *pietas*, Joseph's stature as benefactor of his subordinates as influenced by the Augustan notion of *pater patriae*, the less than sumptuous meal that Joseph prepared for his guests as a nod toward Augustus' program limiting luxury, and even Pharaoh's bestowal of a ring and chain upon Joseph in pledging fidelity as a reference to the Roman idea of *fides*. These concepts had extensive spread among ancient societies. Philo did not require Roman ideology to bring them to mind.

Oertelt provides a thoughtful and effective segment on Philo's presentation of Joseph as dreamer and dream-interpreter. On the surface, a disconnect exists between *De Somniis* II and *De Josepho*. The former represents Joseph as puffed-up by his own dreams, an index of his boastfulness and abandonment to vacuous glory. The latter underscores his wisdom and insight into the dreams of others. Oertelt takes this supposed contradiction to a different plane of understanding by analyzing both tracts as reflections of the discernment and the willfulness of the statesman and tyrant respectively. The deeper meaning emerges in comprehending how the tyrant misleads his people through false expectations and how the ideal statesman instructs his people through interpreting their aspirations. Oertelt observes quite tellingly that neither treatise reckons dream interpretation as forecasting the future but rather as finding significance in the present.

The celebrated scene of Joseph's reconciliation with his brothers receives a comparable analysis as reflecting the qualities of a political leader. But here Oertel's case seems somewhat strained. Philo paints an emotional Joseph when the reunion occurs; he bursts into tears no fewer than three times. He manages to shield these outbursts from his brothers, but the impression he leaves does not easily square with that of the Stoic statesman or righteous judge who controls his feelings, as Oertelt interprets it. Joseph has more dimensions than just the political.

The book does an effective job of drawing out Philo's thinking on the characteristics of political leadership that can be forces for good or ill. In this way, it serves to soften the ostensible contradictions between the divergent portraits of Joseph and thus to see them both as serving the broader interests of Philonic political theory. The question of how to reconcile the contrasting representations thus loses much of its urgency. That may spare us a considerable amount of unnecessary future scholarship on the subject. But a different question does still possess some relevance. If Philo's treatments of Joseph aimed at developing a blueprint for proper governance of the state, to whom were these tracts directed? Who constituted the expected or presumed audience? That issue is mentioned once only in passing by Oertelt and never pursued. Do her proposals of intersection with Roman conceptualizations imply that Philo looked to a Roman readership? Or do the frequent references to Greek philosophy suggest an audience of Hellenized Jews in Alexandria? This would make an important difference in our understanding of the trajectory of the tracts.

Oertelt may overemphasize the political dimensions of Philo's rewriting of the biblical Joseph narrative. But the book develops its thesis with consistency and force. It represents a careful, well researched, and effective presentation of this important aspect of Philo's thought.

Erich S. Gruen
University of California, Berkeley

SARAH PEARCE, ed. *The Image and Its Prohibition in Jewish Antiquity*. Journal of Jewish Studies Supplement Series 2. Oxford: Journal of Jewish Studies, 2013. 288 pages. ISBN 978-0-9575228-0-0. Price: £55/$90.

This essential collection, edited by Sarah Pearce, is the most up to date and critical discussion of the variegated forms of ancient Jewish polemic against the worship of objects other than God. The formation of a discourse around the second commandment is essential for thinking about ancient Jewish practice, ritual, and for thinking about representations of God. What is monotheism? What is the place of image in ancient Israel and ancient Judaism? How are we to understand iconic representation in the history of Judaism from antiquity and beyond? How can we conceptualize the conflicting attitudes towards textual and material representations of divinity? These are the questions at the heart of *The Image and Its Prohibition in Jewish Antiquity*.

This volume, the second in the Journal for Jewish Studies' new Supplement Series, comprises ten essays (all in English), ranging in length from 10 to 28 pages, first delivered at the annual meeting of the British Association for Jewish Studies in September 2010. In addition to the 50 full-color images interspersed throughout the text, this handsome publication includes an introductory essay by Sarah Pearce (1–9) summarizing the contributors' arguments and contextualizing them within the last century of scholarship and archaeological discovery.

The volume opens with Philip Alexander's "Reflections on Word versus Image as Ways of Mediating the Divine Presence in Judaism." This essay offers a theological framework for thinking about Judaism's prohibition on images, on the one hand, and its production of images throughout history, on the other. For Alexander, the second commandment is normative. Though there were stricter and more liberal interpretations of the prohibition in antiquity, all "agreed that a visual image was a totally unacceptable way of representing to the community God's presence in the world" (14).[1] If this is the case, where do the mosaic synagogue floors of Beth Alpha, Hammat Tiberias, and Na'aran, or the frescoes on the walls at Dura Europos, filled as they are with depictions of humans, animals, and gods, fit in? In Alexander's account, they are evidence not for the diversity of Jewish practice but of its failure. He argues that Judaism "followed a well-known trajectory of religious development from 'primitive' animism" to transcendent monotheism (18–19). Thus, the figural art of late antiquity is said to have "*invaded* the religious" sphere of Jewish life, and up to the present day, Judaism "had to *struggle* with the *lure* of images" (22, emphasis added). The periodic violation of the aniconic principle enshrined in the second commandment is mitigated for Alexander not by the "blatantly casuistical" justifications for images put forth by various rabbinic voices (11) but by the supposed primacy of the text in ancient Judaism. Whether it is in a building or on page, Jewish art "*illustrates* scenes from the sacred history; it is essentially Art in the service of the Word" (22). This echoes Gregory the Great's apology for Christian art: it is subordinate to the written word, a pedagogical aid for those who, in their weakness of mind, need it.[2] In Alexander's framework, the history of Jewish art in antiquity is the history of the regretful transgression of the second commandment and the eventual realization—glimpsed by the mystical tradition—that images, be they words or figures, are inadequate mediators of divine presence. Only action—the performance of *mitzvot*—is a sure path to the divine (26).

Many of the subsequent essays in this collection can be seen as responses to the normative vision articulated by Alexander's piece. H.G.M. Williamson's contribution, "Was There an Image of the Deity in the First Temple?" does not go so far as to say that an image ever stood in the Holy of Holies, but it does argue that images of God, and of Asherah, "may have been introduced and removed over the course of centuries"—much like side chapels dedicated to various Christian saints, "any one of whom might become the object of individual devotion by some even while being

[1] For an alternative view, see Martin Goodman, "The Jewish Image of God in Late Antiquity," in *Jewish Culture and Society Under the Christian Roman Empire*, ed. Richard Kalmin and Seth Schwartz (Leuven: Peeters, 2003), 133–45.

[2] *Letters* 11.13. See also Basil of Caesarea, *Homily* 19.

disapproved by others" (37). Margaret H. Williams' essay, "The Menorah in a Sepulchral Context: a Protective, Apotropaic Symbol?" goes further, contesting the claim that the menorah was merely a marker of Jewish identity in the Late Second Temple period. Instead, she asks us to consider the possibility that "certain funerary practices of a magical nature prevalent in Graeco-Roman society were adopted by the Jews" (88). Among these was the prophylactic use of the menorah on tombs and ossuaries to "invoke" God and his protection for the deceased (80–82). Williams views these images not merely as illustrations or reminders but as themselves efficacious and possessive of agency.

Zeev Weiss's contribution, "Images and Figural Representations in the Urban Galilee: Defining Limits in Times of Shifting Borders," draws attention to the recent discovery of six fragments of "three-dimensional statues in what is believed to have been a Jewish city" (141). It is tempting to dismiss these remains as pagan and thus preserve the traditional image of an aniconic Judaism, but as Weiss reminds us, the archaeological evidence from the second century and later "could also be attributed to a transformation in the attitude of the Jewish population" (134). To be sure, several Jewish writers from the Second Temple period—Philo in the *Legatio*, Josephus in both the *Bellum* and *Antiquitates*, Luke's description of Paul in Acts 17:16—are invested in the portrayal of Jews as uncompromisingly aniconic, and scholarship has by and large accepted this picture as normative for all of ancient Judaism. Weiss asks us to imagine not only that the Jews of late antique Sepphoris "did not object" to the installation of three-dimensional statues in the public spaces of their city but that "some might have even enjoyed their beauty when entering the local bathhouse or the monumental theatre" (144). Tessa Rajak's essay, "The Synagogue Paintings of Dura-Europos: Triumphalism and Competition," continues this thought experiment through a meditation on the imagery of the third-century Dura synagogue. She argues quite convincingly that the frescoes share in the "common artistic idiom" of the rest of the city "with an ease that bespeaks more than the mechanical fact of the common workshops and artisans or of pattern books" (103). Yet through this shared idiom, the synagogue's art—Ezekiel's dry bones, the widow of Zarephat, the fall of Dagon—claims a distinctiveness for Judaism over against other religions.

We see this phenomenon in texts, as well. Jane Heath's extraordinarily insightful piece, "Greek and Jewish Visual Piety: Ptolemy's Gifts in the *Letter of Aristeas*," focuses on the letter's counterintuitive "decision to use a genre"—ekphrasis—"that was developed, favoured and theorized in the Greco-Roman world and that is defined by an intense, sustained interest in the visual appreciation of 'works of human hands'" (39). That is, in the letter's very attempt to argue for Jewish distinctiveness, it comes to resemble more and more its Greek opponents. Recent work by Nathaniel Levtow, Jason von Ehrenkrook, and Laura Nasrallah has also noted this phenomenon.[3]

The confluence of "pagan" and Jewish thought on the question of idols is likewise taken up in Aron Sterk's contribution, "The Letter of Annas to Seneca: A Late Antique Jewish Exhortation in Dialogue with Roman Paganism." Sterk has done extensive work on this Latin text, arguing that it was written by a philosophically educated and imperially connected fourth-century Jew, Annas (171), perhaps in response to the pseudonymous correspondence between Paul and Seneca. The letter affords us a rare glimpse into Jewish engagement with pagan thought during the ascendancy of imperial Christianity. Sterk helpfully includes the Latin of the letter as well as a fresh English translation.

The relation of Jewish and Greco-Roman thought and practice is explored further in Sacha Stern's essay, "Images in Late Antique Palestine: Jewish and Graeco-Roman Views." Stern revisits an argument he had made previously about whether the rabbinic distinction between worshipped and not-worshipped objects (as, e.g., in *m.Avodah Zarah* 3:4) corresponded to a distinction made in the Greco-Roman world. Yaron Eliav has claimed that it did, whereas Seth Schwartz has argued that the distinction is a rabbinic invention. In the present article, Stern splits the difference of these two positions, noting that evidence for such a distinction is found almost entirely in *Roman* sources. In the Greek east, by contrast, "the distinction may have been more blurred, if indeed existent at all" (127). Midway through his essay, Stern asks "to what extent one can assume that attitudes towards images were standard in the pagan world" (123). He gestures towards the implications of this question when he states that it is "impossible to capture the wide-ranging interpretations" ancient viewers gave to art (113), and he could press this issue even further. Perhaps it is not a matter of the distinction existing in one region and not another, or one language group and not another. After all, any such distinction is an ideal, a construct imposed on practices that were surely far more complicated.

Laliv Clenman's contribution, "The Faceless Idol and Images of Terror in Rabbinic Tradition on the *Molekh*," takes up the themes of vision,

[3] N. Levtow, *Images of Others: Iconic Politics in Ancient Israel* (Winona Lake, IN: Eisenbrauns, 2008); J. von Ehrenkrook, *Sculpting Idolatry in Flavian Rome: (An)Iconic Rhetoric in the Writings of Flavius Josephus* (Atlanta: Society of Biblical Literature, 2011); L, Nasrallah, *Christian Responses to Roman Art and Architecture: The Second Century Amid the Spaces of Empire* (New York: Cambridge University Press, 2010).

spectacle, and invisibility through a close reading of biblical and rabbinic texts related to the Molekh. Despite the Levitical command to watch carefully for Molekh rituals, biblical texts are notably silent on what, exactly, this rival deity and its worship look like. While some rabbinic texts maintain the "facelessness" of the Molekh idol, others make Molekh worship visible through "explicit, gory, violent and sexualized" imagery that is not easily unseen once read (164). Thus the Molekh is both invisible and hypervisible, hidden yet unable to be forgotten.

Finally, perhaps of most immediate interest to readers of the *Studia Philonica,* Sarah Pearce's "Philo of Alexandria on the Second Commandment" is devoted to thinking about Philo's creative exegesis and higher levels of reading. She writes: "What has been missing thus far in scholarship on Philo and his attitude towards art and the second commandment is serious attention to the fact that Philo approaches these subjects, first and foremost, as a creative exegete of Scripture" (52). What is the character of Philo's creative exegesis? Peder Borgen figures prominently in Pearce's essay, but we would suggest that she goes well beyond his approach. Borgen considers all interpretation to be external to scripture and thus relegates it to the level of rewritten bible. What is missing in his study, but what is present in Pearce's essay, is the transformative character of Philo's work, which ultimately blurs the lines between scripture and interpretation. Philo's readings draw creatively on resources available to him in his Graeco-Roman environment—the philosophical denigration of material cult, for instance—in order to transform the scriptures he is reading. Finally, Pearce's own reading of Philo's *De Decalogo* is integrated into the way she is thinking about Philo's broader exegetical project on the Law of Moses. Philo's *De Decalogo* is essential to understanding Philo's allegorical project, his exegetical project and, in general, his transformation and rethinking of ancient Jewish theology.

In some sense, what is at stake in this volume is the status and characterization of monotheism. These essays demonstrate that the narrative around deity and materiality is far more complicated and at the center of this debate is none other than Philo of Alexandria. Moreover, it is ever more important to get the deeper meaning right—because what is at stake is that it is not fitting that human beings, who have been formed through the working of divine power, should themselves try to give form to divine. This is an essential and field-defining collection which is to be celebrated, assigned, and critically engaged.

Hindy Najman
University of Oxford

Sonja Anderson
Yale University

Otto Kaiser, *Studien zu Philo von Alexandrien*. Edited by Markus Witte. Beihefte zur Zeitschrift für die alttestamentliche Wissenschaft 501. Berlin/Boston: Walter de Gruyter, 2017. vi + 174 pages. Hardcover. ISBN 9783110494570. Price $140, 99,95 Euros.

Markus Witte has collected five previously published essays (chapters one, three, four, five, and seven) and three unpublished essays (chapters two, six, and eight) of Otto Kaiser on the thought of Philo. Kaiser is an internationally recognized Old Testament scholar who is best known for his three-volume *Der Prophet Jesaja* (1960–1973), his three volume *Grundriss der Einleitung in die kanonischen und deuterokanonischen Schriften des Alten* Testaments (1992–1994), and his three-volume *Der Gott des Alten Testament: Theologie des Alten Testaments* (1993–2003). Since the 1970s he has extended these interests into the world of Second Temple Judaism and in recent years published two monographs on Philo: *Das höchste Gut: Philos Hochschätzung der Freundschaft im Horizont ihrer antiken Geltung* (2015) and *Philo von Alexandrien: denkender Glaube, eine Einführung* (2015). The present collection is intended to serve as a companion volume Kaiser's introduction to Philo.

The essays fall into three major parts: the first chapter is an introduction to Philo, chapters two-four address Philo's cosmology and religion, and chapters five through eight explore the Alexandrian's ethics. The format and the basic approach in each chapter are similar. The essays in parts one and two typically open with a summary of Philo's work as an exegete and philosopher (chapters one, two, three, and five)—with some understandable overlap; the essays in part three begin with an overview of the issue that the essay will explore (chapters four, six, seven, and eight). In all cases Kaiser works through the Philonic and other ancient texts carefully. He situates the major Philonic texts he evaluates within the framework of Philo's interpretation of the biblical text (rather than ignoring which biblical text Philo's is interpreting). He helps the reader by supplying subheadings for each unit of analysis, a practice that results in a large number of subheadings for some chapters, e.g., chapters three, five, six and seven average 11.5 subheadings per chapter. The analyses of texts are his own and are thorough. The most significant limitation is that, although he has consulted a large body of secondary literature, there are major omissions of recent work on the topics that he addresses. Readers should not assume that he has engaged all of the relevant secondary literature, but read his essays along with other treatments.

The first chapter serves as an overview of Philo's work and interpretative method. Kaiser opens by placing Philo's works in three periods (pp. 10–11): he situates the Allegorical Commentary (AC) in the first; *QGE* in the second, followed by an interim period in which Philo produced *Opif.*, *Flacc.*,

Legat., and the *Hypoth.*; and the Exposition in the third. The philosophical treatises come last (pp. 10–11). This follows the famous analysis of Leopold Cohn ("Einleitung und Chronologie der Schriften Philos," *Philologus* 7 [1899]: 385–436, esp. 432–434) and the more recent work of myself ("'Prolific in Expression and Broad in Thought': Internal References to Philo's Allegorical Commentary and Exposition of the Law," *Euphrosyne* 40 [2012]: 55–76, esp. 57–60) and Maren Niehoff (*Jewish Exegesis and Homeric Scholarship in Alexandria* [New York: Cambridge University Press, 2011], 169–185) in placing the Exposition after the AC. The placement of *QGE* between them is curious: Abraham Terian ("The Priority of the *Quaestiones* among Philo's Exegetical Commentaries," in *Both Literal and Allegorical: Studies in Philo of Alexandria's* Questions and Answers on Genesis and Exodus, ed. David M. Hay; BJS 233 [Atlanta: Scholars Press, 1991], 29–46; idem, *Quaestiones et solutiones in Exodum. I et II e versione armeniaca et fragmenta graeca*, PAPM 34C [Paris: Éditions du Cerf, 1992], 27–51) and I ("Philo's *Quaestiones*: Prolegomena or Afterthought," *Both Literal and Allegorical*, 99–123) have argued that *QGE* precede the AC, while Maren Niehoff places *QGE* last (*Jewish Exegesis and Homeric Scholarship*, 152–168). While the sequence can be debated—and there may well have been overlap—Kaiser's analysis omits the contemporary discussion of the placement of *QGE*. He is not entirely consistent and later places *QGE* prior to the AC (p. 64). His summary of Philo's work as an exegete and discussions of metaphor and allegory are solid, especially the discussion of metaphor.

The second through the fourth chapters examine aspects of Philo's cosmology. Chapter two explores his cosmology proper by comparing Philo to Eudorus, something that should be done more frequently. Eudorus considered the world to be eternal, while Philo insisted that it was created. In other words, Eudorus read the *Timaeus* figuratively, while Philo read it literally—two well known interpretations among Middle Platonists. The treatment is solid, although in my view the two agreed on the ontological dependence of the world upon God—a point that Kaiser does not emphasize. A reader should also be aware of the work of Mauro Bonazza on Eudorus and Philo (e.g., Mauro Bonnazi, "Towards Transcendence: Philo and the Renewal of Platonism in the Early Imperial Age," in *Philo of Alexandria and Post-Aristotelian Philosophy*, ed. Francesca Alesse; SPhA 5 [Leiden/Boston: Brill, 2008], 233–251) which is never noted. Chapter three is an excellent overview of the cosmological significance of the high priest in Philo: it is one of the most comprehensive recent treatments. It builds on the material in *Spec.* 1, but includes all of the significant Philonic texts. Chapter four turns to prayer in Philo. Kaiser analyzes Philo's use of the Psalter and four important texts (*Plant.* 46–60; *Migr* 121–124; *QG* 1.70; 4.70).

He suggests that Philo used the Psalter to pray based on Philo's incorporation of the language of the Psalter in his exegesis (p.68), although it is better to conclude that Philo's use was primarily exegetical. Here his failure to take recent work into account limits the value of his analysis. In particular, he should have consulted David Runia's analysis of Philo's use of the Psalter ("Philo's Reading of the Psalms," *SPhiloA* 13 [2001]: 102–121) and Peder Borgen's treatment of prayer ("Two Philonic Prayers and their Contexts: An Analysis of *Who is the Heir of Divine Things* (*Her.*) 24–29 and *Against Flaccus* (*Flacc.*) 170–175," *NTS* 45 [1999]: 291–309).

The fifth through the eighth chapters explore different aspects of Philo's ethics. Chapter five tackles virtues and passions. The treatment is solid, although once again, it omits any interaction with the major recent work on the passions (see David Winston, "Philo of Alexandria on the Rational and Irrational Emotions," in *Passions and Moral Progress in Greco-Roman Thought,* ed. John T. Fitzgerald [London/New York: Routledge, 2008], 201–220) or specific virtues (e.g., Katell Berthelot, *Philanthropia judiaca: le débat autour de la 'misanthropie' des lois juives dans l'antiquité,* JSJSup 76 [Leiden: Brill, 2003], on φιλανθρωπία and Gregory E. Sterling, "'The Queen of the Virtues': Piety in Philo of Alexandria," *SPhiloA* 18 [2006]: 103–24, on εὐσέβεια). Chapter six explores the topics of hope and joy versus sorrow and fear. Kaiser makes a good case for the translation of δέος as Angst (p. 107). The analysis is an important contribution to the wider current discussions about lives well lived. Chapter seven turns to the issues of sickness and health, important topics that have not been widely explored by Philonists, but which Kaiser had earlier explored in the OT. The eighth and final chapter is a brief treatment of the role of death. Although Kaiser knows the work of Emma Wasserman and Dieter Zeller on the death of the soul, he never engages them.

This collection thus has merit and limitations. The strength of the collection is that provides the analyses of a first-rate scholar who has carefully and sympathetically read Philo on issues of great importance. The limitation of the collection is that Kaiser did not engage some of the important contemporary debates. While this is a real limitation, I would much rather read a fresh analysis of Philo than a collection of arguments with scholars that does not provide an original reading. It is particularly refreshing to read analyses by an eminent Old Testament scholar, since most Philonists were trained in fields that cover later periods.

Gregory E. Sterling
Yale Divinity Schools

TROELS ENGBERG-PEDERSEN, ed. *From Stoicism to Platonism: The Development of Philosophy, 100 BCE–100 CE*. Cambridge: Cambridge University Press, 2017. x + 399 pages. ISBN 978-1-107-16619-6. Price £90/$120.

This conference volume contains sixteen papers delivered in August 2014 at the Danish Royal Academy of Sciences in Copenhagen. Troels Engberg-Pedersen assembles a well-known group of international scholars in the fields of Hellenistic philosophy, Hellenistic Judaism, and Early Christianity. The contributors investigate the interaction between Stoicism and Platonism from 100 BCE to 100 CE. Engberg-Pedersen offers an introduction, followed by eleven papers discussing "pagan" philosophers, and three covering Hellenistic Jewish works, and two on early Christian texts.

The principle point of investigation is to determine the precise *interaction* between Stoicism and Platonism. A series of recent publications have questioned whether "eclecticism" is an appropriate term to describe the period,[1] or whether we should view the first centuries as a period of "transition" at all.[2] It could be that Platonism was already well-defined at the beginning of the period, and that it did not form its identity by taking on doctrines from other schools.[3] Or it could be that Platonists, Stoics, and Aristotelians sought to triangulate their traditions with Plato as the reference point.[4] To assume strict scholastic boundaries, therefore, might reflect modern presuppositions more than ancient evidence.[5] The title of the volume suggests Pedersen's own assumption that Stoicism dominated the philosophical scene in about 100 BCE, with this influence gradually giving way to Platonism. Several contributors challenge this fundamental assumption (e.g., Boys-Stones).

[1] Caution toward "eclecticism" as a helpful category begins primarily with John Dillon and Anthony A. Long, eds., *The Question of "Eclecticism": Studies in Later Greek Philosophy* (Berkeley: University of California Press, 1988).

[2] The question is taken up already in A.G. Long, ed., *Plato and the Stoics* (Cambridge: Cambridge University Press, 2013).

[3] George Boys-Stones in the volume being reviewed is emphatic that Platonism was already well-formed by the time of Antiochus of Ascalon (67–79).

[4] Cf. David Sedley, "The School from Zeno to Arius Didymus" in *The Cambridge Companion to the Stoics*, ed. Brad Inwood (Cambridge: Cambridge University Press, 2003), 7–32; Richard Sorabji, "Introduction" in *Greek and Roman Philosophy 100 BC–200 AD*, ed. Richard Sorabji and Robert W. Sharples, Bulletin of Classical Studies Supplement 94 (London: Institute of Classical Studies, University of London, 2007), 1:1–32.

[5] The point is made forcefully in Myrto Hatzimichali, *Potamo of Alexandria and the Emergence of Eclecticism in Late Hellenistic Philosophy* (Cambridge: Cambridge University Press, 2011).

The collection opens with a summary essay by the editor. A.G. Long next discusses Posidonius' original theory (so he concludes) of "affective movements" ("Plato, Chrysippus, and Posidonius' Theory of Affective Movements," 27–46), and Malcolm Schofield surveys Cicero's use and critique of Plato ("Cicero's Plato," 47–66). George Boys-Stones discusses Eudorus' critique of Aristotle's *Categories*, finding Aristotle to have perverted Plato ("Are We Nearly There Yet? Eudorus on Aristotle's *Categories*," 67–79).

Two chapters treat the doxography of "Arius Didymus." Myrto Hatzimichali discusses Stoic, Platonist, and Aristotelian interaction in Arius Didymus, specifically treating assimilation to God and whether virtue is sufficient for happiness ("Stoicism and Platonism in 'Arius Didymus,'" 80–99). Next, Christopher Gill discusses "*Oikeiōsis* in Stoicism, Antiochus, and Arius Didymus" (100–119), claiming Antiochus attempts to co-opt the Stoic doctrine for Platonism. Mauro Bonazzi treats more generally "The Platonist Appropriation of Stoic Epistemology" (120–41), suggesting the dogmatic Platonists tended to incorporate Stoic features in order to oppose the Skeptics, who presented a far more serious threat. Gretchen Reydams-Schils traces "'Becoming Like God' in Platonism and Stoicism" (142–58), finding in Alcinous, for example, an incorporation of Stoic terminology, but not necessarily Stoicized Platonism.

Two chapters in the volume treat Philo's philosophical contributions explicitly. In the first, David Runia discusses the neglected *Prov.* 1 ("From Stoicism to Platonism: The Difficult Case of Philo of Alexandria's *De Providentia* I," 159–78). After a brief introduction, Runia analyzes Philo's use of Platonism and Stoicism in the treatise, with frequent comparisons to *Aet.* Philo blends both philosophical traditions, drawing technical terminology and arguments from the Stoics, but retaining a Platonist framework in his cosmology and theology. Philo's principle opposition is to Stoic determinism and the eternity of the world, but his scriptural sensibilities lead him to subvert both traditions to Moses.

A major theme of *Prov.* 1 (and *Aet.*) is God's punitive providence, which, although dependent on Stoic terminology, is worked out along Platonist (Mosaic) lines. Philo, Runia states, "does not necessarily envisage the total destruction of the cosmos as attributed to the Stoics in *Aet.* 8, but rather a threatened purging of the parts of the cosmos through the action of natural catastrophes and elemental change (cf. *Aet.* 146–9)" (176–77). This latter position squares with Plato, but is attributed to Moses (*Aet.* 19). What we have, then, is a clear knowledge of both Platonism and Stoicism, but a subversion of both to Judaism.

Carlos Lévy authors the second essay focusing directly on Philo ("From Cicero to Philo of Alexandria: Ascending and Descending Axes in the Interpretation of Platonism and Stoicism," 179–97). Lévy treats the argument of *Aet.* systematically, and utilizes Cicero's critique of Stoicism as a basis of comparison (his twofold "ascending" and "descending" critique). Like Cicero, Philo regards Stoic departures from Plato to be either slight adjustments or outright errors. It seems Philo's principle objections to the Stoics, again, lie in cosmology and theology. Stoic terminology could be usefully employed, but only when undergirded by Platonic transcendence. Lévy reaches a similar conclusion to Runia, stressing that all Greek philosophy in *Aet.* is subjected to Philo's Judaism, which remains his controlling "philosophical" influence.

Next, Gregory Sterling discusses the interaction between Stoicism and Platonism in the Wisdom of Solomon ("The Love of Wisdom: Middle Platonism and Stoicism in the Wisdom of Solomon," 198–213). Although Wisdom and Philo accept the immortality of the soul from the Platonists, their rationale for biblical miracles assumes the Stoic possibility of the transformation of elements. Wisdom also utilizes Stoic terminology to describe the "intelligent spirit" (πνεῦμα νοερόν), but applies it to the second universal principle, allowing for the Platonic transcendence of God.

Turning to the period after Philo, A.A. Long treats "Seneca and Epictetus on Body, Mind, and Dualism" (214–30), and concludes neither turns to Plato or to the Academic tradition in a way that would indicate their Platonizing of Stoicism. Stanley Stowers next treats "The Dilemma of Paul's Physics: Features Stoic-Platonist or Platonist-Stoic?" (231–53), and attempts to emphasize the more Platonic elements in Paul's thinking (without denying the influence of Stoicism). Brad Inwood deals with "The Legacy of Musonius Rufus" (254–76), and opposes the common view that Musonius was a Stoic, viewing him more appropriately as a Cynic. Harold Attridge discusses naming in early Christianity ("Stoic and Platonic Reflections on Naming in Early Christian Circles: Or, What's in a Name?" 277–95), concluding that a Platonic framework explains how Jesus could be the unique Christian solution to the problem of the unknowability of the transcendent God. In the next chapter, Jan Opsomer discusses Plutarch's polemic against the Stoics, and suggests he is opposed to Stoic doctrine only insofar as he regards it as a departure from Plato ("Is Plutarch Really Hostile to the Stoics?" 296–321). In the final essay, Charles Brittain treats the "Peripatetic Appropriation of *Oikeiōsis*: Alexander, *Mantissa* Chapter 17" (322). Although the essay of Alexander falls outside the chronological scope of the book, Brittain treats it as an important source on Peripatetic ethics of the first century CE.

In addition to the chapters focusing on *Prov.* 1 and *Aet.*, other discussions of Philo can be located in this volume. Two essays include subsections on Philo, the first on "Philo and Paul" (Stowers, 242–46), and the second on "Philo's Stoic Platonism" (Attridge, 277–83). In addition, Sterling's essay includes many references to Philo in comparison with the Wisdom of Solomon. Several chapters also deal with Philonic themes. Christopher Gill's essay on οἰκείωσις establishes the important Platonist background for Philo's own critique of the Stoic doctrine.[6] Mauro Bonazzi's discussion of the Middle Platonic identification of Ideas with the Stoic ἔννοιαι impacts Philo in ways scholars have not yet fully investigated (126–27). Gretchen Reydams-Schils also offers background important for Philo's understanding of the ethical ideal of ὁμοίωσις θεῷ.

As with Cambridge volumes in general, this book is well-edited. I found one misspelling (the Greek transliteration *expyrōsis* instead of *ekpyrōsis*, p. 191), and one grammatical mistake ("what they really means," p. 331). But these errors are minor. The book is an important collection from world-class scholars, and represents an advancement in our understanding of both Platonism and Stoicism from 100 BCE to 100 CE. We look forward to further publications clarifying this obscure period in ancient philosophy.

As a welcome surprise, Philonic works are referenced more in this volume (287 times) than those of any other ancient author, with the exception of Cicero (289 times). This fact alone testifies to the respect Philo is receiving in the world of modern scholarship. And although most of the contributors are focused elsewhere, a most relevant insight for Philonic studies is the general Platonist tendency to appropriate Stoic terminology without altering (in their minds) Platonism. Perhaps Philo would have agreed with Plutarch: where the Stoics got it right, they prove to be proper expositors of Plato, but where they got it wrong, they are perverters of the master. But Philo would claim Plato got it right only insofar as he was a student of Moses.

Justin M. Rogers
Freed-Hardeman University
Henderson, Tennessee

[6] On Philo's critique of the Stoic version of οἰκείωσις see Carlos Lévy, "Éthique de l'immanence, éthique de la transcendence: le problème de l' *oikeiôsis* chez Philon," in Carlos Lévy, ed., *Philon d'Alexandrie et le langage de la philosophie,* Monothéismes et Philosophie (Turnhout: Brepols, 1998), 153–64.

Karin Metzler (ed.), *Prokop von Gaza Eclogarum in libros historicos Veteris Testamenti epitome. Teil 1: Der Genesiskommentar*, Die griechischen christlichen Schriftsteller der ersten Jahrhunderte N.F. 22. Berlin: De Gruyter, 2015. clxv + 490 pages. Hardcover. ISBN 978-3-11-040872-0. Price €139.95.

Karin Metzler, *Prokop von Gaza Der Genesiskommentar. Aus den „Eclogarum in libros historicos Veteris Testamenti epitome" übersetzt und mit Anmerkungen versehen*, Die griechischen christlichen Schriftsteller der ersten Jahrhunderte N.F. 23. Berlin: De Gruyter, 2016. lvi + 570 pages. Hardcover. ISBN 978-3-11-044276-2. Price €119.95.

The publication in twenty-first century of the (partial) *editio princeps* of a major Greek Patristic scriptural commentary is a rare and most welcome event. In the past two years the German Patristic scholar and Byzantinist Karin Metzler has published an edition and translation of the Commentary on Genesis by Procopius of Gaza (c. 465–c. 529) in two volumes. This work is the first part of a much larger commentary, often (misleadingly) called the *Catena on the Octateuch*, none of which so far has been edited in a modern critical edition. The two volumes are designed to be used together. It will be worthwhile first to give a description of their contents.

Volume 1 contains the Greek text in a critical edition that meets with the most exacting standards of current scholarship. Its introduction of more than 150 pages first introduces the author and his work. Metzler argues that it should not be regarded as an (anonymized) Catena, but rather as a Commentary (more on this below). She briefly describes his method of working and purpose, adding some speculations on the libraries that he might have used for his massive project. The reader is then given an overview of previous scholarship on this work. The only previous edition of any value was that of Cardinal Angelo Mai, who edited the work up to Gen 18:3 on the basis of inferior manuscripts. For the remainder of the work it was only possible to consult a Latin translation of the entire work published by Conrad Klauser in 1555. So for the part of the work from Gen 18:3 onwards (a little less than half the entire work) the Greek text is edited for the first time.

Next the Introduction gives a detailed analysis of the manuscript tradition. By far the most important witness is the ninth cent. Munich codex in the Bavarian State Library (gr. 358), which contains the entire work (some loose pages which Klauser had removed from it were rediscovered by Lidia Perria in Basel in the late 80's). There are five additional independent mss. and thirteen dependent mss. of variable quality. Three mss. have been lost, of which one was used by Mai. All in all, it is possible to produce a reliable stemma of the manuscript transmission of the work (diagram on p. lxxxviii).

The critical edition has two main apparatuses, the apparatus fontium and the apparatus criticus. In the former the editor indicates all the sources used by Procopius (these are also indicated in an abbreviated form on the inner margin of the text) to the extent that she (building on previous scholars) has been able to identify them (a large number remain unidentified, although sometimes an educated guess is possible). In a lengthy section of the Introduction a list is presented of all these sources (including Philo), demonstrating the remarkable breadth of Procopius' compilation. The discussion of these sources is one of the most interesting aspects of the edition. The sigla, the principles used in editing the Greek text and an extensive bibliography of primary and secondary works round off the Introduction.

The Greek text is divided into pericopes in accordance with the biblical text being commented on. The biblical text itself is cited for each pericope, but most often not fully. The text is then numbered according to the lines of the pericope. So, for example, the fragment on Cain's anger from Philo *QG* 1.63 on p. 165 (lines 76–78) can be referred to as *CommGen* 4,2:76–78 according to German convention (English convention would prefer *CommGen* 4:2.76–78). The volume concludes with restricted indexation focusing mainly on lists of biblical texts, deviant mss. readings of these texts, and etymologies of scriptural names.

We turn now to volume 2. The introductory section for the translation volume is much shorter and in discussing the author, genre, sources, and purpose of the work covers some of the same ground. A section on doubts regarding the authenticity of the work (groundless in Metzler's opinion) and a scenario on how the work might have originated add to what was already presented in vol. 1. The aim of the translation, we read, is to convey its content to the Greekless reader and also offer interpretative assistance to the reader who is able to study the Greek text.

The greater part of the volume is devoted to the translation, following the pericopes of Procopius' commentary and accompanied by very limited annotation. The sources of the commentary are indicated only in the most summary fashion, no doubt on purpose, since this information is suppressed by the author himself. This means that in order to discover which material Procopius is incorporating, the reader must consult the very full index of authors at the end of the volume, which also serves as the most important index for vol. 1. The volume ends with four pages of corrigenda to vol. 1, largely taken up by a new method of citing Eusebius of Emesa's Genesis commentary in its Armenian version.

Years of intimate study of Procopius's commentary have enabled the editor–translator to develop an interpretation of the work's method and purpose which will now be the starting-point for further research. It is crucial, she argues, to distinguish between three different works, two which have survived and one that is lost. The last-mentioned of these is the so-called "Urkatene" (original catena), a massive compilation of excerpts from patristic and other writings—primarily but not exclusively commentaries—ranging from Philo and Josephus in the first century through to Cyril of Alexandria in the fifth, and covering both the Alexandrian and the Antiochene schools of exegesis. The genre of the catena (Latin for "chain") links together brief excerpts from these sources, giving on most occasions only the name of the author, sometimes accompanied by an epithet such as "bishop" and quite seldom by the name of the work where the excerpt is taken from. The no longer extant "Urkatene" was the basis for the *Catenae on Genesis and Exodus* (as well as other bible books), which have been preserved and were masterfully edited by Françoise Petit (see my review article, *SPhiloA* 11 [1999] 113–120).

In the fourteen line prooemium to his entire work Procopius explains that previously he had collected together the scriptural interpretations of the Fathers and others from their commentaries and various kinds of works. But when he started to put these all together he decided that the collected mass of material was too great and that it needed to be compressed. So, when excerpts agreed with each other he selected just a single representative text, but when they added a distinctive element he included them in a brief form, so that the entire work formed a single body "as though we as a single person alone presented the utterances of all." In the remainder of the work, therefore, Procopius seamlessly and very adroitly stitched together all the excerpts that he selected for inclusion, omitting all names and references, so that—apart from the cited biblical texts—it seems to be his own work, but in fact it is massive compilation of the interpretative efforts of generations of exegetes and other writers such as chroniclers. It is apparent that his work and the *Catena* are based on the same original collection, for they contain much material in common. However, in preparing his work Procopius must have done additional reading and collected extra material, for his work is quite a bit richer than the *Catena*, although at the same time it often abbreviates the excerpts found in the other work. It is possible that he himself was the compiler of the "Urkatene" or may have been involved in that project, which probably took place in the Episcopal library of Caesarea. This possibility is not unlikely, according to the author, but it cannot be proven.

What genre, then, does Procopius's work belong to? It combines the characteristics of three genres. It is based on the method of the catena. It is also in a sense an epitome, since it is an abbreviated version of previous works. This is indicated by its tradition title, Ἐκλογῶν ἐπιτομή ("abridgement of excerpts"). But Metzler argues—perhaps controversially—that it is also, and primarily, a commentary, hence the title she chooses for the entire work, *Commentary on Genesis*. In terms of its form it does indeed proceed as a running commentary, citing the biblical text lemma by lemma, making comments and answering questions raised by that text. But in terms of its content it is most unusual, because although on the surface it appears to be the author's work, in actual fact *none* of its contents are the original thought of its compiler, but in all cases the work of previous writers. The fourteen lines of the prooemium referred to above constitute the only time he speaks in his own person. Even the introduction is drawn from other writers (mostly unidentified, quite likely Origen). As Metzler points out (vol. 1, p. xiii), Procopius' work is the result of the canonization of a corpus of biblical exposition, consisting mainly of the church fathers, but also including Philo and just a little of Josepus, in which differences were accepted and controversies avoided. Procopius is not the first author to use this method. It already appears in the *Commentary on Genesis* attributed to Ps.Eustathius and to be dated to the end of the fourth or beginning of the fifth century (and also includes Philonic material).

What then is the significance of this new edition for Philonic studies? Procopius' Genesis commentary contains copious excerpts from Philo, but exclusively from the *Quaestiones in Genesim*, a work that he no doubt had access to via the Library of Caesarea. In Metzler's edition there are 106 Philonic excerpts, compared to only fifty-six in the *Catena*, so it is almost certain that Procopius must have done additional reading of Philo's work when preparing his Commentary. I only found one clear instance of a text in the *Catena* which he passed over, *QG* 4.168. This is a tribute to the thoroughness with which he worked when putting all his excerpts together and it also demonstrates that he regarded the Philonic material as distinctive and worth including in virtually every case. Since we no longer have the complete work in the Greek original, this makes his evidence all the more valuable. Essentially all this material was already included by Françoise Petit in her splendid edition of the fragments of *QG* and *QE* in the French translation series (1978). Petit had to collect and cite the Procopian texts in their unedited form, but she did this very thoroughly. I could not find any texts identified as Philonic in the new edition that are not already present in Petit's collection, though in one or two instances Metzler is less strict than Petit and includes texts that Petit left out (examples at *CommGen*

17:2.20–21 (the *quaestio* of *QG* 3.52) and 25:27.4–7 (rejected by Petit, cf. her note on *QG* 4.165).

The new edition will facilitate Philonic studies in many ways. It allows the Procopian material to be more readily and much better studied. Not only can this material now be much more easily referred to, but it can also now be seen in the perspective of the entire work, which is available not only in a superb critical edition, but also has been translated for easier reference and understanding. The place of Procopius in the reception of Philo's writings can now be determined with greater precision. This review is not the place to start on such research. But one conclusion can already be reached. Procopius' incorporation of anonymized Philonic texts in a canonical collection of Patristic exegesis is conclusive proof that they had entered the mainstream of Christian thought. Beyond any doubt Philo had become part of the Christian exegetical tradition. He was a *Christianus honoris causa*.

Karin Metzler is warmly to be thanked and congratulated on completing this magnificent work of intricate and detailed scholarship, the result of more than a decade of dedicated research. The Deutsche Forschungsgemeinschaft too must receive thanks for its generous financial support of the project, as well as the publisher Walter de Gruyter who has so expertly facilitated its publication. All scholars working in the field of Patristic exegesis, including Philonists, are greatly in her (and their) debt.

David Runia
Australian Catholic University
The University of Melbourne,
Australia

The Studia Philonica Annual 29 (2017): 265–70

NEWS AND NOTES

The Philo of Alexandria Group of the Society for Biblical Literature

At the Society of Biblical Literature 2016 Annual Meeting in San Antonio, Texas (November 19–22), the Philo of Alexandria Seminar held three sessions. The first, whose theme was "The Knowledge of God in Philo of Alexandria," was presided over by Sean Adams of the University of Glasgow. Speakers and presentations were: Mark Hamilton (Abilene Christian University); "Divine (Dis)embodiment as an Aspect of Divine Otherness in Philo"; Ilaria L. E. Ramelli (Catholic University, Angelicum, and Oxford University); "The Knowledge of God and the Dialectics of Apophatic Theology: Philo between Scripture and the Platonic Tradition"; Sharon Weisser (Tel Aviv University); "Knowing God by Analogy: Philo of Alexandria's Proofs for the Existence of God in the Context of the Debate around Stoic Theology in the Roman Period"; and Tyler A. Stewart (Marquette University), "Theological Suicide: Evil and the Imperception of God."

A second session, devoted to "Reincarnation and Afterlife in Philo and His World," was presided over by Torrey Seland, an Independent Scholar from Norway. Speakers and presentations were: Sami Yli-Karjanmaa (University of Helsinki), "Philo's Position on Reincarnation"; David Runia (University of Melbourne), "Does Philo Accept the Doctrine of Reincarnation?"; Rainer Hirsch-Luipold (Universität Bern-Université de Berne), "Afterlife and Reincarnation in Plutarch"; and Jeffrey Trumbower (Saint Michael's College, Vermont), "Closing the Door on Reincarnation in Early Christianity: Limiting the Options." Finally, the third session, presided over by Scott Mackie, an Independent Scholar, was devoted to a commentary being prepared by Michael Cover on Philo's *De Mutatione Nominum* for the Philo of Alexandria Commentary Series. Speakers and presentations included Michael Cover (Marquette University), "Philo's *De mutatione nominum*: Sample Commentary, Exegetical Structure, and Its Place in the 'Abrahamic Cycle' of the Allegorical Commentary"; Gregory Sterling (Yale Divinity School), "What's in a Name? The Place of *De mutatione nominum* in Philo's Allegorical Commentary"; James Royse (Claremont, California), "The Text of Philo's *De mutatione nominum*"; Frederick Brenk (Pontifical Biblical Institute, Rome), "A Name by Any Name? The Allegorizing Etymologies of

Philo and Plutarch"; and Michel Barnes (Marquette University), "Divine Powers in *De mutatione nominum* and Patristic Reception."

Presentations in all three sessions elicited stimulating comments and discussion. Those wishing to read the Seminar papers can find them online at http://torreys.org/philo_seminar_papers/, a website graciously hosted by Torrey Seland.

Although the Philo Seminar is the only SBL program unit dedicated specifically to Philo, the SBL Annual Meeting program typically includes several other individual papers offered in sessions of other program units. This year, however, the Wisdom and Apocalypticism Section devoted an entire panel to "Philo vis-à-vis Wisdom and Apocalypticism." Presided over by Matthew Goff of Florida State University, the session comprised the following speakers and presentations: Ellen Birnbaum (Cambridge, Massachusetts), "Is There Wisdom in Philo's Rationales for the Book of Genesis?"; Michael Cover (Marquette University), "'Consecrating All the Excellences of Speech' (*Mut.* 220): Philo on the Right Use of Apocalyptic Tragedy and Gnomic Wisdom"; Archie Wright (Regent University), "Questions of Eschatology and Other Apocalyptic Themes in Philo's Demonology"; and Gregory E. Sterling (Yale Divinity School), "When Ontology Meets Eschatology."

Finally, on Monday evening, November 21, Philo Seminar members and friends gathered in the Wine Cellar of Zinc Bistro for a special event to honor David Runia—leading Philo scholar, founding editor of *The Studia Philonica Annual*, and one of the Annual's current editors—with a Festschrift on the occasion of his retirement as Master of Queen's College at the University of Melbourne. In presenting him with this Festschrift, its editor Gregory Sterling, who together with Runia now also edits this Annual, recounted how closely entwined the careers of these two friends and colleagues have been. Also offering tributes were Ellen Birnbaum, Sarah Pearce, and James R. Royse. Responding, the honorand described how years ago he had become involved with the Philo of Alexandria Group at SBL. Taken all together, especially with the input of Sterling and Runia, the various remarks amounted to an oral history of important developments in Philonic scholarship since the Philo Institute suspended activities over three decades ago (see Earle Hilgert, "The Philo Institute, *Studia Philonica*, and Their Diadochoi," in vol. 13 of *The Studia Philonica Annual* [2001] = *In the Spirit of Faith: Studies in Philo and Early Christianity in Honor of David Hay*, ed. D. T. Runia and G. E. Sterling, 13–24).

Readers can learn more about David Runia in his Festschrift, vol. 28 of *The Studia Philonica Annu*al (2016). Readers can also learn more about the event in his honor, the Festschrift itself, and the SBL session on "Philo vis-à-vis Wisdom and Apocalypticism" in several individual posts (which include pictures) by Torrey Seland, online at https://biblicalresources.wordpress.com/2016/12/.

Congratulations, Professor Runia!

Ellen Birnbaum
Cambridge, MA

Philonic Study in Contemporary China

Alongside the rapid growth of Christian churches in China, two noteworthy academic movements have developed in response to the needs of the times: the scholastic phenomenon of Sino-Christian theology, and the movement to sinicize Christianity launched by Chinese state church officials. Chinese scholars in each of these two areas are engaged in Philonic research, in order to explore the modern significance of classic Jewish and Christian theology in providing an academic reference point for both the development of ecclesiastic ecosystems and also the religious decision-making of the government.

Professor Wang Xiaochao, a senior professor and the deputy Director of the Institute for the Study of Morality and Religion in Tsinghua University, who has been committed to researching in the classic Greco-Roman philosophy for many years, is a leading representative of Philonic study in contemporary China. In 1998 he translated and published Philo's *On the Creation, Allegorical Interpretation* (Institute of Sino-Christian Studies, Hong Kong, ISBN 962-8322-14-1). He subsequently published several academic articles: *On the Two Ways of the Emergence of Greco-Judaism Philosophy* (Foreign Philosophy, the Commercial Press, No. 16, 2004.), *On the Reading and Interpretation of Philo to the Bible* (Tsinghua Philosophical Almanac, 2002, Hebei University Press, 2001), *Philo's Logos: The Outcome of Greco-Roman Culture and Hebrew Culture* (the Journal of Zhejiang University, No. 5, 2000), etc.

In recent years, Professor Wang has begun to translate the complete works of Philo. He was awarded a national social science foundation grant for this translation project in 2015. He expects the translation will yield good fruits in the Chinese Philonic study, not only to widen the area of the Chinese study of ancient philosophy, Judaism, and Early Christianity, but also to promote the indigenization and contextualization of the Western Classics in China.

In addition, Professor Wang Xiaochao has started to build academic connections with Philonic scholars outside of China. In late 2015, with the help of the Hong Kong Institute of Sino-Christian studies, he invited Professor Gregory E. Sterling to deliver a lecture at Tsinghua University, an initial foray into enabling his students to learn much more from the prominent experts of Philonic study. Following that, his two doctoral students have come to Yale Divinity School to receive some academic instruction and training from Professor Sterling. As a result, one student has recently published a journal article briefly introducing the state of the field and its prospects in western academia to the Chinese academic peers.[1]

For Professor Wang Xiaochao, another important development has been the creation of a small library at Tsinghua for collecting resources on Philonic studies. Professor Wang and his colleagues hope to continue to expand academic communication and cooperation with the western academics in the future to promote a second brand-new example of "western wisdom spreading to the east (西学东渐)."

Yilin Xie
Ph.D. Candidate in the Department of
Philosophy at Tsinghua University
Beijing, China

[1] 谢伊霖：《斐洛研究述评》,《宗教学研究》, 2017（01），页216–228.

Philo in Venice

For more than one reason Venice is an important city for Philo studies. It is it the home of the San Lazzaro monastery of the Mechitarist fathers, where some of the most valuable manuscripts of the Armenian Philo are housed and where the scholars J. B. Aucher and G. Zarbhanalean prepared their editions of the text of those Philonic works translated into Armenian. It is also the location of the famed Bibliotheca Nazionale Marciana, which contains no less than twelve manuscripts ranging from the 10th to the 16th century that contain Philonic texts. Five of these, including the mss. B and H frequently referred to by Cohn and Wendland in the critical apparatus of their *editio maior*, were the possession of Cardinal Bessarion, who donated his collection of manuscripts and books to the city of Venice in 1468.

Earlier this year the American scholar and long-time Venetian resident Jarrod Michael Broderick published an extended article entitled "Custodian of Wisdom: The Marciana Reading Room and the Transcendent Knowledge of God," in the journal *Studi Veneziani* 73 (2016) 15–94. His thesis is that the twenty-one roundels of the ceiling of the Reading room, painted by seven different artists, should be interpreted as a coherent program that gives expression of the academic interests, moral values, and political ideals of Venice at a particular time in its history. The ceiling in its entirety thus conveys a pedagogic message. The core of this message is formed by the second to fifth groups of three roundels, which portray humanity's quest for a transcendent understanding of reality. The initial group of three roundels viewed on entering the room, painted by Giovanni de Mio, "form a theological prologue which privileges the 'Mosaic philosophy' of Philo of Alexandria as a means of reconciling Hellenistic thought with Christian doctrine and subsuming the philosophy that underpins the entire program into an acceptable religious framework" (p. 19). Specifically, two of the paintings deal with the origin of the sensible world and would seem to be influenced by Philonic thought, showing the generation of the intelligible cosmos and the existence of the models for the corporeal world within the Divine Intellect. Another contains tablets of the Mosaic Law as a revelation of God's knowledge. Broderick notes that the library contains the codices of Philo's works mentioned above and that the first printed editions of these works appears in the decades preceding its construction. (In a private communication he also informs me that the coverage of 15th and 16th cent. printed books which refer to Philo in Goodhart and Goodenough's bibliography is very incomplete.)

If this bold thesis is correct, we have a splendid example of Philonism influencing the iconography of high Renaissance art. And it is an example that can be visited today. Broderick is not only a scholar, but also organises historical guided tours to Venice, as you can discover by consulting the website venicescapes.org. It will surely inspire you to wish to visit the remarkable city that *inter alia multa* also played an important role in the *Nachleben* of Philo's writings and thought.

David T. Runia
Ocean Grove, Australia

Vale Louis Feldman (1926–2017)

All students of ancient Judaism will be saddened to hear of the passing of Louis H. Feldman, for many years a leading scholar in the field. For more than sixty years he taught at Yeshiva University, New York, where he was the Abraham Wouk Family Professor of Classics and Literature. Though best known as a Josephus scholar, he had a formidable knowledge of Philo as well. In 1962 he published a bibliography of Philo and Josephus scholarship covering the years 1937 to 1962. His exhaustive knowledge of

Hellenistic Judaism is displayed in his monograph *Jew and Gentile in the Ancient World* (1993), in which Philo is a constant point of reference. From 2001 he wrote a lengthy series of articles in which he examined Philo's treatment of characters and episodes in the Pentateuch. Much of this research is brought together in his study *Philo's Portrayal of Moses in the Context of Ancient Judaism* (2007). A personal interpretation of Philo's version of Judaism is given in his article "Philo and the dangers of philosophizing" published in the *FS Zev Garber* (2009). Professor Feldman was a familiar figure at meetings of the Society of Biblical Literature, where he would regularly attend sessions of the Philo seminar. He presented a paper on prophecy to the Seminar in 1988 and in 2002 published an article in *The Studia Philonica Annual*.

We extend our sincerest condolences to his family and his many students around the world.

David T. Runia
Ocean Grove, Australia

The Studia Philonica Annual 28 (2017): 271–73

NOTES ON CONTRIBUTORS

Marta ALESSO, is Titular Professor of Greek language and literature in the Faculty of Human Sciences at the National University of La Pampa, Argentina. Her postal address is Pestalozzi 625, 6300 Santa Rosa, La Pampa, ARGENTINA; her electronic address is alessomarta@gmail.com.

SONJA ANDERSON is Assistant Professor of Religion at Carleton College. Her postal address is Department of Religion, Carleton College, 1 North College Street, Northfield, MN 55057-4001, U.S.A.; her electronic address is sanderson2@carleton.edu.

ELLEN BIRNBAUM has taught at several Boston-area institutions, including Boston University, Brandeis, and Harvard. Her postal address is 78 Porter Road, Cambridge, MA 02140, U.S.A.; her electronic address is ebirnbaum78@gmail.com.

RONALD R. COX is Blanche E. Seaver Professor of Religion in Pepperdine University's Seaver College. His postal address is Religion and Philosophy Division, Pepperdine University, Malibu, CA 90263-4352, U.S.A.; his electronic address is ronald.cox@pepperdine.edu.

ERIC J. DEMEUSE is a PhD candidate in theology at Marquette University in Milwaukee, Wisconsin. His current postal address is Marquette Hall, 1217 W. Wisconsin Ave., Milwaukee, WI 53233, U.S.A.; his electronic address is ericjdemeuse@gmail.com.

ALBERT C. GELJON teaches classical languages at the Christelijke Gymnasium in Utrecht. His postal address is Gazellestraat 138, 3523 SZ Utrecht, THE NETHERLANDS; his electronic address is ageljon@xs4all.nl.

ERICH S. GRUEN is Gladys Rehard Wood Professor of History and Classics Emeritus at the University of California, Berkeley. His postal address is 1045 Mariposa Ave, Berkeley, CA 94707, U.S.A; his electronic address is gruene@berkeley.edu.

HELEEN M. KEIZER is Dean of Academic Affairs at the Istituto Superiore di Osteopatia in Milan, ITALY. Her postal address is Via Guerrazzi 3, 20900 Monza (MB), ITALY; her electronic address is h.m.keizer@virgilio.it.

JUTTA LEONHARDT-BALZER is Senior Lecturer at the University of Aberdeen, UK. Her postal address is King's Quadrangle, University of Aberdeen, Aberdeen AB24 3UB, UNITED KINGDOM; her electronic address is j.leonhardt-balzer@abdn.ac.uk.

JEROME MOREAU teaches Humanities in Lyon, France. His postal address is 13, rue Désirée, 69001 Lyon, FRANCE; his electronic address is jermoreau@icloud.com.

HINDY NAJMAN is the Oriel and Laing Professor of the Interpretation of Holy Scripture in Oriel College at the University of Oxford. Her postal address is Oriel College, Oriel Square, Oxford Ox1 4ew, UNITED KINGDOM; her electronic address is hindy.najman@oriel.ox.ac.uk.

MAREN R. NIEHOFF is Professor in the Department of Jewish Thought at the Hebrew University, Jerusalem. Her postal address is Department of Jewish Thought, Hebrew University, Mt. Scopus, Jerusalem 91905, ISRAEL; her electronic address is msmaren@mscc.huji.ac.il.

YAKIR PAZ is a Fellow at the Martin Buber Society of Fellows in the Humanities and Social Sciences at the Hebrew University of Jerusalem. His postal address is Mandel Building, Mount Scopus, Jerusalem, 9190501, ISRAEL. His electronic address is yakirpaz@gmail.com.

SARAH J. K. PEARCE is Ian Karten Professor of Jewish Studies at the University of Southampton. Her postal address is Department of History, Faculty of Humanities, Avenue Campus, Highfield, Southampton SO17 1BF, UNITED KINGDOM; her electronic address is sjp2@soton.ac.uk.

JUSTIN ROGERS is an Assistant Professor of Biblical Studies at Freed-Hardeman University. His postal address is FHU Box 2, Henderson, TN 38340-7326, U.S.A.; his electronic address is jrogers@fhu.edu.

GEERT ROSKAM is Professor of Greek in the Faculty of Arts at the Katholieke Universiteit Leuven, Belgium. His postal address is Blijde-Inkomststraat 21, bus 3318, B-3000 Leuven, BELGIUM; his electronic address is geert.roskam@kuleuven.be.

JAMES R. ROYSE is a Visiting Scholar at the Claremont School of Theology. His postal address is P.O. Box 567, Claremont, CA 91711-0567, U.S.A.; his electronic address is jamesrroyse@hotmail.com.

DAVID T. RUNIA is Director of the Institute for Religion and Critical Inquiry, Australian Catholic University, Melbourne. He is also a Professorial Fellow in the School of Historical and Philosophical Studies at the University of Melbourne. His postal address is 4 Woodlands Drive, Ocean Grove VIC 3226, AUSTRALIA; his electronic address is dtrunia@gmail.com.

TORREY SELAND is Professor Emeritus of The School of Mission and Theology, Stavanger, NORWAY. His postal address is Milorgveien 41, 3035 Drammen, NORWAY; his electronic address is torreys@gmail.com.

GREGORY E. STERLING is the Lillian Claus Professor of New Testament and the Reverend Henry L. Slack Dean of the Yale Divinity School. His postal address is 409 Prospect Street, New Haven, CT 06511, U.S.A.; his electronic address is gregory.sterling@yale.edu.

SHARON WEISSER is Lecturer at the Department of Philosophy, Tel Aviv University. Her postal address is The Department of Philosophy, Tel Aviv University, P.O.B. 39040, Ramat Aviv, Tel-Aviv 69978, ISRAEL; her electronic address is weisser@post.tau.ac.il.

SAMI YLI-KARJANMAA is an Academy of Finland Postdoctoral Researcher in the Faculty of Theology at the University of Helsinki. His postal address is Asemalammentie 103, FI-41370 Kuusa, FINLAND; his electronic address is sami.yli-karjanmaa@helsinki.fi.

The Studia Philonica Annual 29 (2017): 274–81

INSTRUCTIONS TO CONTRIBUTORS

Articles and book reviews can only be considered for publication in *The Studia Philonica Annual* if they rigorously conform to the guidelines established by the editorial board. For further information see also the website of the Annual:

http://divinity.yale.edu/philo-alexandria

1. *The Studia Philonica Annual* accepts articles for publication in the area v to Judaism and classical culture (and not on primarily historical subjects). The languages in which the articles may be published are English, French and German. Translations from Italian or Dutch into English can be arranged at a modest cost to the author.

2. Articles and reviews are to be sent to the editors in electronic form as email attachments. The preferred word processor is Microsoft Word. Users of other word processors are requested to submit a copy exported in a format compatible with Word, e.g. in RTF format. Manuscripts should be double-spaced, including the notes. Words should be italicized when required, not underlined. Quotes five lines or longer should be indented and may be single-spaced. Texts in Greek must be submitted in SBL Greek and texts in Hebrew in SBL Hebrew (both available at no cost from the SBL website). In all cases a PDF version of the document must be sent together with the word processing file. No handwritten Greek or Hebrew can be accepted. Authors are requested not to vocalize their Hebrew (except when necessary) and to keep their use of this language to a reasonable minimum. It should always be borne in mind that not all readers of the Annual can be expected to read Greek or Hebrew. Transliteration is permitted for incidental terms. If other language fonts need to be used, the font must be sent with the manuscript or contact should be sought with SBL Press.

3. Authors are encouraged to use inclusive language wherever possible, avoiding terms such as "man" and "mankind" when referring to humanity in general.

4. For the preparation of articles and book reviews the Annual follows the guidelines of the *SBL Handbook of Style*, Second Edition, Atlanta: SBL Press, 2014. Here are examples of how a monograph, a monograph in a series, an edited volume, an article in an edited volume, and a journal

article are to be cited in notes (different conventions apply for bibliographies):

Joan E. Taylor, *Jewish Women Philosophers of First-Century Alexandria—Philo's 'Therapeutae' Reconsidered* (Oxford: Oxford University Press, 2003), 123.

Ellen Birnbaum, *The Place of Judaism in Philo's Thought: Israel, Jews, and Proselytes*, BJS 290, SPhiloM 2 (Atlanta: Scholars Press, 1996), 134.

Gerard P. Luttikhuizen, ed., *Eve's Children: The Biblical Stories Retold and Interpreted in Jewish and Christian Traditions*, Themes in Biblical Narrative 5 (Leiden: Brill, 2003), 145.

G. Bolognesi, "Marginal Notes on the Armenian Translation of the *Quaestiones et Solutiones in Genesim* by Philo," in *Studies on the Ancient Armenian Version of Philo's* Works, ed. Sara Mancini Lombardi and Paola Pontani, SPhA 6 (Leiden: Brill, 2011), 45–50.

James R. Royse, "Jeremiah Markland's Contribution to the Textual Criticism of Philo," *SPhiloA* 16 (2004): 50–60.

Note that abbreviations are used in the notes and also in bibliographies. Numbers should be given in full for ancient texts, for example, *Aet.* 107–110; for references to modern publications the conventions of the *SBL Handbook of Style* should be followed (see p. 18). When joining up numbers in all textual and bibliographical references, the en dash should be used and not the hyphen, that is, 50–60, not 50-60. For publishing houses only the first location is given. Submissions which do not conform to these guidelines will be returned to the authors for re-submission.

5. The following abbreviations are to be used in both articles and book reviews.

(a) Philonic treatises are to be abbreviated according to the following list. Numbering follows the edition of Cohn and Wendland, using Arabic numbers only and full stops rather than colons (e.g., *Spec.* 4.123). Note that *De Providentia* should be cited according to Aucher's edition, and not the LCL translation of the fragments by F. H. Colson.

Abr.	*De Abrahamo*
Aet.	*De aeternitate mundi*
Agr.	*De agricultura*
Anim.	*De animalibus*
Cher.	*De Cherubim*
Contempl.	*De vita contemplativa*
Conf.	*De confusione linguarum*
Congr.	*De congressu eruditionis gratia*
Decal.	*De Decalogo*
Deo	*De Deo*
Det.	*Quod deterius potiori insidiari soleat*
Deus	*Quod Deus sit immutabilis*
Ebr.	*De ebrietate*
Flacc.	*In Flaccum*

Fug.	*De fuga et inventione*
Gig.	*De gigantibus*
Her.	*Quis rerum divinarum heres sit*
Hypoth.	*Hypothetica*
Ios.	*De Iosepho*
Leg. 1–3	*Legum allegoriae* I, II, III
Legat.	*Legatio ad Gaium*
Migr.	*De migratione Abrahami*
Mos. 1–2	*De vita Moysis* I, II
Mut.	*De mutatione nominum*
Opif.	*De opificio mundi*
Plant.	*De plantatione*
Post.	*De posteritate Caini*
Praem.	*De praemiis et poenis, De exsecrationibus*
Prob.	*Quod omnis probus liber sit*
Prov. 1–2	*De Providentia* I, II
QE 1–2	*Quaestiones et solutiones in Exodum* I, II
QG 1–4	*Quaestiones et solutiones in Genesim* I, II, III, IV
Sacr.	*De sacrificiis Abelis et Caini*
Sobr.	*De sobrietate*
Somn. 1–2	*De somniis* I, II
Spec. 1–4	*De specialibus legibus* I, II, III, IV
Virt.	*De virtutibus*

(b) Standard works of Philonic scholarship are abbreviated as follows:

G-G	Howard L. Goodhart and Erwin R. Goodenough, "A General Bibliography of Philo Judaeus." In Erwin R. Goodenough, *The Politics of Philo Judaeus: Practice and Theory* (New Haven: Yale University Press, 1938; repr. Georg Olms: Hildesheim, 1967), 125–321.
PCH	*Philo von Alexandria: die Werke in deutscher Übersetzung*. Edited by Leopold Cohn, Isaac Heinemann *et al.* 7 vols. (Breslau: M & H Marcus Verlag; Berlin: de Gruyter, 1909–1964).
PCW	*Philonis Alexandrini opera quae supersunt*. Edited by Leopoldus Cohn, Paulus Wendland et Sigismundus Reiter. 6 vols. (Berlin: Georg Reimer, 1896–1915).
PLCL	*Philo in Ten Volumes (and Two Supplementary Volumes)*. English translation by F. H. Colson, G. H. Whitaker (and R. Marcus), 12 vols., Loeb Classical Library. (London: William Heinemann; Cambridge, MA: Harvard University Press, 1929–1962).
PACS	Philo of Alexandria Commentary Series
PAPM	*Les œuvres de Philon d'Alexandrie*. French translation under the general editorship of Roger Arnaldez, Jean Pouilloux, and Claude Mondésert (Paris: Cerf, 1961–1992).
R-R	Roberto Radice and David T. Runia, *Philo of Alexandria: An Annotated Bibliography 1937–1986*, VCSup 8 (Leiden: Brill 1988).

RRS	David T. Runia, *Philo of Alexandria: An Annotated Bibliography 1987–1996*, VCSup 57 (Leiden: Brill 2000).
RRS2	David T. Runia, *Philo of Alexandria: An Annotated Bibliography 1997–2006*, VCSup 109 (Leiden: Brill 2012).
SPhA	Studies in Philo of Alexandria
SPhAMA	Studies in Philo of Alexandria and Mediterranean Antiquity
SPhilo	*Studia Philonica*
SPhiloA	*The Studia Philonica Annual*
SPhiloM	Studia Philonica Monographs

(c) References to biblical authors and texts and to ancient authors and writings are to be abbreviated as recommended in the *SBL Handbook of Style* §8.2–3. Note that biblical books are not italicized and that between chapter and verse a colon is placed (but for non-biblical references colons should not be used). Abbreviations should be used for biblical books when they are followed by chapter or chapter and verse unless the book is the first word in a sentence. Authors writing in German or French should follow their own conventions for biblical citations.

(d) For giving dates the abbreviations BCE and CE are preferred and should be printed in regular large caps.

(e) Journals, monograph series, source collections, and standard reference works are to be be abbreviated in accordance with the recommendations listed in *The SBL Handbook of Style* §8.4. The following list contains a selection of the more important abbreviations, along with a few abbreviations of classical and philosophical journals and standard reference books not furnished in the list.

ABD	*The Anchor Bible Dictionary*, 6 vols. New York, 1992
AC	*L'Antiquité Classique*
ACW	Ancient Christian Writers
AGJU	Arbeiten zur Geschichte des antiken Judentums und des Urchristentums
AJP	*American Journal of Philology*
AJSL	*American Journal of Semitic Languages*
ALGHJ	Arbeiten zur Literatur und Geschichte des hellenistischen Judentums
ANRW	*Aufstieg und Niedergang der römischen Welt*
AP	*L'Année Philologique*
BDAG	Bauer, W., F. W. Danker, W. F. Arndt, and F. W. Gingrich. *A Greek-English Lexicon of the New Testament and Other Early Christian Literature*. 3rd ed. Chicago: University of Chicago Press, 1999
BETL	Bibliotheca Ephemeridum Theologicarum Lovaniensium
BO	Bibliotheca Orientalis
BJRL	*Bulletin of the John Rylands Library*
BJS	Brown Judaic Studies
BMCR	*Bryn Mawr Classical Review* (electronic)

BZAW	Beihefte zur Zeitschrift für die alttestamentliche Wissenschaft
BZNW	Beihefte zur Zeitschrift für die neutestamentliche Wissenschaft
BZRGG	Beihefte zur Zeitschrift für Religions- und Geistesgeschichte
CBQ	*The Catholic Biblical Quarterly*
CBQMS	The Catholic Biblical Quarterly. Monograph Series
CCSG	Corpus Christianorum Series Graeca, Turnhout
CCSL	Corpus Christianorum Series Latina, Turnhout
CIG	*Corpus Inscriptionum Graecarum*. Edited by A. Boeckh. 4 vols. in 8. Berlin, 1828–1877
CIJ	*Corpus Inscriptionum Judaicarum*. Edited by J. B. Frey. 2 vols. Rome, 1936–1952
CIL	*Corpus Inscriptionum Latinarum*. Berlin, 1862–
CIS	*Corpus Inscriptionum Semiticarum*. Paris, 1881–1962
CP	*Classical Philology*
CPJ	*Corpus Papyrorum Judaicarum*. Edited by V. Tcherikover and A. Fuks. 3 vols. Cambridge MA, 1957–64
ClQ	*The Classical Quarterly*
CR	*The Classical Review*
CRINT	Compendia Rerum Iudaicarum ad Novum Testamentum
CPG	*Clavis Patrum Graecorum*. Edited by M. Geerard, 5 vols. and suppl. vol. Turnhout, 1974–1998
CPL	*Clavis Patrum Latinorum*. Edited by E. Dekkers. 3rd ed. Turnhout, 1995
CSCO	Corpus Scriptorum Christianorum Orientalium
CWS	Classics of Western Spirituality
DissAb	Dissertation Abstracts
DBSup	*Dictionnaire de la Bible*, Supplément. Paris, 1928–
DPhA	R. Goulet, ed., *Dictionnaire des philosophes antiques*, Paris, 1989–
DSpir	*Dictionnaire de Spiritualité*, 17 vols. Paris, 1932–1995
EBR	*Encyclopedia of the Bible and Its Reception*. Edited by Hans-Josef Klauck *et al*. Berlin: de Gruyter, 2009-
EncJud	*Encyclopaedia Judaica*, 16 vols. Jerusalem, 1972
EPRO	Études préliminaires aux religions orientales dans l'Empire romain
FAT	Forschungen zum Alten Testament
FGH	*Fragmente der Griechische Historiker*. Edited by F. Jacoby *et al.* Leiden, 1954–
FRLANT	Forschungen zur Religion und Literatur des Alten und Neuen Testaments
GCS	Die griechischen christlichen Schriftsteller, Leipzig
GLAJJ	M. Stern, *Greek and Latin Authors on Jews and Judaism*. 3 vols. Jerusalem, 1974–1984
GRBS	*Greek, Roman and Byzantine Studies*
HKNT	Handkommentar zum Neuen Testament, Tübingen
HNT	Handbuch zum Neuen Testament, Tübingen
HR	*History of Religions*
HTR	*Harvard Theological Review*
HUCA	*Hebrew Union College Annual*
JAAR	*Journal of the American Academy of Religion*
JAOS	*Journal of the American Oriental Society*
JAC	*Jahrbuch für Antike und Christentum*
JBL	*Journal of Biblical Literature*
JHI	*Journal of the History of Ideas*

JHS	*The Journal of Hellenic Studies*
JJS	*The Journal of Jewish Studies*
JQR	*The Jewish Quarterly Review*
JR	*The Journal of Religion*
JRS	*The Journal of Roman Studies*
JSHRZ	Jüdische Schriften aus hellenistisch-römischer Zeit
JSJ	*Journal for the Study of Judaism in the Persian, Hellenistic and Roman Periods*
JSJSup	Supplements to the Journal for the Study of Judaism
JSNT	*Journal for the Study of the New Testament*
JSNTSup	Journal for the Study of the New Testament. Supplement Series
JSOT	*Journal for the Study of the Old Testament*
JSOTSup	Journal for the Study of the Old Testament. Supplement Series
JSP	*Journal for the Study of the Pseudepigrapha and Related Literature*
JSS	*Journal of Semitic Studies*
JTS	*The Journal of Theological Studies*
KBL	L. Koehler and W. Baumgartner, *Lexicon in Veteris Testamenti libros*. 3 vols. 3rd ed. Leiden, 1967–1983
KS	*Kirjath Sepher*
LCL	Loeb Classical Library
LSJ	*A Greek-English Lexicon*. Edited by H. G. Liddell, R. Scott, H. S. Jones. 9th ed. with revised suppl. Oxford, 1996
MGWJ	*Monatsschrift für Geschichte und Wissenschaft des Judentums*
NCE	*New Catholic Encyclopedia*, 15 vols. New York, 1967
NETS	New English Translation of the Septuagint. Edited by Albert Pietersma and Ben Wright. New York: Oxford University Press, 2007
NHS	Nag Hammadi Studies
NT	*Novum Testamentum*
NovTSup	Supplements to Novum Testamentum
NTA	*New Testament Abstracts*
NTOA	Novum Testamentum et Orbis Antiquus
NTS	*New Testament Studies*
ODJ	*The Oxford Dictionary of Judaism*. Edited by R.J.Z. Werblowsky and G. Wigoder. New York 1997
OGIS	*Orientis Graeci inscriptiones selectae*
OLD	*The Oxford Latin Dictionary*. Edited by P. G. W. Glare. Oxford, 1982
OTP	*The Old Testament Pseudepigrapha*. Edited by J. H. Charlesworth. 2 vols. New York London, 1983 1985
PAAJR	*Proceedings of the American Academy for Jewish Research*
PAL	*Philon d'Alexandrie: Lyon 11–15 Septembre 1966*. Éditions du CNRS, Paris, 1967
PG	Patrologiae cursus completus: series Graeca. Edited by J. P. Migne. 162 vols. Paris, 1857–1912
PGL	*A Patristic Greek Lexicon*. Edited by G. W. H. Lampe. Oxford, 1961
PhA	Philosophia Antiqua
PL	Patrologiae cursus completus: series Latina. Edited by J. P. Migne. 221 vols. Paris, 1844–1864
PTS	Patristische Texte und Studien
PW	Pauly-Wissowa-Kroll, *Real-Encyclopaedie der classischen Altertumswissenschaft*. 49 vols. Munich, 1980
PWSup	Supplement to PW

RAC	*Reallexikon für Antike und Christentum*
RB	*Revue Biblique*
REA	*Revue des Études Anciennes*
REArm	*Revue des Études Arméniennes*
REAug	*Revue des Études Augustiniennes*
REG	*Revue des Études Grecques*
REJ	*Revue des Études Juives*
REL	*Revue des Études Latines*
RevQ	*Revue de Qumran*
RGG	*Die Religion in Geschichte und Gegenwart*, 7 vols. 3rd edition Tübingen, 1957–1965
RhM	*Rheinisches Museum für Philologie*
RHR	*Revue de l'histoire des religions*
RSR	*Revue des Sciences Religieuses*
RVV	Religionsgeschichtliche Versuche und Vorarbeiten
Str-B	H. L. Strack and P. Billerbeck, *Kommentar zum Neuen Testament aus Talmud und Midrasch*. 6 vols. Munich, 1922–1961
SBLDS	Society of Biblical Literature Dissertation Series
SBLMS	Society of Biblical Literature Monograph Series
SBLSP	Society of Biblical Literature Seminar Papers
SBLTT	Society of Biblical Literature Texts and Translations
SC	Sources Chrétiennes
SCS	Septuagint and Cognate Studies
Sem	*Semitica*
SHJP	E. Schürer, *The History of the Jewish People in the Age of Jesus Christ*. Revised edition. 3 vols. in 4. Edinburgh, 1973–1987
SJLA	Studies in Judaism in Late Antiquity
SNTSMS	Society for New Testament Studies. Monograph Series
SR	*Studies in Religion*
ST	*Studia Theologica*
STAC	Studies and Texts in Antiquity and Judaism
SUNT	Studien zur Umwelt des Neuen Testaments
SVF	*Stoicorum veterum fragmenta*. Edited by J. von Arnim. 4 vols. Leipzig, 1903–1924
TDNT	*Theological Dictionary of the New Testament*. 10 vols. Grand Rapids, 1964–1976
THKNT	Theologischer Handkommentar zum Neuen Testament, Berlin
TRE	*Theologische Realenzyklopädie*, Berlin
TSAJ	Texte und Studien zum Antike Judentum
TU	Texte und Untersuchungen zur Geschichte der altchristlichen Literatur, Berlin
TWNT	*Theologisches Wörterbuch zum Neuen Testament*. 10 vols. Stuttgart 1933–1979.
TZ	*Theologische Zeitschrift*
VC	*Vigiliae Christianae*
VCSup	Supplements to Vigiliae Christianae
VT	*Vetus Testamentum*
WMANT	Wissenschaftliche Monographien zum Alten und Neuen Testament
WUNT	Wissenschaftliche Untersuchungen zum Neuen Testament
YJS	*Yale Jewish Studies*
ZAW	*Zeitschrift für die alttestamentliche Wissenschaft*

ZKG	*Zeitschrift für Kirchengeschichte*
ZKT	*Zeitschrift für Katholische Theologie*
ZNW	*Zeitschrift für die neutestamentliche Wissenschaft*
ZPE	*Zeitschrift für Papyrologie und Epigraphik*
ZRGG	*Zeitschrift für Religions- und Geistesgeschichte*

www.ingramcontent.com/pod-product-compliance
Lightning Source LLC
Chambersburg PA
CBHW030810100426
42814CB00002B/72

* 9 7 8 1 6 2 8 3 7 1 9 3 2 *